THE NEW AUTOBIOGRAPHY
RICHARD BRANSON

Finding My Virginity

Virgin BOOKS

1 3 5 7 9 10 8 6 4 2

Virgin Books, an imprint of Ebury Publishing,
20 Vauxhall Bridge Road,
London SW1V 2SA

Virgin Books is part of the Penguin Random House group of companies whose
addresses can be found at global.penguinrandomhouse.com

Penguin
Random House
UK

First published in the United Kingdom by Virgin Books in 2017
This edition first published in the United Kingdom by Virgin Books in 2018

www.penguin.co.uk

A CIP catalogue record for this book is available from the British Library

ISBN 9780753556139

Printed and bound in Great Britain by Clays Ltd, Elcograf S.p.A.

Penguin Random House is committed to a sustainable future for our business,
our readers and our planet. This book is made from Forest Stewardship Council®
certified paper.

Contents

Dedicated to my parents Ted and Eve, who made me who I am. To my sisters Lindy and Vanessa, who have always been there for me. To my wife Joan, who makes every day an adventure. To my children Holly and Sam, who dream of an even brighter future. And to my grandchildren, Etta, Artie, Eva-Deia and Bluey, who make me want to turn our dreams into reality.

———————————

A special thank you to Greg Rose for helping me pull this project together. Greg has spent years getting to know my life, my mind (and my tennis serve!) and searched through countless unburnt notebooks and memories for us to bring this book to life.

Prologue

You can only lose your virginity once. But in every aspect of my life – building businesses, raising my family, embarking upon adventures – I try to do things for the first time every day.

When I first published *Losing My Virginity*, in 1998, I wasn't at all prepared for the reaction. I expected the business community, some newspaper reviewers and a few autobiography readers to pick it up, but before I knew it the book had taken off. *Losing My Virginity* is still the most common object handed to me (except a mobile for a selfie), usually by a person with a pen and a smile. I have written short updates to my autobiography over the years, but so much has happened in the past two decades that I realised I needed to write a sequel.

I was pondering the right time to do this when I came across my old notes for *Student* magazine's launch in the archive. I rubbed the dust away to double-check the date – the notes really were from 1967. What better way to mark fifty years since I started out in business than by sharing everything that has happened and all I have learned over the decades? This book highlights incidents from my early days, but it concentrates on the past twenty years, the time I have been finding my virginity all over again.

Finding My Virginity kicks on from where *Losing My Virginity* left off, at the dawn of the new millennium. By 1999 people thought we had done everything and there was nowhere else left for us to expand, no new challenges for me to embark upon. But being involved in running a company like Virgin is never a question of sitting back, it's about constant reinvention as the world changes, and as do I. This is the story of the last two decades, told through one of the most dynamic brands in the world. My home has moved from a houseboat to a paradise island, while my company has grown from a UK business to a global brand. My dream of flying private citizens to space has gone from a childhood fantasy to the brink of reality, and my focus has shifted from battling bigger rivals to changing business for good. In this time I've experienced joy, heartbreak, hurricanes, business (and other) highs, grief, records, doubt and my toughest ever crisis. It's been a rollercoaster ride and I have no intention of getting off any time soon. There have been many more adventures in the year since I finished this book, so I've written more chapters about the devastating hurricanes that destroyed our home and much of the Caribbean, our exciting new businesses, including Virgin Hyperloop, and of course getting very, very close to space with Virgin Galactic's latest progress.

Fifteen years after *Losing My Virginity*'s publication, Zach Galifinakis asked me: 'Is your book a play on the name of your company, or the first time you had sex?' 'Both,' I answered. This time around, I considered giving my book an even more risqué title. That it was factually accurate only made it more tempting. My alternative name for the book you are reading? *Losing My Virginity: The Second Entry*. I also considered *Virginity Lost*, a nod to the title of John Milton's epic *Paradise Lost*, but it felt too negative. I view life as one big adventure; I'm always learning, and finding new things to try and challenges to overcome. I'm still finding my virginity every day. But now that I am a grand-dude to four wonderful grandchildren – Etta, Artie, Eva-Deia and Bluey – I look at my life in a new way.

Whether you are running a company or simply living your life, hopefully you can learn from my mistakes and put a smile on your face along the way. A reviewer described *Losing My Virginity* as the first autobiography in which the author had written an exposé of himself. I hope *Finding My Virginity* will be similar. If your life is one long success story it won't make for a good read. What's more, you're most likely a liar. We all have ups and downs, trials and tribulations, failures and triumphs: we just hope to come out stronger on the other side.

The late Steve Jobs, the entrepreneur I most admire, said: 'My favourite things in life don't cost any money. It's really clear that the most precious resource we all have is time.' That thought has been on my mind as I write this book, thinking back to all the good times and tough times behind me, and looking forward with wonder at what lies ahead. I've always lived every day as if it's my last, fiercely loving my family and friends and trying to make a positive difference. We only get one life, and this is mine.

I hope you enjoy finding out how I did it for the first time – all over again.

1 1999

Necker Island, New Year's Eve, 1998. I was in my bedroom, trying to make an urgent to-do list. As I stared at the blank piece of paper in front of me, across a sandy path a song Prince released in 1982 was booming around the Great House on repeat. It was a song that let everyone know 1998 was nearly over and the ball was about to drop on the last year of the millennium: 1999.

The New Year's festivities were in full swing. My daughter Holly was leading the celebrations with our family and friends. I could hear the clink of glasses as my wife Joan toasted with friends while our fourteen-year-old son Sam ran around getting under her feet. They were the familiar sounds of family life and ones that I was grateful to hear after my adventures of the previous weeks.

Five days earlier, on Boxing Day, I had arrived on the island fresh from my last ballooning adventure. I was lucky to be alive. On 18 December, Steve Fossett and I had set off from Marrakech in the hope of completing a record-breaking round-the-world trip. What had followed was a mixture of high-stakes adventure and diplomacy – pulling in favours as our balloon had veered over Libyan airspace, then having our approval to fly over China rescinded before being reinstated as we made our way over Nepal. Finally, having got close to crossing the Pacific, the winds blew us back, forcing us to land in the ocean near Hawaii. I'd made it there for Christmas, then flew on to Necker Island the following day.

Back in the security of home, with the end of the year approaching and the end of the millennium looming, I found myself both reflecting back and looking forwards. As so often during my life as an entrepreneur, I really had no idea what was coming next. I had created and sold the biggest independent record label on the planet, and fought doggedly to build Virgin Atlantic into the best airline in the world. The Virgin Group had grown from a couple of companies to more than a hundred and I had gone from a struggling hippy to a proud father and businessman. My mind was starting to wander to other projects, fresh ambitions and bigger dreams. Within the space of twelve months we would launch nine different companies and begin turning Virgin into the all-encompassing global brand it is today. It was time for a new start, and to look to the stars.

*

How do you go about becoming a millionaire? I'm often asked this question and ever since I founded Virgin Atlantic in 1984 my answer has been the same: 'Start as a billionaire and launch a new airline.'

The first fifteen years of Virgin Atlantic had been a topsy-turvy tale of excitement, innovation and survival. We had taken the might of British Airways head on and, unlike the airlines that came before us, lived to tell the tale. In fact, we won one of the largest libel cases in British history after BA's Dirty Tricks campaign tried to put us out of business. It was a campaign that most people within the industry knew by another name altogether: Operation Barbara. Why was it called that? Because Barbara Cartland had written a lot of novels about virgins getting screwed.

As we emerged from this most challenging of periods, I had clear skies for the first time in a while, exploring new horizons for the Virgin brand. Many experts will tell you it tends to take a year to get a business off the ground, from the initial idea through planning, market research, development and launch. Personally, I've always disregarded this rule. As far as I'm concerned, anyone following it should pull their finger out.

When I was a wide-eyed teenager our mail-order record company was set up in a couple of days, and even more complex businesses like Virgin Atlantic went from idea to lift-off in a matter of weeks. Generally, we like to work fast: try ideas, see if they stick, and, if they don't, quickly move on to the next one.

I work best when my mind is able to jump from one topic to the next in quick succession. It keeps things lively, and it's amazing how often good ideas for one company come out of another completely unrelated business. As I took a step back from the day-to-day running of Virgin Atlantic, I was able to concentrate on what was next for Virgin. As it turns out, there was more than even I had ever imagined.

The turn of the century was to prove unprecedentedly productive, even by our standards. After my first wave as a records impresario and second as an airline founder, the third wave of my career as a global entrepreneur was about to begin in earnest. Some of the companies, namely Virgin Blue (now Australia), virginmoney.com, Virgin Wines and Virgin Mobile Australia have gone on to become big success stories. We had already launched the likes of Virgin Clothing, Virgin Brides, Virgin Cola, Virgin Vodka and Virgin Vie cosmetics by this point, all of which would disappear in the next few years. But failures didn't put me off at all. They had all been fun to get stuck into, and we'd learned a lot of important lessons.

Some businesses quickly turned into far less successful operations. Virgin Cars, our automobile company, was effective for a few years but overnight became unworkable. Our business model of purchasing cars, mostly from the Netherlands and Belgium, and importing them to sell into the UK was destroyed by a combination of restrictive practices by the big carmakers and changing currency values. V.Shop, small record stores we launched after rebranding Our Price, never got off the ground, while there were similar stories for Virgin Student, Virgin Energy and Virgin

Travelstore. The dot.com bubble was still going strong, but we hadn't quite got the hang of it. Because our core businesses remained solid, the brand wasn't derailed by these smaller failures. I was also able to spend even more time with my young family and enjoy life a little more. I didn't feel I had so much to prove, and was getting more comfortable in my own skin. If the odd business didn't work out, I was confident there would be another on the way.

We were beginning to see which core areas we could expand the brand into, but it was still taking time for me to understand how flexible the Virgin brand was, the areas where it could bend successfully, and the areas where it would break. The sweet spot was always where we could differentiate from the competition, in service and in product, and where there was a real appetite for change. We were still a long way from creating the more structured strategy we have today, but it was one hell of a ride finding out what worked.

With the financial clout we had gained from selling Virgin Records and the profile lift our battles against BA had inadvertently given us, Virgin Atlantic continued to grow in popularity and profit. I was determined for us to capitalise. Our fleet grew to twenty-eight jets, and by the end of 1999 we had agreed a deal to sell 49 per cent of the company to Singapore Airlines for £600 million in cash. This would give more opportunity to invest in new businesses and reinvest in Virgin Atlantic's customer experience, while maintaining a controlling stake in our airline. We had already become the first airline in the world to introduce seatback video across our fleet. Now we became the worldwide launch customer for the new Airbus A340-600 and introduced new successful routes everywhere from Las Vegas to St Lucia, Delhi to Barbados and Shanghai to Cape Town.

I began to enjoy flying Virgin Atlantic even more when we created the first ever double beds in the air in business class, and could even continue my meetings mid-flight when we launched Earth Calling in-seat call service via passengers' mobile phones. Now there really was no escape for my team from phone calls at all hours! Thankfully for them, we also introduced the first ever in-flight bars. It's amazing who you can get talking to and what you can get discussing over a few drinks at 30,000 feet. I've heard hundreds of business pitches at our sky-high bars over the years and several have gone on to become successful companies. As for matchmaking, there are few things I love more than setting up a couple while they sip a drink above the clouds. And at least one hit single has been written at the bar, while birds go flying at the speed of sound outside the window . . .

One morning in September 1999 I was woken up at four in the morning to learn that BA was having a little trouble with a big wheel. BA was paying big money to be the sponsor of the new London Eye, but its launch was fraught with technical problems. When they were finally ready to launch it, ahead of celebrating the millennium, they were unable to erect the wheel. We just so happened to own an airship company nearby in the Home Counties, so I got on the phone to the team.

'We need to scramble a blimp,' I told them. 'How quickly can you get one to the Thames?'

With the world's press assembled and the wheel lying limply on the South Bank lawn, our blimp hovered directly above, proudly displaying the legend 'BA CAN'T GET IT UP'. We got the headlines that night at BA's expense – literally! The photo also coincided with the same day BA's share price plunged to a new record low.

The following year, I pulled BA's tail again when we revamped our free in-flight massages for Upper Class customers. Right outside Heathrow Airport, we installed a giant poster stating 'BA Don't Give A Shiatsu'. In just five words we showcased our effervescence, cheekiness and great service. That, to me, is what Virgin is all about. It's crucial in this job not to take yourself too seriously and people appreciate it when they see a bit of humour and personality shining through. One thing I've learned over the years is that the average customer is usually far smarter – and more appreciative of a joke – than big businesses give them credit for.

*

When I founded the airline Lord King from British Airways said that I was 'too old to rock, too young to fly'. Fifteen years on, where was I now? It was a question I was asking myself, not just from a business sense, but as a father, too. My children, one not yet born, the other tiny when Virgin Atlantic started, were growing up and already making those first steps towards leaving home.

We had never planned to send the children to boarding school; I had suffered such dreadful experiences there myself. But as Holly approached sixteen we discussed the option seriously. Holly was keen to try out full-term boarding, and we compromised on her going to school in Oxford, which was close to where we lived then, but far enough away for Holly to gain some independence.

Choosing a school for your children should be a process of careful thought and contemplation: in our case, we managed to find the right choice by getting lost instead. Joan and I had an appointment at a school in Oxford we were considering for Sam and Holly. But having driven to the school, it turned out we had the wrong one altogether.

Popping inside and realising it was not an open day, we bumped straight into the headmaster, David Christie. Rather than show us where to go, he insisted on whisking us around on a whirlwind tour of his school instead. The tour and his passion for the school were very impressive indeed. It had, until recently, been an all-boys' school up to Sixth Form, but was now taking girls. There was a progressive air about the place, an unstuffy feel compared to the crammers I had experienced. By the time we left, both children were bound for St Edwards. It was a real sliding-doors moment in more ways than one: as it turns out, a young boy named Freddie Andrewes, whom Holly would get to know rather well in the coming years, was already studying at St Edwards.

When Holly was later named the school's first female Head of School I was overflowing with pride. But I was equally pleased that she was making friends, enjoying herself and growing into a fine young woman. She was already acquiring a taste for tackling injustices, and when she came home bemoaning the fact that girls were not allowed to wear trousers I helped her draft a letter to her headmaster demanding equality for all students. It reminded me of when I was at Stowe School, though in my case I would have campaigned for all students not to wear ties.

There were some amusing antiquated perks to being Head of School, one of which was the right to be able to graze your own goat in the school grounds.

'Holly, this is too good an opportunity to miss,' I told her over the kitchen table. 'Whenever you come across absurd rules, take advantage of them.'

'What do you mean?' she asked.

'I think you should buy a goat.'

'Don't be silly, Dad,' she replied, wisely resisting.

As Holly prepared to graduate in 2000, we spent an evening hunched over her desk together working on her big speech to the whole school. I went to see her make the speech and was amazed how she had already become a better public speaker than her dad. She was shy, but concentrated on her words and spoke unwaveringly in her beautiful, clear voice. Not for the first or last time, I wept with pride.

Although sending Holly and Sam to St Edwards was well worth it, it did take some getting used to the children not being at home. I was accustomed to being away from the kids a little, due to travelling with work so much. For Joan, it was a real wrench – to begin with she would cry every day: she missed her babies so much. She took to driving to Oxford quite a lot, and would 'just happen' to pop by the school near midday, and take Holly and Sam out for lunch. Back home, after one of these lunches, there was often no food in the house. I remember standing in the kitchen one evening, rifling through bare cupboards, and saying to Joan: 'Look, I know the kids are gone, but we still need to eat!'

'Well, you know where M&S is, too, Richard,' she replied.

It was a fair point. I got used to driving to Marks & Spencer. But she soon took pity on me!

*

Sitting there on Necker Island on New Year's Eve, staring at my blank piece of paper, I'd decided it was time for a new start, to look to the stars. The following year, I followed up on that decision, literally so, with the setting up of a new company.

My fascination with space first started thirty years earlier. It was 20 July 1969 and I had turned nineteen two days before, still nursing the type of hangover that any teenager celebrating their nineteenth birthday could expect. My father turned on the tiny black-and-white television in our home in Shamley Green and I, along with countless millions, watched the extraordinary sight of images from space being beamed back to earth. More than 238,000 miles above, Apollo 11 had landed on the moon. I was gripped as Neil Armstrong uttered the immortal words: 'That's one small step for man, one giant leap for mankind.' Whether he fluffed his line or not, it was inspirational.

I was instantly convinced I would be going to space one day. I assumed that if NASA could land on the moon, in the near future they would be able to take anybody who wanted to go to space. There was absolutely no doubt in my mind. But when the Apollo missions ended, and the years started to pass without new breakthroughs, space travel felt further away again. Nevertheless, I was sure it was just a matter of time, and my enthusiasm remained undimmed.

In 1999, I was to take the first small steps towards fulfilling my own dream. For all the remarkable travels around the world I took that year, the most exciting journey started with a short stroll from my then home, across the icy greenery of Hyde Park, to a dreary bureaucratic building. I walked into Companies House and officially registered a new company: Virgin Galactic Airways. (Being a born optimist, I also registered Virgin Intergalactic Airways!) I did not know how to start a spaceline – nobody had ever done it before – but I loved the name and the idea thrilled me. It seemed an exciting way to enter a new millennium, looking up to the stars and thinking about how to get up there – and back again.

*

All that, though, was in the future. Back on New Year's Eve it was time to dance with my wife. I put down my pencil, left my to-do list of possibilities on the table and joined our guests downstairs as Prince sang on: 'I was dreamin' when I wrote this, so sue me if I go too fast. But life is just a party and parties weren't meant to last ...'

2 What You See is What You Get

I was one of the first people in the country to use a mobile phone in the 1980s. It weighed more than Holly did at the time and was almost as big. To call it a brick would be disrespectful to bricks. However, by the time their size got more manageable, mobiles spread rapidly and transformed the way we did business. I no longer had to be at certain places at specific times so often, and was free to spend more time with my kids in the great outdoors, or just disappear for a while. I hated being stuck at a desk, and could see how mobiles would be transformative for workforces, providing freedom as well as convenience.

The spark for Virgin Mobile came back in 1999. I was sitting in the kitchen of my Holland Park house, working my way through some correspondence, when Will Whitehorn, my head of communications, came in, waving a piece paper.

'Guess what, Richard. We've won a prize.'

'Oh great. Which one?' I asked.

'Actually ... I've won a prize.' Will put the document – a phone bill – down on the table in front of me. 'You have made me call you and every journalist in the country so often that BT has awarded me a trophy for the highest phone bill in Britain.'

Will's bill got me thinking. No, not that I should bother him less often. But why were we giving BT all the money from so many calls? Why not start our own phone company?

In 1998 global mobile phone sales more than doubled to 162.9 million – we needed to get into the market. But I, along with everybody else, was paying through the nose for the pleasure of using my phone. Lengthy contracts that had huge service charges became the norm. Mobiles had become so useful so quickly that most people just accepted they would be ripped off.

I saw this as a prime opportunity to shake up the market. The Virgin Group was relatively stable and we had cash from Virgin Atlantic's new partnership to invest – mobile was the obvious space to do it in. My one concern was the idea of footing all the costs of a huge infrastructure investment. This, though, was where the really unusual part came in: we wouldn't have to build a whole new network, we would piggyback off one of the existing ones. In 1997 we started a twenty-year partnership with Fast Track, a network ranking the UK's top performing private companies in the *Sunday Times*. I couldn't help but notice many of the successful start-ups, such as Carphone Warehouse, were in the telecoms sector. I asked Stephen Murphy and investment guru Gordon McCallum why we weren't already investing. They were ahead of the game, quickly showing me a Goldman Sachs report about the possibility of MVNOs – mobile virtual network operators. It was filled with jargon that made my head hurt, but, once most of the dozens of acronyms had sunk in, the direction we should take seemed clear: if we could persuade one network to agree, we would rent time and bandwidth on their system, and bring our marketing and customer service expertise to the table.

Once I got the word out that Virgin was interested, we were approached by many networks for partnerships, as well as entrepreneurs with ideas for the mobile space, from handset designers to pager developers. I came across two young men from BT Cellnet with considerable experience in the telecoms industry, Tom Alexander and Joe Steel. After negotiations to form a deal with Cellnet got nowhere, I suggested to Tom that we start a truly different mobile company together.

I invited Tom up to my then home in Kidlington, Oxfordshire, for lunch. In old-fashioned entrepreneur style, we hashed out a plan over the kitchen table. We would launch a pay-as-you-go service, where users would only pay for what they actually used. We would aim at the youth market, appealing to teenagers getting their first phones, as well as slightly older people who had grown up with Virgin and were fed up with being stung by their old providers. And we would use our Virgin Megastores to sell the phones. By this point we had 381 stores worldwide and new flagships in London (Piccadilly Circus), Miami, Glasgow, Strasbourg and Okayama, filled to the brim with the sort of savvy people we could aim our product at. Tom, along with Joe, agreed to leave Cellnet and joined James Kydd from Virgin Drinks as Virgin Mobile's first three employees.

There was just one small problem. These smart young men were, well, too smart. Being dressed neatly in suit and tie was not really the Virgin way.

'Do you really want to come to work dressed like that every morning?' I asked, yanking Tom's tie. 'How do you breathe?'

On their first day working for Virgin Mobile, we had a somewhat unusual initiation ceremony: we took their suits and ties, and, making a small fire, set them alight. As we watched the material go up in flames to cheers all round, I knew we had made the right decision. Now we just had to light a similar fire underneath the mobile phone industry itself.

*

As news of Virgin Mobile leaked out, critics once again suggested we were spreading the Virgin brand too thinly and entering too many sectors in which we lacked expertise. I wasn't worried about that: I saw change as a challenge, and wanted to meet it head on. But what we needed most was a network. One by one the networks rejected us, concerned that they would lose more than they would gain by letting us into the market. Then, finally, the last one we spoke to, One 2 One, agreed to supply their network and we would provide the brand and marketing. On 1 August 1999 we became 50/50 partners with them. But then, out of the blue, One 2 One was sold off by its owners Cable & Wireless to German firm Deutsche Telekom, who rebranded it T-Mobile. For a worrying twenty-four hours it looked like they were going to drop us, so I jumped on a plane to Germany to meet Deutsche Telekom's CEO Ron Sommer. Ron was straightforward and very smart. To my great relief, after an hour of listening to me, he said he understood the vision, and agreed to go ahead with our deal.

T-Mobile matched our investment of £42.5 million and we set about creating one of Britain's biggest start-ups of all time. After we secured bank debt of £100 million, City analysts started putting heady numbers on the value of the company. One even estimated the business was worth £1.36 billion – before we even had our first customer!

'Did they really say billion, not million?' I had to double-check with Will.

I was scratching my head, wondering why we hadn't entered the mobile business earlier.

When it was time to launch the company, I knew I needed an event that grabbed people's attention. At one airline launch I flipped Kate Moss upside down on the wing as the press looked on at Heathrow. 'Richard, I've got no panties on!' she shrieked. I had forgotten it had been raining earlier; I felt my feet slipping and my grip getting looser. For a moment, I thought I was about to drop the most famous supermodel in the world off the side of our jet. I managed to cling on, and I think Kate has just about forgiven me.

For Virgin Mobile I wanted to show this was a network with nothing to hide, which wouldn't screw customers over with hidden charges. What better way than joining seven gorgeous ladies in a huge transparent mobile phone in London's Trafalgar Square? Oh, and we just happened to be completely naked, except for some little orange cushions barely covering our modesty.

'What you see is what you get,' I told the crowds, who got the message and enjoyed a laugh. The Metropolitan Police didn't quite see the joke, though, and we had to make a dash for it, taking our cushions with us.

*

Sometimes the publicity stunts we pull can take even me by surprise. That was the case with the launch of Virgin Mobile in Australia. By November 2000, Virgin Mobile UK had more than 500,000 customers and scooped Mobile Choice's Network of the Year award (not bad, since we didn't actually have a network!). As the Aussie public had embraced our airline so quickly, it made sense to strike while the iron was hot and launch a second mobile company down under. As in Britain, we found an established company, Optus, and agreed a partnership using their network infrastructure and Virgin's branding and customer experience. And, as with the launch of Virgin Mobile in the UK, we wanted an event to get people talking.

The first inkling I got that something unusual was going on was when I was picked up from my hotel, the Holiday Inn in Potts Point, Sydney. I got into a car with chief marketing officer Jean Oelwang, Peter Beikmanis and Catherine Salway for a briefing. I presumed we would be driving to the harbour, but instead we started heading out of the city and into the countryside.

'I thought we were going to do the launch next to Sydney Harbour,' I said.

'Erm, yes, we are,' said Jean, a little too nervously.

As the others in the car exchanged sideways looks, I could tell something was up. The next thing I knew we had arrived in an empty field. It seemed an unusual and unpopulated venue for a business launch. Then I heard the whupp-whupp-whupp of helicopter blades. That made more sense. I stood back in the full force of the wind as the helicopter landed next to the car.

'I think I get the picture.' I was about to climb into the helicopter when Jean pulled me to one side.

'Richard, we probably should have told you this earlier ...'

Jean stood back as one of the helicopter crew put a harness on me. 'You're not actually going in the helicopter. You're going to fly a hundred feet under it.'

That was a new one! I could feel my heart beginning to thump, but nothing ventured and all that. The helicopter crew told me to lie flat on the ground. As I lay down in the soft warmth of the grass, I could feel a bungee rope being attached to my waist.

'Keep still', I was told. 'Keep your head down.'

As I lay there I could hear the blades whirr into action. I was just wondering what Joan would make of my current predicament when, with a jerk, I was lifted off the ground. As I went up I span around and around uncontrollably fast. I tried to get myself into a skydiving position – arms and legs spread-eagled. My face had a fixed expression somewhere between bemusement and, I suspect, terror. Probably closer to terror, thinking about it.

Finally, I got the hang of it, and now we were really moving. I was flying forward through the air, 100 feet below the helicopter at a rapid rate. Over the years, I have often had dreams where I am flapping my arms and flying. Sometimes I soar around Necker, smelling the ocean air. Other times I fly up into space, looking down at the pale blue dot of Earth. Usually, however, I am looking down along Oxford Street, where our first Virgin Records store was, knowing that if I stopped I would crash. I swoop down, knock somebody's hat off and zoom back upwards. Occasionally I wake up falling.

This was as close as I'd get to my dreams in reality. I've never had a more exhilarating experience in my life. I worked out that if I dropped my arm on either side I could even control my direction – to a certain extent. As we approached the city I began to enjoy myself, waving to confused-looking people far below, and feeling more like Peter Pan than ever before. This is what being a bird must feel like, I thought to myself.

The next thing I knew, the imposing structure of Sydney Harbour Bridge was approaching fast in front of me. I tried dropping my arms as I'd just taught myself, but it wasn't going to be enough. I tried shouting to the helicopter pilot to climb higher, but that was just as futile: there was no way he could hear me.

'Higher! Higher!' I shouted.

I'm going to hit the bridge. I was sure of it. What a way to go, I thought, zooming across the sky in a harness before ... SPLAT! A face-first collision with one of Australia's most iconic constructions, like Wile E. Coyote in a Loony Tunes cartoon.

At what felt like the last possible second, the helicopter veered upwards and I narrowly avoided becoming a permanent addition to the side of the bridge. I barely had time to catch my breath as we zipped across it, low enough for me to see the astonished expressions of the bridge walkers looking up. Finally, we landed on top of a giant cage structure next to Sydney Opera House. I was bursting with adrenaline, pumped up after everything I'd just been through. Inside the cage people were dressed in the colours of all of our rivals – there were lots in Australia's highly competitive mobile market. They were wearing handcuffs to signify the long contracts they were locked into by the likes of Vodafone and Telstra, and singing, 'Set us free! Set us free!' I set off some explosive bolts, the cage collapsed and the 'customers' were freed.

'I thought I was a goner for a minute there,' I told Jean afterwards.

'I'm very glad you weren't,' she said reassuringly. 'We hadn't managed to get you insured!'

*

Virgin Mobile became the fastest growing mobile start-up in UK history. We acquired our millionth customer in 2001, an impressive number for a company that had started from scratch as a punt only a couple of years earlier.

But I was eager to capitalise further. On 21 February 2001 I travelled to Cannes for the 3GSM World Congress, where I announced Virgin Mobile as the world's first global mobile virtual network operator. Within the next few years we would launch new, independent mobile companies in ten countries in five continents. With our UK partners T-Mobile, we launched a new service in Northern Ireland. We negotiated a $1 billion joint-venture agreement with Singtel to set up mobile phone operations throughout Asia, the first being Singapore in 2001.

We had plans for Virgin Mobile South Africa, Canada and France to add to the UK and Australia, but the market I was desperate to get the Virgin brand into was one of the most challenging to break: the United States. We approached Sprint and a deal looked likely to go ahead, but they got cold feet at the last minute as the market shrank after 9/11. I phoned Bill Esray, Sprint's CEO, who was opposed to the deal. Our pledge to invest heavily ourselves – to the tune of $187 million over the next few years – showed we were serious. My arguments that the deal was cheap for Sprint, could transform their stuffy image and open up a new, youthful audience were all met with radio silence.

'Look, you need a brand like Virgin,' I ended up telling him. 'Right now, you're the phone company of choice for young Republicans.'

Somehow that did the trick. Bill relented, and in October 2001 we announced a new joint venture with Sprint to offer pay-as-you-go Virgin mobiles in the US. Dan Schulman came on board as CEO and we began preparing our US launch strategy.

Nine months later, once again I was dangling high above the ground, this time from a crane in Times Square. As reporters and tourists gathered below, I ripped off my clothes and threw them into the crowd, a (large!) strategically placed mobile phone covering my privates as I was flanked by six strapping cast members of new Broadway musical *The Full Monty*.

'That was fun. But I preferred the UK launch,' I told Dan afterwards. 'My support act there was all-female rather than all-male!'

The message was the same, though. Greater transparency and simplicity for customers. What you see is what you get. With the help of some irreverent ads, the business began to grow rapidly. Before we knew it, Virgin Mobile USA had broken the record as the fastest company ever to generate over a billion dollars in revenue, within three and a half years of launch. We sold the business to Sprint in December 2009 for £294 million; it continues to grow and remains the largest Virgin Mobile business worldwide.

3 Building a Business from the Back of a Beer Mat

The best ideas don't always need to have detailed financial projections and complicated business proposals behind them. Sometimes they come fully formed on the back of a beer mat. One such idea was the spark that led to the fastest growing Virgin company of all time: Virgin Blue.

The beer mats in question had been scribbled on by Brett Godfrey, who at the time was the chief financial officer for Virgin Express, our European carrier. I've always loved finding talent from within the Virgin family and encouraging people to challenge themselves in new companies within the Group – Brett was a great example. I'd first spotted his potential when he wrote an excellent note to a group of new starters. I began following his progress closely, and saw how he dealt with people in a personable manner and got the best out of them. He was someone who understood the little details of the airline industry that make all the difference; he knew management had to be accessible and visible, so would often get out and about, even rolling his sleeves up with the baggage handlers to heave bags and hear their issues from the frontline. So when the Virgin Express CEO position came up, I thought he was the man to fill the role.

When I called him up from Oxford one Thursday night to offer him the job, however, he turned me down flat.

'I really appreciate the offer,' he explained, 'but I've got two young kids now, and my wife and I have decided to move back to Australia.'

I was disappointed, but accepted his reasoning. 'I always respect a person who puts family first,' I told him. Wishing him all the best, I added: 'If you want to do anything in Australia, let me know and we'll see what we can do.'

There was a pause. 'Funny you should say that,' he replied. 'I've had an idea for a few years now that I'd love you to hear.'

I always like someone ready to seize their chance. 'OK,' I said. 'What is it?'

'Hold on.' I heard a muffled sound on the phone as Brett scrambled around for his notes. 'I've got the idea on the back of some beer mats ...'

Brett began telling me his plan for a low-cost airline in Australia. As the son of a Qantas employee, he knew the ins and outs of the Australian aviation market. He described how he'd sat down for a few pints with another airline expert, Rob Sherrard, who had launched Sherrard Aviation and also given Brett his first job as an accountant. They talked about the rise of low-cost carriers in Europe and the US, and pondered how this model could be translated to the Australian market. At the time, the public were being ripped off thanks to a lack of competition. Qantas was not being challenged by Ansett and had no incentive to improve their service or lower their prices. As flying is the only way to get around most of Australia's vast landscape, Qantas knew they had a captive audience. Brett and Rob's beer mat proposal was to find a way to set them free.

'Well, why don't you put a more detailed plan together? I'm happy to have a look at it,' I said.

Brett's plan was delivered to my door the next morning. I've always liked people who move fast too.

*

If I had to pick any single nation that really understands and breathes the Virgin way of living, it would be Australia. I have always loved visiting the country and spent lots of time down under in my early years, travelling around with my family, playing sport on the beach and in the ocean. I fell in love with the culture, the climate and the people.

When we were looking to expand Virgin Atlantic, one of the first destinations on my hit list was Sydney. I began a campaign to get the government to change their single-designation policy, which was allowing British Airways a monopoly on the route from London to Sydney. The authorities were also determined to protect their traditional home-grown airline, Qantas, whether or not it meant less choice and poorer service for Australians and fewer tourism dollars. I tried again and again, but got nowhere fast – there was no appetite for change, and certainly not for helping a scruffy Englishman from the music business.

At one particularly fruitless meeting with Senator Gareth Evans in May 1988, he made it clear in no uncertain terms that there was not going to be a change of policy. I left the room angry but undeterred, and immediately sent a note to the press explaining what had happened. It ended: 'If Virgin Atlantic was allowed to fly it would stimulate demand on this route, benefiting tourism, small businesses and visiting relatives. Competition must be in everyone's interest. Fortunately though, I'm only 37 and – as long as I don't go down in a balloon – time is on my side!' Well, I did go down in quite a few more balloons, but am still here to tell the tale.

What we really needed was to start a new airline altogether, which was why Brett's idea was so enticing. Looking through his proposal the following day, it was apparent that the numbers added up, the vision was clear and Brett's enthusiasm was infectious. Who says accountants can't be imaginative? Perhaps those few pints helped to get the creative juices flowing! Australia's duopolistic aviation market was exactly the kind Virgin was designed to disrupt. I asked

Brett to fly to Australia to look at the areas I still had some concerns about, in particular ticketing, pilots, terminals, slots, quality planes and staff. Before the week was out he was back, having answered all my questions.

While I was more than satisfied, the Virgin board still needed persuading. They had previously rejected the idea, with Brett telling me he had been close to abandoning the whole concept before I showed interest. This made me even more determined to see it through, but I found myself fighting the same lack of enthusiasm that Brett had faced from Virgin's executives.

'Look at the upsides,' I said in a board meeting. 'Then look at the downsides. The potential is massive; there is risk, but it is manageable.'

One of my main arguments was the element of surprise. None of the Australian airlines would expect a business like ours to compete with them. We were still establishing our brand on the global stage. Nobody would see us coming. After a big battle, I finally convinced them. I met up with Brett in person to tell him the good news. Shaking his hand, I grinned at him.

'Screw it,' I said. 'Let's do it.'

*

'If you've got purple hair and you're working in a butcher's shop and you can still smile after a tough day, you're the kind of cabin crew we're looking for ...'

Our advertising campaign for airline staff was unusual in many ways. Firstly, rather than focusing on the more obvious location of Sydney for recruitment, we set our sights on the Sunshine Coast. Alongside Perth, Brisbane was the fastest growing market in the country, the beaches were a huge attraction and Queensland's government was extremely keen to market a new airline and boost its region's tourism.

Rather than going for experience we wanted to recruit people who wouldn't usually apply for airline jobs. Virgin has always focused on finding the best possible people, and I was determined to set our new airline apart by having the finest staff in the world. We didn't want people who had been working at airlines for years – we needed fresh faces with new ideas. A typical Virgin airline employee is the sort of person who will joke with passengers and smile, not just nod their head and say: 'Yes sir, no sir, three bags full sir.' I shared a story about one occasion when we had a short delay before a Virgin flight and people had to queue up at the gate. One of the passengers jumped the queue and marched up to the desk. Our team member very politely asked him to get back into the queue. He turned on her and said: 'Don't you know who I am?' So she picked up the intercom and announced: 'I have a young man at gate 23, who seems to be lost – he doesn't know who he is.' The other passengers roared with laughter. 'Fuck you!' shouted the self-important man. She kept a straight face and replied: 'I'm afraid you're going to have to get in line for that too, sir!'

The recruitment campaign was a runaway success, and 12,000 people wanting to relocate to Queensland had sent in their CVs.

Our budget to launch the airline was just A\$10 million. That might sound a lot of money but, to put it in context, JetBlue, a low-cost airline in the US, had needed US\$120 million to get off the ground. I was eager for us to use the internet like no airline before us – within six months, 92 per cent of bookings were online. This is normal now, but back in 2000 high street stores and holiday brochures reigned. We were appealing to younger consumers, and reducing our costs too, as transaction fees were far cheaper online. We might have been operating on a tiny budget, but we made up the difference with our enthusiasm, initiative and humour. We decided to call it Virgin Blue, a cheeky word-play on the fact that Aussies call redheads 'bluey'. It appealed to my sense of humour to name our red planes Blue: it also meant I could convince Brett and Rob to dress up as the Blues Brothers for our inaugural flight from Brisbane to Sydney on 31 August 2000.

As the launch date approached, we caused quite a stir by announcing our prices. For a one-way flight from Brisbane to Sydney our flights were more than A$50 cheaper than Qantas's. Their stock price plummeted by A$2 billion. I called Brett excitedly, conscious that delays can ground airlines before they ever take off.

'Are we on target for launch?' I asked. 'Let's do everything we can to get in the air on time and make the most of this.'

Brett remained confident and we stepped up our plans to start flying. With customers rolling in, the team grew from twelve staff in March to 350 in August. With a month to go before lift-off, I was getting calls from management about rising costs. The accountants worried we wouldn't be able to pay our staff, but I was ignoring them, pushing for more investment and urging Brett to plan faster expansion. While Brett was scrabbling to keep the payroll flowing, I signed off on a A$600 million long-term investment to order ten new Boeing 737s. I was eager to take advantage of the splash we were making, especially with the eyes of the world on Australia for the Sydney Olympics.

I dialled into a board meeting to back Brett up. 'Before anyone says anything,' I began, 'I know we're over budget, and I promise you it will be worth it.' Some of those in the room sounded unsure, but I continued to press our case. 'There is no point trying this half-heartedly – we have to really go for it, or give up. Are we giving up?'

On one side of the coin, what we were doing seemed a massive risk. Did I know all the ins and outs of the airline business in Australia? Certainly not. While we had built up a wealth of experience with Virgin Atlantic, this was a whole new market with its own intricacies, complications and absurdities. But at the same time I believed Virgin could succeed in Australia because everybody already knew about us there: Virgin had an incredible 94 per cent brand recognition in the country before we even launched the airline. Beyond the brand recognition, there was massive overlap in our values and outlook to build on as well: it may be a cliché to suggest Australians know how to have fun and we do, too, but it's true. They work hard, play hard and don't take themselves too seriously, all of which rang plenty of bells.

We knew there was an appetite for us to get up in the air, though, and we were determined to satisfy it. We also knew that our rivals weren't ready for us. From the outset we had caught them off guard, and began making inroads on their market share. My instinct was proved right: our customers loved our approach, our staff were incredibly enthusiastic and it was the most successful start to a business we'd ever had. In less than a year, we'd welcomed our millionth passenger on board.

*

It didn't take long, however, for our Australian rivals to fight back and then attempt to take us out of business. Qantas introduced a new low-cost service to counter our growth, undercutting our fares at a loss and increasing capacity on routes we were doing well on. Putting more seats on a route than there are passengers means both companies will lose money – there will simply be too many empty seats to cover costs. As a business tactic, it's something of a power play: bigger players can suck in these losses, accept a short-term hit and try to bankrupt their rivals. Then it's back to business as usual, robbing flyers of the benefits of innovation and competition.

As for Ansett, they were struggling badly. As well as the disruption our entrance into the market had caused, they were desperately trying to replace an ageing fleet and modernise their service. Passengers were deserting in droves, and we were there to pick them up. At the same time we were expanding, too, moving smoothly into the New Zealand market with flights from Christchurch to Brisbane on our new Pacific Blue service. Air New Zealand, who part-owned Ansett, needed to respond. Rather than try to undercut like Qantas, their strategy was to take us off the table in a different way.

In June 2001, just ten months after our inaugural flight, their CEO Gary Toomey began floating the idea of buying Virgin Blue. After an initial meeting, he took Brett to dinner at a Chinese restaurant in the Crown Casino in Melbourne. Out of the blue, he made an offer for our airline: seventy million dollars.

'You mean seventy million *US* dollars?' asked Brett.

'Yes, I think we can do that,' Gary replied.

It was an astonishing offer. Our little company, which still had only five jets and an estimated market share of about 4 per cent, had grown from a A$10 million investment to a A$120 million valuation in under a year.

Brett excused himself and called me from the restaurant payphone with the news. I was back in Holland Park going through my post when he phoned.

'Seventy million dollars?' I sat upright in my chair. '*Seventy*, not seventeen?'

'Seventy,' Brett confirmed. 'And US dollars. Not Australian.'

I thought for a few seconds. 'Turn it down,' I said. 'It's an unbelievable offer – nobody really expected us to make a penny. But it could still be undervaluing us.'

The Virgin Group board were less certain. They were understandably keen to see such a quick and large return on our investment. The unknown question was precisely what Ansett were thinking – were they running scared? At a management meeting, Brett told his team he thought Ansett would disappear within three years. Everybody laughed. But then, while our profits kept rising, Ansett began making greater redundancies and suffering from more Qantas flights squeezing their routes. Two months after we'd turned down that initial offer, they informally came back to the table, this time suggesting a joint venture. Now Qantas CEO Geoff Dixon joined the party: he told the press his airline was considering acquiring Virgin Blue – something we dismissed outright. We were there to compete with the behemoth, not join it.

Ansett, by contrast, was a different situation. For the right price, perhaps there was a deal to be done. We ran the numbers at our Brisbane office, but they still didn't seem to add up. Getting rid of Virgin Blue would only reduce Ansett's losses by about A$200,000 a day, which we thought was probably one-fifth of what they were losing. This turned out to be a very low estimate.

'There must be a bigger move coming,' concluded Brett.

Indeed there was. The call came towards the start of September as I was about to leave the office. I sat back down as I heard who was on the other end of the line: the CEO of Singapore Airlines, Dr C. K. Cheong.

As Dr Cheong chatted away, it all began to make sense. Singapore was already a partner of Virgin's since paying £600 million for a 49 per cent stake in Virgin Atlantic in 1999. Ironically, we reinvested some of that money to start Virgin Blue – we even offered Singapore the option of becoming partners in our Australian airline for A$10 million, but they declined. However, Virgin Atlantic weren't the only airline that Singapore had a stake in: they also owned 20 per cent of Ansett, and needed to protect their investment.

Cheong's proposal was straightforward. They wanted to buy Virgin Blue outright – and for a lot more than A$10 million.

'Richard, you and I have been friends for many years,' Dr Cheong told me. 'Which is why we are formally offering a very generous A$250 million for Virgin Blue.'

It was a bigger offer than I could ever have imagined. But it was also one that came with a deadline. And also with a warning.

'You have twenty-four hours to make up your minds.' Dr Cheong made it clear they wanted us out of the way, and backed it up with hard cash – and a threat for good measure. 'If you refuse, I promise the Singapore government will unleash huge investment into Ansett, and destroy Virgin Blue within six months.'

I thought it all over on a sleepless flight to Australia. As evening fell on 3 September, my mind was racing. I got back to the Potts Point Holiday Inn in Sydney, where all the

Virgin Blue cabin crew were staying, around 10 p.m. Brett and his management team – Rob Sherrard, Amanda Bolger and David Huttner – were waiting for me at a table in the corner.

I joined them for a beer to discuss what we should do. Brett was quite emotional, surrounded by his staff, and argued that we shouldn't throw all of this away for what, admittedly, was an awful lot of money. The team estimated Virgin Blue was worth double what Ansett were offering. And if we did take the money, Brett wasn't going to hang around.

'I couldn't stay on if we did the deal,' he told me. 'I wouldn't be able to look the team in the eye; they would know we had sold them out.'

Brett and his team weren't the only ones trying to convince me not to sell. At one point in the discussions, Derryn Hinch, the well-known Australian broadcaster and now a senator, even turned up.

'What do you think Australians will think if I sell?' I asked him.

'They will think you're a lying prick,' he told me in no uncertain terms. 'Anything else you do in Australia for the next hundred years will bring back memories of your sell-out.'

But this decision wasn't as clear cut as Brett and Derryn made out. It wasn't just Virgin Blue I had to consider: I had the whole Virgin Group to think about. I spent a long night pacing up and down my hotel room hashing out the options in my head. I was torn. The Virgin Group could certainly use the money to reinvest, and I couldn't argue with the logic of cashing out a quarter of a billion Australian dollars, twenty-five times what we had initially put in.

But I didn't like being threatened – especially by Virgin Atlantic's partner! Plus, something about the offer didn't quite add up. Why were Ansett's parent company Singapore Airlines so keen to give Virgin Blue, a relatively small player, so much money to go away? Were they really going to use the might of the Singapore government to put us out of business? If so, resisting would be akin to starting a bleeding competition with a blood bank – we'd never win. But the sheer size of their offer smacked of desperation. Could Ansett be in greater trouble than we realised? Maybe even on the verge of bankruptcy? For them to offer us A$250 million made me think we might just have all the cards in our hand.

Early the following morning I flew to Melbourne airport. We had informed the Australian media that I had a major announcement to make, and they were out in force to hear what I had to say. It wasn't just the media, either. Rumours were by now flying around about a possible deal, and lots of our staff were standing at the back of the Domestic Express Terminal. There were a lot of nerves in that room and, as I stood up on a podium, I could feel the room go silent – it was one of those cut-the-atmosphere-with-a-knife moments. I caught the eye of a couple of cabin crew leaning on the wall at the back of the crowd. They looked terrible: as tired as I was from the lack of sleep the night before.

'I've got some good news and some bad news,' I said, lifting up a big cheque as I spoke. 'I've had a fantastic time in Australia. The good news is we have done well with Virgin Blue. We've made twenty-five times our investment in a year. I have this cheque for A$250 million for the airline ... The bad news is it is a sad day for Australia and for competition. I'm back off to England. It's sad that we are selling today, but it's an offer we can't refuse.' As the cameras zoomed in on the amount, I could see a Bloomberg reporter speaking loudly into her mobile phone: 'He's selling, he's selling, get the story up!' Within moments, the story was live on ABC's website as well as out on the wires. At the back of the room, some of the ladies from Virgin Blue were crying their eyes out. I decided it was time to put them out of their misery.

'Oh, fuck it, I'm only joking!' I ripped the cheque into tiny pieces and threw it into the air. 'I'm sorry for upsetting my staff who were not in on the joke. But we're here to stay!'

At the back of the room, our staff cheered and I walked over to hug them. But for others in the room, the news was too late – the original story was already spreading throughout the world and they were on a damage limitation exercise to stop it spreading further.

The Bloomberg reporter, now ashen-faced, was shouting into her phone. 'He's not selling! Kill the story!'

I went over to her to try and apologise.

'I'll lose my job because of that. You are so irresponsible; you made me put out a false report!'

I got down on the floor and kissed her feet, begging for forgiveness. It was a surreal end to a crazy couple of days.

*

Singapore Airlines, it transpired, had been bluffing. They had no cards in their hand, let alone the royal flush of the Singapore government that they had threatened. The very next day they turned down an offer to buy all of Ansett for one dollar, and withdrew all their support. After failing to buy Virgin Blue, they knew that continuing to bail out Ansett was throwing good money after bad. The following day, Qantas turned down the same offer. It seemed Ansett was losing far more than we ever imagined – around A$50 million per week – and Air New Zealand needed to ditch their share before they went down with it. The following week, Ansett declared bankruptcy.

Looking back, I think most people would have taken the money. Certainly, everyone at Virgin Group wanted to – it would have been an extraordinary return on investment. But emotionally – and I do most things on emotion – it would have felt like selling one's own child. Staying at the Holiday Inn at Potts Point with all the cabin crew certainly influenced me. They were such a delightful, fun team. In the end, the idea of selling them out was just too strange. It felt fitting that the company which started over a few beers was saved by a conversation over a few more.

4 Let's Get Physical

I seem to have experienced more than my fair share of fires over the years. Our childhood home caught fire. Our then home in Holland Park caught fire. Our old cricket pavilion in Oxford was burnt to the ground. Our trans-Pacific balloon burst into flames and, of course, the Great House on Necker was destroyed by a blaze in a tropical lightning storm. But one of the worst such incidents preceded the call I took in August 1999 from Frank Reed, one of the duo behind our new venture Virgin Active. We were about to open the first of our gyms after months and years of hard work and preparation. But then disaster struck.

'You won't believe it,' Frank sounded distraught. 'The club has burnt down.'

Two years earlier I had met Frank along with his business partner Matthew Bucknall at my home in Holland Park. It was a summer's day, and I was sitting in the sunshine, scribbling some notes for my first autobiography, *Losing My Virginity*, when they arrived. Matthew and Frank were casually dressed and relaxed in demeanour. But behind all that they clearly had ambition, too.

'We're going to build you another billion-dollar business,' said Matthew.

I was obviously sceptical at first. This was a period when Virgin were investing in all sorts of sectors and companies. My house had become something of a revolving door of business pitches, with every fresh-faced young hopeful believing their business idea was bound to make them a fortune. I always applauded the optimism, but knew from experience that nine times out of ten the workable plan to make it happen didn't exist.

'And here's the plan of how we're going to do it,' added Frank.

There was something about them that made me sit up and listen. Very quickly I realised Matthew and Frank had the know-how to back up their confidence. They presented to me their vision to create the world's most loved health club brand. I had presumed their idea was limited to gyms in the UK, but they explained how they saw this brand expanding globally. This was my kind of thinking. I was keen for Virgin to continue growing our presence around the world, and it was great to see how important the brand's values were to their strategy.

'We want to create the first global comprehensive consumer-led branded health and fitness facility,' Matthew explained, 'readily accessible to a wide socio-demographic group at a price consumers are willing and able to pay.'

'Well, that's a bit of a mouthful,' I laughed. 'As a dyslexic, let me see if I've got this right. You want to create a great global Virgin health club chain that most people can afford?'

'Sorry, Richard. Yes!'

The pair talked for a further hour without interruption from me – a very rare feat. As they outlined their vision, I leaned back in my chair and put my scruffy pair of rubber-soled Timberlands on the table. Matthew and Frank must have been panicking at my lack of feedback as they pitched. They might even have thought I was being rude. In reality, I was taken by their vision and loved the idea of Virgin moving into fitness.

'Well, what do you think?' asked Matthew, glancing sideways at his business partner.

I leaned back in my chair, and let him wait a little longer, before I allowed a grin to spread across my face.

'I think it's absolutely fuckin' brilliant. I'd love to do it with you.' Their expressions relaxed, and I heard them sigh with relief.

*

Matthew and Frank got to work immediately. I asked them to spend the next year travelling the globe. I wanted them to visit all the leading health clubs worldwide, see what they were doing well, what they were doing poorly and how we could do it all far better.

'I will cover all the expense on the condition that when you return you create the very best health clubs in the world.'

'That's very generous of you,' Matthew thanked me.

I waved that away. 'Obviously,' I laughed, 'it helps that we own an airline!'

The health club market was crowded, and I knew our entrance into it had to be done right.

Whenever I had been to health clubs in the UK, I always came away disappointed. The changing rooms were always cramped. The equipment was dated. And the prices were exorbitantly high. It felt like a chore working out, which is why I rarely did: I much preferred to exercise in the great outdoors. We needed to come up with a new business model to change that, which started by focusing on the customers.

It quickly became clear how Frank and Matthew's skills complemented each other. Frank went to work on the design and branding. He came up with startlingly simple, beautiful design plans, which would give members clear sight lines throughout the clubs and bright, friendly atmospheres to work out in. Matthew, meanwhile, explored locations for the first Virgin Active health club. I presumed they would plump for London, but they came up with a prime location in the north of England – Preston. That surprised me: a low-key launch in Lancashire was a long way from 'blowing up' the Coca-Cola sign in Times Square to launch Virgin Cola.

But Matthew and Frank knew what they were doing. Virgin Active wasn't the right business for me to be jumping off buildings or flying balloons to announce our arrival; as they explained, gyms worked on steady word-of-mouth growth. If there's one thing I've learned, it's to trust people to make their own decisions, so I let them get on with it.

Mind you, it took me a while to get my head round Matthew's explanation of their reasoning behind the plans for the next club locations.

'I've developed an ingenious demographic modelling system to pinpoint exact coordinates where it makes sense to invest in new health clubs,' he told me at one catch-up meeting.

'That sounds great, Matthew. What the hell does it mean?'

Everyone uses data to plot customer demographics now, but in 1999 he may as well have been talking Double Dutch to me.

'Did you ever play Battleships as a kid?' he asked.

'Of course.'

'Well, it's like playing Battleships.'

Now I understood. Put simply, we used surveys to pinpoint the specific locations where gaps in the market existed with lots of potential customers living nearby.

Frank and Matthew were like the left- and right-hand side of the brain working in unison. Frank was so up and down that we got hold of a biorhythms device and jokingly pretended to track his mood swings. On the other side, Matthew was the steady hand on the tiller. When it came to the first Virgin Active stars of the year party, it made perfect sense for them to dress up as Batman and Robin. Frank got one over on Matthew by presenting him with his Robin costume just minutes before the event started. It happened to be several sizes too small for a man six foot three inches tall! I was just happy that somebody else had drawn the short straw out of the fancy-dress box for once.

*

'I've made my money on the site, I believe in what you're doing – this is my present to Preston.'

The location we secured for our first gym came with the blessing of its former owner. It was the last available property on a site with the first Warner Bros multiplex cinema and was initially intended to be a bingo hall. But then the owner heard our pitch and was sold on the purpose of Virgin Active. He told us his father had recently suffered a heart attack, and he fully supported our vision of getting Prestonians to live more active lifestyles.

We had originally scheduled to open our first club in February 1999, but, as is often the case, there were delays with building and design work. The press were openly questioning what we were doing, entering a crowded fitness market with one gym in what some London papers considered an unfashionable part of England.

In the original business plan, I had written: 'It will be the attention to detail and the 100 different touches that will distinguish Virgin Active from the competition.' Does the music and atmosphere in the club inspire people to pedal a little faster? Is the pool the right temperature? Are the towels laid out for everyone? What we'd created achieved all of that, and then some. Firstly, the staff we'd hired had the Virgin spirit. You can never fake a genuine smile, and when I met them I could see their enthusiasm. And secondly, all of the pain points I hated about gyms had been addressed head on. The light, spacious, open-plan design allowed members to see exactly what they were getting when they walked through the door. And the showers were as good as, if not better than, those in people's homes. Certainly, they were better than the one on my houseboat!

So, by August 1999 we were ready to open our first family-friendly, open-space health club – until disaster struck. Matthew explained how the fire had swept through the gym, doing tens of thousands of pounds' worth of damage. Thankfully nobody was hurt. But it put our opening back months and months. On top of this, we had a full team to continue paying and no money coming in.

It's easy to feel downhearted in such a situation. Instead, we sought out the benefits. While we began the rebuild, the staff threw themselves into engaging with the community, shouting our simple principles from the rooftops – literally in some cases. By the time we opened the club, we did so with 5,500 members. Just a few years earlier, LivingWell were charging £300 as an individual joining fee. By contrast, Virgin Active had no joining fee and no long-term contracts. There are no barriers to entry, no roadblocks to exit, no locked doors and no hidden extras. As we ripped the old models to shreds, we were loved by our customers and hated by the industry with a passion.

5 How to Start a Train Company

When it first became public knowledge in the early 1990s that Virgin were interested in setting up a train company, the powers that be were, to put it politely, less than enthusiastic. Or to put it less politely, as the British Rail CEO John Welsby did, after leaving a meeting with me and unaware the intercom was on outside my then home, 'I'll be in my grave before that fucker gets his logo on my trains!'

The idea of running my own train company had first come to mind in September 1991. I was in Tokyo, looking for locations to open a new Virgin Megastore. After doing my various recces, I jumped on the Shinkansen, the bullet train, bound for Japan's historic former capital of Kyoto. The journey was a revelation. It wasn't just the speed, as we whizzed through the Japanese countryside at 199mph, it was also the excellent service, the vending machines, the entertainment – much of it reminiscent of the plane journeys Virgin Atlantic had pioneered. It made me wonder why the trains in the UK were so bad by comparison.

Back in London a few days later, I was interviewed by the *Sunday Telegraph*'s transport correspondent, Toby Helm. He asked Will Whitehorn and me if Virgin were interested in operating our own train service.

'Well, are we?' I said to Will, remembering the contrast with my Japanese experience. 'It certainly needs improving.'

After the interview, we spent a couple of days looking into it a bit more, learning about the government's proposals to privatise British Rail.

'Tell Toby we are interested,' I told Will. 'Let's fly a kite. It can't do any harm.'

Forty-eight hours later, the *Sunday Telegraph* was emblazoned with the headline 'VIRGIN TO GO INTO TRAINS'. The momentum now matched that of a bullet train: I was already searching for a CEO and a management team by the time the phone starting ringing off the hook on Monday morning, with scores of potential partners. It turned out there was an awful lot of interest in Virgin Trains and we hadn't even registered the name yet!

I began meeting officials, including John Welsby. He visited my house at the time and within seconds of walking in made it very clear that he opposed any sort of privatisation of the railways. By the time he left, I knew his disapproval applied to me in particular. And this was confirmed when he strolled out of the meeting and turned to his colleague, not realising the intercom was going to broadcast his colourful comments to the entire office.

Regardless of John's strong opinions, the Virgin Rail Group put bids together for both the CrossCountry and InterCity West Coast franchises. We promised new diesel Voyager trains, to be built by Bombardier, on the CrossCountry line's criss-crossing route around the UK. When we won the bid in November 1997, I was both ecstatic and excited about the possibilities. The following year, I predicted in *Losing My Virginity* that Virgin Trains would come to be seen as one of the best things we ever did.

*

In the first years after my forecast, however, many people thought precisely the opposite. It didn't take long to appreciate the size of the challenge we had taken on and for me to wonder why I had decided to try and run my own train company. Put simply, the railways were in a bad, bad way, both organisationally and on the tracks. The infrastructure was half the size it had been in 1946 when the Labour government nationalised the railways, and there had been very little investment since.

We took over running the CrossCountry route in January 1998, the same month we beat off competition from Stagecoach and Sea Containers to win Britain's premier track, the West Coast franchise, too. One of the first decisions we had to take concerned rolling stock. After discovering that 300mph Maglev trains wouldn't suit the size and shape of Britain's railways and would produce high emissions and electricity costs, I flew to Italy in May 1998 to see if tilting trains could work. I travelled on a Pendolino ETR 460 from Turin to Rome and was amazed at how smoothly we zipped through the countryside.

Bringing Pendolinos to the UK was controversial, however. British Rail had tried and failed to introduce tilting trains on the West Coast back in 1981, with their Advanced Passenger Trains quickly being nicknamed Accident Prone Trains. The press dubbed them 'queasy rider' as reporters on board were sick, while technical problems cost taxpayers millions of pounds. If the railways had still been nationalised, a government official would have lost his job for even suggesting bringing back tilting trains. But as an entrepreneurial company, it was a decision that Virgin was able to make.

Convinced that Pendolinos were now the best choice, I signed two of the biggest deals in Virgin's history. First, Brian Souter, the chairman of Stagecoach, got in touch and we agreed a deal for his more experienced company to pay £158 million for a 49 per cent stake in Virgin Trains. Next, we agreed a £1.85 billion deal for Alstom to build us a fleet of tilting, safe, lightweight, energy-efficient trains. Given the money involved, Alstom were surprised by the simplicity of our instructions. They were used to extremely lengthy, restrictive briefs that ruled out most creativity. Instead, all I told them was what speed the trains needed to go, how often they needed to run and how we wanted them to look. We left the details to them.

'You're the technical experts,' I wrote to them. 'I want you to use your expertise.'

Next, I headed over to Old Dalby, near Melton Mowbray, where we had electrified the track for testing. I was standing on the platform to watch the tilting train for myself when I decided to take a closer look. There was a man pressing a button on a laptop in each carriage to tilt the train, and I wanted to see what he was doing. Not thinking, I jumped over the barrier, straight onto the track with 25,000 volts charged overhead.

'Richard! What the hell are you doing?' Tony Collins, who worked for Alstom and would go on to become Virgin Trains' CEO, was screaming at me as I hopped onto the train. He was right to do so: it was only by luck that I didn't step on the wrong track: if I had, I would have used up yet another of my (far more than) nine lives!

Aside from the trains and the tracks, the other main challenge was changing the culture of staff, many of whom had worked under British Rail for decades. When we started the West Coast franchise we found a British Rail procedure manual in the office. It detailed rules and regulations for everything, even including how close your carpet was officially allowed to be from the skirting board. There wasn't exactly a get-up-and-go spirit around the place and I was initially worried they wouldn't be able to adapt to such a radically different setup. But as it turned out, the staff became one of our greatest assets: they embraced every change we implemented.

*

Events, though, were to conspire against us as we started the new millennium. On 17 October 2000 the tragic Hatfield GNER rail crash took place, killing four people and injuring seventy. In the aftermath, speed restrictions were introduced across all rail operators over the entire country. A year later, things got worse. In the weeks following 9/11, Railtrack, which was a public company, went into administration and its shareholders lost all their money. This was to cost taxpayers £1.25 billion a year in additional infrastructure costs.

The British government created Network Rail, a not-for-dividend private company, to manage the chaotic infrastructure. Very quickly, however, Network Rail was in disarray, too. They told us they could not deliver the promised upgrades on time, the cost of the upgrades was quadrupling and our Pendolino top speed was cut to 125mph – all of which made our proposed journeys longer and less frequent. It was a massive blow.

After long negotiations, both the West Coast and Virgin CrossCountry franchises were suspended in 2002 in favour of management contracts (agreements to run, maintain and manage the line, with minimal disruption to passengers, until new franchise terms were agreed). Eventually, we lost the CrossCountry franchise to Arriva, who bid more when it was retendered in 2007. It felt like a huge missed opportunity. We had never really had a chance to drive a good business on this higgledy-piggledy route. Just as we began turning it around, it was gone.

I was determined the same wouldn't happen on the West Coast Main Line. By the time we signed the management contract we had already delivered the first Pendolino, on budget and on time. In November 2001 I stood in Alstom's chilly Birmingham factory and proudly looked on as Joan, who usually avoids such occasions, named our new train *Lady Joan*. As we sat together that night watching the *Six O'Clock News*, Joan squeezed my hand as the newsreader said: 'Virgin has delivered on its promises.' She knew how much this project meant to me personally, and, as ever, was right by my side.

'By the way,' she added, 'you know the name of the train is wrong?'

'What? No, it isn't.'

'Yes, it is. The wife of a knight doesn't use her forename in her title. I'm actually Lady Branson – not Lady Joan.'

'You're pulling my leg.'

'I'm not. Look it up.'

I did – she was right, of course.

In mid-2003 I sat in the latest of a seemingly never-ending series of meetings with ministers and officials from the UK government's Department for Transport. We were discussing the finer details for renegotiating Virgin Trains' franchise, and were going around in circles. On my way to one particular meeting I had spotted a game of Sam's on the kitchen table and stuck it in my bag. As the meeting dragged interminably on, I decided to bring it out to loosen everyone up.

'Let's play a little game,' I said, to bewilderment around the table. 'Just hold these in your hands; this won't hurt a bit . . .' I explained the rules of the game and what was about to happen. 'I'm going to ask some questions. If you answer correctly, the buck passes to the next person. If you get them wrong, you will get electrocuted. OK?'

Patrick McCall, Virgin Trains' executive co-chairman, looked on a bit nervously. I couldn't decide if the ministers looked bemused or simply terrified – probably a bit of both! It might sound extreme, but I needed to find some way of injecting a spark into proceedings.

Something needed to happen because by this point we were not making money and were losing goodwill in our brand. I felt we were victims of our own success with our other Virgin companies. Because people had seen instant improvement in service with businesses like Virgin Atlantic and Virgin Money, passengers expected an overnight transformation to take place as soon as the trains took on our name. The difference there, though, was that we started those businesses from scratch, and could build up the culture, practices and experiences in a bespoke way. With Virgin Trains, we inherited outdated facilities and old-fashioned working models. For all our efforts, by the end of 2003 Virgin Trains was still a long way from being on track.

*

It wasn't until September 2004 that a full timetable of our 125mph Pendolinos was finally ready to go into service. A week before the first customer train journey, we did a trial run of the Pendolino from London to Manchester. Prime Minister Tony Blair joined me at London's Euston Station to mark the entry of tilting trains into service.

I was delighted when the train arrived in one hour and fifty-three minutes, knocking fifteen minutes off the record time for a London–Manchester journey. We had reason to be confident the first commercial service would go off without a hitch, too. But then our flagship *Royal Scot* train broke down at Carlisle with a wheel problem, causing a two-hour delay. Only two of seventy-eight tilting services had any issues, but that was enough for some people to predict the end of Virgin Trains before it really got going. 'Euston, we have a problem . . .' was the infamous *Daily Mail* line.

But after this rather inglorious opening, the Pendolinos and the team came into their own. In the first week we hit 82 per cent punctuality, 10 per cent up on targets, and only four of 2,010 services were cancelled. It was not perfect, but it was a good start. Slowly but surely we began to turn things around. 'General mood of passengers is that it worked well and will steadily improve,' I wrote in my notebook.

And that is precisely what happened. Tony Collins took over as CEO in 2004 after years of superb work from Chris Green, and by 2008 we were named the UK's best train company by the Institute of Customer Service – an accolade that would have sounded utterly implausible a few years earlier. We had finally delivered on our promises.

6 Answering Madiba's Call

I was in the bath when Nelson Mandela rang. The tub belonged to friends of mine, and was situated in their English country house where I was staying. I was having a proper soak, plenty of bubbles, and was relaxing to the point that I almost didn't answer the phone. But, somehow, when Madiba rang, wherever you were, you always took the call.

'Richard,' Madiba said, ignoring the sounds of splashing in the background and getting straight to the point, 'you said that you wanted to help out in South Africa ...'

Madiba and I had recently spent time together in Cape Town putting on an incredible concert to raise awareness about AIDS. I had just got back from South Africa, so I presumed he wanted to follow up on that.

'Yes, Madiba. You know I'm happy to help,' I responded, brushing the bubbles off the telephone cord.

'Well, we have a problem. Our biggest health business, the Health & Racquet Club, is about to collapse.' He explained that 5,000 people were going to lose their jobs and that a company that was one of the symbols of South African growth and progress was going under. 'Do you think you could save it?' he asked. 'Do you think you could save the people?'

'I'm sure we can do something.' I tried to sound more assured than I was feeling. 'I'll be back on the next plane to Africa.'

As it happened, I knew more about the Health &
Racquet Club chain than Madiba might have realised. As
Virgin Active had expanded in the UK, we had been in the
process of buying a couple of their clubs from Healthland
International, the overseas branch of the overall company,
LeisureNet. The discussions, however, had taken a
sharply different turn when Heathland suggested that,
rather than two clubs, we took over fifty leases from them
in one go.

It had been a tempting offer. The gyms were high-quality
and it meant we could achieve scale overnight. I was over
on Necker, running up quite a phone bill debating it back
and forth with Peter Norris, an adviser for Virgin Group and
Virgin Active. It got to 2 a.m. back in England, and Peter
and I were both sorely tempted to do the deal. But I could
tell from something in Matthew Bucknall's voice that he
wasn't convinced.

'It looks a good deal on paper,' he said, clearing his throat,
'but it's not as easy as it sounds. The model they have presented just doesn't stack up.'

'In that case we're not going to do it,' I decided. 'Let's all
get some sleep.'

After we declined the Healthland deal, they soon went
into receivership. As Matthew had rightly deduced, their
business model had some fundamental flaws. They hadn't
forecast properly and ran out of cash, which was why they
had knocked on our door. There was a domino effect, and
very quickly LeisureNet was placed under a liquidation
order. That put seventy-six Health & Racquet Club gyms
across South Africa, with more than 900,000 members, on
the verge of going under, too.

As I put the phone down on Madiba, I had no idea what
we could practically do, whether there was a viable business opportunity, or if the call would cost us millions of
pounds. But I respected his desire to support his people and
wholeheartedly wanted to help.

*

South Africa is a place I have always had a lot of affection for, and had got to know particularly well in the early years of the new millennium.

One corner of the country I had long ago fallen in love with was Ulusaba, part of the Sabi Sand Reserve in Kruger National Park. Ulusaba means 'place of little fear' in the local Shangaan tribe's language and it was easy to see why. The first time Joan and I visited, we stayed in a tiny little makeshift treehouse, creaking and wobbling high above the plain with a stunning view of the waterhole below. This was a gathering point for all manner of animals, from rhinos to gazelles, buffalos to hyenas. Throughout the park there were leopards, elephants, hippos, lions and giraffes marauding below. There were also painted wolves. Often known as wild dogs, these creatures hunt in packs with incredible guile and cunning, and have a fierce sense of family loyalty and solidarity. There are usually bigger, faster, stronger predators ready to steal their meal – or their young – but working together they can fight them off. Forget the Big Five (although magnificent lions, African elephants, Cape buffalos, leopards and rhinoceros can all be found roaming Ulusaba): these creatures quickly became my favourite animals in the bush.

It was a magical place. Lying there looking up at the stars in the indigo sky, I felt I had discovered another little piece of paradise. I set about buying Ulusaba, with a view to turning it into a luxury reserve for people to visit and support the local community. With Karl and Llane Langdon at the helm, we have developed Ulusaba into a haven for wildlife as well as a beacon for the surrounding region. Today we employ 107 team members, of whom seventy-six are from the local villages. Their income is able to support an estimated 540 individuals in around sixty families. What's more, those who become rangers and trackers are sponsored to study for Field Guides Association of Southern Africa accreditation, and, as ever, we promote our best staff from within. The park has become an integral part of the community, especially since we launched Pride 'n' Purpose, a scheme to support local people by building schools, backing regional education schemes and creating health clinics.

In 2000 we visited Ulusaba to mark the official launch of Virgin Limited Edition, our collection of spectacular hide-aways, which also includes Necker Island and Kasbah Tamadot in Morocco. I have acquired each place in different ways over the years – I became the lease holder of our former London property the Roof Gardens after a bouncer refused me entry for wearing jeans and looking too scruffy. I bought the place the next day, and gently informed the bouncer to let me in regardless of my clothing. He turned out to be a delightful gentleman and ended up working for us for another three decades.

There is another side to South Africa. At the same time as developing the Ulusaba resort, I was also spending more time in South Africa working with our foundation Virgin Unite, specifically tackling the escalating HIV/AIDS crisis there. I travelled across the country to see the situation up close, and was horrified by what I found. There were huge advertisements for funeral services along every road. Inside the hospices were rows of beds filled with people dying from HIV/AIDS. More terminally ill people lay slumped in corridors, waiting for others to die before they could fit into beds. The scale of the problem was utterly catastrophic.

The most infuriating thing about this misery was that much of it was entirely preventable. Raising awareness of ways to prevent HIV spreading and ending discrimination against people who were HIV positive should be possible. We created videos, made by Africans and translated into several languages, to show how the HIV/AIDS drugs worked to help the human immune system. We urged the African National Congress, which had been so inspirational in helping to build a new South Africa, to accept that HIV and AIDS were linked, and start helping to solve the problem. In 2003, we also helped to organise a wonderful concert in Cape Town with Nelson Mandela, using the number he wore during his eighteen years of imprisonment, 46664, as a rallying call for the HIV/AIDS movement.

When Joan and I first visited Ulusaba it was the landscape and rich variety of wildlife which had struck us. This time, we returned again with a very different focus: the people who lived there and the staff who worked for us. We launched the Bhubezi Community Health Centre, where more than 100,000 people from Ulusaba's surrounding community could get free treatment and testing for HIV, AIDS and other issues. At the same time, across the Virgin Group, we created a 0 per cent challenge, pledging that no one else who works for us should ever die from AIDS. Gathering all the staff together at Ulusaba, Joan and I kick-started the project by being tested for HIV in front of them. It was a different sort of launch from the ones I was normally involved in, but one of those that I was most proud of.

*

'Excuse me, sir? Do you enjoy visiting the gym?'

Never afraid to roll up my sleeves and get stuck into a bit of selling myself, I walked the floors of a Johannesburg shopping centre. The centre was pristine and shiny, and populated by people like the local businessman I'd just accosted.

'Yes, I do,' the man said, doing that double shake of the head of recognition, as he realised who I was.

'Have you heard about the new gym that we're opening near here next month?'

'I have.' The businessman paused. I watched a smile flicker across his lips. 'But I won't be joining your gym until you release your special last-minute deal.'

'There won't be a special last-minute deal,' I assured him, shaking his hand. 'I hope to see you at Virgin Active next month.'

The day after my bathtub chat with Nelson Mandela, Matthew, Frank and I flew to Johannesburg to see first-hand what the Health & Racquet Club chain was like, and whether my promise to Madiba was going to be a potential opportunity or a financial black hole.

Over the next five days, the three of us visited nearly all of the seventy-six clubs in the chain. To my relief, I liked what we saw. Yes, they were starved of investment and running into disrepair, but the clubs were also spacious, the staff were helpful and there was plenty of potential for growth. I could see there was a real chance of saving most of the jobs and turning our little health club business into an international force in one fell swoop.

We put together a rescue package, which would see all Health & Racquet clubs rebranded as Virgin Active. I called Madiba to tell him the good news and explained how the team which ran our health clubs in the UK would look after operations in South Africa, too.

'Oh, you have health clubs already?' he asked me.

I had assumed Mandela knew we ran gyms, but he had simply gone with his instinct when he called me.

In March 2001 we acquired all seventy-six Health & Racquet clubs in South Africa for R319.6 million (£24.5m), paying £11.6m in equity and raising the rest from financial partners Nedbank. There were lots of challenges as we expanded rapidly, but the most difficult part was accurately measuring how many people were using the gyms. The previous business model had seen members pay large fees up front for lifetime membership. This was fine in the short term, with healthy cash flow being used to fund expansion into new properties, which in turn bring new membership fees. However, when you have lots of gyms open and can't expand any more, the costs keep rising and the profits start dropping. When the music stops, you need somewhere to sit down.

We announced we would cancel all membership contracts and operate using our UK model. This meant no long-term contracts and great value monthly fees. The initial reaction, however, was not good. The South African public had such an emotional connection to Health & Racquet that it would take us a long time to shake off that legacy. I spent a lot of early 2001 in South Africa, giving away free Virgin Atlantic flights and building up support in the country, which fortunately already had plenty of trust in the Virgin brand.

We set ourselves an ambitious target of 300,000 Virgin Active South Africa members by the end of the first year. As the weeks until our relaunch ticked away, this looked increasingly untenable. The weekend before we were due to take over, we had only signed up 50,000 members. By the end of that weekend, we had 80,000. It was enough to keep us ticking over, and, as we fixed problems in underperforming gyms and reinvested in new features, numbers continued to grow, albeit slowly.

For the opening of the Melrose Arch club in Johannesburg, an occasion I'll never forget, we were joined by Nelson Mandela. As he arrived, I noticed that he was hobbling slightly.

'Are you OK?' I asked.

'It's my knees,' he explained. 'They sometimes hurt from being in prison on Robben Island. The many, many hours breaking rocks.'

Not that they stopped him dancing with delight alongside our staff in the gym minutes later. It was an inspiring sight to watch him wandering through the club and seeing how his mere presence lit up people's lives. If it hadn't been for Madiba's call, these people wouldn't have jobs. This was just a tiny example of the hope and help he gave to South Africa and the world. He was a genuine entrepreneur as well as a monumental leader. Once the launch had finished, he sat down with our family for a meal and was already on the lookout for another way to support his wonderful charities.

'That was a delightful lunch,' he thanked me, with a glint of mischief in his eye. 'Now, last week I saw Bill Gates and he gave us $50 million ...' Ouch!

7 'What do you call a Virgin employee with a tie? The defendant'

I have never liked wearing a suit. In the early 2000s, I had to dress formally for two very different reasons – and for two different types of court.

The reason for the first occasion arrived in a very official-looking letter, which was delivered to me on Necker. It was the kind of letter that had summons written all over it, but when I opened it, it wasn't the sort I was expecting. Instead, I read that the Queen was inviting me to become a Knight of the British Empire. Nobody was more surprised than I was.

Being included in the New Year's Day Honours List for services to entrepreneurship felt all the more remarkable for my involvement in what had happened in 1977 on Queen Elizabeth II's Silver Jubilee. Back then, I had signed The Sex Pistols – the notorious punk band who had been dropped by EMI and A&M in a matter of months – to Virgin Records. It had been smart business all round: for The Sex Pistols, Virgin were the only label able to handle their outrageous behaviour without having shareholders to shock; for Virgin, it helped to reinvent our image away from the 'Earls Court hippies' that others in the music business had branded us.

By the time we signed The Sex Pistols in May 1977, the band had already achieved notoriety by swearing live on national television in front of shocked audiences. But their first single for Virgin was even more provocative: 'God Save the Queen' was the anti-Jubilee anthem, released to coincide with the national celebrations. With its lyrics about 'a fascist regime' and 'she ain't no human being', the record was banned by the BBC and kept off the top of the charts by the powers that be – but everyone knew it was really number one.

To celebrate, we threw a boat party along the Thames. As the boat reached the House of Commons, the band blasted out 'God Save the Queen'. At which point the police, who had been following the boat, piled on board and in the melee that followed arrested The Pistols' manager, Malcolm McLaren, as he shouted 'Fascist pigs' at them. Given all of that, and my role as a thorn in the side of the establishment, it had never crossed my mind that twenty-three years later I might be knighted.

It had also never occurred to me that I might one day need to wear a morning suit. Rather than rocking the boat again, I thought I'd better look the part for Buckingham Palace. To begin with, it didn't go well. Joan came into our bedroom in Holland Park and had to stifle her giggles at my wonky collar and my failed attempts at looking smart. But with her help, I was soon looking half-decent.

Even so, it was a strange feeling, going to Buckingham Palace with all the full pomp and splendour of the investiture ceremony. It took place in the State Ballroom, the largest room in the Palace, thirty-six metres long and feeling almost as high, and opulent, decorated in white and gold: the sort of room that makes you feel as though you're stepping into a fairy tale. In the ceremony itself, those receiving awards wait in a side room to be called forward, one by one, by the Lord Chamberlain. As the National Anthem and then a series of military tunes are played, each award is given. And for the knight, there is a knighting stool – made of crimson velvet and gold thread. You kneel forward on one knee, bow your head and are then touched on each shoulder with the knighting sword.

As I stood in that side chamber, waiting for the Lord Chamberlain to call me forward, I felt quite nervous. Would Her Highness remember my involvement with 'God Save the Queen'? I suddenly became worried that when I bowed my head to be knighted with her sword on my shoulder, she might take her revenge and lop off my head! As my name was called and I walked through the grand doors into the ballroom, it was difficult to take it all in. Looking across at the audience of invited guests, I felt a mixture of pride and bemusement that I had ended up here.

Thankfully for my nerves, it was Prince Charles who did the honours rather than the Queen. He couldn't have been nicer, and the subject of punk rock didn't come up once. I left the palace with my head still on my shoulders. Together with my family we headed to a party I had put on for the other honours recipients. As I arrived, a reporter asked me how it felt to be a Knight of the Realm.

'It feels great,' I told him. 'It's going to feel odd sleeping with a Lady, though.'

Noting Joan's less than impressed reaction, I was reminded of the old adage that behind every great man is a great woman . . . rolling her eyes.

*

The second time I had to dress formally was in slightly less pleasant circumstances: it was to settle an ongoing dispute between Virgin Mobile and T-Mobile.

I dislike going to court almost as much as I dislike wearing suits. Back when I was starting out, I'd scribbled the words 'we don't need lawyers' in my notebook, and underlined them for good measure. Court cases can keep me up at night with worry and there have been numerous occasions over the years where we've had to go and defend ourselves, from linguistic arguments through to libel trials.

My first experience was back in 1970 when I was arrested under the 1899 Indecent Advertisements Act for using the words 'venereal disease' in our Student Advisory Centre leaflets, to encourage young people to get sexual health check-ups. After a day in the dock, we were given a nominal fine of £7, but as a result the outmoded law was eventually changed. Next was the infamous Sex Pistols case in 1977, when we were taken to court for displaying the band's album title, *Never Mind the Bollocks*, in our Nottingham record store window. We won that case when a professor of linguistics testified for us that 'bollocks' was a nickname for priests – before revealing he was a priest himself!

Virgin Atlantic's Dirty Tricks battle with British Airways ended with us winning the biggest libel settlement in British history in 1993, which we distributed equally to all our staff. It became known as the BA Christmas Bonus. Five years later, we won £100,000 damages in a libel suit against the CEO of lottery company GTECH. We've got a clean record of winning all our important cases. But I learned over the years how time-consuming and unpleasant the process is, even if you do end up on top. I was in no mood for another day in court – and not just because I hate wearing a tie. But the situation with T-Mobile was so serious, there was no other option.

The shame was that Virgin Mobile was actually doing really well. By 2003, Virgin Mobile UK was turning over more than £1 million a day. As such, we were already looking into floating the business on the Stock Exchange. Our partners, T-Mobile, were very happy with the way things were going – or so I thought. It all changed with the arrival of a new T-Mobile UK managing director, Harris Jones, from America. Mr Jones took a very different view of the situation: he saw our relative inexperience in the mobile market as an opportunity, and decided to try to snatch our 50 per cent share in a company now worth more than $1 billion. He claimed he was upset that T-Mobile had to pay us a marketing fee worth around £4.56 a month for every Virgin Mobile customer. The deal was written as plain as day in our contract. But this didn't stop T-Mobile calling in their high-powered lawyers and threatening us with court if we didn't change the agreement. I thought it was disgraceful, and we immediately took legal advice. Our team felt we were on very strong ground and we began working out our response.

However, we were in an acutely difficult position, because, as we didn't own our own infrastructure or masts, we relied on T-Mobile to provide service for our 2.4 million customers. I started spending many hours a day on the phone going over technicalities. Attempts to resolve the situation took place in a Leicester Square office. It was somewhat ironically called The Communications Building, but there was very little real communicating going on. Meetings became incredibly tense, with representatives from both sides speaking statements pre-approved by lawyers into microphones hanging from the ceiling.

We began to suspect T-Mobile were leaking details to the press, but it was impossible to discuss this at board meetings because T-Mobile were on the board! As rumours of a legal battle spread, Gordon McCallum from our head office joked to me: 'What do you call a Virgin employee with a tie? The defendant.'

As was typical at the time, Virgin Group's cash flow was running low, with money disappearing fast into Virgin Atlantic among others. We could ill afford an expensive legal battle. T-Mobile asked us outright to cut the marketing fee payments. We debated whether it was worth conceding substantial amounts of money for the sake of saving the relationship. In the end, we decided on principle to stand firm.

'We're in the right here. I'm not being bullied by them,' I told the team.

Once we gave them our response, T-Mobile attempted to break our partnership by activating a so-called 'no-fault' termination clause. If successful, it would have given them all our shares worth over half a billion pounds for just £1. A date in court became inevitable.

*

On the morning of the High Court case, I felt even more nervous than I had been at Buckingham Palace – and equally ill at ease in my suit and tie. Although our lawyers felt our case was a good one, you can never be certain how a judge will rule and interpret the law. I knew that if we lost the position of the whole Virgin Group would have been on shaky ground. The stakes were that high.

Inside the courtroom, the wait for the ruling from Mr Justice Cooke was excruciating. As he cleared his throat to deliver the verdict, I willed him to make what I thought was the right decision. As it turned out, his conclusions were better than I could have hoped and worse than T-Mobile dared believe possible. The judge not only saw our side of the story, he was actually appalled by T-Mobile's behaviour.

'In my judgement,' he said, 'their behaviour was not acceptable commercial conduct ... T-Mobile took the view that its commercial interests took precedence over the rights and wrongs of the situation ... That, in my judgement, is a course of conduct which is deserving of moral condemnation.'

As I breathed a huge sigh of relief, the good news continued. Instead of T-Mobile being given our shares for £1, as they had demanded, the judge ordered them to give us all of their shares – worth £500 million – for £1. What's more, they were made to pay the costs of both sides, as well as the damages. A bad day for T-Mobile just got worse. By taking us to court, they had ended up losing well over half a billion pounds.

The following day I had a telephone call from the head of T-Mobile's owners, Deutsche Telekom. He was really charming, genuinely mortified by what had happened and invited me over to their headquarters in Bonn so he could apologise in person. He told me he was going to fire Harris Jones and that he accepted the court's judgement.

'I hope we can enter into another commercial deal going forward,' he said.

I was impressed and admired his pragmatism: even though he had lost half a billion, he wanted to at least rescue something from it. I came away feeling that we could continue working with T-Mobile. A new managing director, Brian McBride, took over from Mr Jones at T-Mobile in the UK. He was keen to move on, and we soon negotiated a new commercial arrangement. Virgin Group took over 100 per cent ownership of the company and T-Mobile secured a long-term distribution deal. Virgin Group got complete control of Virgin Mobile, while T-Mobile received improved network compensation and would earn up to £100 million if we decided to float the business in the next two and a half years. T-Mobile would continue to provide network coverage for Virgin Mobile for at least ten years, but non-exclusively, so we now had the option of bringing in other telecoms partners, too. As you can imagine, all parties checked that new contract extremely thoroughly!

As for the £1 we paid them for our half a billion pounds' worth of shares? Brian McBride framed the coin and put it on his office wall at T-Mobile.

8 The World Turned Upside Down

Holly was just three years old when she first told us she wanted to be a doctor. Joan was driving to Kidlington from London, on a glorious spring day in the Oxfordshire countryside, when Holly made the bold announcement. I suspected the influence of our lovely London neighbour Dr Peter Emerson, whom Holly had always adored, behind her plans.

'That's lovely, darling,' Joan turned round to look at our daughter. 'But to be a doctor takes a lot of training. You'll have to study for a long time.'

'I don't mind,' Holly said.

'Plus you'll have to leave home to do it.'

At this, I could see Holly's face fall in the rear-view mirror.

'Oh,' she said. 'I don't want to leave you and Dad!'

'Just wait until you're older,' Joan laughed. 'By the time you have to leave home you'll be happy to!'

A decade and a half later and I found myself driving Holly and the family. This time, there was slightly less room in the vehicle: my three-year-old daughter was now nineteen, and the car was packed full of all her essential belongings. We were on our way from Oxford to London, where Holly had a place at University College London to study medicine.

It was an emotional time for us, preparing to say goodbye to our little girl, even though she wouldn't be too far away.

Considering my own struggles with education – I dropped out of school at fifteen – I was incredibly proud of Holly for having done so well at school. I have always thought that Holly and Sam have been fortunate to inherit the best features of both of their parents, and not take on some of my own flaws (obviously my darling wife does not have any flaws!).

As Holly was growing up it was clear to Joan and me that she was very single-minded and bright, just like her mum. She was also independent and adventurous, but perhaps a little more grounded than I had been at her tender age – or any age for that matter. She excelled at schoolwork and had a real talent for science and maths, subjects I've never really got to grips with.

The drive into London came at the end of one of those summers when everything seemed to feel in a good place. We'd spent it together as a family on Necker, and I'd enjoyed quality time playing with the kids and catching up with my parents. Having finished school the year before, Holly had been away on her gap year in Canada, learning to be a ski instructor, and it was great to have all the family back together for those summer months. I knew that things would be different come the autumn, and was determined to make the most of that precious time.

As well as the family, the business was also in a good place. I took the opportunity of the summer break to take stock and go through the books. We had agreed a more methodical strategy for investing in new businesses, acting as a branded venture capital company and investing in areas that truly suited us. While not every move worked, the likes of Virgin Mobile and Virgin Blue were off to incredible starts as our fastest growing companies ever. Virgin Active had risen quickly to become the world's third largest health chain. What's more, in 2001 Virgin Atlantic were the only profitable airline flying across the North Atlantic. I concluded that the Virgin Group was the healthiest it had ever been and felt unusually content.

I felt slightly less pleased when we got to Holly's new student digs – Ramsey Hall, right on Tottenham Court Road. The problem was the difficulty I had in trying to build the desk I'd bought Holly from IKEA the day before. The furniture brand's founder Ingvar Kamprad was dyslexic like me, so everything from their unusual product names to visual manuals was down to his unique way of looking at the world. But I still couldn't make head or tail of the instructions, and soon everyone was chipping in with an opinion on how it should be put together.

'I told you we should have got a MALM desk,' was Joan's unhelpful comment as we looked at the pile of wooden parts and metal screws in front of us.

'I thought we had.'

'This is a GALANT.'

'What's the difference?' I obviously didn't speak IKEA.

'I'm not sure, but it looked a bit easier to put together.'

'Just pass me that Allen key,' I said, trying to sound as though I knew what I was doing, even though I had no idea.

With Holly trying to help and Sam wisely keeping well away from the chaos, I carried on, to no avail. In the end, we decided to go out for dinner, and return to the construction conundrum on a full stomach. That seemed to do the trick, and we were able to leave Holly with her desk up and in more or less one piece.

Right from the start, Holly settled in well at university. She immediately fell in love with her course, and met new people who would become lifelong friends. She was a diligent daughter, too, in phoning home regularly and coming back to Oxford for weekends. I would often find her and Sam upstairs playing computer games on the Nintendo just as they had always done, especially Holly's favourite, Donkey Kong Country. But she understandably came on fewer family trips, and, as parents, we had to adjust to her new life.

Sadly, it wasn't going to be the only change I had to get used to that month.

*

On Tuesday 11 September 2001, I caught the Eurostar to Brussels for what I expected to be a relatively humdrum day giving a speech to Members of the European Parliament about the need for pro-competitive legislation in the automobile industry.

I had just started my speech when I noticed an assistant pass a note to the committee chairman. I'll never forget the look on his face as he read the note. I immediately knew something was wrong and paused as he stood up to relay the news to the room.

'Terrorists have attacked New York,' he announced to the shock of everyone present. 'A number of aircraft are involved.' As everyone in the room started exchanging worried glances, murmuring to each other and reaching for their phones, the chairman continued. 'This building could be a target for another attack. If anybody wants to leave, you are of course welcome to.'

I watched as the murmuring grew louder and a number of people got up and walked out. The vast majority, though, stayed.

'What do you think, Richard?' the chairman asked me. 'Are you happy to proceed?'

Like everyone else gathered, I had no idea how serious the situation really was. Given the number of people who had decided to remain, I felt I had to continue. Somehow I struggled through my speech as quickly as possible; all the while my mind was thousands of miles away. Were any of our planes involved? I didn't have any details, but knew instinctively we had a crisis on our hands. Within the hour, I was on the Eurostar back to London, desperately trying to get through to my team on the phone.

Will Whitehorn was the first to call. 'It looks like terrorists have taken over four aircraft,' he told me as the train sped away from Paris. 'The Twin Towers have just come down and there could be over 10,000 dead. Reports are also coming in of other aircraft being hijacked. They've closed US airspace. In your absence, we turned Virgin's planes back. Only three had passed the point of no return. Since then they've shut US airspace. I suggest we talk in more detail once you're back and gather tomorrow morning first thing at Holland Park.'

My instant reaction was utter horror at the sheer scale of the attack and immediate concern for everyone in New York. A woman in the seat next to me cried while frantically trying to get through to friends and family in the US on her phone. As I did what little I could to comfort her, I began mentally listing the people I knew in the city. Hoping against hope that they were OK, tears were soon streaming down my face at the magnitude of what was taking place.

When I got back to the office, I watched the horrific footage of the planes hitting the Twin Towers for the first time. Images of people jumping out of the buildings soon followed. At that moment, all my businesses and the fact I had an airline to run faded into insignificance. Nothing else mattered much after seeing that.

Instead, I went home to see my wife and kids and check they were OK. Joan had been in Oxford having lunch with friends when Holly had called with the news.

'Get to the television now!' she'd told her.

Joan described how she had viewed the attacks in horror in a little clothes shop next door to the restaurant.

'It felt like watching a computer game,' she told me, as we huddled together on the sofa. 'It didn't seem real.'

I thought once again how lucky I was to have my family. And how short and precious life can be.

*

The following morning, as heavy as my heart was I knew that business had to go on. Virgin Atlantic's management team, led by Steve Ridgway, had already initiated emergency protocol by the time Will, Richard Bowker, Patrick McCall, Mark Poole, Simon Wright and I gathered in my living room for a dawn crisis meeting.

As well as the terrible human and emotional loss, there were severe business implications and many thousands of jobs at stake. The decision by the team to turn our aircraft around had been a wise one, and we saved lots of money by having the planes grounded in the UK. The situation would also have been even worse if our deal to sell 49 per cent of the business to Singapore Airlines hadn't gone through the year before. But even so, the overall picture was potentially precipitous. We estimated cancelled US flights and customer drop-off meant our airline would lose £1.5 million per day. Within a few months, we could be looking at losses of hundreds of millions of pounds.

I began making calls. Firstly, I spoke to our bankers to assure them our cash position remained solid. Then I called our rivals at British Airways and other airlines to discuss a common-sense approach to the crisis. BA head Rod Eddington was helpful as we suggested working together to urge the government to support all UK airlines once US airspace reopened.

'Good on ya, mate!' he agreed, confiding that BA were expecting an £8 million daily loss.

Going straight in to bat, I called Transport Secretary Stephen Byers to implore the government to stand up for UK airlines' interests. I knew that our competitors in the States were already getting huge support and cash handouts from the US government. They also had the luxury of going into Chapter 11 administration if necessary. This would mean they could declare bankruptcy while continuing to operate, only partially paying back debts and effectively wiping the slate clean. This was never an option for us in the UK. I told Stephen that we needed decisive action from government if we were going to get through this.

That one day was to change our business instantaneously. Difficult decisions had to be made internally. In the coming days we had to renegotiate our bank lending and aircraft contracts and restructure. Over the next few months, capacity to the US was cut by one-third, and we began expanding into markets such as India, China and Nigeria. We flew larger planes, such as 747-400s, on busier routes to Africa and shifted the smaller aircraft like airbuses to North Atlantic flights.

But the ramifications didn't stop there. To keep the business afloat, we were forced to make more than 1,200 people at Virgin Atlantic redundant – the first mass redundancy I'd ever had to authorise. Handwriting many of the redundancy letters with Steve, and speaking personally to as many of our people as possible, was one of the hardest and most painful things I've ever done. I was devastated so many people had to suffer such hardship.

At the same time, I knew there was little choice. In extreme situations like this, you have to move quickly. If we didn't lose the few, we could have lost everybody. It was that serious. To their eternal credit, the team took the bad news with remarkable class and professionalism. Lots of older and part-time employees offered to make way voluntarily, while we offered unpaid leave and gave part-time work where we could. We promised those who lost their jobs they would be the first we'd rehire when the airline recovered – and thankfully most did return in the next couple of years.

Ensuring Virgin Atlantic's survival was paramount – if the company went bankrupt, the heart of the Virgin Group would be ripped out. As a result, anything not bolted down was up for sale. Selling one thing to pay for another and juggling assets with cash reminded me of playing Monopoly: we could have done with collecting £200 every time we passed Go! Instead, we ended up selling some small hotels in the UK, including Raymond Blanc's Le Manoir aux Quat'Saisons in Oxford. Most agonisingly for my family, we were forced to sell our favourite holiday escape, La Residencia in Deia, Mallorca. All the while, I kept thinking of Evel Knievel's famous quip he once told me: 'Made $60 million in my lifetime, spent $61 million.'

As 2001 became 2002, my upbeat mood of the previous summer had vanished completely. I felt low, upset at having to sell businesses and lose people, and demoralised as the world appeared to be heading towards war in the wake of 11 September. I tried to spend lots of quality time with my family and made an effort to be cheerful and visible around our staff. They, I have to say, were fantastic. It would have been understandable if morale had dropped, but everyone pulled together and worked harder than ever.

Even during these direst of times, we continued to attempt to innovate and improve things for those flying with us. We became the first airline to install bullet-proof doors in our cockpits. The Kevlar doors meant our passengers knew they were that little bit safer on our planes: it was a policy that was soon adopted by other airlines. At the same time, I tried to do what I could to those affected by 9/11: we offered complimentary flight tickets to New York for dozens of grieving relatives of those lost on that terrible day.

Throughout, I tried to lead by example. As soon as US airspace reopened I flew to see New York mayor Rudy Giuliani, and encouraged others to resume flying to the Big Apple. The mayor handled the crisis with grace and I offered to throw a party for him at the Roof Gardens in London to raise further funds to support New York. On 13 February 2002 Sir Paul McCartney graciously agreed to perform to help raise money for the recovery efforts. As Paul, Rudy and our guests gathered around the piano for a singalong of 'Let It Be', for the first time in a long while there was a hint of optimism in the air.

Tensions within the business were still running high however. In the months that followed, we continued to adapt Virgin Atlantic's business model still further and began a big push into the Caribbean markets. Such was the continuing pressure that when one of our executives questioned this strategy, I was uncharacteristically short with him.

'We've got to send the planes somewhere!' I snapped at him.

The tough aviation conditions had little impact in Australia. With Ansett in voluntary administration, we seized the opportunity and were able to expand rapidly, taking over their terminals and slots. We had 3,000 wonderful staff, forty-one Boeing 737s flying millions of satisfied customers and more than 30 per cent of the market. On 8 December 2003 we floated Virgin Blue on the stock market for A$2.3 billion. A$2.3 billion! This, the same airline we'd started with A$10 million only four years earlier, and had rejected a A$250 million offer for only two years previously.

The Australian aviation landscape was changing, and I pressed ahead with getting the British rights to fly to Australia with Virgin Atlantic, expanding our reach in the country. All sorts of so-called airline experts came out of the woodwork, claiming our plans were a 'lot of hot air'. I knew they were being planted by Qantas, so I wrote to the *Australian* and challenged their CEO Geoff Dixon. If Virgin Atlantic were flying to Australia within eighteen months, he would have to serve as cabin crew on our inaugural flight. If we didn't enter the market, I would wear a Qantas outfit on their plane from London to Australia. To top it off, we Photoshopped a picture of Geoff's head onto the body of a beautiful lady in a Virgin uniform.

'We're running an airline,' Geoff wrote back to me, 'not a circus.'

I didn't mind a jot – Qantas shares dropped by 3 per cent and Virgin Atlantic began flying to Australia in December 2004 – just in time to win the bet, though I'm yet to see Geoff in drag!

For Virgin Atlantic's core business, meanwhile, the new strategy was working. To our relief, the markets began to settle down. I remained very hands on because I loved working with the airline team and felt personally responsible for it. I wanted to do everything I could to generate more jobs and re-hire more people. I carried on writing and sending handwritten letters to staff, and continued to lobby ministers to secure additional slots for us at Heathrow. I made sure I was on every inaugural flight to get our routes off to the best possible start, and stayed in the same hotels as the staff to keep my ear to the ground on how things were really going.

Throughout, I liaised regularly with Steve Ridgway. He is a personal friend, whom I had met when we took on the

Virgin Atlantic Challenger expeditions, breaking world records together. He was incredibly creative, quickly moved through the ranks to become chief executive and coped brilliantly with the 9/11 crisis. He was smart enough to surround himself with top-quality people, such as Julie Southern, who took on lots of hard negotiations with the likes of Boeing and Airbus.

*

Aviation has never been the same since that September day. Looking back, I think we coped as well as we could have done. I am proud of the way both Virgin and also the airline industry more generally pulled together.

Back in Holland Park in the aftermath of the attacks, the September sunshine gave way to gloomy skies that matched our moods. Such was the dizzying pace of events that I had completely forgotten a photographer had an appointment that evening to take some pictures of Will and me for a National Portrait Gallery exhibition, 'Managing Partners'. I half hoped they might have forgotten, too, but they turned up, and we trudged outside to a bench to have our photo taken. Will and I were both feeling very bleak and preoccupied, hadn't slept in two days, and looked extremely bleary-eyed. I've still got the photo that went up in the gallery, and it captures all too well our overwhelming feelings, shared by so many, of those dark days: of uncertainty, of sheer exhaustion and, most of all, of sadness.

9 The Elders

Back in 1968, I'd created my first business, *Student* magazine, to protest against the Vietnam War. Along with the rest of the magazine staff I took part in the October march to the American Embassy in Grosvenor Square. We chanted about the US President Lyndon B. Johnson – 'Hey! Hey! LBJ! How many kids did you kill today?' – as I marched alongside Vanessa Redgrave and Tariq Ali. The experience had been an exhilarating one – at least until the police got heavy-handed and I had to dash across the square, narrowly avoiding the baton charge.

Thirty-five years later, I was on another historic march, campaigning against another unjust war. This time, the conflict was the coming one in Iraq and the US President driving it, George W. Bush, supported by the British Prime Minister, Tony Blair. On 15 February 2003, I was one of the thirty million people in 800 cities around the world protesting against the Iraq War. The march in London I joined wove its way from two starting points on Gower Street and the Embankment towards Hyde Park: the BBC estimated that over a million people took part. It was a march made up from all walks of life: from veteran marchers like me to those who'd never been on a march before; friends and whole families, rather than the usual suspects. Compared to the Vietnam marches it was far better organised and completely peaceful.

Such was the volume of protestors taking part that the march itself was incredibly slow – stopping and starting as we made our way through the London streets. As I walked, I thought of the words of Nelson Mandela: 'Our human compassion binds us the one to the other – not in pity or patronisingly, but as human beings who have learnt how to turn our common suffering into hope for the future.'

The strength of feeling against a new, disastrous war that day was incredibly powerful. Despite an absence of support from the international community and the public, the war-mongering machine was moving forward with unstoppable force. Like many people around the world, I desperately wanted to do something to prevent another pointless war. I remembered the first Gulf War in 1990, when I was spurred into action by the same feelings of hopelessness and anger. Then we ran relief flights to Jordan, and flew to Iraq with medical supplies. Saddam Hussein handed over women, children and sick hostages to us in one of the most nerve-wracking but rewarding journeys of my life. The question was, what could I do to make a difference now?

*

This had been an issue I had been thinking about more generally long before the pull to war had begun. A couple of years before, Bill Gates and his wonderful wife Melinda had flown out to spend the Easter holidays on Necker Island. I have long been inspired by Bill for his computing genius but in particular his compassion. I was in awe of how he had transformed his life from focusing upon Microsoft, a business that had changed the world, to looking at how to give back to others.

Bill has an acutely sharp brain and a unique way of looking at the world. He hones in on specifics and is an expert on subjects ranging from gaming to global health. Melinda is an incredibly smart woman, too. She told us all about her research into malaria, AIDS and tuberculosis and it was fascinating watching Bill listen and learn from his wife. He asked lots of questions and it was interesting to have another avid note-taker around. He can be chatty, but would certainly agree with Doug Larson's quote: 'Wisdom is the reward you get for a lifetime of listening when you'd have preferred to talk.'

Spending time with him, I wrote in my notebook: 'I never thought I'd be in awe of anyone, but I have to admit – what he's achieved is nothing short of breathtaking'.

Bill and I are very different characters, but have a lot more in common than our notebooks and cheque books. We held a delightful Easter egg hunt and the children loved finding the chocolate treats buried around the island. We got talking about water sports and I was pleasantly surprised to learn that he used to race sailing boats.

'I thought you would be too busy on computers to get out on the water,' I joked.

I wasn't laughing for long. Heading out into the ocean, we raced around the British Virgin Islands, where Bill proved his sea legs and gave me a run for my money! We were equally well matched on the tennis court, as well, where our match was tied at two sets each.

'Let's call it an honourable draw,' I suggested, overcoming my competitive instinct in the name of friendship.

Something else we had in common was our shared respect for Nelson Mandela. Over dinner, a fish supper whipped up and eaten at a table on the tennis court, we got talking about how Bill and Melinda's Foundation was trying to make a lasting impact. Bill told me that meeting Mandela had changed his life. He contrasted Mandela with Tabo Mbeki, who had followed him as South African President. He said that Mbeki not only refused to believe that anti-retroviral drugs would help HIV/AIDS patients, but had also turned down a $50 million grant from Bill.

'Mandela taught me about living,' said Bill. He went on to explain how meeting the most respected person in the world had set him on a new path, combining the spheres of capitalism and charity. Once again, it got me thinking about how to bridge these two worlds.

'How do you manage it?' I asked Bill. 'You're a hands-on sort of guy. So how do you juggle the foundation with Microsoft?'

'I don't. I now spend far more time on our charitable work; it's not that I enjoy Microsoft any less – it's just the right thing to do.'

This struck a chord with me. By the end of Bill and Melinda's stay, I felt similarly inspired. I wanted to follow suit, and find a way to shift my own focus further towards doing my part in helping others.

*

One possible way of doing that had come up a couple of years before that, in conversation with another great mind: the rock singer Peter Gabriel. Peter is a good friend and I always enjoy chatting to him: we know how to get each other thinking creatively, and throw around lots of different ideas. In 1999, Peter had a vision of bringing together some of the world's most respected people to communicate collectively through the internet and use technology as a tool for good. I had another idea about uniting a group of Elders to tackle conflicts in the world. Over the course of a few conversations we moulded the two ideas together.

I invited Nelson Mandela over for dinner with the two of us and our families, and we brought up our plan. Mandela thought it was very exciting, but he wasn't convinced we had developed the concept enough.

'How will it work practically?' he asked. 'I'm sure there will be the will, but will there be a way?'

Then, in 2003, war in Iraq looked increasingly likely. I had closely followed the reports coming out from the UN weapons inspectors and it appeared that the evidence for an invasion did not add up. My instinct was that war would be a dreadful mistake and there must be an alternative solution. Most people wanted Saddam Hussein to step down, but there had to be a better way of achieving this than killing potentially hundreds of thousands of people and unsettling the whole of the Middle East. Idi Amin had been persuaded to step down from Uganda in 1979 to live in exile in Saudi Arabia for the rest of his life, bringing peace and stability to Uganda. Perhaps the same could be done with Saddam.

I was trying to think who in the world could persuade Saddam to step down, when I came back to the Elders' idea that Peter and I had discussed. One person came to mind: Mandela had spoken out against the prospect of war. I called him up again to see if he could help and sent him the following note:

Dear Madiba,

America and Britain have definitely decided to go to war. Inevitably there will be many civilian casualties. I believe there may be only one way to stop a war in Iraq and I believe you may be the only person in the world to achieve it. If Saddam Hussein could be persuaded to retire to Libya (or somewhere else), with full immunity, I do not believe it would be possible for America to press ahead with war. If he were to make this sacrifice to avoid his people going through yet more suffering, it would enhance his reputation considerably. The personal alternative will be the fate of Noriega, Milošević or worse. Knowing your close relationship with President Qaddafi and the respect with which you are held in Iraq you are perhaps the only person who could organise this. I believe that you would have the credibility to persuade Saddam Hussein to step down. By flying out with you – to, say Libya – he could leave with his head held high. It would be the best thing he could ever do for his people. If it helps you I would be happy to send you a plane to take you there and back (hopefully via Libya!)

Kind regards as always,
Richard.

Mandela responded positively, agreeing to fly to Iraq on the condition that Kofi Annan, the Secretary-General of the United Nations, joined him. I contacted Kofi, who also agreed readily. Now we went into overdrive organising the trip details. We had to keep the plans top secret, because there were concerns President Bush would start the war even earlier if the US found out. I had real hope that Madiba and Kofi could make Saddam see sense. We had two pilots on standby and a Learjet ready on a runway in Johannesburg to take them to Iraq. But a couple of days before they were due to fly, Allied bombs started falling on Baghdad. Our efforts were too late: a terrible war that has affected millions of people – and still does – began.

Like millions of others, I felt helpless, heartbroken and terribly frustrated. There had to be a case for compromise and communication rather than guns and bombs, but we didn't get to make it. A paranoid part of me still wonders whether secret services intercepted our plans and alerted President Bush to Mandela and Kofi's visit, given that the bombing started slightly earlier than anticipated. Would anything have come of their visit? It's impossible to say for sure, but, certainly, there was a chance. I turned my attention to doing what I could to help in other ways, including flying a relief mission to Basra to deliver more than sixty tonnes of medical supplies. Mike Abunalla, an Iraqi exile, proudly piloted the flight. It was overwhelmingly sad seeing up close the suffering Iraq's people were going through.

As the fighting raged, I spent a lot of time thinking about what else I could do as a business person to help reduce suffering in the world. Ever since my meeting with Bill and Melinda Gates in 2001, I had been pondering how to build my own foundation in a uniquely Virgin way. We already gave lots to charities, but it was a scattergun approach. I felt we could do more by focusing on some key subjects.

As with any other business, I started to search around for people to make it happen. It just so happened that Jean Oelwang at Virgin Mobile Australia had a long history in the charitable sector and was keen to get back into non-profit work. I called her up and we discussed how I saw a new type of organisation working – not as a charity simply offering out donations, but a real force for good uniting people to change their own communities and the wider world. Her vision chimed with my own.

'I love it. Let's do it. How soon can you move to London?' I asked.

Later, Jean told me she danced around the room packing her bags as soon as I hung up the phone. We spent the first six months listening to our staff, experts in the non-profit sector, governments and customers to build the purpose of this new venture. Our staff came up with the logo, the structure and even the name: Virgin Unite.

*

If I had to give one reason why I have been fortunate enough to experience some success, it would be my knack of bringing together wonderful people. I had seen this up close while in South Africa when I engineered a meeting between Mandela and the Dalai Lama, who had never met and whose people worried about it being deemed too political. Staying a few blocks away from each other, it was the only opportunity for these two great spirits to meet. We managed to organise it and it was magical. This meeting reinforced my belief in the idea Peter and I had about forming a group of independent global elders.

Although it hadn't worked with Iraq, I kept returning to the concept of a global village of Elders, who would be able to speak out on the most challenging issues facing the world and command the respect of those in power. I talked this through with Jean, trying to work out how it could work practically. The only solution we could think of was for Mandela himself to personally unite these Elders – only he had the love and respect to bring together such a group of formidable people.

I was very conscious that Mandela had gone into retirement after so many years of unrelenting service for his country, his people and the world: he had announced an unofficial 'don't call me, I'll call you' policy. Therefore, I felt nervous as Peter and I refined our ideas into a letter to send to him, breaking the rule. But we believed there was no alternative: without Mandela and Graça's blessing, the Elders would not have the essential validity to move forward.

So we wrote, 'An idea – yes, I'm sorry – another idea ...'

As well you know, in an African village there are elders who the rest of the village look up to. We believe that the Global Village needs to equally tap into our elders. You told us then that it had been easier for you to gain the trust of the generals negotiating in Rwanda, as they said talking to you was like talking to a father.

We would like to set up a small body of the most respected 'Elders' in the world and as you are accepted as the most respected figure of all today, we would ask that you become the father figure to this organisation and the first Elder.

We would suggest that the Elders are initially chosen by yourself, and then in the future chosen by the world community, giving them added legitimacy on the world stage. None of them would be current politicians.

The Council of Elders would comprise 12 men and women. Four of these could stand down every three years. The new four could be voted in from a shortlist selected by the Elders through channels like the internet, television, post and email. They would represent a broad spectrum of the world's people.

I appreciate that you would have difficulty finding much time yourself but it would give enormous credibility to the future of the Elders if you were to give it your blessing and be its founding father. I would pledge myself to find the time and resources to help organise it behind the scenes and to make sure it became a force for good in the world and hopefully continues for many years to come.

Kind regards, Richard.

The next day I was again taking a bath when I got another call from Madiba. 'Graça and I would love to accept. We love the idea. Come to Africa and let's work out who the twelve most respected people in the world are to form the Elders.' Peter and I were overjoyed. From that day on, I decided never to get out of my bath!

10 'They're building a spaceship!'

If a Virgin Atlantic pilot hadn't wandered into the wrong hangar by mistake, Virgin Galactic might never have happened. That pilot was Alex Tai and the hangar in question was in the Mojave Desert in California. If that doesn't sound science fiction enough, what he discovered in the hangar was even more so: an almost completed spaceship.

The hangar and spaceship belonged to the aircraft designer Burt Rutan and his company Scaled Composites. I had first come across Burt during my hot-air ballooning adventures in the 1980s. Before crossing the Atlantic in a balloon in 1987, I went out to Burt's California base to ask for his advice on issues such as pressurised capsules and aerodynamics. I began to learn more about his designs, including bizarre planes that looked more like doodles in a student's notebook. They had odd names like the Long-EZm, the VariEze and the Quickie – branding wasn't Burt's strong point.

Fifteen years later, I got in touch with Burt again, this time over the Virgin Atlantic GlobalFlyer project. The aim of the project was to build and fly a single-seat, all-carbon-composite aeroplane around the world, non-stop, without refuelling. For years I had been trying to convince Boeing and Airbus to build their most widely used planes out of carbon fibre: as well as massively reducing CO_2 emissions, it made economic sense, as these planes would use far less fuel. After several years passed marked by inaction from the big aeroplane manufacturers, we decided to prove to them it could be done. Steve Fossett, who had been by my side on our around-the-world balloon flight attempt in 1998, would fly the plane. Burt would design it.

In mid-2002, Alex Tai happened to be in Mojave after a flight from London to Los Angeles. We had been tipped off by Steve Fossett that, as well as building the Virgin Atlantic GlobalFlyer, Burt had a secret project on the go in another hangar. When Alex wandered into the wrong hangar, Building 75, we discovered what it was. Once Will heard about it, he was on the phone to me in a flash, his voice flush with excitement.

'Richard, fuck the GlobalFlyer. They're building a fucking spaceship!'

It sounded too good to be true. For twelve years we had been all round the world looking for a genius designer to get our space dreams off the ground, and now we'd bumped into one by mistake, while we were working on another project two doors away. It didn't take much persuasion for me to head out to the desert and see it for myself. On the way over, I reread Tom Wolfe's classic book *The Right Stuff*, the story of early space travel, and I could feel my excitement building.

The Mojave Desert has a long history of being home to experimental flying: it was where Chuck Yeagar had broken the sound barrier in an X-1 and where Bob White flew the X-15. It is also a spectacular place: hot and dry with the rich blues of the never-ending skies contrasted with the yellows and starched greens of the landscape, dotted throughout with cacti and the striking silhouettes of the native Joshua trees. Burt's house is no less spectacular: a pyramid in the desert that rises out of the horizon like something out of a film set. Inside, his home is decorated with murals of ancient Egyptian civilisation – interspersed between the images and the pharaohs and gods was the odd alien face. I was clearly in the right place.

As we sat down in the pyramid, I asked Burt for more details about his vehicle, which he called SpaceShipOne.

'It's simple, really,' he said. I was expecting some sort of detailed blueprint, but instead Burt pulled out a napkin. A man after my own heart! It turned out that Burt had quite an extensive collection of napkins he'd sketched ideas down on. The drawing for SpaceShipOne was on napkin number 316, while a sketch of the mothership WhiteKnightOne was on napkin 318. I resisted the overwhelming urge to ask what was on napkin number 317 – it may have been another spaceship design, or perhaps just a ketchup stain.

Burt explained that his aim for SpaceShipOne was to win the Ansari XPRIZE. Launched in May 1996, this was the largest prize offered in history, with $10 million going to whoever could meet its near-impossible criteria. The winner would be the first private team to build and launch a spacecraft capable of carrying a person into space. Oh, and they had to do it twice within two weeks. No pressure! In total, there were twenty-six teams from seven different nations competing for the prize – not just the money, but also the prestige of being the first, the fastest, the highest and the best.

Burt then explained the unique design of his system. He wasn't particularly inspired by the NASA Mercury and Apollo launches I had seen on the television all those years ago. There was no massive rocket to shoot the spaceship upwards, and no dramatic ten-to-one countdown before boosters would be ignited. Instead, Burt looked back further to the X Series rocket planes that had smashed the sound barrier for the US Air Force, just down the road at Edwards Air Base. Aeroplanes like the X-15 had been hitched to B-52 bombers and released from great heights, saving fuel and allowing them to zoom arrow-like to the edge of space.

Burt and his napkin designs had their own spin on the concept. WhiteKnightOne would act as an ultra-light mothership, being able to hold the heavy load of SpaceShipOne tethered underneath it. It would carry the spaceship up to a great height and then release her from the heavens. Now came the truly inspired part. The biggest problem with space travel had never been getting into space, but getting back down to earth safely. Burt believed he had devised a new system for SpaceShipOne that could solve this issue. After being dropped from WhiteKnightOne, the spaceship would rocket upwards until it reached its peak height in space. Once it was ready to return, its unique feathering system would come into play. SpaceShipOne's wings would be unlocked and be able to adjust position to fold upwards. This would effectively turn the ship into a giant shuttlecock as it began re-entry into the atmosphere. Rather than plummeting at breakneck speed, it would glide down gently and smoothly before landing back on the runway it had left a few hours earlier, soft as a feather.

It sounded brilliant, but I knew this would be extraordinarily expensive to create. This is where Paul Allen, the visionary Microsoft co-founder, came in. He too loved space travel; he knew the names of the Mercury 7 astronauts by heart and wanted to become one himself. He also craved taking on insurmountable challenges, and was similarly convinced about Burt's genius. Burt told me that he originally had several meetings with Paul. He had decided not to ask him for an investment until he believed in the project so much that if he had the cash he would have put it in himself. Finally, Burt turned to Paul and spoke with iron-fisted conviction.

'I know I can do this and I want to do this now.'

Paul leaned over, shook Burt's hand and said: 'We're going to do it then. Now.'

Paul agreed to put in around $25 million, giving the programme enough financial clout to compete with rival projects from the US, UK, Russia, Argentina, Romania and Canada. Paul never got on Burt's back about spending too much money, even as timelines overran and costs increased exponentially. Both Burt and Paul were convinced they had a good shot at winning the XPRIZE and that was good enough for me. We quickly agreed for Virgin to sponsor the Mojave Aerospace Ventures team, and for the spaceship to have the Virgin logo on its tail. The advantage I had was that neither Paul nor Burt had a consumer company to promote, so they were happy for us to get involved.

Plus I don't think I would have taken no for an answer!

*

On 21 June 2004 I was back in the Mojave Desert, along with an assorted crowd of hundreds of space enthusiasts, locals, scientists, families and students. Since Virgin had come on board as a sponsor, SpaceShipOne's development had continued to progress. On 17 December the previous year, the 100th anniversary of the Wright brothers' first powered flight, the craft had made its first rocket-powered flight. Piloted by Brian Binnie, it became the first privately built craft to go supersonic. Now, after a further six months of technical refinements, the vehicle was ready to make its first attempt at flying into space. Or as Burt told *Time* magazine before the flight: 'I've been to two goat ropings and a county fair, and I've never seen anything like this before.'

Mike Melvill, an affable sixty-four-year-old test pilot from Scaled Composites, was at the controls. Mike wore very distinctive glasses that helped him to exude calm: I could have done with some of those glasses myself. As per Burt's original plan, SpaceShipOne was taken up by WhiteKnightOne, being flown by Brian Binnie. He took Mike to the prearranged height and the gathered crowd held its breath for the countdown.

'Release, release, release!' As the command rang out, we watched as the spaceship first dropped from beneath the mothership then shot up at an acute angle. So far, so good. But then, as the g-forces grew, the spaceship rolled 90 degrees to the left, which was absolutely not part of the plan. In Mike's desperate struggle to correct the problem, the ship then rolled 90 degrees right. There was clearly an issue with the main control system, and SpaceShipOne wasn't able to reach as steep an incline as intended. Back down in the desert, we feared the worst. It was going to be touch and go whether Mike would be able to land the spaceship safely again, let alone reach space. Then, just as all seemed lost, the backup controls kicked into gear and he guided the ship up, up, up. It reached its peak at an altitude of 100.4 kilometres – well beyond NASA's official definition of space, but just a shade beyond the higher boundary required by the XPRIZE milestone. To applause and cheers of relief, the spacecraft had done its job – by no more than the length of an athletics track.

There was still a lot of work to be done. But while there were many issues that needed resolving before we attempted the two XPRIZE flights in quick succession, the overall signs were good. With the big days a matter of weeks away, I began looking to the future. Paul Allen and I both lived in Holland Park, London, at the time, so I popped round to his house for a cup of tea. Paul's house was quiet and sparse, very different from the bustling atmosphere in my home, where people were always coming and going and the kids were running around. In a similar way, Paul and I have very different business philosophies: while I often talk ahead of myself and overshare, Paul keeps his cards closer to his chest. I remember coming out of a meeting with him and his staff crowding around me. 'What did he say to you?' they wanted to know.

I asked Paul what he planned to do with the spaceship if it was successful. To my horror, he said he wanted to put it in the Smithsonian once it had accomplished his dream, securing its place in aviation's historic canon.

'You can't do that,' I said. 'What you are doing is incredible, but you're missing out on the bigger opportunity here. The government isn't going to start sending people to space again – it's up to us. If you put SpaceShipOne in a museum, we're losing the chance of a lifetime – of many lifetimes.'

'What are you suggesting, then?' Paul asked.

'I'm talking about developing Virgin Galactic as a consumer brand,' I explained. 'Virgin runs businesses for people. We go into a market where the public is not being served well, and drastically improve it. What better or bigger market than space?'

I knew that some of the technology could be really useful for Virgin going forward. I told Paul we would be happy to pay a royalty on using the technology that had been developed. Paul liked the idea and understood the logic, though he still wanted to put SpaceShipOne and WhiteKnightOne in the Smithsonian. I understood, anxious to close the licensing agreement. I couldn't believe we were the only company interested – there should have been a line out of the door! Paul was good enough to shake hands on a deal right there in his kitchen.

*

On 29 September 2004, I stood out on the tarmac in Mojave looking at SpaceShipOne glowing white and red in the blazing sun. I couldn't stand still. The big test – our shot at winning the XPRIZE – had arrived. A couple of days earlier, I had arrived to officially announce our new business: Virgin Galactic. I said that if SpaceShipOne won the XPRIZE, we would engage Scaled Composites to develop a much larger new mothership and spaceship – WhiteKnightTwo and SpaceShipTwo – with the aim of launching passengers into space. I would be the first passenger. Reservations would open very soon, I announced, with customers putting down a full $200,000 deposit in advance, though this would be fully refundable until Virgin Galactic was ready to fly passengers to space. My announcement caused quite a stir and there was huge interest in what we were attempting. Now all we needed was for the team to win the XPRIZE.

Mike Melvill took the first of the two flights stipulated by the competition rules. As we watched SpaceShipOne drop from the mothership and blast off into the stratosphere, I wondered whether we were more scared watching back on earth than Mike was striving for space. He had plenty of reasons to be terrified; the ride was far from smooth. At 170,000 feet the spaceship went into a series of vertical rolls, spinning a record twenty-nine times up to 300,000 feet. It was out of control, speeding faster than a bullet out of the earth's atmosphere. How Mike didn't pass out I'll never know. But the system worked, the spaceship went up into space at 102.9 kilometres and Mike got back to earth in one piece.

When he climbed out of the cockpit to great relief and applause, I asked him how it felt to see the wonder of space.

'It felt like a religious experience,' he told me, seeing the curvature of the earth alone in a tiny ship. He had felt the beginnings of what is known as the overview effect, a shift in awareness whereby astronauts realise just how fragile and precious life back on earth really is. Even Mike's calm exterior cracked a little at feeling that.

Five days later, it was time for the second flight. After so much spinning on the first test, there were yet more issues to solve in precious little time. Yet the Scaled team remained confident: the spinning, though scary, also showed the strength of the spaceship and how much pressure it could withstand. When it came time for Scaled to decide who would be the pilot this time around, Brian Binnie got the nod.

That morning, I stood in the Control Room feeling nervous as Brian climbed into SpaceShipOne. As calm as Brian had looked, many of us in the control room were the exact opposite. The stakes felt high: this was an-all-or-nothing moment for us. If the XPRIZE was not won, it would be unlikely that Virgin Galactic could get started. As I hoped and wished that Brian would get SpaceShipOne high enough to win the prize, another even more serious concern took over. What if he didn't make it back at all? But it was too late to think that: for this flight, we were beyond the point of no return.

The spaceship looked stunningly beautiful as it was released to fly solo without a hitch. WhiteKnightTwo bounced up and its pilot Mike Melvill flew the mothership out of the way. After six seconds of free fall, Brian ignited the rocket motor at around 46,000 feet. With unbelievable power, the spaceship reached full thrust within a fraction of a second. It began its rocket-powered ascent as smoothly as one can expect from a test vehicle zooming at super-sonic speeds. Within a dozen seconds the sound barrier was passed. After one minute the ship was approaching 5,000 kilometres per hour and the sky began to change colour. From the milky blues of the California sky, the view turned darker, moving through navy past grey into pitch black.

Suddenly, we lost radio contact. Burt still looked relaxed, but I saw his expression darken as the silent seconds ticked on. After what seemed like an eternity, the radio crackled into life and Brian's voice reverberated around the room – up in the outer atmosphere, everything was fine. The relief was palpable. I exchanged sideways glances with Alex and Will, and Paul and I breathed out almighty sighs in unison. After about eighty seconds the engine shut off, and deep silence made the darkness feel blacker still. Out of Brian's window, the curvature of the earth shone clear and bright. Gravity disappeared from the cockpit, and he knew he was in space. Before SpaceShipOne deployed its feathering system, it reached its top-level altitude of a record 112.2 kilometres above the earth, smashing the required target. The XPRIZE had been won.

When SpaceShipOne landed in triumph, there was a lot of hugging with the family, a few tears and smiles all round. I had the great honour of shaking the pilots' hands and congratulating them on a job well done. Somebody told me it was the forty-seventh anniversary of the launch of Sputnik 1, the first artificial satellite to orbit the earth. We were truly standing on the shoulders of giants.

I clambered up on top of a pick-up truck with the pilots, Burt, Paul and the team. As we waved to the crowd, high-fived and embraced, a chilling rule in the XPRIZE regulations came to mind. It stated that the pilots had to stay alive for at least twenty-four hours after their flight in order for the result to stand. I noticed that the roof of the pick-up was very slippery indeed, especially as we began jolting around, spraying champagne. As we stood atop this greasy moving vehicle, I couldn't help but glance at Brian, hoping he wouldn't fall off and kill himself. I noticed Burt was making the same eyes at Paul and me. Later, he told me: 'I was more afraid that one of the billionaires would fall off than the pilot who had to stay alive for us to win $10 million!'

We agreed to contract Scaled Composites to begin work on our new space programme; but we would also build our own team from scratch to ultimately take over Scaled's work. Then we had to think about taking reservations, navigating our way through all manner of rules and regulations, and working out how all this fitted in with everything else happening in the Virgin world. We didn't know how it would all work, but I was convinced we would be creating hundreds of jobs, and inspiring millions of dreams. I realised that with the barriers broken, and two commercial astronauts receiving their wings, I was one (small) step closer myself. Suddenly it was very likely that our family, our friends and thousands of others would have the chance to go to space in our lifetimes. Before the XPRIZE came along, I had almost given up hope of ever going. Now I was convinced my spaceman fantasy was not far from becoming reality. But rather than worry about the detail for now, I took another moment to look up at the skies, basking in the wonder of space, closer than ever before.

The most incredible day turned into the most outrageous of nights. It seemed as though everybody in Mojave was crammed into the Mariah Inn's tiny bar. I was hugging anybody within grabbing distance. I even proposed to the Iranian astronaut Anousheh Ansari on behalf of my son, forgetting she was already married! 'Come on, you are very beautiful, Sam is very handsome, we are all very happy – let's cap the night off!' President George W. Bush called the team from on board Air Force One and congratulated everyone. He was delighted to know the spirit of adventure and entrepreneurship was thriving in America. We resisted the temptation to suggest our aircraft was better than his – let alone our space programme!

Since the first person went into space in 1961, fewer than 500 others have followed, most of them male, white and

English-speaking. It was great that those lucky hundreds had made it out of the atmosphere, but I was excited that we could help many more people from different countries, cultures and languages. As the cost per NASA space shuttle launch had grown to approximately $1.5 billion, we knew it was up to the new commercial space industry we were inventing to create the astronauts of the future. In a few glorious, high-octane seconds, SpaceShipOne had ushered in a brave new era of space innovation. For the first time, the sky was no longer the limit. Now, the really hard work began. There was a multi-billion dollar private space industry just waiting for us to kick-start it. Virgin Galactic had lift-off.

11 An Englishman in America

For a long time when I travelled to the US the most common question I got asked in the street was: 'Hey, are you that guy from *Friends*?' Indeed, I did sell a union flag hat to Joey and chat with Chandler in an episode of the classic sitcom, but it's been quite a while since anybody asked me about it. Now, I am far more likely to be quizzed about Virgin America, our start-up US airline. When we began, nobody gave us a chance. The very idea of starting a new US airline in the post-9/11 climate was enough to get them rolling in the aisles and window seats. We were the first US domestic airline to form after 9/11, and most expert observers expected us to be the first to close down, too.

Whenever I flew in America I encountered the same problems I used to find with international travel. The service was poor, prices were high, the entertainment was almost non-existent, the food was barely edible and the customers were missing out. It felt like an accepted truth that cross-country American flights were something to be endured rather than enjoyed. We saw it as a real chance to disrupt a sector where we already had expertise, in a key market where the Virgin brand was loved, but had room to expand. Why not make flying good again, instead of treating customers like cattle?

In early 2004, we tasked a tiny team in New York to turn Virgin America into a functioning airline. Fred Reid came on board as CEO. The team's first decision was where to base our fledgling airline. We considered several cities, from Washington, DC, to Boston, but against accepted wisdom we chose San Francisco. The arguments against were numerous: the airport was overcrowded and needed investment; the weather was foggy and unreliable; the labour market was tough. But I was amazed when I realised such a thriving location, with Silicon Valley on its doorstep and tourists all year round, didn't have a home-town airline. Befitting their new home, Virgin America had a start-up mentality from the beginning. After some long, hard months, we introduced our first plane to the world in October 2006. As a nod to another group formed in San Francisco, we called it Jefferson Airplane after the legendary band.

There is a lot more to launching an airline than simply putting a plane on the runway, however. That is particularly true in the US, where legislation is especially stringent. For a country that prides itself as the freest marketplace in the world, it certainly has some of the strictest regulations. Our competitors, who just possibly had their bottom lines in mind more than a sense of patriotism, began questioning our 'American-ness'. They tried to paint me as an eccentric British entrepreneur who had no place meddling in US business. I was happy to subscribe to the first half of the description, but the second complaint was plainly ridiculous. By law, non-Americans may not own more than 25 per cent of the voting shares of a US airline, a ruling that we were careful to stick to. While we licensed the Virgin brand and considered Virgin America very much part of the family, the Virgin Group did not control the airline. But by objecting relentlessly, our competitors managed to delay our launch and cost us tens of millions of dollars at the same time.

They also forced us to lose our brilliant CEO, with Department of Transportation regulators demanding Fred Reid's removal by February 2008 as a condition of granting our certificate to start flights. Because I'd interviewed Fred for the job on Necker Island, he was deemed too close to me: some rivals even claimed I had hired him as a puppet

CEO while I would run the business. Despite the accusations, Fred remained incredibly upbeat.

'Well, my sell-by-date is coming up, we better get moving,' he said at his last meeting.

I gave him a hug and thanked him for his superb work, but everyone was frustrated. By mid-2006 we had a fully employed staff, customers-in-waiting and planes sitting on the tarmac unable to fly.

In the end, it was the wonderful American people who got us off the ground. In January 2007, we took to the streets of San Francisco, explained what our airline was all about and let the public decide for themselves whether they wanted the option of flying with us. By May, more than 75,000 letters had been sent to Congress on our behalf. It turned out we were 'American' enough after all, and we finally got approval to fly from the Department of Transportation.

Delighted, we began selling tickets in July, gearing up for our inaugural flight the following month. Passengers were signing up in droves and our planes and teammates were raring to go. We arranged a big press push to celebrate our launch, with inaugural flights from New York and Los Angeles landing in San Francisco simultaneously. There was just one problem, though: while we had permission to fly in theory, the actual Department of Transportation certificate had yet to materialise.

On 7 August, the day before the planned inaugurals, there was still no sign of the paperwork. I was being interviewed in the Virgin Atlantic lounge at JFK in New York, determined not to let slip we were still worried we'd never get off the ground. It was touch and go, but, finally, we got a call from our counsel. Their message was short but sweet: 'The eagle has landed.' I jumped out of my seat, cheered and ordered champagne all round, even though it was ten in the morning. Our inaugural flights from New York and Los Angeles took off and Virgin America was go.

*

After launching more services between Washington, San Francisco and Los Angeles, we began flying the route I was most excited about: Las Vegas. In the UK, they describe Vegas as the city where even your accent is an aphrodisiac, and I wouldn't argue with that. It's a place I always love visiting, letting my hair down and having a blast.

As I travelled to the West Coast ahead of our inaugural flight to Vegas on 10 October, I had no idea what the team had in mind for our launch. I had given them a single piece of guidance in what they came up with: 'There's only one way to announce anything in Vegas – by being completely over the top.'

'We won't disappoint,' promised Abby Lunardini, Virgin America's head of communications.

A while earlier, I had been ordained as a minister in the Universal Life Church. It was surprisingly simple to get accreditation online. But I hadn't yet had the chance to use the powers vested in me to declare a couple husband and wife. With Vegas being the capital of quickie marriages and outlandish decisions, we decided our inaugural flight to Sin City would be the perfect place to hold the world's first wedding at 35,000 feet. The willing couple happened to be our marketing director and his fiancée, and they were only too happy to tie the knot in between the aisles. The wedding was a great success and a lovely way of both celebrating our employees and showing the world that we intended to do things differently.

By the time we got to Las Vegas we were in celebratory mood and a crowd greeted us as we reached the Palms Hotel and Casino. I was looking forward to meeting the local team and perhaps having a quick flutter. The comms team, however, had other plans for me: hosting a wedding at 35,000 feet, it turned out, was just for starters. I'd told them to come up with something over the top – I just hadn't anticipated that the something going over the top, literally so, might be me.

Before we went through the front doors of the Palms Hotel, I saw lots of people craning their necks, looking upwards. I couldn't see what they were looking at: the only thing I noticed was how incredibly windy it was. Then the penny dropped: I would be dropping from up there. I turned to Abby and Christine Choi, our New York-based comms director.

'Am I about to do what I think I'm about to do?'

'We thought it would be fun if you jumped off the top of the Palms Casino,' Abby explained. 'We've got a ceremony set up at the bottom, hosted by the magicians Penn and Teller, and all of the city's press are waiting for you to jump into it.'

I hadn't been warned, presumably because the team were (rightly!) worried I might say no. I took another peek outside. If anything, the wind was picking up: the palm trees were blowing at right angles and I estimated the wind was raging at close to 50mph. Suddenly, the building looming above me started to look very high indeed. A bell started ringing in my head: *Say no, Richard. This is crazy. Tell them you're not going to do it and walk away.* But, of course, it wasn't quite as simple as that: there was a lot of press there, and expectations were, well, about as high as the Fantasy Tower at the top of the Palms Hotel. I put on a tuxedo and got in a lift, which took forever to go up what felt like hundreds of floors. When I reached the top, I stepped out onto the roof of the hotel. I took a deep breath, and allowed myself to be strapped into a harness. I got halfway up onto the platform to jump, then changed my mind. It just felt too windy. I unclipped myself, turned around and got right back in the lift again.

Abby and Christine looked about as petrified as I did, but for different reasons.

'We're getting fired, aren't we?' said Abby.

'I need some time by myself to think it over,' I said. 'Call me in my room in fifteen minutes.'

For the next quarter of an hour I paced alone in my suite, debating what I should do. I could soon hear murmuring coming from outside the door: clearly, everyone thought I'd bottled it. Sometimes the bravest thing to do is to say no –

especially if you are putting your life at risk. The many times I have had near-death experiences jumping out of balloons and being rescued from the ocean also came to mind. Compared to those, jumping off a building didn't seem so bad. But I couldn't shake this feeling in my bones that something was going to go horribly wrong.

As the fifteen minutes were up, Abby knocked on my door.

'Richard, we appreciate you don't want to jump, but will you please just come back up to the roof for a few photos with the press?' I guessed what that meant!

When I made it up back onto the roof, there were walls all around blocking off the gale.

'Hey, it's not that windy after all,' someone said.

Maybe they're right, I thought. Perhaps the weather was calming down. Perhaps I was making a lot of fuss over nothing. My normal approach to life is to say screw it, let's do it, and that's what won. I decided I couldn't let everyone down. In what seemed like no time at all, I was back in the harness and climbing on top of the wall, staring down at the 407-foot drop.

'Jump! Jump! Jump!'

Far below me, Penn and Teller were whipping the audience into a frenzy. I awkwardly manoeuvred myself into position. Suddenly the protection from the walls disappeared, and I felt the full force of the wind. Who said the weather was calming down? It shook me from side to side. After hesitating for so long, I didn't hang about at the point of release. I waved, gritted my teeth and jumped.

Almost as soon as I was airborne I realised I'd made a bad decision. There was no way I could control my speed or change direction. The wind was whipping through my hair as I hurtled through the air. Below me, Teller was shouting: 'Whoa! Slow down, slow down!' But there was nothing I could do.

Travelling at over 100mph, the wind picked me up and smashed me painfully hard into the side of the building. Fortunately I hadn't spun around, so it was my backside that hit the wall rather than my head. It completely ripped the back of my jeans off, cut my legs and arm open and badly bruised my hand. As I finally started to slow down, the searing pain mixed with acute embarrassment and I hung there in mid-air like a rag doll, feeling an absolute fool. I slowly twirled around and the crowd gasped at the sight of me holding my bleeding bottom in both hands, a look of agony on my face. I reached the ground and the compere handed me a microphone as I struggled out of the harness. I tried to wave at the crowd but my hand was throbbing too much. I must admit, my speech was not one of my better performances. I shoved the mic firmly back into Teller's hand and meekly limped off the stage.

After spending a couple of hours with medics, I joined our guests and tried to put on a brave face. I wasn't in the mood to celebrate or mingle, but it was the only option: my arse was hurting so much that I couldn't sit down. But, looking on the bright side, it could have been a lot worse. What's more, at least everyone knew Virgin America had arrived in Las Vegas – even if we had landed with a bump!

*

After the Las Vegas launch we continued to grow Virgin America aggressively. November 2007 was an important moment for the business, with David Cush coming on board as CEO, bringing a wealth of experience after more than twenty-two years at American Airlines. While I love promoting from within, sometimes it is incredibly effective to bring in somebody who knows a sector inside out, has a fresh perspective and is hungry to work on a new and exciting project. He surrounded himself with great Virgin people and between them they understood the Virgin way immediately – to focus on superior customer service, innovative products and design and empowering staff. One of the most satisfying elements of Virgin America's growth has been hearing so much praise for how unique our team is. 'You don't look like a pilot,' said a passenger as one of our pilots walked through

San Francisco airport. 'Thanks very much,' he replied. Word of mouth about the airline continued to spread. In 2011 we won Condé Nast's prestigious Best Domestic Airline award for the fourth of what is now ten years running. Besides the crew, what I loved most was the unique, mood-lit cabins, created by Adam Wells, who now heads design for Virgin Galactic.

But despite the public and critical acclaim, we were still struggling to get the airport slots we needed, fuel costs were rising and competitors were attacking us from all sides. Although revenues grew 43 per cent to over $1 billion, we still made a $27.4 million operating loss in 2011. Profit felt a long way off. We launched services from Seattle to Los Angeles and New York to Las Vegas, with West Coast flights to Boston quickly following. While expanding, many companies experience growing pains. But we were determined to live up to our promise to be the most innovative airline around, even as we grew into new markets. We created the first on-demand dining experience in US aviation, and then the advancement I really loved came into play: we became the first airline to offer fleet-wide WiFi.

While I believe in switching off from devices and relaxing without distractions, flying is often the perfect time to get some work done. I have spent thousands of flights waiting to get to the other side to complete a deal, share some news, or even talk to my family. Now, I could do it all from the comfort of my seat at 35,000 feet. As the only airline that calls California home, it made sense for us to be at the vanguard of new technological developments. As *Wired* described us, we are 'a million dollar iPod – that flies'.

When we opened our new terminal in San Francisco International Airport we wanted to christen the runways with a Virgin America flight alongside Virgin Galactic. The regulations for this unprecedented twin flight seemed insurmountable, but somehow we got Federal Aviation Administration approval. Before take-off, the atmosphere on board the Virgin America plane was electric. We auctioned seats on the flight to support Galactic Unite (the not-for-profit arm of Virgin Galactic) and KIPP charter schools, and invited some of the kids from the programme, from aspiring engineers to young flyers, budding mathematicians to fledgling entrepreneurs.

It was one of the most spectacular experiences of my life, looking out of the window of our plane to see our spaceship riding alongside, then glancing back inside at the awestruck faces of so many children. I sat next to the Lieutenant Governor of California, Gavin Newsom, watching our spaceship flying gracefully close to the window as we circled above the gleaming Golden Gate Bridge. We urged some of the middle-school kids to climb over us and wave at the Virgin Galactic pilots.

It was as though we were staring out into the future. We could practically see Scaled Composites pilot Mark 'Forger' Stuckey, who went on to join the Virgin Galactic team in 2015, smiling from WhiteKnightTwo's cockpit. Everybody on the plane whooped and cheered, knowing we were part of history in the making. We landed side by side on the airport's dual runways, the first passengers to arrive at the terminal. It was fitting that the Virgin America plane was named *My Other Ride's A Spaceship* – perhaps my favourite ever name for an aircraft. Some of the students had never been on a plane before, let alone seen a spaceship. I'm sure the experience showed that space is a very real part of their future and encouraged them to dream big.

'I hope some of you grow up to become astronauts or pilots,' I said. 'Or both.'

*

You can tell a lot about an airline from its safety video. Most were safe and dreadfully dull. We wanted to create a video that got people's attention, helped them remember the important details and entertained them. Together with Virgin Produced, Virgin America created the first ever safety video set entirely to music and performed in dance. Millions of views and several awards later, the most gratifying response is still seeing the smiles on passengers' faces every time the video comes on. The Safety Dance can now be seen on dance floors, in airport terminals, all over the internet, in bedrooms and, of course, on planes. One of our team even performs the Safety Dance live in-flight and taught me the moves. I may not be quite as coordinated as some of the team, but I gave it a good go.

This kind of thing is great for building morale, as well as showing the public what we are about. I always try to make sure everyone keeps their sense of humour through it all. Virgin America has provided plenty of opportunities for that. I've made it a habit to hide inside the overhead luggage holds, encouraging the crew to do likewise. When guests board and open the holds, we greet them with a friendly, 'Good morning, sir. Can I take your bag?'

But despite these lighter moments, the challenges to make Virgin America a success continued. In their wisdom, the US competition authorities somehow let the six largest airlines in the US become three giant airlines. Through sheer size, they dominate the market and control slots in key airports, stifling competition and innovation. The industry response bore this theory out: in nearly every major survey of US airlines, United came out last, while Virgin America was top of the pile. Size rarely equates to quality.

By 2013 Virgin America had been applying to get the necessary slots for five years to enter Newark airport and begin operations there. Every time, the authorities told us there were no slots available. In reality, the incumbent airlines were squatting on capacity – running small planes at a loss – in order to keep the competition out. We got a foot in the door when American Airlines went into Chapter 11 of the United States Bankruptcy Code and we secured a few of their slots. Once we began operating, fares from Newark to California dropped by 40 per cent. I was hopeful we could expand further, but somehow United were awarded a new batch of slots.

I felt their sole aim was to push Virgin America out of the market place – whatever the cost. I publicly called them out on it and we lobbied behind the scenes to get flyers a better deal, asking the Department of Transportation to end the practice of squatting on capacity. We got our Newark slots, but were still wary that the competition would do everything they could to maintain their monopolies and keep us out of their markets.

12 The Rebel Billionaire

I met Ivana Trump a year before I met Donald Trump in the early 1990s. She was handing out the prizes at the Business Traveller Awards in London. Upon receiving the top airline award from her, I exuberantly picked her up and turned her upside down for a light-hearted photo. She took it well, dined with us later, cancelled her British Airways ticket and returned to the States on Virgin Atlantic. The following day's headlines said 'Virgin turns up Trumps again at Business Traveller Awards'. A while later, Donald invited me to lunch at his apartment in Manhattan.

I was intrigued. The invitation had come somewhat out of the blue. I turned up to an apartment that was undoubtedly opulent, but not as flashy as I had anticipated. That was not the only part of the lunch that didn't turn out as expected. Even before the starters had arrived, Donald was warming to what he wanted to talk to me about: the various people he was planning to take revenge on for refusing his request for help.

'I phoned ten people for financial help when I was in trouble,' he said. 'Five of those people said they wouldn't help me.' This rejection had not gone down well: Donald went on to spend the rest of this bizarre lunch telling me how he was going to dedicate his life to destroying those five people.

'I don't think that's the best way of spending your time,' I told him when I could get a word in. 'This is going to eat you up, and do more damage to you than them. Isn't this just a waste of time and effort? You'd be far better forgiving them.'

Donald just shook his head and carried on explaining at length how and why he was going to destroy each of them in turn. 'These people didn't help me when I needed them. They turned their back on me,' he continued to vent.

'That's a shame,' I offered. 'But isn't life too short to waste on petty squabbles?'

As I tried to eat my chicken soup, I couldn't help questioning why on earth he was telling me this. As he continued to run through his list of main offenders in detail, I wondered if he was going to ask me for help. If he had, I would have become the sixth person on his list.

'I really don't think these people have done anything to deserve this,' I said. 'There must be a better way to occupy your life?'

I came to regret those words later, when he announced he was going to run for President!

As I went down in the lift, I had an idea for making a film about a businessman out to destroy five people, and the methods he uses. But I decided that it would be too far-fetched, and no one would believe anybody could be so crass. I remember contrasting it with a subsequent lunch I had with Hillary Clinton, which we spent talking about education reform, drug policy, women's rights, conflicts around the world and criminal justice reform. She was a great listener as well as a very eloquent speaker.

As far as Donald Trump is concerned, the meeting was a completely wasted opportunity. I left his apartment feeling quite sorry for him.

*

I didn't hear from Donald Trump after that meal for over a decade. Then, in 2004, my television show *The Rebel Billionaire* went on air.

I've always had a love of adventure, whether that was climbing trees as a child or mountains as an adult. That has fed into my working life, too: adventure has always been a huge part of the Virgin brand, and one of the main reasons why we have been able to expand so widely and continually for so long. So when Fox offered me the opportunity to host a TV show designed to encourage the adventurous streaks in other entrepreneurs, it was an easy decision to accept.

The Rebel Billionaire was a business reality show with a twist. While I appreciated shows such as *The Apprentice* for bringing the idea of entrepreneurship to a wider audience, I had never wanted to get involved myself. Shows like this tend to be edited to focus upon people's worst, most negative characteristics. *The Rebel Billionaire*, by contrast, promised to be different. Rather than setting the contestants business tasks, I would instead be able to share my experiences through extreme adventures.

Videos started flooding in with participants pitching why they should be on the show. One of the applications stood out right away, from a woman called Sara Blakely who had started a new company called Spanx in her basement. She was concise, had a clear vision for her business and seemed like fun. Another excellent video came from a guy called Shawn Nelson who ran a versatile, modern furniture company named Lovesac. They both made the list of the sixteen final contestants.

We started filming the twelve shows in November 2004. We began by assembling all the contestants at Heathrow in London, where they were met by an elderly taxi driver, who was to drive them to my then home in Oxford. The taxi driver, who had a very bad limp and a walking stick in his hand, observed the contestants closely. When the contestants arrived in Oxfordshire, he surreptitiously took notes on which of them made him carry the luggage out of the taxi. Were they friendly, or were they rude? Did they engage in conversation or ignore him? Then, that evening over dinner, the taxi driver walked in to meet everybody. He pulled off his mask to reveal ... it was me all along! There were gasps from the contestants, especially the two who had been most unpleasant to the man they thought was just a taxi driver. Sixteen contestants immediately became fourteen and they found themselves driven back to the airport (though not by me this time).

The series took myself and contestants around the world, with the challenges continuing everywhere from Morocco to South Africa. All the while, I whittled down the contestants based on their decision making, bravery and leadership skills. The last characteristic was particularly important, as I had kept the grand prize a secret. As well as winning $1 million, they would be handed the keys to the whole Virgin Group, becoming president for three months. This also upped the stakes for me – I had to find somebody who could help us run hundreds of companies.

A particularly telling episode took place at Victoria Falls, on the Zambezi River, on the border between Zambia and Zimbabwe. The point of the exercise was to see if the contestants had the courage and good sense to say no. It is very important to take risks in life and business, but they need to be calculated – there is no point risking your neck for something with little chance of success (as I'd learned the hard way in Vegas!).

I asked one of the contestants, Sam Heshmati, to join me in a special NASA-designed barrel and plunge 170 feet over the waterfall. Sam hardly blinked as a crane lowered us down into the river's rapid current. We counted down from ten for the barrel to be released, sweat pouring off our faces. As we reached five he exhaled deeply, a look of fear in his eyes. I realised he was willing to go through with it. A split second before we were due to drop, I screamed 'Stop!' I made Sam look down and stare at the rocks below, which would have ripped our bodies to shreds.

'You were three seconds from death,' I told him, before sending him home. 'Question things more! You shouldn't blindly accept a leader's advice.'

That wasn't even the most dangerous challenge: that dubious honour goes to walking a plank between two hot-air balloons while flying 10,000 feet above the ground. After most of the contestants made it across, Tim Hudson and Sara hesitated and opted to use the safety wires instead. To allow them to redeem themselves, I challenged them to climb a ladder up to the top of the balloon, where I would meet them.

This meant that I had to haul myself up a swinging 100-foot rope ladder as well. With nothing but the distant ground beneath my feet, my heart was in my mouth as the rope wobbled in the wind. It was as though the ladder had concertinaed out, hundreds of rungs long, and seemed tougher than any mountain I'd ever climbed. I made it to the top, though, where I composed myself in the manner of an English country gentleman, sat down at a table and poured three cups of tea. Tim climbed up next, without too much drama, but Sara was afraid of heights and struggled terribly. Just as she was about to reach the summit, she slipped and almost fell through a vent. It was with some relief that we all were able to sit down, hurl the now luke-warm tea down our necks and race back down before the balloon ran out of fuel.

Sara had impressed me with her attitude as much as her business plans, and it was no surprise that she made it to the final. But in the end, I decided Shawn could benefit most from winning, as his talent was so raw. As we stood on the balcony of the Great House on Necker, however, I had a final twist in store for him. I took out the $1 million cheque and held it just out of his reach.

'You've got a choice,' I told him. 'You can take the money, or toss a coin for an even bigger prize.'

Shawn's final dilemma summed up the show. The pro-gramme had been about adventure, but also about understanding the risks, and learning when to say no. It's one thing being bold; it's another altogether risking your future on pure chance.

Shawn, I could see, was torn over his decision. 'What would you do, Richard?' he asked.

'It's up to you,' I replied.

To me, the answer was obvious, but it was for Shawn to work out for himself. As he paced up and down the terrace, I could see he wanted to show off (and make better television) by gambling. But was that moment of adrenaline really worth throwing away the chance to transform his company, and the lives of his employees? Finally, he was ready.

'I'll take the cheque,' he told me.

I gladly handed it over. 'If you had gone for the coin toss,' I told him, 'I would have lost all respect for you.'

Shawn learned a lot on the show, and took his experiences back to Lovesac, which has grown into one of the world's top furniture companies. And while Sara didn't win the show, I gave her an additional $750,000 to start her own foundation supporting women through entrepreneurship and education. As well as growing her charity, Sara built her business, Spanx, into an industry creating 'shapewear' brand. They sold $4 million worth of products in their first year without even having a website and Sara became the youngest woman in the world to create a billion-dollar company on her own. She has gone on to become the first individual woman to join Bill Gates and Warren Buffett's Giving Pledge (my family and I have also joined, pledging to give half of all proceeds we take out of Virgin Group to good causes). Not bad for someone who started her company because she 'wanted to make her butt look even better'!

Sara and I are now good friends and she joined me on the judging panel for Virgin Media Business' pitching contest for start-ups, VOOM. It was really satisfying seeing her pass on the expertise she has learned from her years in business.

'It's just like the old days,' I told her. 'Except we're on the floor – not the top of a balloon.'

*

While *The Rebel Billionaire* was an absolute blast to make, was a beneficial experience for all the people involved and, hopefully, made for some entertaining television, not everyone was impressed with the show. Donald Trump, by now the host of *The Apprentice*, did not take kindly to having a rival, however friendly and well-meaning.

When I did the press rounds to promote the show, I was inevitably asked how my programme differed from *The Apprentice*.

'It's more about adventure and entrepreneurship than confrontation and boardroom dealing,' I'd explain.

I was also regularly asked how my management style compared to Donald's. Each time, my answer was the same: we had very different personalities. I didn't say anything false or mean about him, merely pointing out our contrasting personas. Donald, however, didn't see it that way. He began making horrid, personal comments about me in the press. When I ignored these, he wrote to me directly, firing off the following letter on 12 November 2004:

Dear Richard,

... now that I have watched your show, I wish you came to me and asked my advice – I would have told you not to bother. You have no television persona and, as I found out with others a long time ago, if it's not there there's not a thing in the world you can do about it. At least your dismal ratings can now allow you to concentrate on your airline which, I am sure, needs every ounce of your energy. It is obviously a terrible business and I can't imagine, with fuel prices etc., that you can be doing any better in it than anyone else. Like television, you should try to get out of the airline business too, as soon as possible! Actually, I wonder out loud how you can be anywhere close to a billionaire and be in that business. Perhaps the title of your show, *The Rebel Billionaire*, is misleading?

In any event, do not use me to promote your rapidly sinking show – you are a big boy, try doing it yourself!

Sincerely,
Donald J. Trump

I couldn't help but respond to that. As politely as possible, I replied five days later:

Dear Donald,

Thanks for your note. I think if you look carefully through the press cuttings, I have actually avoided 'nasty' comments. I have enjoyed the time we have spent together and would not denigrate you personally.

Having said that, every interviewer has asked what differentiates us. Since I disagree with some of your 10 rules for success, I've cited two of those. Your advice for people not to shake hands – and your advice that you should go all out to get your own back on anyone who crosses you. I believe my thoughts to be honest, fair comment. I told you the same when we had lunch together and you told me that you were going to spend whatever it took to get your own back on those who had not returned your calls and had not helped you when you were near bankruptcy. I believed it was a waste of your talent and energy and is not the best advice to give budding entrepreneurs.

I have read what I believe can be construed as 'nasty' comments from you about myself in the press over the last couple of weeks and – although tempted – have to date decided not to respond to them and to rise above them. Suffice to say that I have created six billion dollar empires in six completely different sectors and I think that that qualifies Fox to title this show 'The Rebel Billionaire' (in the airline business alone – that you cite – I have made over $2 billion in personal shares I have sold in Virgin Atlantic and Virgin Blue and still own 51 per cent and 25 per cent respectively). Perhaps you could re-read what I have said to date and decide whether it's worth us remaining as friends – or alternatively, you adding me to your list of enemies! It's your call.

Kind regards, Richard.

I didn't get a reply for another decade. I guess my name was added to that list!

*

It wasn't until 2015 that I heard from Donald again. Now he was making headlines for a different reason: as a candidate for the Republican nomination for President of the United

States. Whenever I saw Mr Trump's rabble-rousing speeches on television, or heard his poll numbers were surging, I thought back to our bizarre meeting. Then I remembered our later correspondence. Could this man really be a serious contender for the White House? It appeared so.

On 22 September 2015 I received another note from Donald Trump's office. I was sitting at the Temple on Necker Island when I opened it, with some apprehension: 'Good afternoon Mr. Branson. As per Mr. Trump's request, please see the attached note. Thank you!' I looked at the sender's name, took a sip of tea and opened the attachment, wondering what on earth it could be. Inside, I found an article from the 15 September edition of the *Los Angeles Times* about the burgeoning commercial space industry. Under the heading 'Astronomical Undertakings', Jeff Bezos, Elon Musk and I were profiled. Donald Trump had taken a black Sharpie pen and drawn a big arrow pointing at my photo, before writing the words 'RICHARD – GREAT!'

My immediate suspicion was that Jeff and Elon would have received identical notes. Laughing, I turned to my assistant Helen Clarke and said: 'You have to take your hat off to Donald for having the time to do things like this!'

More notes of a similar nature followed, including invitations to his box at Flushing Meadows for the US Open. Normally I'm a great believer in people befriending those they've fallen out with, but on this occasion I must admit I was sceptical of the timing. If he'd sent his note any time during the decade before his presidential bid, I might have attended. Donald seemed to have forgotten his nasty earlier letters. Instead, he seemed so keen to recruit high-profile people to support his presidential bid that he had taken to flattery via email. If he had taken a quick look into my advocacy work on anything from refugees to drug reform, gun control to climate change, he would have realised I was one business person his divisive rhetoric and bullying behaviour would not impress.

I suspect he never anticipated his presidential campaign would go as far as it did, and was as surprised as anybody when he began to look like a serious candidate for the presidency. There have been times throughout history when fears about immigration and unstable economies have been exploited by demagogues, using falsehoods and hate to stir up unrest. This was no different. 'I would like to see an entrepreneur become President one day,' I wrote. 'I believe entrepreneurial thinking is incredibly valuable in leaders, and there are many entrepreneurs who I would be delighted to see in power – just not this one.'

Would I ever support Trump? No. But would I try to talk to him about issues I care about, from climate change to criminal justice reform, and encourage him to take a better approach? Of course. As I told him all those years ago, life is too short for enemies and the spirit of forgiveness is far stronger than the spirit of revenge.

Would Donald agree? Sadly, I doubt it.

13 Crossing the Channel

Dover, June 2004. It was a glorious summer morning as I crunched my way down onto the beach, feeling somewhat overdressed. As the seagulls circled and squawked overhead, I hoped that they would decide not to treat my black dinner jacket and bow tie as target practice. The same went for the equally black vehicle waiting in front of me: the sleek, top-of-the-range, open-top sports car design of the Gibbs Aquada. On land, the vehicle had an amazing turn of speed, and, as I climbed in, I turned the ignition to hear the low, powerful thrum of its engine: this was a vehicle that could accelerate into the distance at the tap of the pedal. But the car's speed wasn't its defining feature. After a quick rev, I waved to the assembled crowd of well-wishers and then, feeling only slightly nervous, drove it straight into the sea.

Ever since I had watched *Thunderbirds* as a teenager back in the 1960s, I had wondered when aquatic cars would become a reality. Now, forty years later, the amphibious cars of the show had been turned from toys into something real. I'd wanted to do something special to mark the twentieth anniversary of Virgin Atlantic's launch, and this seemed the perfect opportunity to fulfil a childhood dream. We'd borrowed Gibbs Technologies' Aquada and now the challenge was set: not just to see whether it would float, but whether I could make it into *The Guinness Book of Records* for the fastest crossing of the English Channel by an amphibious vehicle.

Driving a vehicle into the water, amphibious or not, is the oddest sensation. It's completely counter-intuitive to every driving instinct and lesson you've ever had. For all the power of the Aquada's engine, I drove it into the water tentatively, half expecting to see seawater beginning to seep in. But, to my relief, the inside of the vehicle remained dry.

'It's working!' I shouted in delight, and pressed down on the accelerator. Within a matter of seconds, I heard the whirr of the car's wheels retracting and the boat began to shoot forwards. At that moment, with perfect timing, a Virgin Atlantic Airbus jet completed a flyover low above us. Our anniversary was celebrated: now all I had to do was claim the record.

As Dover and its white cliffs disappeared in the rear-view mirror, I was enjoying myself. The previous record for crossing the Channel in such a vehicle had stood since the 1960s at six hours. But with the Aquada having a top speed on the water of 30mph, I was confident we could smash that, especially as the howling wind was behind us. In sea mode, the car's accelerator worked as a throttle, and it was surprisingly smooth to ride – even if it did come down with an almighty splash as you hit a big wave.

About halfway across we got into the heart of the Channel's busy shipping lanes. Here, the water was choppier, a situation not helped by the close proximity of boatloads of reporters. As I watched the ferries go by, I could see the great ripples they were causing, and the waves heading in our direction. I gripped the steering wheel, braced myself and – SMACK! – the waves whooshed straight over the top of us. I was absolutely soaked – but somehow the car was still afloat and we were able to continue speeding towards our destination.

Before I knew it Calais was in sight. As we got closer, the dots on the beach became people, and I could see the town's mayor at the head of a group of reporters and well-wishers. To applause, I steered the Aquada onto a ramp on the beach.

'It was absolutely flawless,' I told the press. 'I wasn't worried about sinking for a moment,' I fibbed, still dripping wet and looking the worse for wear in my soggy James Bond dinner jacket.

The journey had taken just one hour, forty minutes and six seconds, beating the previous record by over four hours. It's a record that, at the time of writing, still holds: a decade later, the then presenters of *Top Gear* decided to pick up the gauntlet and try to beat my world record. Jeremy Clarkson, James May and Richard Hammond built their own amphibious vehicle – essentially a souped-up pick-up truck that just about floated – and began the hazardous journey across the Channel. As they teetered along dangerously somewhere between England and France, the Coast Guard intercepted them, flying overhead and demanding an explanation.

'Our intentions are to go across the Channel faster than "Beardy' Branson"!' replied Clarkson at full volume. But despite the Coast Guard wishing them 'bon voyage' they made it across the Channel a few hours outside my record time.

I'd loved driving the Aquada and agreed to be the first customer, preparing to cough up about £75,000 for the car. I had visions of driving it around the British Virgin Islands reefs, hopping between Necker and Moskito islands. But then the company mysteriously took it off the market, straight after our record-breaking crossing. Interest was at an all-time high, and no explanation was given. I presumed there must be a major technical or financial problem, as the company just seemed to disappear. Then, eight years later in February 2012, all became clear. I picked up the *Metro* newspaper and saw photos of a 'high-speed Amphitruck' making 'a splash on the Potomac River in Washington DC. The quirky military vehicle travels at speeds of up to 30mph and can go from water to land at the touch of a button.' It wasn't just Jeremy Clarkson who had been watching our world-record attempt with interest: the US military had seen the success of the crossing and bought up the rights to the Aquada immediately.

*

At the same time as the Amphitruck was making its public debut, my mind was back on the English Channel, thinking about another way of crossing it to add to my list of world records. As well as the amphibious crossing, I also hold records for an assortment of different challenges, including the First Pacific Crossing by Hot-air Balloon, the First Transatlantic Crossing by Hot-air Balloon, the Fastest Crossing of the Atlantic in a Boat, the Most Followers on LinkedIn and, rather bizarrely, the Richest Reality TV Presenter! In 2012, Sam and I hatched a plan to break three Guinness World Records in one day by kitesurfing across the English Channel with family and friends. We wanted to achieve the largest group crossing; Sam had his heart set on becoming the fastest person across, while I planned to become the oldest person to do so. The record for Sam to beat was two and a half hours, while the group had to beat four hours. As for me, I just had to make it across in one piece!

Over the years kitesurfing has become something of an obsession for me. I first learned to kitesurf in the very early days of the sport's development. I was taught here on Necker, back when it was lethally dangerous and you felt you could be pulled for 100 feet or so underwater or dragged across the beach. You just had two strings attached to a kite, and you had to pray you didn't hit anything. I survived without too many injuries and have been hooked ever since. It gets me away from everything, clears my mind, and when I come back I'm completely refreshed and ready for the challenges of the day. Alongside tennis, it's my favourite sport in the world, as many more people are beginning to agree. Wind permitting, I always fit in a kitesurfing session every day on Necker, sometimes just for twenty minutes, but often for a long, five-hour kite across to Anegada and back.

The sport also provides ample opportunities for me to put a smile on people's faces – including my own. One day I was getting ready to go kitesurfing when Denni Parkinson, a delightful South African model, came up to me with a very unusual request. Her boyfriend, the photographer Stephane

Gautronneau, said he wanted to capture a particular picture, and asked if I would take Denni kitesurfing on my back.

'Would you mind,' Denni asked, 'if I didn't wear any clothes?'

I was a little taken aback for a second, but replied: 'Certainly, as a British knight I would be happy to be of service. I never turn down a damsel in distress.'

By the time we were kitesurfing back towards the beach there was quite a crowd ... including my wife. As I was coming in, I just caught Joan's expression – even from the other end of the beach, I think I could see her wry smile whilst making a face.

'Typical Richard!' she laughed, and walked back up to the house.

Since then, three lovely women and I have broken the Guinness World Record for the most people on a kite at one time: another record to add to those attempted across the English Channel.

By comparison to the amphibious car crossing, the French authorities were less supportive of our world record attempt. We were told that our kitesurf attempt was illegal on health and safety grounds.

'Ask forgiveness, not permission,' I told the group as we prepared for an early morning departure before they could catch us. We gathered on the beach just after dawn, all dressed as pirates to add to the feeling we were on a swash-buckling journey against the odds. I looked at Sam as we got our kites ready on the sand.

'See you on the other side,' he smiled.

'Not if I see you first,' I said. 'I'm going to give you a real run for your money.'

I was confident, maybe not of beating Sam, but certainly of keeping up with the leaders. I just hoped the winds didn't blow us too far off course. Two years earlier we'd had to abandon a similar attempt to mark my sixtieth birthday halfway across, when we fell foul of terrible weather.

This time was just as tough, but Sam got off to a great start. I had chosen too small a kite, which just wasn't responding. Just before the halfway mark of the thirty-mile trip, my kite fell out of the sky and I had to abandon my board. While I was left bobbing in the sea, waiting for a support boat to pick me up, Sam and some of the group steamed on ahead to achieve the fastest crossing, shaving twelve minutes off the record with a time of two hours and eighteen minutes. On top of that, nine of the group made it over – another world record in the bag for the family.

I was delighted for them, but also determined not to let the side down. The next morning, as the rest of the group recovered, I headed back to the beach with Charlie Smith, who used to run water sports on Necker and now works for Larry Page. This time, just the two of us would attempt the reverse journey, from England to France.

As we entered the water the wind direction and speed kept fluctuating, making kitesurfing very challenging. The waves were enormous and 40mph winds shook through our bones. To make matters worse, the wind finally settled directly behind us, which was the last thing I wanted. I had trained on a kite in every type of weather except downwind situations – now I had to cross the English Channel downwind in heavy waves. Again and again, my board was swept away from me, as the wind was going in the opposite direction to the tide: Charlie had a tracking device on, which showed I crashed 110 times during the journey.

I was fortunate to have Charlie with me, an exceptional kiter and good friend who worked unbelievably hard that day. As I was thrown underwater repeatedly, the temperature was dropping and the warm waters of the British Virgin Islands felt a million miles away. I must admit I kept looking at the support boat and came close to stopping. But I didn't want to let Charlie or anybody else down – plus I wanted that world record. As we approached the busiest shipping lane in the world, I prayed I wouldn't lose my board in front of a ship. We sank into the water and waited for a really fast boat to pass, then followed in its wake, just making it across before the next one came along. I was completely and utterly exhausted.

After what felt like days, but was actually less than four hours, the French coast was finally in sight. I got a burst of speed as we reached the shallows and I allowed myself a smile – one that soon disappeared as we reached the beach. There was no victory party this time, just a helicopter full of angry French policemen circling overhead, with what looked like machine guns. The waves were crashing onto the beach with such force that there was no way we could swim back to the support boats – we had to land. I was shivering with cold as we stepped onto the beach, but managed to say "Allo 'Allo'! as the policemen marched over, angrily telling us our crossing had been illegal.

'I thought anybody could swim in the sea?' I argued.

As we stood there shivering, the *gendarmes* remained locked in conversation on their phones, deciding what to do with us.

'Can you just take us to the cells so we can warm up for the night?' I asked, only half joking.

Thankfully we were so sorry looking they took pity on us. 'I assure you, Monsieur Branson, the food is far superior in our restaurants than in our prisons!' They gave us a very firm warning never to do it again.

'I can assure you,' I said, 'I have no intention of another attempt.'

After drying off, we found one of those nice restaurants they had mentioned. I didn't really mind what we ate, as long as it was hot. I had got my record as the oldest person to cross the Channel on a kiteboard, and felt even more admiration for Sam and the family for getting across in record time: it had taken me three hours and forty-five minutes to kiteboard from Dymchurch in Kent, to Wimereux in northern France. As we sat eating some hearty soup, I reflected on how wonderful it was for the family to have set three world records in two days, and how lucky I was not to have been arrested!

14 Steve

Pushing the limits of flying and stretching the technology to take us into space offers those who take part remarkable, never-to-be-forgotten experiences. But those rewards come with a risk attached, and in the mid-noughties I was devastated to lose several heroic men in two separate accidents.

In February 2005, I'd turned my attention away from Virgin Galactic and back to the project that had led to us working with Burt Rutan – the Virgin Atlantic GlobalFlyer. I travelled down to Salinas in Kansas and was met by a crowd of thousands on a freezing landing strip, looking up at the majestic plane. As Steve Fossett and I stood on the runway, I took a moment to marvel at the sheer strangeness of what we had built. The GlobalFlyer had a single jet engine above a short casing in the middle, with the tiny cockpit in front of it. Steve would have a few feet of space to sit in while he flew around the world without stopping. To either side he could see twin tail booms mounted, making up a thirty-five-metre wingspan, with every part of the plane built with ultra-lightweight material. If we could pull this off, it could revolutionise the way planes were built, and save massively on CO_2 emissions.

As Steve got into the cockpit I jumped into a chase plane to follow his progress from the air and held my breath for the big take-off. Steve expertly guided the plane off the runway and it flew magnificently from the get-go. It was exhilarating flying behind, watching this unique machine zip through the air in front of us. I was already envisaging converting this technology to our commercial jets in the future. But then the GlobalFlyer began to lose lots of fuel very quickly; next the GPS system faltered. I was nervous, I have to confess, but had full confidence in Steve's ability at the controls. He was extraordinarily calm under pressure, as he had shown on countless other adventures, including becoming the first person to fly a helium balloon around the world solo. Even so, it was alarming when I could no longer follow Steve's progress in the chase plane. When it got to the morning of 1 March, I had to stop in Toronto to launch Virgin Mobile Canada, and was dumped onto the tarmac at the airport as Steve flew off overhead.

Back in the Mojave Desert, Burt and his team were frantically calculating whether the Virgin Atlantic GlobalFlyer had enough fuel to continue the challenge. The wind was playing in our favour; if the jet stream remained strong, Steve could still make it. Nearly three days after he left, with almost no sleep, no respite and no landings, he glided back onto the tarmac in Salinas. He had set a world record for the longest non-stop flight in history: 26,389.3 miles in sixty-seven hours.

Boeing and Airbus were quickly in touch and visited Scaled's factory to see how they had developed the aircraft. They were astounded that a plane built out of carbon-composite material could fly around the world non-stop, using less fuel per hour than a four-wheel truck. They set about developing their own versions and now planes like the Airbus A350 and Boeing 787 are largely made of carbon-composite material. Years later Virgin Atlantic ended up buying them from both companies. This is saving incredible quantities of CO_2 being pumped into the air, and giving airlines big cost savings to pass on to passengers. Steve went on to complete two more world record-breaking flights in the Virgin Atlantic GlobalFlyer, which were among an amazing 116 records he set in five different sports. I joked with him that he was making me look bad. 'You're on track to break the record for the most records broken, Steve. Slow down, I've always had my eye on that record!'

But Steve's record-breaking triumphs were soon followed by tragedy. A year later he disappeared while flying over the Great Basin Desert in Nevada. I was distraught and hoped against hope he was alive. We helped coordinate efforts to find him, praying that such a hardy adventurer could have somehow survived. But as hard as we looked, there was no sign of my friend. When the Civil Air Patrol called off their search on 2 October 2007 after a month with no breakthrough, we continued the search using Google Earth's new satellite imagery technology. Sadly, there was to be no miracle. On 29 September 2008, a hiker found Steve's identification cards in the Sierra Nevada Mountains in California and remains matching Steve's DNA were later recovered. It's strange how adventurers often die doing something relatively mundane, rather than when they are pushing the limit. Just as T. E. Lawrence (Lawrence of Arabia) died on a motorbike in England, rather than fighting in the Middle East, Steve died flying a normal plane, not while chasing the land-speed record. When you know the dangers, are trained for them and are fully focused, you are usually ready to deal with them. Mistakes can often happen in less dangerous situations.

I had lost one of my finest friends. I went to Steve's memorial service and sat between Neil Armstrong and Buzz Aldrin, who both placed Steve among the world's great adventurers. It was only a few years earlier that Steve had been a commodities broker. He had gone on to inspire millions with his achievements. So many people I have loved and admired have died pursuing what they love. The only comfort is, sadly, just that. One of my last memories of Steve was the inimitable way he delivered the Virgin Atlantic GlobalFlyer to the Smithsonian Institution's permanent collection, after we retired the revolutionary aircraft. Rather than have somebody else handle the logistics, Steve piloted the plane himself, sweeping low over the building as onlookers gazed on in wonder, before he taxied it right to the front door.

There will only ever be one Steve Fossett.

*

At the same time as Steve had been breaking records with the GlobalFlyer, Virgin Galactic was starting to take shape. We signed an historic deal for Scaled Composites to design, build and test the world's first private spaceship for commercial passenger service. If I weigh up everything I have ever taken on, this is the biggest task, and if we can pull it off it will be my proudest achievement.

We had licensed SpaceShipOne's XPRIZE-winning technology from Paul Allen, and agreed to have Scaled Composites build our new eight-seater spaceship and mothership. Now the first step was recruiting our own team to begin building the Virgin Galactic brand, too. In July 2005 Burt and I travelled to the EAA Oshkosh air show in Wisconsin, to announce the formation of The Spaceship Company. This new aerospace production business was established to eventually manufacture Virgin Galactic's future launch aircraft, spaceships and support equipment. Onstage, I spoke about the unique opportunity of demonstrating the commercial viability of manned space exploration. Offstage, I wandered around shaking hands and hearing from fellow space enthusiasts, a giddy grin wide across my face. We were going to develop the world's first commercial, passenger-carrying spaceline.

By the end of 2005 we also reached an agreement with the state of New Mexico for the building of the world's first spaceport. It would cost $200 million to build the spaceport in the south of the state, covering twenty-seven square miles and including a dedicated terminal and hangar, medical facilities, clubhouses, offices and Mission Control. New Mexico's climate, free airspace, low-population density, high altitude and stunning scenery made it the perfect spot from which astronauts could appreciate the wonders of space. But the clincher was the professionalism and enthusiasm of Secretary Rick Homans and his team – they were (almost!) as excited about space as we were.

With our spaceline and spaceport in development, it was time to show our vision of what Virgin Galactic would look like. We brought in design guru Philippe Starck to create a new identity that reflected our project's vision. When I met him he spent a lot of time staring at me intensely.

'Your eyes are perfect,' he said.

'They are?' I asked, flattered but a little confused.

Then he explained his concept around the beautiful image of a nebulous iris, through millions of years of evolution, signifying our opportunity to look back at earth from space. He took images of my own eye and turned them into a logo that really stirred me. Now that we had our branding, I was desperate to show off what our spaceship and mothership would look like, inside and out. I wanted it to be large enough for people to have a real experience in space.

'I don't just want to be strapped tight into a seat in a chunk of metal, blasted to space and back again without seeing anything,' I told the design team. 'I want people to come back changed by what they have witnessed – we need big windows, comfortable seats and the space to float around in zero gravity.'

We debated ships big enough for four, six, even ten people. Burt sent his team on a series of parabolic arc flights so they could get a sense of what was possible in a weightless space. They came back confident they could scale up SpaceShipOne's smaller design into a beautiful, functional, safe aircraft.

As momentum built, we began looking into partnerships with the wider space community. Ever since I had watched the moon landing, NASA had always been the pinnacle of space travel, setting the standard all of us who came after aspired to. Now, as NASA stepped away from manned space travel, we knew they would still play an integral part in space's future. We discussed ideas for how we could work together, finally signing an agreement to collaborate on future manned space technology. They also made their unique facilities at the NASA Ames Research Center in California available to us. More than anything, it was a huge acknowledgement of acceptance from the industry at a very early stage of Virgin Galactic's development.

Then, just when everything seemed to be going perfectly, a tragic accident shook us all.

*

Thursday 26 July 2007 should have been a great day for Virgin Galactic. Stephen Attenborough, who had become Virgin Galactic's first full-time employee when he joined as commercial director, was in New Mexico with Alex Tai as part of the architectural judging panel for the spaceport. He called me with the news that Norman Foster, probably the greatest living architect, and a Brit to boot, had won our global competition to design the world's first spaceport. His otherworldly design made the spaceport feel as if it was emerging mysteriously out of the desert. It was simultaneously an ecologically sound continuation of the landscape and a space-age marvel. I loved it.

Stephen and Alex were driving through the desert to Las Cruces, where we were to make the announcement. As they pulled into a gas station to refuel and grab an ice cream to cool down, the Scaled Composites team called Alex, who immediately called me on Necker. I was just returning from a walk around the island, and answered cheerily, expecting more details about Norman Foster.

It was one of those moments that turned from fun to horror in an instant.

'Richard, you better sit down,' Alex said. 'There has been an explosion in Mojave.'

That day, Scaled Composites had been preparing for a routine 'cold flow' test. At 2.34 p.m. on the north-eastern edge of the Mojave airport, they were testing the propellant flow system for SpaceShipTwo. This did not mean igniting the rocket motor at all, or even lighting a fire – it was simply to examine the rate at which the propellant would flow through a new valve opening. A two-metre-long spherical tank made of carbon fibre was filled with nitrous oxide, which Scaled used to provide the oxygen its rocket fuel needs to burn. It should have been routine: nitrous oxide isn't even usually considered hazardous – you've probably come across it at the dentist as laughing gas – and Burt's team had carried out many similar tests for SpaceShipOne.

But this time it was different.

Seventeen people were there watching the test. Six of them moved back to a control post more than 100 metres away to watch on closed-circuit television, protected by a bunker of earth and a shipping container. The other eleven members of the team moved behind a fence, less than ten metres away from the test site. When the nitrous oxide was ignited, the tank exploded. The sound was likened to a 500-pound bomb. The bottom of the tank broke apart violently, and carbon fibre and concrete from the pad below flew into the air. Shards of carbon fibre ripped into the engineers standing nearby.

More members of the Scaled team were sitting in Building 75, and heard the explosion in the distance. They hardly stirred – it simply sounded like a sonic boom, a fairly common noise in Mojave, which is a busy supersonic flight corridor. But Chuck Coleman, one of Scaled's engineers who was watching the test, somehow stumbled across to the office and began waving his arms and shouting for help. As he spoke, he didn't realise that huge shards of carbon fibre were sticking out of his body.

A great cloud of dust flew up into the Mojave air, concealing the tragic scene. When it settled, the horrible truth of what had happened was revealed. Glenn May, who had been away from Mojave for the previous year and only returned to work at Scaled Composites that week, was dead. His colleagues Todd Ivens and Eric Blackwell were also killed: they were the first fatalities in commercial spaceflight's history. Jason Kramb, Keith Fitzsinger and

Gene Gisin, meanwhile, were all seriously injured and required surgery.

The news was devastating. I sent my deepest sympathies to the loved ones of those who had died, and all those affected. We cancelled our spaceport announcement out of respect and Scaled set about finding out what had happened. Burt, who had been away from Mojave, rushed to the desert. He was distraught – it was the first time in a long and distinguished career in aerospace that he had ever lost anybody. Now he had lost three people in one day. A few weeks later I flew over to see him and found myself face to face with a broken man. He looked as if he had aged twenty years overnight. He was very quiet and all his usual exuberance had been extinguished in a flash. He could hardly walk, had trouble breathing and appeared to be wasting away. He took a lot of the blame on himself for not getting the safety aspects right, and for not being there when the explosion happened. You could see the responsibility physically weighing on his slumped shoulders.

It turned out Burt had developed a serious medical issue and was diagnosed with constrictive pericarditis, a hardening of the sac around the heart. While Burt, as a man of engineering principles, refused to believe the stress from the accident contributed to his condition, I can't help thinking it did. He was literally broken-hearted. His wife Tonya agreed. But they didn't sit around feeling sorry for themselves. Together, they set up a fund to support the families of those who had passed away.

It was vital the cause of the accident was pinpointed so that it could never happen again at Scaled or any other space company. The California Occupational Safety and Health Administration launched an investigation into the accident and Scaled launched their own with experts from across the industry, including representatives from Boeing, Lockheed and Northrop Grumman. The inquiries did not determine exactly what had caused the explosion, but the California State investigation into the accident fined Scaled for failing to observe correct workplace practices.

December 1998
'To be opened only if…' The letter I wrote Joan before my last ballooning adventure – in case I didn't make it back

December 1998
'P.S. love you both <u>very</u> much.' My letter to Sam and Holly before my balloon flight

March 2000
On the steps of Buckingham Palace with Sam, Joan and Holly after being knighted

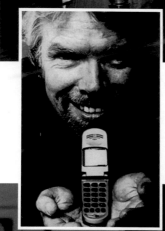

March 2000
Celebrating my knighthood with Mum and Dad
after the ceremony at Buckingham Palace

Circa 2000
The first Virgin Mobile phone –
the technology that changed my life

Circa 2001
Keeping up with Kate Moss, the ultimate work-hard-play-hard model

September 2001
Will Whitehorn and me on a bench in Holland Park, sad and sleepy-eyed after 9/11, sitting for a National Portrait Gallery exhibition on Managing Partners

October 2001
Naked ambition! Announcing Virgin Mobile's arrival in the US

November 2001
Tilting with the Virgin Trains team after unveiling our Pendolino

November 2001
Mission
Impossible
accomplished as
Virgin Trains gets
on track

2002
I'm officially
a banker!
Launching Virgin
Money's first
credit cards

December 2003
With the world's
first privately
built craft to
go to space –
SpaceShipOne

June 2004
Breaking a World Record crossing
the Channel in the world's first
amphibious car

November 2004
A very angry letter from the
future President Trump

TRUMP
THE TRUMP ORGANIZATION

November 12, 2004

Mr. Richard Branson
Virgin Atlantic Airways
The Office   1 9 NOV 2004
Manor Royal Crawley
West Sussex
RH109 NU
United Kingdom

Dear Richard:

I see that you are trying to take me on with your nasty comments, much the same way as Mark Cuban had tried. As you know, Mark went down in flames, his show was unceremoniously cancelled, never to return again. In any event, now that I have watched your show, I wish you came to me and asked my advice — I would have told you not to bother. You have no television persona and, as I found out with others a long time ago, if it's not there there's not a thing in the world you can do about it.

At least your dismal ratings can now allow you to concentrate on your airline which, I am sure, needs every ounce of your energy. It is obviously a terrible business and I can't imagine, with fuel prices etc., that you can be doing any better in it than anyone else. Like television, you should try to get out of the airline business too, as soon as possible! Actually, I wonder out loud how you can be anywhere close to a billionaire and be in that business. Perhaps the title of your show, *The Rebel Billionaire*, is misleading?

In any event, do not use me in order to promote your rapidly sinking show — you are a big boy, try doing it by yourself!

Sincerely,

Donald J. Trump

February 2005
With Steve Fossett
launching the world's
first all carbon-composite
aeroplane to fly around
the world non-stop

2005
Kasbah Tamadot, our magical retreat in Morocco's Atlas Mountains

February 2005
The Virgin Atlantic GlobalFlyer, a world record-breaking
flight that changed aviation forever

Circa 2005
With Dad at Virgin Trains – he and Mum always supported me unconditionally

Circa 2006
Planting a kiss on Arch on Necker Island, where we taught him to swim

Circa 2007
Discussing The Elders with two of South
Africa and the world's great moral leaders,
Nelson Mandela and Archbishop Tutu

2007
A great honour introducing my
family to Nelson Mandela

Circa 2006
Shaking hands on the creation of
The Elders with Nelson Mandela

2006
Virgin Mobile
comes to France

October 2006
Meeting the first
group of students at
the Branson Centre
of Entrepreneurship
South Africa

February 2007
Launching the Virgin Earth
Challenge in London with Al Gore

August 2007
Lift-off! Finally launching Virgin America's first flight, soaring over the Golden Gate Bridge in San Francisco

March 2008
Mum and Dad very much in love and sharing a laugh on Dad's 90th birthday

July 2008
Mum and the mothership named after her, VMS *Eve*, at Virgin Galactic's base in the Mojave Desert

September 2008
Fighting back against
the proposed monopoly
between British Airways and
American Airlines

October 2008
Holly and I hanging out on the
rigging, attempting to break
the world record for the Fastest
Sailboat Crossing of the Atlantic

February 2009
Mooning the
Alaska Airlines
team after
finally getting
permission for
Virgin America
to fly

Circa 2009
Serving drinks on
Virgin America's
pioneering planes

April 2010
Running the London
Marathon dressed as
a giant butterfly

October 2010
With genius
engineer Burt
Rutan, in front of
SpaceShipTwo and
WhiteKnightTwo

November 2010
Dressed up in newspaper for iPad magazine
Project's launch outside Apple in New York

December 2010
Wrangling a herd of Texas longhorn steers
on the tarmac with Virgin America

**VIRGIN AMERICA
IS HERE. DON'T
FLY LIKE CATTLE!**

Circa 2010
Taking a break from
the weights in Virgin
Active UK

April 2011
My Other Ride's a Spaceship. Virgin America flying in tandem with
WhiteKnightTwo and SpaceShipTwo

April 2011
My Other Ride's a Spaceship

Circa 2011
Getting into the spirit with Virgin Active's team at our flagship health club in Soweto

July 2011
Diving with whale sharks off the coast of Mexico to promote ocean conservation – I swam right into one of their mouths

July 2011
Gearing up for the Virgin Active London Triathlon with Nell McAndrew and Melanie C

Handwritten personal letters are so important, they show humanity and character

KENSINGTON PALACE
12.1.93.

Dear Richard,
hurray!
love from Diana x

BARACK OBAMA

Richard, Joan, Holly & Freddie —
Michelle and I could not be more grateful for the extraordinary hospitality you showed us in BVI. Obviously the setting was extraordinary — what we did not fully expect was to come away with a wonderful holiday, but also with wonderful friends that we hope last a lifetime.
I would have gotten this note out sooner, but we wanted to include some gifts for the little ones that took a few weeks to finish. Hope they enjoy them!
Michelle looking forward to seeing you soon, and Richard, don't practice too much before our next competition.

To Richard
from John.
These are new lyrics for the whole song.

Obviously we will not be using all of them — but I think it's TERRIFIC
let me know

Candle in the Wind

Goodbye England's rose
May you ever grow in our hearts
You were the grace that placed itself
Where lives were torn apart
You called out to our country
And you whispered to those in pain
Now you belong to Heaven
And the stars spell out your name

And it seems to me you lived your life
Like a candle in the wind
Never fading with the sunset
When the rain set in
And your footsteps will always fall here
Along England's greenest hills
Your candles burned out long before
Your legend ever will

Loveliness we've lost
These empty days without your smile
This torch we'll always carry
For our nations golden child
And even though we try
The truth brings us to tears
All our words cannot express
The joy you bought us through the years

Goodbye England's rose
From a country lost without your soul
Who'll miss the wings of your compassion
More than you'll ever know

I spent a lot of time soul-searching. I went on a pre-dawn walk by myself on Necker, thinking long and hard about what to do next. After talking to the survivors, as well as the relatives of those who had died, I concluded we should press on.

But we were to continue without another key member. Not long after the investigation, Burt stepped down as the head of Scaled Composites. At the end of 2010, he announced his retirement. Soon after, thirty-six years since the day he arrived in Mojave, he left his pyramid and moved to a ranch in Idaho.

15 Four-Play

Business can sometimes be about being in the right place at the right time. That was the case in April 2005, when I ran – in this case literally – into Simon Duffy, the CEO of cable communications company NTL.

I was in Central Park, New York, making the most of the spring weather by going for a run between meetings: that little bit of exercise helps to keep my mind as well as my body fresh. As I passed by the zoo, miles away in my own world, I bumped into someone coming the other way. As I stopped to apologise, I realised I knew who it was.

'Simon!' I gasped.

'Richard! Small world,' he grinned.

'Yes,' I wheezed, 'but quite a big park.'

We sat down on a nearby bench and caught up. It was a slightly different setup from my usual business meetings, wiping sweat from my beard, wearing somewhat different attire. Simon and I knew each other well; we first met when Thorn EMI acquired Virgin Records in 1992, and we had previously run our internet service provider Virgin.net as a joint venture, before NTL bought it outright in 2004. Simon told me that both NTL and Telewest were struggling to turn around their reputation for poor service, and wanted to make some major changes. He gave me the strong impression that he really respected the Virgin brand. I sensed an opportunity, so I invited him for a less sweaty meeting.

In November 2004, Simon and Shai Weiss met Gordon McCallum and me to dig into the details. Over a pot of tea, Simon introduced Shai, who complimented the mock-up cruise ship on my table – an idea to make cruising appeal to a younger generation (which would come to fruition twelve years later with Virgin Voyages). He told us NTL were merging with Telewest, and he had a proposal that might interest us. Guessing what it might be, I wasn't immediately gripped by the prospect; in a recent survey, NTL had come fiftieth out of fifty when it came to brand loyalty, and Telewest weren't much better, whereas Virgin was the most respected brand in the UK. But what he suggested next caught my attention – his pitch, with no slides or notes, explained they wanted to get rid of the NTL and Telewest brands altogether and call the company Virgin Media.

'Let me get this straight: you are suggesting rebranding your entire business under the Virgin umbrella?'

'Yes – but that's not the really interesting part. The deal would also include Virgin Mobile,' he added. They rightly anticipated Sky entering the broadband space and BT moving into TV, so wanted to get into mobile. With our brand power and wide-ranging offerings, we were the perfect candidate to create a formidable competitor to Sky and BT.

Shai explained how we could launch the world's first 'quad-play' business, offering cable television, broadband internet, landline phones and mobile all in one simple package. Getting people's business across such a broad range of products would mean we could keep costs low and reinvest in infrastructure and services. It sounded amazing: I was ready to be swept away by the idea, but didn't want to let on. We would have a big negotiation ahead. I did my best poker face, nodded a lot, and kept quiet, all the while inside thinking 'whoopee!' at how transformational this business could be for our brand. Just as Virgin Megastores were waning on the high street, this could bring us into the digital world and give us a major presence in people's homes.

My only concern was the terrible customer service reputation that NTL and Telewest had. NTL was hated by the press and, worse, consumers referred to it as NT-Hell. Could our team turn that around like they'd done with British Rail on the West Coast Main Line? Could we turn them from the worst into the best? I believed we could. The deal, though, was far from straightforward. Many of our businesses were joint ventures, usually with us owning 51 per cent. Brand royalties were factored in, but we would charge only a token rate and earn the main money through the equity. This time we put more value on the brand, creating a more predictable way of earning. As well as agreeing a brand royalty, I also wanted to limit the potential damage of putting our name on two companies with the lowest customer satisfaction in the UK.

Long, complicated negotiations began. The four of us reconvened in New York on 11 September 2005, an emotional day to be in the city on the fourth anniversary of the 9/11 attacks, with jets flying overhead. We ironed out the deal over lunch in the Four Seasons then went for a stroll in Central Park, where a reporter promptly spotted me posing for photos with tourists. He asked what I was doing in town and who the businessmen with me were. We were eager to keep the deal secret, so I pushed Simon and Shai away and bluffed my way out of it. 'I'm just in town for the tennis,' I claimed (it was half-true – we saw Roger Federer beat Andre Agassi in his last Grand Slam final at Flushing Meadows that afternoon!) The deal didn't leak and on 4 April 2006 a £962.4 million deal was agreed. We took on 10.7 per cent of the shares in the new business (in exchange for Virgin Mobile), and the whole company would be called Virgin Media. On the day of the announcement, I took out a marker and wrote 'Four-Play' on the wall, rather than the planned 'Quad-Play'. It certainly got people's attention!

The Virgin Media deal set a precedent, which has been replicated and modified for each Virgin business since, protecting the brand, but giving each company space to manoeuvre. Overnight, we had a new UK business with ten million customers and 13,000 employees. But we also had three different companies joined together very quickly, and a huge customer service problem to solve. We placed three Virgin veterans – James Kydd, Ashley Stockwell and Simon

Dornan – to lead the culture in the right direction. We discovered, for instance, that NTL's staff had been dealing with complaints by reading lifeless scripts – it was no wonder customers disliked them. We threw the scripts straight in the bin and gave our staff the freedom to be themselves. With this change and many others, the feedback started to improve, and gradually we started to turn their reputation around.

For the first time, consumers could get everything they needed from one company. In one fell swoop, we became Britain's number one broadband provider and largest mobile virtual network operator, as well as the second biggest pay TV and home phone provider. I felt thrilled that our way-of-life brand would be inside people's homes every day.

*

Virgin Media was about to become the largest Virgin company in the world. While we were very excited, one man was very nervous. One very powerful man: Rupert Murdoch.

Rumours had reached Rupert's son James, CEO of British Sky Broadcasting, that we were about to acquire a majority stake in ITV, Britain's first and largest commercial TV station. It was true. Our new company had more than 90 per cent of the cable market, but when it came to content we were lagging behind. Sky had tapped into Britain's national religion by getting the rights to top-level football – no matter the cost. I thought that ITV was really undervalued at the time, and if we got hold of it we could really make a dent in Sky's TV dominance. The Murdoch family had other ideas. They decided to stop us no matter what it cost them.

On 9 November 2006, we proposed a merger with ITV. Eight days later, BSkyB effectively blocked us by buying a 17.9 per cent stake in ITV, costing Sky's shareholders £940 million purely as an expensive spoiling tactic to stop our deal. I was furious. A few days later I was in Manchester for a last-throw-of-the-dice attempt to revive Virgin Megastores with a new UK music concept, under strict orders not to discuss ITV. As film crews for BBC, ITV and Sky looked on, the first question was: 'What do you really think about BSkyB's deal with ITV?' I looked at the camera, considered how Murdoch already controlled most of Britain's media, and decided to lay it out straight.

'I think that Murdoch is a threat to democracy,' I said.

Expanding on my theme, I went on to add, 'If the *Sun* and the *Sunday Times* and Sky and the *News of the World* all come out in favour of one particular party, the election is going to be won by that particular party. We have got rid of democracy in this country and we might as well let Murdoch decide who is going to be our Prime Minister. His empire should be looked at by competition authorities and it should be decided if it's good for democracy that one person has so much influence.'

The rest of the afternoon went by in a blur, and I soon found myself back in my hotel suite. There was a big, white freestanding bath with cast-iron feet in the middle of the room, and I ran a bath, switching on the television as I jumped in. On *Channel 4 News*, presenter Jon Snow read their opening headline: 'Branson calls Murdoch threat to democracy'.

As the piece finished, my first instinct was to call my dad. 'Did you catch the news?' I asked.

'Of course.'

'Well, what did you think?'

'You know what? I think you did the right thing. Murdoch will respect the fact that you are facing up to him – a bully never expects people to stand their ground.'

I had been nervous but I felt a bit better about it then. In these situations, Dad was the person I would ring because he always gave me great advice – some I would take, some I would (foolishly) ignore. He was the person I wanted to talk to when something good had happened; when something bad happened; when I needed somebody to quietly show off to. He was right about Murdoch; I've met him quite a few times since, and I think there is a sort of mutual respect there. We compete hard in the day but can remain friends after work – as it should be. However, when we challenged Murdoch's blatantly anti-competitive move with the Office of Fair Trading, the press were eager to pitch a fight between us. I admire him as an entrepreneur, but don't respect the views of some of his newspapers or TV channels.

Successive British governments had been afraid to limit Murdoch's dominance because they were afraid he would turn against them in upcoming elections. But on this occasion, the Competition Commission decided it was a deal too far. On 29 January 2008 they ruled that Sky must cut its stake in ITV from 17.9 per cent to below 7.5 per cent. After no end of appeals and arguments, BskyB were forced to sell 10.4 per cent of their stake in ITV on 8 February 2010 at a loss of about £348 million. And I was just delighted we managed to avoid another day in court.

Rupert Murdoch soon had other issues to worry about. In 2011, the Metropolitan Police informed me that my phones, my kids' phones and my neighbours' phones had all been hacked by News Group Newspapers, a wholly-owned subsidiary of News Corp. Like many other phone-hacking victims, as a matter of principle I brought a claim against News Group Newspapers that was settled on financial terms, which included a compensation payment that I donated to charity. I received a letter from them including an apology for their wrong and unlawful invasion of my privacy and for causing harm, distress and suffering.

After the Dirty Tricks of British Airways, which had included private investigators rifling through my bins, I felt saddened that our family's privacy had been invaded again.

*

At heart, I am an entrepreneur, which means I love building businesses and creating new things. In order to keep doing this, however, it sometimes means selling stakes in companies or entire businesses.

This is one part of my life I don't enjoy. I am not a person who harbours regrets, but selling companies has always left

me with an empty feeling. I can still taste the tears streaming down my face after I sold Virgin Records in 1992 to keep
Virgin Atlantic afloat. Selling 49 per cent of Virgin Atlantic
in 1999 was very tough, too, but we needed the funds to
kick-start the early stages of Virgin Active, the expansion of
Virgin Money and the creation of Virgin Mobile. I enjoy the
intensity of the bidding process and the heat of the negotiating table. But, as I believe that a business is nothing more
than a group of people trying to make a difference, selling
always leaves me sad, feeling somehow I have traded
people. So when I do have regrets, it is generally about
upsetting people along the way, or letting anyone down.
Sometimes in business people get hurt. But sometimes, too,
doing a deal is the right thing for all parties.

Since our early battles with Sky, Virgin Media had carved
out a big share of the UK's broadband market. But by the
late 2000s, that market dynamic was changing rapidly. I was
eager for Virgin Media to keep pushing ahead with new
developments rather than resting on their laurels, as I knew
the landscape could alter so quickly. The best example was
landline phones, which had gone from necessity to nui-
sance in a couple of years. Now, having the best broadband
product in the market meant we were perfectly placed to
gain customers as data use grew exponentially. Virgin
Media's network infrastructure and brand power were so
strong that we were able to outstrip Sky and BT.

In 2013, completely out of the blue, John Malone's
Liberty Global approached us with an offer. We were not
looking to sell or reduce our stake, but Liberty Global are
probably the most revered, respected and successful cable
network investor in the world and the deal they were pro-
posing was an enticing one. They offered to buy the
NASDAQ-listed company for $23.3 billion: in addition, we
would retain a stake and the all-important brand.

I've known for a long time that the most valuable thing
we have built is our brand. We'd had success using the
Virgin name to rebrand companies around the world in
many different sectors, but this deal saw us really utilising

the brand to its full potential. Brand power really does set us apart, allowing us to achieve scale without losing personal connection. I'm aware that, as the face of the brand, my own image is tied up in this appeal, too. Ever since my mentor Sir Freddie Laker showed me the benefits of leaders being the visible fronts of businesses, I've been comfortable with this. It works, and if that means me appearing on websites, on posters and in ads, that's fine with me. Liberty Global certainly recognised the benefits, too, and we were able to expand our partnership across the water and launch Virgin Media Ireland together in 2015. We didn't sit back on our proceeds from the Virgin Media deal. We used that Virgin spirit, the new cash and our people to start fresh ventures such as Virgin Hotels, Virgin Sport and Virgin Voyages, and invest in existing ones like Virgin Galactic, all the while pushing the Virgin brand even further outwards.

16 Holly and Sam

hen Holly and Sam were teenagers I took them to Las Vegas to teach them a lesson about the perils of gambling. We had always played cards as a family, usually wild bridge, but never for money. I knew, though, that they were growing up and would be tempted to try gambling soon. Rather than getting themselves into a dangerous situation, I decided to introduce them to the pitfalls of betting personally. Vegas might seem a strange environment to share some fatherly wisdom with your children, but I thought learning a few hard-hitting life lessons in an atmosphere of hedonism and wild abandon could actually be very effective.

We headed to a casino on the strip for the full Vegas experience. Flashing signs and fancy cars outside, the relentless rattle of fruit machines inside. There were croupiers as far as the eye could see: tables of blackjack, poker and the seductive, spinning whirr of the roulette wheel. It was the last that attracted Holly and Sam's eye, so we went over to the table.

'Ok,' I said, 'You've got $40 in casino chips each. I'll place the bets for you. Let's have fun.'

The pair of them looked thrilled, excited at being treated like grown-ups. They sat up at the table and debated whether to go for red or black, or choose a specific number. It didn't last long. Within a matter of minutes, they'd lost all their money.

'Never mind,' I said, putting a fatherly arm around them. Accidentally leaving a couple of remaining chips on the table, we turned away for a drink and the message I'd brought them to Vegas to impart.

'That's the thing about gambling,' I explained. 'Everyone thinks they can win, that this time they might be the lucky one. But, in fact, it takes no time at all for that hard-earned money to disappear into thin air. Actually, that's not quite true.' I waved around at our surroundings: the glitzy chintz of the decor. 'There's a saying in Vegas, the house always wins. And that's true; the only people who make any money out of casinos are the owners. And they make plenty of it.'

Sam and Holly stood there, looking suitably chastened. Good job, I told myself. That was a proper bit of parenting, Richard Branson-style. I was sure the message had hit home. I'd shown that the glamorous image of casinos and the gambling that went with it was nothing but a façade. A dangerous illusion that you'd do well to avoid.

Half an hour later, having finished our drinks, we were ready to head back to our hotel. As we glanced at the table we had been playing roulette on, every person who was sitting there stood up and applauded us. The table was packed, but they ushered us over and let us back into the circle. I had to double-blink – there, in front of us, was a huge pile of winnings stacked up. While we'd had our drinks, the couple of chips we'd left behind on the table had tripled and tripled and tripled into a small fortune!

'Hey! Congratulations, buddy!' one of the other guests patted me on the shoulder.

I was gobsmacked. To my side, Holly and Sam couldn't contain their excitement.

'The house always wins, does it, Dad?' Sam asked, with a smirk.

I decided it would be wrong to take any of the winnings ourselves, and split them between everyone on the table to thank them for letting us know. I then tried in vain to rescue my fatherly advice session with the children.

'Kids,' I argued as we left the casino. 'It's important to remember that there is an exception to every rule.' There was not a murmur from either of them about me giving away their winnings. But as for my fatherly advice? I might as well have been talking to a brick wall. They were too busy grinning to pay any attention. Fast-forward to 2018 and we are turning the iconic Hard Rock Hotel and Casino in Las Vegas into Virgin Hotels, bringing its magic back under the Virgin brand. Sam, Holly and I will have to hit the tables and see if our luck is still in!

*

I know how fortunate we were to offer Holly and Sam many advantages when they were growing up. But when children are born into fortunate circumstances, helping them to develop character and shape their own futures presents its own challenges. As I grow older, I appreciate more and more how my mum helped mould me with tough love, pushing me to extremes and urging me to take risks. I wanted to give Holly and Sam the same freedom to mature, but was always aware it was different for them due to our wealth. There was no getting away from the fact that, whatever they did, there was always a safety net. That has to have an effect on how you approach life, and can easily leave you damaged.

The key to avoiding this was letting them make their own decisions and mistakes, while giving unreserved time, love and support. We always tried not to spoil them, only allowing a few presents and ensuring the ones we gave were useful. Rather than forcing them in any particular direction, we tried to find ways to help them develop a wider understanding of the world.

Ever since he was a child, Sam had often strolled into the house with surprises for us. Whether it was a shaved head, an electric-orange mohawk, or an outlandish outfit, I was rarely shocked and often amused. Joan took a slightly less laissez-faire attitude to Sam's fashion choices, though we always supported him and let him go his own way: I was well aware how many dodgy jumpers I'd thrown on over the years! But when Sam came back from a few months' travelling in 2005, he had a new accessory that even Joan and I found it hard to resist commenting on.

'What exactly do you call that?' asked Joan. We were in the kitchen on Necker catching up, when Joan pointed to Sam's forearm. When Sam had first walked back into our house, we'd tried to keep our cool. Our immediate reaction was not to tell him off or disapprove: instead, we walked out of the room quietly, got over our surprise and tried to carry on as though nothing had happened. But it hadn't taken long for us to crack.

'Go on then, Sam,' I said, 'tell us about the tattoo.'

'Oh, you noticed it?'

'Just in passing,' I fibbed, on tenterhooks to see what the tribal writing on his arm meant. I prayed it wasn't anything offensive.

'It means "Necker" in Sanskrit,' Sam explained to my relief. 'I got it done the traditional way in Thailand.'

I loved it, to the point that it did make us wonder for a second. After Sam had headed out again, I turned to Joan.

'We aren't getting old, are we?'

'I don't know about you, Richard – but I'm certainly not planning to.'

I couldn't help but smile, and begin pondering what tattoo I could get myself.

A while later, Sam came back from further travels and his mum met him at the airport. He got into the car sheepishly, before saying: 'Mum, you know you love me ...'

'What have you done this time?'

He showed her a new tattoo.

Joan smiled and said: 'Well, you've come back in one piece; a tattoo is not so bad.'

The tattoos were just the latest sign of a young man beginning to find his place in the world. I was acutely aware that Sam was growing up and the balance in our relationship was beginning to shift. From the moment he was born Sam had come to all manner of launches, events and parties with me. Often, when the nights were getting late and I wanted to go, I would point to Sam being tired out and make my excuses to leave. 'It looks like it's time for Sam to go to bed, I'd better take him home,' I would say. But as he got further into his teenage years, he was increasingly becoming the life and soul of the parties: now it was Sam using my tiredness as an excuse when he wanted to leave.

Like many young people, Sam hadn't worked out what he wanted to do by the time he left school. I reassured him that was absolutely fine – and natural, too.

'You're nineteen,' I remember telling him in one conversation. 'That only happens once – so enjoy it.'

Sam always had an insatiable thirst for knowledge. We spent many evenings together watching TV documentaries, often Sir David Attenborough's wonderful natural history programmes. During one of these shows, we got talking about Sam's future. I was very keen not to put any pressure on him or his sister, and to let them stand on their own two feet. Like me Sam wasn't particularly academic and told me that school had made him feel like his options were quite narrow.

'Why don't you take a gap year, then?' I suggested. 'You can go out and enjoy some new experiences, have some fun and think about how you want to make your mark in the process. What is there to stop you?'

Sam did just that. He learned to snowboard, travelled through India, spent time in Bali and immersed himself in new cultures with different people. One night he called home with news of his latest plans to head to Sydney.

'You know you're so lucky,' I told him. 'I began my career at fifteen, and never had the chance to do what you're doing.' I knew I was fortunate to be able to travel so much on business, and had seen so many amazing places over the years. But it was rare that I could do what Sam was doing: taking time to travel with no work in mind.

'Well, Dad, why don't you come along?' Sam asked. Throwing my words to him back at me, he added, 'What is there to stop you?'

Which is how I ended up clearing my diary, and found myself flying out to Australia, meeting Sam and his friends in a beautiful beach shack above Rae's in Byron Bay. We played on Wategos Beach in the day, cooked delicious dinners in the evening, took in the local bars at night and enjoyed the odd smoke together, too. I was savouring my own personal gap month!

As I leaned back in a deckchair on the beach one evening, Sam looked over at me, smiling.

'Dad, this is the least I've ever seen you work.'

'Enjoy it while it lasts!' I laughed.

Although I was checking in on things back in the office, the time difference meant I could get to relax more, too. I was able to put work on the back-burner and enjoy the chance to spend some quality time with my son. My only disappointment was my struggle to keep up with Sam and his friends on the surfing. On the first two days, I failed to get one run in. On the third, Sam's friend mentioned that two photographers were hiding in the bushes. With that incentive, I managed to catch the very next wave and glide in to shore, meaning I looked more surfer king than shark fodder on the following day's front pages.

*

Holly, meanwhile, was working enormously hard at University College London to get her degree, and I loved getting her updates on student life. One day she called me up after getting her exam results. She had done really well and I told her how proud I was of her. As she excitedly carried on telling me all about the tests, I had to interrupt her.

'Holly, I'm really sorry,' I told her, 'but I'm going to have to call you back.'

I was debating the role of women in business in front of thousands of people at an event organised by Maria Shriver in California. Although it was a big deal, family always comes first, no matter what, which is why I answered the phone to hear her results. When Holly rang,

I had asked the audience to bear with me as I took the call, and they were happy to play along with it.

'Hang on one second. I want to tell them your results.' I quickly relayed the good news and the crowd gave her a standing ovation.

'Erm, thanks everyone. Dad, I love you, speak to you later.' I put the phone down with a smile. 'Now, where was I?'

As the first (and so far only) member of my immediate family to do so, Holly graduating was a proud moment. Whatever my misgivings about the suitability of higher education for some people, it was absolutely the right option for Holly. Though always an old head on young shoulders, she matured enormously and qualified as a doctor. She had always wanted to help other people and got a job at Chelsea and Westminster Hospital doing just that. It was great having her so close to Virgin's offices in west London: when I was in the UK on business, it meant she could pop in to visit after her shifts.

Despite Holly enjoying her role, I still had an inkling that she might like to join Virgin at some point. After all, we have always been a family business. I genuinely felt that Holly could achieve more and make a bigger positive impact in the world working under the Virgin umbrella; she could use her medical experience, but working with greater financial resources and variously skilled teams of people to make a difference. I asked Joan what she thought of Holly joining: 'It's up to her really,' was her wise reply. 'Holly and Sam can do anything they want to do, as long as it makes them happy.'

As Virgin Unite grew further into areas that interested Holly, such as providing medical aid for people in need and business support for young entrepreneurs, she finally came on board to work with us in an internship role. Holly assured me it would just be for a year, travelling around all the different Virgin companies and getting real-world experience on the front lines of everywhere from Virgin Media to Virgin Atlantic, Virgin Money to Virgin Management. Around this time Peter Norris took on the role of Virgin

Group chairman, and took Holly under his wing in the office. A delightful man of vast experience and always eager to help, he became a mentor to Holly, and I was proud to see her thrive under his guidance. Holly was torn; she had trained hard for many years and loved being a doctor. Giving it up would be a massive step. But the opportunity to build something new was too much to resist. At the end of the year Holly decided that being at Virgin felt natural, and the right thing to do. She joined full time, focusing on people and purpose across our businesses, and has gone on to chair Virgin Unite, taking over from Patrick McCall after 10 years in the role. I am thrilled to have Holly on board.

*

Sam was also stretching his wings, albeit in a different direction. North, to be precise.

At an event at the Roof Gardens in London, the pair of us had the chance to meet up with explorer Will Steger. Will ran Arctic expeditions, which were high-endurance challenges, living in the wilderness for months on end. By now, Sam was twenty-one, very much enjoying life, but still finding his path towards what his calling would be. I thought this could be a wonderful way for him to grow up and learn a lot about himself.

Of course, I didn't present the idea to Sam in that way – who wouldn't run a mile at such talk from their dad? Instead I spoke about what an adventure it would be, and that we could take on some of it together. Sam also wanted to draw attention to climate change, a problem he was already acutely aware of from my dealings with former US Vice-President Al Gore, and the documentaries we watched together. This was a chance for us to see its effects up close and personal.

In March 2007, Will invited me to come on the first week of his Global Warming 101 expedition with Sam and a group of about twenty young people, travelling 1,200 miles from the south of Baffin Island to Igloolik. I joined the team at

Clyde River, a small community on the northern coast on Baffin Island, where the Inuit people continue to live the way they have for centuries. On the first night the Inuit villagers threw a welcoming party for us in what was effectively a very large, cold shed. In the centre of the floor they had laid out an incredibly generous feast with raw reindeer, caribou heads, raw fish, seals and fermented walrus, which had been buried under the snow for a month. We had to go forward in turn and cut off a chunk of raw meat. I was dreading my turn. It was not easy to swallow but we had to do it in order not to offend. I chewed with my thumbs up, trying to hide my expression as the partially frozen seal melted in my mouth. It was all a far cry from the Roof Gardens where we'd first met Will.

The next day we got up at 6 a.m. – not that it was ever easy to tell what time of day it was that far north – to melt the ice covering our tents and coats. Then, as the sun was coming up, we headed off down the most exquisite ice valley. I had a leg injury so sat on the sled with sixteen baying dogs ahead of us, while Sam ran behind. The landscape remained unchanged for hours on end, but it was always breathtaking: the sweep of the ice and the mountains, the sharpness of the white against the crisp blue of the sky.

Not everything was beautiful about the location: going to the toilet in such surroundings was also something else. As the temperature was so low, between -10 degrees C and -25 degrees C with wind chill, there were times when your excrement froze before reaching the ground. Coupled with that, you would have to constantly monitor all around in case polar bears sneaked up on you whatever you were doing.

We had a beautiful week together sleeping under the stars, before I left the group and the hard work for Sam really began. He was to stay for another two weeks. They battled through hazardous hills of ice with their dogs and sledges. The team had to survive the practicalities of living in the ice, and learn how to catch and eat raw fish. Later, Sam joined Will and a group of young explorers on a longer, more arduous journey across the Arctic to raise awareness about climate change.

I'm certainly not a believer in sending people to the army or even to strict boarding schools – as I had to do – but to go through hardship and overcome it is incredibly good for you. When Sam returned he said it was one of the best experiences of his life.

'If you can handle a trip like that,' I told him, 'you will be able to cope with pretty well anything.'

As a smile spread across Sam's now bearded face, I realised that my son had gone away a boy and come back a man.

17 The Elders Assemble

Every January, the world's great and the good gather together in the Swiss mountain resort of Davos for the World Economic Forum. It is a coming together of both political and business leaders, and an opportunity to catch up with old friends, make some new ones, and above all to debate, discuss and share the latest ideas. There's something about the crispness of the Swiss air, the crunch of the snow underfoot and the compactness of the setting that really helps to crystallise ideas.

In January 2006, Jean Oelwang and I flew in late one evening to join them. As the shadows of the Swiss mountains spread out in the moonlight below, I mulled over what we were there to achieve. Rather than a business idea, we were there to push our concept of the Elders, and to see who we could persuade to come on board. I was both excited and a little nervous at the prospect: normally when I start a business there are rival companies which aren't working the way I would, and I use their (bad) example to inspire my new vision. But with the Elders this was going to be very different – nothing remotely like this had been done before. Peter Gabriel, Jean and I brought together an amazing team to work on incubating the project, with documentary maker Andrea Barron and Peace Direct's Scilla Elworthy among many volunteering their time to shape the idea. But now we needed wider help.

Over the next three days, Jean, Peter and I pitched hard for support. We didn't just need people with deep pockets – they also had to understand and believe in our vision.

I managed to persuade a variety of wonderful souls to get on board, including the futurist Peter Schwartz and his wife, AKQA founder Ajaz Ahmed, Jimmy Wales from Wikipedia and Larry Brilliant from Google.org. One lady came into a meeting and I offered my seat to her. She turned out to be Pam Omidyar from Humanity United, who has gone on to commit millions to the Elders.

'I've never forgotten your courtesy,' she told me years later.

There is a lesson there. Good manners cost nothing: little kindnesses will take you a long way.

Six months later, in July 2006, in somewhat different weather conditions, I was hosting three back-to-back gatherings on Necker Island. As well as business leaders, philanthropists and politicians, we also invited two people Nelson Mandela was earmarking as potential Elders: President Jimmy Carter and Archbishop Desmond Tutu. We met each morning in the Temple, a stunning construction next to my house with 360-degree views of the ocean and a great long table to sit and debate at: the perfect location to inspire what we were trying to achieve.

I moved around the groups, trying to get people animated about the Elders concept. We discussed its purpose, what areas it should focus upon, how it should be governed and structured. On the first morning, I announced, 'From now on, there is a ban on PowerPoint. It just gets in the way and bores the audience. Everybody has to speak from the heart.' Jean later told me she had been up all night preparing her PowerPoint presentation. Instead she gave her vision of the Elders as I'd hoped she would: expertly and with real passion. Peter and then I got up and explained why we believed this was the most important thing we had done in our lives.

I thought the meeting was going swimmingly, but then Jimmy Carter stood up, dusted down his white shirt and cleared his distinctive, airy voice.

'I'm sorry, Richard. I appreciate your intentions, but I just don't see how this is going to work.'

I felt shaken by his intervention. This was a man I had grown up revering, the only US President not to go to war, and a wise and honest statesman who understood how the world worked. If he didn't think the Elders was a good idea, then what the hell were we all doing there?

I ushered Jean and Peter into my very small office. We all felt deeply disappointed, and I was embarrassed that we might have brought all these remarkable people together for nothing. But then Peter suggested we could look at this the other way around, as an opportunity.

'We're overcomplicating this,' he argued. 'Why don't we ask them what they think could work?'

Peter and I had only ever wanted to be facilitators and supporters. We realised that we needed to give them a sense of ownership, and the chance to shape their own organisation. Regaining my composure, I went back out to the assembled guests.

'If this is going to work,' I told them, 'we all have to trust each other, and be completely open. I don't know how to do this. Peter doesn't either. I don't think any of us do alone – but together we might have a chance.'

At this point, Archbishop Tutu – 'just call me Arch' – backed me up.

'When we started South Africa's Truth and Reconciliation Commission, we didn't know how to go about it either,' he remembered, to nods all round. 'We just started, and together built it into something that could work.'

From funding options to issues to focus on, targets to governance structure, a brutally honest discussion on how the Elders truly could make a difference began. Later, I watched as Arch and President Carter sat down under a tree on Turtle Beach, overlooking the ocean, and drafted the first values and core principles of the group together.

'The Elders represent an independent voice,' they wrote, 'not bound by the interests of any nation, government or institution. We are committed to promoting the shared interests of humanity, and the universal human rights we all share. We believe that in any conflict, it is important to listen to everyone – no matter how unpalatable or unpopular this may be. We aim to act boldly, speaking difficult truths and tackling taboos.'

At the end of the two weeks, President Carter stood up and gave a magnificent presentation about the potential of the Elders. He said that, while the UN had a crucial role to play in conflict resolution, the Elders could have a far bigger impact. 'It could be fiercely independent and move quickly; it wouldn't be beholden to big countries; and it could base all decisions on moral authority rather than political impact.'

I watched on in awe. Ever since that moment, both he and Arch have been behind the idea 100 per cent.

*

While Archbishop Tutu was helping us to pull the Elders together, back in his native South Africa an issue was rearing its head that I didn't feel I could ignore. Despite the hope and awareness the 46664 concert in South Africa had raised, I was getting increasingly frustrated with the inaction of the South African government to tackle HIV/AIDS. There just didn't seem to be the political will to act in the face of a disease that was killing hundreds of thousands of people.

Then, in August 2006, South Africa's health minister, Manto Tshabalala-Msimang, went to an international AIDS conference in Toronto and stated that HIV could be cured with potatoes, beetroot, garlic and lemon. It was maddening. I went back to South Africa on 26 October to visit a number of community homes for AIDS orphans with an organisation called Starfish. I remained preoccupied with the South African government's inaction.

Before I went onstage at a charity event in Mupmalanga, I turned to Jean Oelwang and said, 'I've got to say something.'

'If you do speak out,' she warned, 'you could get kicked out of South Africa. We'd be letting down so many people who we are working with here.'

I understood, but was so angry that I couldn't let it lie. When I stood up, I pushed my prepared speech aside and did what I'd told those at the Elders meeting on Necker to do: speak from the heart. I began by praising South African President Mbeki and the ANC for all they'd done against apartheid. But then I called for them to be indicted for crimes against humanity for letting so many people die. By denying antiretroviral drugs they were killing their own people. This was a crime I felt made President Mbeki and his health minister, who fully deserved the nickname Dr Beetroot, guilty of genocide. That sounds like strong words, but in 2008 a Harvard study found Mbeki's policy of blocking the provision of medication to AIDS patients was responsible for an estimated 330,000 unnecessary deaths and more than 35,000 HIV-infected births.

Never one to duck a fight, I went on national TV to continue to make my point. 'If you go to America or Britain,' I told the interviewer, 'people don't die of AIDS any more. But you have a government in South Africa whose health minister still advocates garlic as a cure and a president who is not much better as far as AIDS is concerned. It's just too sad for words.'

To my surprise, and his great credit, President Mbeki had the grace to send a long handwritten reply, which I'm told he sat up all night composing. 'Because of the respect and regards I and many others in our country have for you,' he wrote, 'we take with the greatest seriousness the grave accusation you allegedly made.' Mbeki vigorously defended his HIV/AIDS strategy, but requested that I meet him and his health minister, and said he was willing to hear me out.

After canvassing opinion from a wide range of experts on what could be done to help change South Africa's health policies, I replied on 6 November. I apologised for speaking so emotionally after a very disturbing visit to a rural community being torn apart by HIV/AIDS and said the whole world needed to get behind the South African government: 'We certainly don't have all the answers,' I wrote, 'and fully respect that the issues are far more complicated than anyone outside South Africa will ever understand.' I promised to support the country in whatever way I could and offered to meet him that month.

President Mbeki's response was to handwrite a lengthy reply from the heart himself, explaining how his upbringing and life had led him to draw such terrible conclusions about HIV. He wrote about what he felt needed to be done to combat the problem, as well as address South Africa's lack of job opportunities. He then told me of the desperate problems they faced in alleviating decades of poverty. He said that black South Africans 'hope that, one day, they will have ready access to the health facilities that would help them fully recover their health when they became gravely ill'. 'We are who and what we are as a people,' he wrote, 'because of respect for, and unqualified devotion to, the ethical and humanist principle that "umuntu ngumuntu ngabanye" – every human being thrives as a human being because others thrive as human beings!'

I was touched, too, as he went on to suggest meeting his elderly mother: 'My mother turned 90 in February this year. She lives still in the rural neighbourhood where I was born, and remains as mentally alert as ever. Again, God willing, you will one day have an opportunity to meet her at her rural home. If this were ever to happen, I hope that you would listen carefully to what she would tell you about disease and death among the rural people who have been her closest neighbours for many decades.' I was humbled he had taken the time to write such a personal letter and I took heart in its basic message of humanity. 'Your honesty and sincerity in your letter have truly helped me understand more deeply your perspective,' I replied. I added that I would be delighted to meet his mother to hear her views, and asked if I could bring along my mum to share the experience: 'My mother is now 81 and is also a pretty formidable lady. I'm sure the two of them would get on well.'

We continued to exchange letters, and I suggested an idea for a Centre for Disease Control in Africa as something positive to come out of our correspondence. It was bizarre that the continent that most needed such a Centre didn't have one. Furthermore, on 1 December, the South African government made a World AIDS Day announcement using the tagline Stop HIV and AIDS and Keep the Promise. There was a long way to go, but, hopefully, mindsets were changing. We went through weeks of meetings with the ANC government, and after lots of negotiating ironed out the details so that the Centre for Disease Control could be launched.

But the day before President Mbeki was to announce the centre he was given a vote of no confidence by the ANC National Executive Committee and forced to resign. When President Jacob Zuma took over he agreed to move the Centre for Disease Control forward. He asked me to join him at a press conference to announce it, which I did – but that was the last we heard from him. We contacted the government regularly to try to push the project ahead, but, sadly, nothing happened. Without the personal drive of Mbeki to make it happen, there was no longer the political will to move forward.

While the Centre for Disease Control did not open, the Bhubezi Community Health Centre is going strong. I have returned to Bhubezi many times over the past decade. It is always a delight to see many thousands of people getting the care they need.

I know that it's a drop in the ocean, but in the past 10 years the Centre has received over 325,000 patient visits, tested nearly 25,000 people for HIV/AIDS (40 per cent tested positive and, where appropriate, started receiving free life-saving anti-retroviral treatment). And the Centre doesn't just provide support for people suffering from life-threatening illnesses; it has become a community centre point, and a place where all manner of health advice and support is given. There are also visiting health groups, such as the Starkey Hearing Foundation, who provide hearing aids to people in remote areas.

Some of the most moving moments of my life have been in Bhubezi fitting hearing aids to people who have lost their hearing. So far, the Starkey Foundation has fitted nearly two million hearing aids, changing people's lives in the process. On a visit in 2015, I shared a really special moment with the very first girl I helped to fit with a hearing aid that day. She smiled up at me as I attached the device, and we went through the simple steps to tune it. When my voice got through to her and she heard sound for the very first time, she screeched with joy – a sound that will stay with me forever.

*

By May 2007, Mandela and Graça had decided on a list of twelve proposed Elders. Leaving the bustle of Jo'burg behind for the serenity of the bush, we flew to Ulusaba for Nelson Mandela's first address to them. It was a magical, over-whelming moment: as Mandela began walking up the hill, the pathway turned into a cacophony of noise and emotion as our staff spontaneously burst into song. Mandela danced along in a trademark multi-coloured shirt, holding hands with the locals.

The wind continued to be with us: when Kofi Annan, travelling on UN commitments, video conferenced in, Mandela asked him simply: 'Would you become an Elder?'

'How can I say no when you have me on the screen?' Kofi laughed. 'Of course I'm in.'

The finances fell into place, too. We set ourselves challenges to raise the money needed to cover the costs of running the Elders for three years: $18 million. I was so convinced by the idea that it was easier than expected to convince others.

We chose 18 July, Mandela's eighty-ninth birthday, for the launch at Constitution Hill in Jo'burg. Originally a prison during the apartheid years, it had been transformed into the home of South Africa's Constitutional Court. As I walked down a long hallway lined with artwork created during the Truth and Reconciliation movement, I stopped as I came upon a beautiful memorial to the people who had been kept imprisoned there. A sprawling series of crosses were etched along the wall – one for every day of Mandela's twenty-seven years in jail. I knew we had chosen the right place to introduce this new force for peace in the world.

Many of the Elders were there: Mandela and his wife Graça Machel, Kofi Annan, President Carter, former President of Ireland Mary Robinson, Archbishop Desmond Tutu, and Grameen Bank founder and Nobel Peace prize-winner Muhammad Yunus. Also named as Elders, but watching from afar, were Self-Employed Women's Association of India founder Ela Bhatt, former Norwegian Prime Minister Gro Harlem Brundtland, former Algerian Foreign Minister Lakhdar Brahimi and former Brazilian President Fernando Henrique Cardoso.

Panic struck as two generators blew before we started the launch. I frantically ran backstage to find Miles Peckham had organised a third. Then Peter and I introduced the Elders concept, before he performed a heart-stopping rendition of 'Biko'. President Carter and Kofi spoke eloquently, while Arch's speech made us laugh and cry: 'We owe our freedom to extraordinary people,' he told the assembled crowd. 'The bad, the evil, doesn't have the last word. It is ultimately goodness and laughter and joy and caring and compassion.'

Madiba, meanwhile, made the most stirring speech I have heard in my life. 'Let us call them Global Elders, not because of their age, but because of their individual and collective wisdom. This group derives its strength not from political, economic or military power, but from the independence and integrity of those who are here. I believe that, with your experience and your energies, and your profound commitment to building a better world, the Elders can become a fiercely independent and robust force for good, tackling complex and intractable issues.'

They were powerful words, powerfully spoken: like everyone in the room, I was deeply moved. It was so rewarding to be there to witness it. It was rewarding, too, to see how quickly the Elders moved into action following the launch. They quickly convened and began outlining a plan of action together, starting with a first trip to learn more about the humanitarian situation in Darfur and see how they could help. Our idea had come to life: the Elders had assembled.

18 Climate Change

In late summer 2006, Al Gore asked if I would see him for a meeting. We had never met before, so arranged to get together in London for breakfast. After he'd finished speaking, I didn't feel like eating any more.

Strange as it might sound for a man in the process of setting up his third airline, I was becoming increasingly preoccupied with a seemingly contradictory subject: climate change. But that meeting with Al Gore took my concerns further. It wasn't a social call – he was there to show me the world was staring a global disaster in the face and doing nowhere near enough about it. And show me he did. I had already been looking into the subject, but nothing prepared me for the impact Al's presentation made. Will Whitehorn and Jean Oelwang sat quietly alongside me, listening intently, and we were all shocked by what Al said. His words were so clear and his evidence so overwhelming that I knew we had to start acting before it was too late.

Al's presentation went on to become the powerful documentary *An Inconvenient Truth*, which brought climate change to the attention of millions of people. He was eager for a business leader to speak out on the problem, and encourage other CEOs to follow suit.

'You are in a position to make a difference,' he told me. 'If you can make a giant step forward other people will follow.'

After Al left, I did some soul-searching. How can a businessman who runs three airlines and a trainline commit to helping lead the fight against climate change? I went back

to my previous research into the issue, reading the likes of
The Skeptical Environmentalist by Bjørn Lomborg and James
Lovelock's Gaia books. I went to meet Jim Lovelock and his
analysis only reinforced my changing view. There is no
doubt humans are increasing the amount of CO_2 and other
greenhouse gases in the atmosphere at an exponential rate,
and that the ever-thickening blanket around the earth that
this creates is driving up temperatures. It was clear to me
that unless more was done the consequences would pose
potentially catastrophic risks to the earth's environment,
economies, species, cultures and people. I thought about
what kind of planet my generation wanted to leave to my
children's children. My conclusion was that we had to do all
we could to help.

But how I could I do that? I decided that for the next few
years we should divert all of the dividend profits made by
the Virgin Group from our transportation businesses to
investments in renewables research and developing new
clean technologies – sustainable, low-carbon transport fuels
in particular. As you may have established by now, I believe
strongly in people. Entrepreneurship has helped create
many of the wonders of the world today, and it can help us
overcome many of our challenges for a better tomorrow.
New initiatives could help us get to the root of the problem.

I was then invited by President Bill Clinton to speak at
the Clinton Global Initiative coming up in September. Bill
is a shrewd operator and never misses a trick: after I agreed
to attend, he called me asking if there was any particular
pledge I would like to make. I realised this would be the
perfect opportunity to share my plan and when I explained
it to President Clinton, he was delighted, and decided to
make the announcement the centrepiece of his event.

On 21 September I was in the Sheraton Hotel in Midtown,
New York, when President Clinton took to the stage and
gave me a glowing introduction. In front of an audience
including Bill Gates, French President Jacques Chirac,
Rupert Murdoch and Warren Buffett, he described me as
'one of the most interesting, creative, genuinely committed

people I have ever known'. I was flattered, or at least I would have been if I hadn't missed my cue and was in the loo at the time!

As the assembled leaders looked around to see where I was, I finally made it onstage and ran through our plan: 'What we've decided to do is to put any proceeds received by the Virgin Group from our transportation businesses into tackling environmental issues,' I said. Unaware of the impending global financial crisis, in an interview afterwards I estimated these profits could be as high as $3 billion over the next decade.

'Our generation has inherited an incredibly beautiful world from our parents and they from their parents,' I argued. 'It is in our hands whether our children and their children inherit the same world. We must not be the generation responsible for irreversibly damaging the environment.' I discussed our new venture, Virgin Fuels, which would invest in biofuels and other innovations to develop clean aviation fuel. Together with Shai Weiss and Evan Lovell from Virgin Group, we decided to expand from biofuels development to more environment-focused investments, setting up Virgin Green Fund in early 2007. This independent private equity firm would invest growth capital in the renewable energy and resource efficiency sector more broadly.

'The only way global warming is going to be beaten is to invest in new fuels (and energy) that can actually replace fossil fuels,' I concluded.

*

Climate change has not been the only major issue that has concerned me in recent years: the matter of drugs has continued to energise me, and lead me to taking up a role as a Global Drug Commissioner.

When I was growing up in the sixties and launching a record label, drugs were never far away. Our stores became places where young people could hang out and listen to music. I was one of thousands of young people who would join friends on a beanbag, listening to the latest Pink Floyd record and sharing a spliff. But aside from the occasional joint, I was never really much of a user myself: my work and adventures have always given me much more of a buzz.

One exception came when I travelled to Jamaica in 1974 to convince Peter Tosh to sign for Virgin Records. I felt Peter was the only person in reggae as talented as Bob Marley, and when I heard he was leaving the Wailers and going solo I was determined to sign him. I flew to Jamaica, found out where Peter lived and knocked on his front door. There was no answer, but I could hear noises inside the house. I sat down on the dusty ground outside and waited for what seemed like three days. From people coming and going, I got the impression that Peter knew I was outside, and was testing how keen I was to sign him. Eventually he came to the door.

'I guess you better come in,' he boomed, offering me the floor in his living room. He then disappeared into the hall, before returning with an enormous box of ganga. I sat there, goggle-eyed as he rolled the longest spliff I've ever seen. We stayed up (well, lay prostrate on the floor!) for two days, which was how long it took to empty the box. Somehow, I passed his initiation test and he signed to Virgin Records. The following year we released *Legalize It*, his pro-marijuana anthem.

While Peter used marijuana both recreationally and creatively, many other musicians were becoming reliant on much harder drugs. I've seen plenty of people struggle with addiction, including some of our artists, from Sid Vicious to Boy George. As I grew older I began to see how their addictions were made so much worse by the ongoing criminalisation of drug users. The amount spent on enforcing drug laws – more than $100 billion a year – is equivalent to the amount spent globally on foreign aid. But instead of helping, this extraordinary sum is being used to fund a war against people, to enormous human, economic and social cost around the world. Hundreds of thousands of people have been criminalised, and hundreds of thousands more have been killed. The war on drugs has also effectively kick-started the $320 billion a year criminal drug industry, fuelled terrorism – and done nothing to reduce drug production, supply and use.

My own experiences strengthened my conviction that drug addiction and abuse should be treated as a public health issue, not a criminal problem. As the century turned, I continued to speak out and quickly learned that many around me felt the same way, but were afraid to raise their voice. In this climate, I saw a need for more evidence-based drug policies to spread throughout the world. The key would be proving to governments, who did not want to hear it, that the war on drugs had failed and that there was a better approach.

In 2010, I was invited by former President of Brazil Fernando Henrique Cardoso to join the newly formed Global Commission on Drug Policy. This unprecedented group began carrying out an enormous amount of research into worldwide drug policies. Many of the members had seen the results of draconian laws first-hand as presidents and prime ministers of countries including Colombia, Mexico, Switzerland and Greece, and were determined to make amends for not doing more when they were in power. Kofi Annan also joined us, alongside the likes of Paul Volcker, former chairman of the US Federal Reserve and George Shultz, former US Secretary of State. In the years to come, leaders from Chile, the Czech Republic, the UK, Portugal, Peru, India, Pakistan, Poland and America joined the Commission and evidence continued to build.

As the only business leader on the Commission, I came at the problem from an entrepreneurial standpoint. When I attended Commission meetings, from Switzerland to the US, I would state what I would do if it were a business: 'The war on drugs is killing millions of people, and putting billions of dollars into the pockets of drug lords,' I argued at a meeting at MoMA in New York. 'If the war on drugs was a business, I would have shut it down decades ago, and tried something else. It's time the world did exactly that.'

The new millennium had brought some radical changes rooted in the realisation that business as usual was not an option. From Switzerland to South America, new evidence-based policies to treat drugs as a health issue were put into practice. I was particularly taken with Portugal, which in 2001 became the first European country to officially abolish all criminal penalties for personal possession of drugs, including marijuana, cocaine, heroin and methamphetamines. In December 2011, I visited the country on behalf of the Global Commission to congratulate the Portuguese on the success of their drug policies and see their impact first-hand. Nothing is straightforward when it comes to drugs, but the figures here are persuasive. I saw people with drug addictions being treated with therapy, rather than slung in jail. The number of people seeking treatment for drug addiction had more than doubled. The majority of heroin addicts dropped their habit and became useful members of society again (whilst in America, where prohibition reigns strong, the number of people now dying from opioid overdoses every year is higher than that of US soldiers killed in the Vietnam War).

By June 2011 we were ready to release our first report, calling for a major paradigm shift in global drug policy. Backed by solid evidence and announced by experienced leaders, we demanded an end to the criminalisation, marginalisation and stigmatisation of people who use drugs but who do no harm to others. In its stead, we urged countries to ensure that human rights and harm reduction policies were enforced, for people who use drugs as well as those involved in the lower ends of illegal drug markets, from petty sellers to farmers. We also encouraged governments to experiment with legal regulation of drugs (especially cannabis) to safeguard the health and security of their citizens.

Announcing the report, I said: 'The war on drugs has failed to cut drug usage, but has filled our jails, cost millions in taxpayer dollars, fuelled organised crime and caused thousands of deaths. We need a new approach, one that takes the power out of the hands of organised crime and treats people with addiction problems like patients, not criminals. The one thing we cannot afford to do is go on pretending the war on drugs is working.'

I was very proud when Sam and his production company Sundog Pictures went on to make a documentary following the Commission's work and depicting the failed war on drugs in all its horror. *Breaking the Taboo* quickly amassed millions of views online and continues to stream on Netflix, convincing more people that the war on drugs must end. We hosted community discussions at screenings of *Breaking the Taboo* everywhere I visited, bringing drug policy reform to the mainstream in Morocco, Sweden, Ukraine and multiple US cities.

Change was beginning to happen, but not quickly enough: by 2015 the Global Commission on Drug Policy had been calling for drugs to be treated as a health issue, not a criminal problem, for five years. There were signs of progress, especially with marijuana in the US. Then it was announced that in April 2016 the first special session of the United Nations General Assembly to discuss drug policy would be held for eighteen years. It was a perfect opportunity to frankly debate the war on drugs and its devastating negative impacts on people and communities everywhere.

Ahead of this, I was thrilled to get word that the United Nations Office on Drugs and Crime (UNODC), which has shaped much of global drug policy for decades, was intending to make a major statement. In an embargoed press release circulated to the BBC, myself and others, I learned that UNODC were intending to call on governments around the world to decriminalise drug use and possession for personal consumption for all drugs. It was massive news. I wrote a response to share once UNODC launched the document at the International Harm reduction conference in Malaysia on 18 October. I also carried out embargoed interviews with the BBC and other press, where I applauded the organisation for choosing a new path of sensible, evidence-based policy: 'This is a refreshing shift that could go a long way to finally end the needless criminalisation of millions of drug users around the world,' I drafted. 'My colleagues on the Global Commission on Drug Policy and I could not be more delighted.'

On the eve of the conference, however, I learned UNODC were distancing themselves from their own release. My sources told me that politics had got in the way and at least one global superpower was pressuring them to backtrack.

'It looks as if Russia is strong-arming the UN into cutting the release,' our advocacy director Matthias Stausberg told me. Russia is committed to a hardline approach on drugs and has roadblocked progressive policy reform before.

'Is there anything we can do?' I asked.

'It doesn't look like it. Our contacts say many at the UN are supportive of this move and want the story to come out. But they are going to bury it before it ever sees daylight.'

I paused for a moment. We already had the report. What was to stop us sharing it? Sure, embargoes, protocol, international relations. But this was important. This document could legitimately help to save lives.

'Fuck it,' I said. 'If the UN won't release it, I will. Let's post the whole paper anyway and commend them for their good work – even though they've bottled it.'

UNODC claimed, very half-heartedly, that the paper was not final or authorised– despite releasing it to the BBC and others! But they were too late – the cat was out of the bag. International media picked up my blog and before long the document was on the front pages of newspapers and websites globally. I looked at Twitter and saw thousands of people sharing a picture of global and local experts on the closing day of the Harm Reduction International conference in Kuala Lumpur, waving copies of the paper in the air, calling on UNODC to endorse and release it formally.

When the UN special session on drugs rolled around, I was in New York to witness far too little progress being made. Shaped heavily by prohibitionist countries like Egypt and Russia, it was more political farce than meaningful force. The session lacked the teeth to write a new chapter in global drug policy. Elsewhere, change continues regardless.

Champions of reform, like the Czech Republic, Mexico, Switzerland, Colombia, Uruguay, Jamaica, the Netherlands and Norway continue to stand up and I hope that more global powers will join them in creating lasting, meaningful, evidence-based reform of global drug control policy.

Would I leak another paper if I thought it would move things along? Absolutely!

*

Many people ask why I don't just give my money to charity, rather than investing in new technology to tackle climate change. The answer should be clear for any entrepreneur. Throwing money at a problem without having a clearly defined purpose will never solve anything. I wanted to find entrepreneurial solutions to this enormous challenge, and create long-term change. I believe the way to do this is by challenging existing conventions and coming up with innovative new ways to do business. Early pioneers in new sectors often get their fingers burnt leading the way for others, and we were no exception. Investing during the worst financial crisis of our time, many investments in areas such as biofuels were not successful.

But fast-forward to 2017 and really exciting breakthroughs are happening. For instance, Virgin Atlantic's ongoing partnership with LanzaTech to develop commercially viable low carbon fuel is getting close. For the first time ever, 1,500 US gallons of jet fuel have been produced from 'Lanzanol' – LanzaTech's low-carbon ethanol. This is the world's first jet fuel derived from waste industrial gases from steel mills (that would otherwise go up chimneys) via a fermentation process. The alcohol-to-jet fuel has passed all its initial performance tests with flying colours, and could result in carbon savings of 65 per cent compared to conventional jet fuel – a real game-changer for aviation. The jet fuel is scheduled for a first-of-its-kind 'proving flight' in 2017 – if successful, we will seek approval to use the fuel on routine commercial flights. This would also help pave the way for

LanzaTech to fund and build their first commercial jet fuel plant, hopefully in the UK, to supply fuel to Virgin Atlantic.

There are many other promising areas of development for cleaner flight today. First and foremost, there's efficiency. In July 2016, Virgin Atlantic announced a $4.4 billion investment in a dozen new Airbus A350-100 aircraft. These have 30 per cent lower carbon emissions than the Boeing 747-400 aircraft they're replacing. One way to kickstart innovation towards solving seemingly intractable problems is by setting challenges like the Ansari XPRIZE. And similar thinking was behind the Virgin Earth Challenge, a $25 million prize for scalable and sustainable ways of removing greenhouse gases from the atmosphere.

The idea, like so many good ones, came from my wife Joan. We were sitting in the kitchen on Necker talking about climate change, when she got straight to the point.

'There must be some genius out there who can remove the carbon from the atmosphere,' she sighed.

'There probably is,' I agreed. 'But how do we find them?'

'Why don't you offer a prize?' she replied.

That's exactly what we did, bringing on board experts Dr James Hansen, Tim Flannery, Jim Lovelock, Crispin Tickell and Al Gore to act as judges alongside me. Within a year of the challenge's February 2007 launch more than 3,000 proposals had been delivered to my desk. Today it stands at over 10,000. After lengthy technical analysis, we have narrowed more than 2,000 thorough and sincere applications down to eleven hopefuls. It is not an easy prize to win. The rules of the challenge are designed to ask not just if they work, but how they will get to scale in the real world. Although we are looking for that eureka moment, perhaps it is a prize that no one will win. It is more likely that the world will get on top of the problem through thousands of different initiatives. But it's worth a try, giving everyone a beacon to strive for.

We went on to launch the non-profit Carbon War Room to tackle climate change through practical business solutions. It has now merged with the Rocky Mountain Institute (RMI), marrying the Carbon War Room's bold and agile entrepreneurial approach with RMI's scale, experience and expertise. They are at the forefront of an energy revolution that can unlock the greatest wealth-creating opportunity in modern history. We've also joined Bill Gates' Breakthrough Energy Coalition to stimulate reliable, affordable energy for the world. We're investing in new energy technologies, working with more than twenty countries towards a carbonless future.

Much more work needs to be done across the board if we are to meet our climate targets, and work together to create a better, more just, prosperous future for the planet and its people. We haven't yet had the breakthroughs I've hoped for, but we have seen progress. In the meantime, the cost of wind, solar and battery power continues to reduce, moving us towards a world that one day could and should be powered by clean energy.

Ten years after launching the Virgin Earth Challenge, on 29 April 2017 I travelled to the People's Climate March in Washington. Alongside Al Gore and 200,000 people of all ages, we joined together to call for ambitious action against climate change. There was such positive energy and I particularly loved the creativity and humour of so many handmade signs. Among those I carried were: 'Treat the planet like it's Earth – not Uranus!' and 'If you screw us we multiply!'

Soon after we marched, President Trump took the US out of the Paris Agreement, a decision that could have catastrophic effects for the world's climate and wellbeing. It is a policy of 'America first. Earth last', that will hurt everyone – Americans included. Climate change does not respect international borders, it imperils us all.

However, the reaction was remarkable. A few years earlier, we had formed the B Team, an organisation of leaders committed to a plan B for business. Now, the B Team, the Elders, RMI/Carbon War Room and business leaders globally reaffirmed their commitment to putting people and the planet alongside profit. The battle against climate change is being waged by a growing collective of businesses, individuals, officials, governments who understand this is the most important fight of our lives and will reap the $1 trillion opportunity it unlocks. At Virgin, we will continue to invest in renewable energy, to explore new clean fuels for our airlines, to invest in energy efficiency. For instance, one very exciting Rocky Mountain Institute/ Carbon War Room initiative is working with various governments in Africa and the Caribbean to help achieve clean energy access.

Paul Polman, my fellow B Team leaders and I were doing everything we could to convince more business leaders to raise their voices on this crucial issue. I contacted Elon Musk, who sat on the White House advisory council, to use his influence to convince President Trump not to make a terrible mistake.

'Elon, can you intervene?' I emailed my friend.

'I certainly will resign [from the advisory council] if the US withdraws from the Paris Agreement, but it is not clear whether threatening to do so will help or hurt. I will certainly strongly imply that I will have no choice but to do so. This is really fucking killing me btw. Goddamn it.'

'*Implying* stronger. Agreed. Hope not necessary. Thank you.' Sadly, it was necessary, and Elon left the council when the US left the Paris Agreement.

It remains to be seen what long-term damage the Trump administration will do to the environment, among other issues. While in Washington I also attended an event on the tented lawn of the *Atlantic* chairman David Bradley and his philanthropist wife Katherine. I was seated at the same table as US Secretary of Defense James 'Mad Dog' Mattis. That very night, President Trump's ninety-ninth day in office, North Korea fired a missile that fell into the ocean. I thought to myself: as long as Mad Dog is sitting here eating his salad and not in a bunker, we know the world is not at war! After dinner I went over to President Obama's house to catch up, wishing my host was still in charge over at the White House.

19 Back on Track

I was in the cinema in Zermatt, Switzerland, when my phone started to vibrate. We were over there on a family skiing holiday in February 2007, and had taken a break from the slopes to catch a film. As is my usual way on family time, I ignored the phone. I took a big handful of popcorn and munched away as the movie continued. But then the phone vibrated again. And again. And again. Something, I sensed, wasn't quite right.

Shuffling past Joan and the kids, apologising to some Swiss cinema-goers as I squeezed by, I reached the end of the dark aisle. For some reason, the thought had entered my head that there was a problem with one of our planes, so I was surprised to pull my BlackBerry out to see that it was Virgin Trains' CEO Tony Collins ringing. Returning the call, I left the auditorium to hear what Tony had to say.

'There has been a major crash at Grayrigg in Cumbria,' he said, getting straight to the point. 'I don't know how many people are hurt, or if there are any fatalities, but it doesn't sound good.'

I knew immediately that I had to get there as quickly as possible. 'Tony, I'm so sorry to hear that. I'm on my way right now,' I said.

I went back into the cinema, apologising again as I squeezed past to whisper to Joan and the kids what had happened. We hurried back to the hotel and after a torturous journey arrived in Manchester at five o'clock the next morning. At the airport, Tony and Will were waiting for me, and together we drove to the scene of the accident.

It was cold and dark as we headed out into the depths of the countryside. Approaching the scene of the crash, we got out of the car and finished the last part of the journey on foot. The scene was a jarring mix of contrasts: sweeping across the landscape were the lush, green Cumbrian hills, but then, emerging out of this idyllic vision, the nightmare of an upturned train with the Virgin logo sticking up in the air appeared from down the bankside.

As we walked along the track, Tony and some of the waiting officials filled me in on what was known about the accident so far. The previous evening's 17:30 service from London Euston had set off on time for Glasgow Central, with 105 passengers and four members of staff on board. At 8.15 p.m., the Pendolino was coming down the track past Grayrigg at its planned speed of 95mph, when it suddenly hit a set of points. The derailment brought down the overhead line equipment, and passengers reported the train rocking forcefully before it fell sideways and carriages were thrown from the track down a thirty-foot embankment. Local farmers reached the scene first, and were joined by more than a dozen ambulances and 500 rescuers, along with mountain rescue teams, police, air force and search-and-rescue helicopters, plus five fire engines. The rain was pouring down on the dark, muddy field, but they worked tirelessly through the night to evacuate the passengers.

By the time I arrived officials had got everybody out of the train and were trying to clear the track and get it reopened. It was cordoned off with the police patrolling on all sides, and I stepped through the police tape as Tony pointed out the faulty bolts. Then we made our way towards where a small crowd was huddling.

'What are you doing here, Richard?' a man asked.

'Where else would I be?' I answered. This was our company, our team and our passengers – I wanted to do everything I could to help them. 'If it was my daughter, or my son on this train, I would like to think the owner of the business would be here,' I told him.

My heart sank as I was told that an elderly lady had died in the accident. The family of Margaret Masson, an eighty-four-year-old Glaswegian, was in Royal Preston Hospital morgue. I went straight there to be with the family and we had a big hug, which I find is the best possible thing to do in such situations. We spoke quietly for a short time and then I went to visit our train driver, Iain Black, and the families of five passengers who were seriously injured. Thankfully they all made full recoveries. Next, I went over to Grayrigg Primary School, which had been turned into an emergency meeting point, met with passengers and thanked our staff who had worked through the night.

There's no question, the key thing after a major disaster is to get there quickly, deal with it head on and be both sympathetic and honest. Handling the aftermath of an accident involving your company is one of the hardest things a leader can do. I wouldn't wish it on anybody. But, as hard as it is, it is nothing compared to what the loved ones of people who have died or been injured are going through.

Having run airlines for several decades without serious incident, it is always something that is in the back of my mind. Whenever I get a call late at night, my first thought is that something bad has happened. The burden of leading companies that have people's lives in their care is simply a part of being a leader. But in moments like this it weighs very heavily indeed. Whatever the situation, I do feel completely responsible when things go wrong. At the end of the day, it is my name above the shop. I get more than my fair share of credit when things go well and more than my fair share of blame when things go badly. I try to learn from both.

We learned that the points had been poorly maintained and left unchecked by Network Rail: they were scheduled to have been inspected five days earlier, but Network Rail had failed to do so. After ensuring we had done everything we practically could to help the situation, I went to speak at a makeshift press conference in the middle of a field. I was expecting there to be some animosity towards us, or at least misunderstanding and misplaced blame. Instead, there was nothing but support. Although we were certain the accident was not our fault, we thought it would be in bad taste to criticise Network Rail. John Armitt, Network Rail's CEO, responded with integrity, stating clearly from the onset that his organisation was to blame. I praised our brave train driver: 'He's carried on sitting in his carriage for nearly half a mile, running the train on the stone – he could have tried to get back and protect himself but he didn't, and he's ended up quite badly injured. He is a definitely a hero.'

Investigators told us the accident could have been far worse, with more injuries and fatalities, if it wasn't for the strength of our Pendolino. After the accident, our relationship with Network Rail improved, and the public responded with support, too. They had seen how well the team handled an extremely tough situation.

*

The public response to the aftermath of the Grayrigg crash showed how far perceptions of Virgin Trains had changed since we'd been awarded West Coast Main Line franchise back in 1997. Over the next decade and a half, we had transformed that service from a clapped-out national embarrassment into the most used, most frequent railway in Europe. We took the line from thirteen million passengers a year at the start of the franchise to 91 per cent satisfaction scores by 2012 and the busiest mixed-use railway in Europe with thirty-eight million passengers in 2017.

When bidding for the franchise opened up again in 2012 we were confident of being given the contract once more, and made an aggressive but realistic bid to take the line forward. We outlined plans to grow annual passenger numbers to forty-nine million by 2026, adding more state-of-the-art Pendolino trains and delivering a proposed £4.8 billon premium to the government. The main rival bid for the line came from FirstGroup, who claimed they could pay the government £5.5 billion and grow customer numbers to sixty-six million. From our knowledge of the line, we thought their plan was unrealistic. Not only that, but they had form on this sort of thing, and the government, passengers and taxpayers had suffered because of it before. Previously, FirstGroup had bid for the Great Western franchise with high premium payments, more than £1 billion loaded towards the end of the franchise period. They then withdrew from the franchise agreement before substantial payments were due. They made irresponsible bids, and if it all went wrong they would simply hand back the keys, having made a lot of money beforehand. It was like someone overpaying considerably for the freehold of a house, agreeing to pay a tiny percentage up front, arranging to live in it for ten years, then leaving before the bulk of the money was due. No owner in their right mind would accept such an offer. I am always willing to take risks, but they have to be calculated, not reckless.

I assumed the DfT would agree. So when they announced in August 2012 that the West Coast Main Line franchise would be handed to FirstGroup, I was flabbergasted. I stared in disbelief when I saw the news flash up on the screen in the Temple on Necker, then reached for my phone to call Patrick McCall and see what he made of it.

'This just doesn't make sense,' he agreed. 'They can't fit that many people on the trains – the numbers just don't add up.'

As the days went by, it was all I could think about. As more details emerged about FirstGroup's bid, it only confirmed our suspicion that the decision was nonsensical. I wrote to Prime Minister David Cameron and Chancellor George Osborne, as well as Transport Secretary Justine Greening, questioning the decision. I wouldn't let it go for the simple reason that I believed we were right and could continue to make a difference. If we lost the West Coast Main Line, we would have no other franchise and thousands of wonderful employees would no longer be part of Virgin. The thought made me feel sick to my stomach.

We continued weighing up our options, one of which was to request a judicial review of the decision and take the DfT to the High Court. As I've said, I hate going through the courts, but at least it would force the DfT to provide us with more information about the other bids and the process. We brought in expert legal counsel to evaluate our chances of winning if we opted to challenge the DfT's decision. We were advised by our QC that our chances of success were less than 10 per cent. Peter Norris, the Group chairman, our CEO Josh Bayliss and COO Ian Woods were against taking legal action. They thought it would be a waste of good money.

Did I really want to challenge the government? I trust my senior team absolutely, but when an issue really digs deep under my skin I won't let it go. I was sure we were being screwed over, and I didn't want to give up without a fight. I felt responsible for all of our team, who could well lose their jobs if we bowed out. At the same time, I knew there was a danger of looking like a bad loser if we continued to argue our case. Reputation is everything, and I had to weigh the risk of looking petty against the hope of changing the government's mind.

But the way our staff reacted out on the platforms, in offices, streets and homes convinced me to carry on. A groundswell of outrage was growing. Ross McKillop, a regular customer of both Virgin Trains and FirstGroup, set up an independent online petition calling for the government to reconsider their decision. The e-petition got 180,000 signatures in a matter of days, forcing the government to raise the issue in Parliament. Meanwhile, the tide was turning in the press, whose tune was changing from amusement at our predicament to bemusement about the decision. Prominent customers like Lord Alan Sugar, Piers Morgan, Jamie Oliver, Eddie Izzard, Rio Ferdinand, Stephen Fry, Dermot O'Leary, Mo Farah and even some MPs took to social media urging their followers to sign the petition. 'Something dodgy about Virgin Trains losing their franchise?'

questioned Stephen Fry. It all helped and soon we had the most signed e-petition in UK history.

Then Justine Greening was replaced by Patrick McLoughlin as Secretary of State for Transport. I wondered what had really been going on behind closed doors. In each meeting we would ask for details of what was happening and be met with pairs of eyes staring down at their shoes. There were rumours in the press that there was an 'anyone but Branson' agenda among some of the DfT staff, and the bids really hadn't been judged on their merits. After fifteen years of working together to transform the railway, I still felt like the outsider, the wild card who didn't belong. Usually I am comfortable with that billing, but I was damned if my persona was going to bring a good business and a lot of great people down. Had they really reverted back to the original 'that fucker isn't getting his logo on my trains' bias?

Throughout all of this, Brian Souter, Martin Griffiths and their team at Stagecoach were tremendously supportive. We'd experienced many ups and downs, but after two decades in business together we had a lot of mutual trust, and they backed our judgement. With the deadline looming for the decision to get rubber-stamped, I gathered the team at Sam and Holly's home in Kidlington. Patrick, Josh, Peter, our comms director Nick Fox and Tony Collins were sitting in the living room, crowded around the coffee table looking at an old Alice in Wonderland chess set. I wondered if somebody at the DfT had gone down the rabbit hole when making their decision, and whether they thought it was me behaving like the Mad Hatter.

I went around the table, asking each person for his view. We started a logical discussion, but there was understandably some disagreement; frustration was bubbling to the surface, and we had to act fast. Both our chairman and chief executive thought we should throw in the towel and retire gracefully from the dispute. They argued the risk to the brand was too great. Did the public really just think I was crying about losing my train set? The atmosphere was getting increasingly tense.

At this point, Joan appeared from the kitchen with a tray in hand. 'Boys, I think you all need a little break. Why don't you have a cup of tea and a KitKat?'

Sure enough, there were chocolate bars and tea on the tray and we sat back to gather our thoughts for a moment. I got up and kissed Joan.

'You always know the right thing to do in an emergency,' I told her.

I felt calmer, and turned to Tony, who had been quiet all through the meeting. 'What do you think?' I asked him. 'You know this company better than anyone.'

He paused for a moment. 'I really think there is a smoking gun in the DfT,' he said. 'The more we look at the numbers, the more it looks like FirstGroup are taking the mickey.' Patrick, who led the battle with the government, agreed too.

I leaned back, put down my cup of tea and knew I had made up my mind. 'It's not a smoking gun. It's a fucking nuclear arsenal!' I hadn't felt this angry about something since BA's Dirty Tricks. 'We've come this far,' I told the room, 'I believe we're right, and our job's not finished. Screw it, let's do it.'

I rarely overrule my two top executives, but ultimately, as shareholder, the buck stops with me. On this occasion I made a judgement call and told the lawyers to proceed with the judicial review.

*

A few weeks later, I was pacing the corridors of Virgin Trains' backroom office deep inside Euston Station, as I prepped to give evidence to the Commons Transport Committee. Graphs and figures were swimming before my eyes. There is so much jargon within the rail industry that I was worried about mistaking one acronym for another, or mixing up some figures. I usually consider my dyslexia an advantage in business, but when I was questioning the government's sums it would not do to get my own muddled up.

There was a crowd outside Parliament as we arrived at Westminster, but I was too nervous about my speech to take much notice. I sat outside the chamber, sweating despite the chilly autumnal weather, furiously scribbling some last-minute edits in the margins of my notes. 'Our bid is the best for the railways and for the country,' I wrote along the top of my paper, and underlined it. As I was called to appear, I took a deep breath and walked in to see a square table filled with suits. I couldn't help feeling that the majority of people staring back at me thought we were behaving out of turn. But after thanking the committee for hearing us out, I frankly outlined our views.

'Good afternoon, Madam Chair,' I began. 'I'd like to give a brief summary of our position. Virgin Trains believes if this decision is allowed to stand, it will be bad for the country and passengers on the West Coast Main Line, and bad for passengers on other franchises. A successful West Coast franchise is vital for this country. A bad decision is bad for the UK. Based on an analysis of the two bids, we believe Virgin will offer more and – just as importantly – that it is deliverable and more financially robust. For instance, we plan £800 million of investments with new trains; improved stations and more routes on offer sooner.'

I described our frustrations with the bidding process, but how this instance was of a different magnitude. 'Sadly, the mechanism which the DfT uses to assess the bids doesn't allow FirstGroup's bid to be judged directly against the other bids or against realistic targets. This is the fourth time that we have lost a competitive tender – twice on the East Coast and once on Cross-Country. But this is the first time we have chosen to contest it and we have not taken the decision lightly.

'Since National Express handed back the keys after the East Coast collapse,' I continued, 'we have been in talks with the DfT about how to improve the process and prevent this being repeated. We have met three successive

Secretaries of State for Transport – all to no avail. But there is an opportunity now to ensure no repeat of these fiascos. And we are convinced it needs more than a pause in the West Coast process – that is just a sticking plaster. The entire franchising process and structure is so fundamentally flawed that we recommend that the current rules and regulations for franchising are completely reviewed and the West Coast franchise competition is delayed until this has been completed. There is simply too much at stake for rail passengers and the taxpayer to make the wrong decision here with the wrong structure. My partners at Stagecoach and I are happy to run the current franchise on a not-for-profit basis until such a process has been completed. We are confident with better franchise rules the government would receive better bids for this and for other franchises.'

It was a long statement and the reaction was polite but short.

'Thank you, Mr Branson,' said the committee chairwoman. When the hearing finished, I left none the wiser about what they would decide to do. But I felt a little better knowing we had done all we could.

Over the coming days there were no new developments, and the date for our court appearance, in the first week of October, crept ever closer. I was in New York on 1 October for some speaking engagements with Virgin Unite, when Helen walked into my hotel room.

'Patrick McLoughlin's secretary has just been on the phone,' she told me. 'He wants to speak to you at 7 p.m. – midnight in the UK.'

I cancelled my plans and brought Josh and Nick, who were in the city, too, over to my hotel. At 7 p.m. on the dot the phone rang.

'Richard, I want to start by apologising on behalf of the Department,' said the minister. 'We've discovered significant technical flaws in the way the franchise process was conducted. There have been deeply regrettable and completely unacceptable mistakes made by my Department in the way it managed the process. Because of this, we are cancelling the competition to run trains on the West Coast Main Line.'

I tried desperately hard to stop myself from whooping down the phone at him.

'I understand,' I said, keeping my best poker face on while Nick, Josh and Greg Rose looked on.

'We are no longer contesting the judicial review sought by Virgin Trains Ltd in the High Court,' the minister continued. 'I will be making an announcement shortly, but I wanted to tell you first.'

As I hung up, I turned to the expectant faces in the hotel room, puffed out my cheeks and summoned a frown. 'Well ... that's that. At least we tried.' I couldn't hold my smile in any longer. 'We won! They're cancelling the competition!' It was such a relief to know we had been right, that we wouldn't be letting our staff down and that the public would know the truth.

We presumed we would continue to run the line while the DfT sorted itself out, but we didn't know how long for or on what terms. I flew to the UK to see the staff – I wanted to thank them in person for their unwavering support. We eventually signed a management agreement to begin on 9 December 2012, which has now been extended into 2018. The new franchise deal boosted payments to the taxpayer by 58 per cent, guaranteeing more than £430 million will be paid to government. As I made the announcement at Euston, representatives from the DfT watched on from the platform – they even brought a cake. It was a remarkable turnaround from what just months earlier had been a toxic relationship.

The franchise is firmly back on track, and in July 2015 we reached 400 million customer journeys on the West Coast Main Line. I felt extremely proud when we were named Best Rail Operator at the 2014 and 2015 Business Travel Awards – both years we wouldn't have been running the franchise if we hadn't contested the DfT's decision. All of which just goes to show: you should never give up on something you believe in.

20 Becoming a Banker

One of the iconic images of the 2007–8 financial crisis in the UK was the majestic old clock ticking away at Northern Rock's headquarters in Newcastle while people queued around the block to take out their savings during the run on the banks. It was fitting, then, that a few years later, in January 2012, I was hanging out of the window next to the famous clock to celebrate Virgin Money's purchase of the company. However, it nearly all went horribly wrong. Eager for the press below to get a great photo, I hung a long way out of the window. I leaned out a touch too far and felt myself slipping forward. For a split second I thought I was going to fall out from the top storey of the building, before, thankfully, somebody behind yanked on my shirt and pulled me back in. It was a moment where everything could have gone wrong but ended up OK in the end – a bit like the story of Virgin's purchase of Northern Rock itself.

*

Throughout 2007, it had become increasingly clear that the global economy was in trouble. Sensing what was coming, I had sold all my personal shareholdings in the stock market for cash. By August, the banking sector was in crisis. Then, in September, I was sitting on Necker watching the BBC's Robert Peston standing outside Northern Rock's iconic branch in Newcastle, explaining how the bank was on the verge of collapse. One commentator said: 'What this bank needs is someone like Richard Branson to sort it out.'

Now there's an idea, I thought.

Ten years earlier, in October 1997, I found myself dressed up in a bowler hat and pinstripe suit, cutting a red ribbon and introducing the world to Virgin Money. I was officially a banker.

How the hell had that happened? One of the main reasons was Rowan Gormley, who had suggested Virgin get into financial services in his very first meeting.

'Why on earth would we do that?' I asked.

'Simple really. Nobody trusts banks. Everyone trusts Virgin.'

The other main reason was Jayne-Anne Gadhia, who ran our bank from day one. After building our Virgin One accounts up to 70,000 customers and £3.75 billion in mortgages, we sold our 25 per cent stake to our partners RBS for £45 million. Sadly, Jayne-Anne and many of her team had to move to RBS as part of the deal (Virgin Money continued with our other products under Rowan's leadership). By 2007, we were providing all sorts of products from a price comparison site to credit cards, savings and investments. We had taken 100 per cent ownership of the company in April 2004, buying the remaining 50 per cent stake for £90 million from AMP/HHG. Entering the mortgage market had been next on our list. Here I was delighted to be able to call again on Jayne-Anne. Over at RBS, she had become increasingly disillusioned with the irresponsible behaviour of Sir Fred Goodwin and co. Then she remembered a long-standing offer I had made for her to return. When she called and explained the situation, I kept her waiting for about a millisecond before offering her and all her team their jobs back. Jayne-Anne and eighty-two of her staff returned to the fold within the week. She had the bit between her teeth, and a plan to build a new One account to take on the mortgage market. I called her up from Necker Island simply to say: 'Welcome home.'

While I was watching Robert Peston on the BBC news, Jayne-Anne was back in Edinburgh, getting a facial at the Stobo Castle health spa. Beneath the slices of cucumber resting on her eyes, similar thoughts about Northern Rock were going through her head. Cucumber off, she sent an email to Gordon McCallum and Stephen Murphy, outlining how we could help the people suffering in the crisis, and build our business at the same time. 'Whatever happens,' she wrote, 'I think we should do some research into who people would trust with financial services now. I bet the answer will be Richard Branson. I know that all this sounds pretty batty, but on the other hand – discontinuities in the system make it right for change – and I think we could do something.'

Stephen Murphy and Gordon McCallum were initially less convinced: 'batty' was one of their milder words for her ideas. But after speaking to Peter Norris, who had run Barings Bank, we began looking into it seriously. By 13 September 2007 it was clear to everyone just how bad the situation was: the first run on a bank in the UK since Queen Victoria sat on the throne took place. But while the news concentrated on the back of the long, snaking queues, I had my eye on the front. The staff of Northern Rock, working round the clock, displayed superb professionalism in a desperate situation. I was impressed, and thought they deserved a brighter future.

I began top-secret talks to gather investors and form an equity consortium – 'dialling for dollars' as the team affectionately called it. On 12 October, I headed to the Stock Exchange with Jayne-Anne and Nick Fox to submit our bid. We offered to put £1.25 billion of new cash into the bank, on top of Virgin Money as a business. It was a good deal for existing shareholders, who could recoup their investment on excellent terms in the future, and for the public, too. We would repay the taxpayer in full before taking any profit. We estimated Virgin Money would lose £300 million by early 2009, break even in 2010 and grow the following year.

If those sound like big sums, they were: this was the biggest risk the Virgin Group had ever taken. In a business that I was still very new to, this worried me. Could the brand stretch this far? Would we ever really be accepted by the banking establishment? If I was younger, I wouldn't have given it a second thought. But now I gave myself space to think it over. Having weighed up the downside, I decided to press on. After protracted negotiations, on 26 November Northern Rock named our consortium as its preferred bidder. When the Bank of England and the FSA both declared us their preferred bidder, too, the signs looked good that the deal would go through.

*

Nothing, however, is straightforward in banking, particularly when politics comes into play. In January 2008, Gordon Brown, then British Prime Minister, asked me to join him on a trade mission to China with some representatives of leading British businesses. Virgin was looking to expand more in the Far East and I was happy to go. There were forty journalists on the trip, and they quickly framed it as 'Branson and Brown's sweetheart deal'. Before I had a chance to change clothes in my Beijing hotel room, there were cartoons in newspapers showing Gordon and me in each other's pockets. In fact Gordon and I spoke a grand total of one sentence to each other on the flight, but the idea stuck.

While I rushed over to the Great Hall of the People on Tiananmen Square to deliver a speech, back in the UK Liberal Democrat Deputy Leader Vince Cable was standing up in the House of Commons and using parliamentary privilege to say that I was not a fit person to run a bank. Whether I was fit or not, the idea that I was going to actively run the bank on a day-to-day basis was frankly ridiculous. I had no intention of doing so, which was why I had assembled an outstanding team of banking professionals to manage Virgin Money. Regardless, Mr Cable claimed I was 'nationalising the risk and privatising the profit'.

Cable was against the deal in principle, but made his opposition personal, too. My past was catching up with me. When I was nineteen I made one of the most stupid decisions of my life, selling records intended for export to

British customers, and not paying tax on them. I was caught, thrown in jail overnight and fined three times the tax I had not paid. HM Customs & Excise didn't press charges, I did not get a criminal record and I vowed to myself never again to do anything that would mean I couldn't sleep with a clear conscience at night. I decided to share the story myself so other people could learn from it, so I didn't have any skeletons in my closet, and so I wouldn't forget it. Thirty-six years later, however, it seemed I wasn't the only one who remembered my mistake.

While the debate raged on about whether Northern Rock should be nationalised, I was still extremely confident the government would do the best thing for the bank and the country. As the pressure and criticism continued, we were asked to increase our government guarantees and put in up to £200 million extra in equity warrants. The risk of the deal was skyrocketing, while the prospect of any returns was nose-diving. Unsurprisingly, rival bids from private equity groups disappeared at this prospect, but we held firm. We seemed to be the only option for the government.

Then, at 2 p.m. on 17 February, Gordon Brown and Alistair Darling announced the nationalisation of Northern Rock. Ironically, given where the spark of the idea had come from, I found out from watching a BBC news report. I was livid. I had seen Chancellor Alistair Darling early in the process and he had agreed to let me know the final decision personally. Now here I was learning about it from the TV. I phoned Patrick McCall, who was working on the deal for Virgin Group.

'The deal's off – they're nationalising,' I said.

'Very funny, Richard. I'm not falling for that.' He thought it was a wind-up.

'I'm serious, turn on BBC1.'

Patrick switched on his television to see a report on Northern Rock, but still couldn't believe it: 'How the hell have you got the BBC in on the joke?'

Eventually, Gordon Brown telephoned me to explain their decision and requested that I didn't make too much fuss. I was fuming, and began writing a stinging opinion piece about shady dealings at Downing Street as soon as I got off the phone. I saw sense before hitting Send, though, realising little good could come of this – there is no point burning bridges. Instead, I jumped in a boat from Necker to Moskito Island, where we were looking at a new sustainability project. As Dr Daniel Kammen talked me through computer modelling for solar panels, my mind was elsewhere.

'I've just heard that they're nationalising Northern Rock,' I interrupted him. 'So if it's all right with you, I think I'm going to get drunk.'

'Gordon Brown may come to grasp a truth I learned long ago,' Jonathan Calder subsequently wrote in the *New Statesman*. 'There is nothing more dangerous than a disappointed Virgin.' His joke wasn't too far off the mark. While we were frustrated at missing out on Northern Rock, we pushed on with other plans for Virgin Money. I was always looking for new opportunities to expand the brand, though not all of them were as enticing as they first appeared. In the mid-2000s lots of people were excited about a new commodity that Goldman Sachs wanted to invest in. I had never heard of it, found it quite confusing and balked at the amount of money required. We decided to bide our time and get more details. As we investigated the deal further, I grew even more sceptical about the damage it could do to our brand, and we turned it down.

I forgot all about these commodities until the real estate lending crash sent the financial world into disarray. Suddenly the commodities were all anybody was talking about: subprime mortgages. Many experts placed lots of the blame for the crash on subprimes, and Goldman Sachs were fined $550 million by the US Securities and Exchange Commission. As well as forking out the second biggest penalty ever paid by a Wall Street company, Goldman Sachs also had to state that its subprimes marketing material – the same documents we had been looking at – had misled investors with incomplete information. It was a timely reminder to always examine every aspect of a deal, and go with your instinct if it doesn't feel right.

*

As it turned out, losing our Northern Rock bid in 2008 may well have been a blessing in disguise. After the bid, we concentrated on expanding Virgin Money's existing services, while our international brand also grew around the world. But when a new Conservative government came to power, Chancellor George Osborne announced Northern Rock was being put up for sale to the private sector in June 2011. We decided to enter the fray again. We made a jumbo-sized bid of £747 million – a nice number for an airline owner. We had put the best package together, and this time the government agreed.

In November the deal was announced for Virgin Money to buy Northern Rock. The deal brought us huge scale overnight: 2,100 employees, seventy-five Northern Rock branches, one million customers, a £14 billion mortgage book and a £16 billion retail deposit book. The combination of Virgin Money and Northern Rock fitted really well together. We already had credit cards, investments and insurance offerings, and now added mortgages, savings and current accounts. The combination meant we had a platform to grow, and no need to merge or cut jobs. We pledged to make no compulsory redundancies. Now we could make a real challenger bank that would be strong, stable and a true test for the big boys.

We made Newcastle upon Tyne the operational headquarters of our savings and mortgages business and embraced the local culture. I went to Virgin Money's offices in Gosforth to get to know the staff, then travelled up to Edinburgh to meet more of the team. On the way back down to London we made a detour into the store in Norwich, before I raced back to the capital to speak on a panel about ending the war on drugs. It was one of those moments when I just had to laugh at the paradoxes of my life. I must be the only person in history to go from launching a bank to calling for marijuana to be legalised in the time it takes to open a current account – or roll a joint.

The deal was done hours before the biggest football match of Newcastle United's season so far against Manchester United. We rushed to a local printer and got some stick-on logos to paste onto the front of the Newcastle shirts. Alan Pardew was the team's manager, which felt like a good sign. He was a star player in Crystal Palace's team in 1990, the first football club Virgin had sponsored. Back then, we had one Virgin Atlantic plane at Gatwick and I was searching for ways to get the word out about our airline. We heard Crystal Palace were looking for a sponsor at very short notice and offered £10,000 to back the team – an amount that wouldn't cover a player's daily wages now. The unfancied Palace team, led by their fearsome strike force of Ian Wright and Mark Bright, made it all the way to the FA Cup Final. With the Virgin logo flying proudly on their shirts, they took Manchester United to a replay. I'm not usually much of a football fan, but was cheering wildly as Wright bagged a brace at Wembley. The replay meant even more coverage, and was probably the best ten grand we ever spent. Fast-forward to January 2012, and Newcastle beat Man United 3–0 live on Sky Sports, and everyone knew Virgin Money had arrived, too.

Now we had a large presence back on the high street, I was determined we would be drastically different from the tired old banks still lining the streets. I hated the glass windows that blocked customers from bank tellers. I wanted Virgin Money to feel as close as possible to Virgin Records and Virgin Megastores – places in which you were comfortable relaxing and meeting friends. Why should the experience of buying a financial product be worse than buying a record?

'Why can't we take the glass screens out of every branch?' I asked Jayne-Anne.

'It's because the staff are worried about safety and bank robberies,' she explained.

I wasn't to be deterred, however. 'But when was the last robbery and how much cash do we keep in the banks?' Eventually the team relented and we took out the glass, freeing up the branches.

Then Jayne-Anne mentioned an RBS store she had visited in Edinburgh decades before, called The Ladies Branch. It was a bank that doubled as a tearoom, with free drinks, calming music and even complimentary paracetamol! All the customers were women – and so were the staff. It was all rather sexist, but there was the germ of a good idea there. We decided to launch our own Virgin Money Lounges, taking inspiration from Virgin Atlantic's Clubhouses and providing a unique banking experience. The main difference is that no banking actually takes place in the Lounges. They are instead places to meet friends, enjoy free refreshments and complimentary WiFi, relax during a busy day, or take the kids to play. We hold book talks, exhibitions and charity events, and even have a grand piano in each Lounge to celebrate our musical heritage. It's basically a private members' club, where the only condition for entry is being a Virgin Money customer.

Most of the Lounge visitors appreciate the extra effort so much that they become extremely loyal customers across the road in the bank. Don't tell our competitors, but in the cities where we have Lounges alongside branches, sales are nearly 300 per cent higher than anywhere else. One young businesswoman, Jessica Bannister, regularly takes her young son to our Norwich Lounge and gets her work done there. She wrote me a letter in June 2015 that summed it up: 'I feel supported, I feel known, I feel a sense of community and belonging. I've already taken out every account I could with you because I believe and want to support your ethos and I tell everyone about what an incredible place this is.' No other bank gets feedback like that.

Jayne-Anne spent the next couple of years bedding Virgin Money down. Staff morale was sky-high, customers were flocking in and we continued to expand. In July 2012 we bought £465 million worth of mortgage assets from the government – these were from the 'bad bank' side of Northern Rock. A journalist asked me why we were buying the 'bad bank' – 'To make it good, of course!' I told him. More investment followed in January 2013 when we picked up £1 billion of credit card assets from MBNA, adding £363 million more the following year.

Our little bank was growing up.

21 Planes and Mergers

O ne question I am often asked is which company is my favourite. Founders, just like parents, shouldn't have favourites – we love all of our kids equally. But if you promise not to tell anyone, I'll admit to you, Virgin Atlantic will always have an extra special place in my heart. Can you imagine me still running a record label, in my sixties? Virgin Atlantic was the jump-off point from which I built a whole world to live, love and laugh within. As I said in 2012, 'We have no plans to disappear. Virgin Atlantic was my baby twenty-eight years ago when we set up with just one plane. Like all children, they never really stop being your babies and Virgin Atlantic is still much cherished.'

In the mid-2000s, with so much other stuff going on, I was thankful the airline, which had taken up so much of my time, energy and passion, was relatively stable and enjoying several years of growth. But there was more trouble brewing. In 2007, I got a call from the Civil Aviation Authority asking for a meeting – that was curious enough, but when the officials who came swore me to secrecy I knew something was up.

The officials told me a few individuals within Virgin Atlantic had been colluding with their counterparts at British Airways. Our management had found out about it and immediately reported it to the CAA.

'Tell me this is a wind-up?' I turned to Virgin Atlantic CEO Steve Ridgway.

Surely nobody would be foolish enough to forget the golden rule – never talk to your competitors unless there is a formal process. I was shocked. I knew nothing about it and would of course have stopped it immediately. But rather than being a misunderstanding, the accusations were true; it turned out there had been a couple of discussions around fuel surcharges on long-haul flights. Virgin Atlantic was granted immunity for immediately reporting this to the Civil Aviation Authority when they found out about them, but I still felt very uncomfortable with the whole episode. Several people at BA lost their jobs, and some of them could have gone to prison. BA were fined £121.5 million by the Office of Fair Trading. Later, the US Department of Justice fined them a further £148 million.

Will Whitehorn found out years later that BA's management learned of the discussions twenty-four hours after we had, and their lawyers were about to go to the CAA, too. A former board director at BA told Will: 'You guys did the right thing.' If ever a lesson had to be learned about the folly of even accidentally talking with your competitors, this was it.

While I believed both sides were to blame in that case, Virgin Atlantic and British Airways were somewhat further apart on the latter's plans to merge with American Airlines. For more than a decade, BA tried to form a partnership with AA, which we fiercely contested. This partnership could lead to anti-trust immunity under US law, which would allow legal collusion on pricing, substantially reduce competition and potentially put Virgin Atlantic out of business.

If I was king for a day, I would ensure competition laws were more strictly adhered to. I believe small is beautiful, and the more companies competing, the better. BA were essentially requesting permission to fix prices and schedules, as well as share marketing and operational data – activity that would normally be illegal. It was an unholy alliance. Two separate attempts were blocked, as we protested and the competition authorities held firm against BA's considerable lobbying power.

Then, in September 2008, the BA/AA deal looked to be back on the table. The 'Open Skies' agreement, allowing any European Union or US airline to fly between any point in the EU and the USA, had become active in March. It paved the way for approving alliances between UK and US airlines, without increasing competition at all. BA/AA would dwarf the capacity of rival alliances. Allowing the two biggest carriers on the planet to merge would create a hugely uneven playing field. The deal would also damage the UK economy, with Heathrow's position as Europe's number one hub under threat with fewer airlines operating there. We were determined to stop it going ahead, and had common sense and evidence on our side.

On the opposite side was BA's new head, Willie Walsh, who seemed determined to make this a personal battle between the two of us. I had no idea what I had done to upset him, but he had held a grudge for as long as I could remember. I didn't know Willie personally, but I knew his organisation was trying to put my airline out of business. So we fought back the best way we knew how – by making sure everyone knew the tricks they were trying to pull.

I went to Heathrow and we launched the No Way BA/AA campaign, slapping the slogan loud and proud on the side of our planes, as well as on advertising around the world. If allowed to proceed, what was already a near-monopoly for BA would become a complete monopoly with AA. They would have highly dominant market shares on key routes, including 100 per cent on Heathrow to Dallas/Fort Worth, 80 per cent to Boston, 70 per cent to Miami, 67 per cent to Chicago and 62 per cent to JFK. Yet, to my surprise, their lobbying seemed to be working with the regulators.

In August 2009, on the first anniversary of BA and AA applying for permission to tie up, I sent a letter to President Obama warning him how dangerous the merger would be for consumers. 'Your Administration is nearing a defining moment in US airline competition policy,' I wrote. 'Never before has the US Government approved an anti-trust immunity application where barriers to entry are so significant that any new meaningful competitive entry is virtually impossible. Now, more than ever, consumers are counting on you to put their interests first.'

On this occasion, he didn't intervene. I met President Obama a little later at the White House, but we kept our brief discussion to sharing updates on the Elders, international relations and drug reform. There was a persistent story going around that we nipped out onto the South Lawn after I offered to share a spliff with the President. I assure you that, despite our shared belief in marijuana regulation, it was just a rumour! As for the tie-up between BA and AA, I could only hope the proposals would go up in smoke.

*

Virgin Atlantic wasn't the only one of our airlines facing difficulties. On the other side of the world, Virgin Blue were discovering that there was nowhere to hide in Australia's tough airline business.

When we had scaled Virgin Blue, we were careful to stay smart and efficient. At its peak, Ansett had 16,000 staff catering for ten million passengers. By the time we hit fifteen million passengers, we still only had 4,000 people working for us. Virgin Blue had grown into a real competitor in the leisure sector, and were becoming more respected for our customer experience as well as the reliability and fun for which Virgin is always known.

But our main competitor, Qantas, attacked us by expanding their own low-cost airline. I believed, for us to combat this, we needed to answer back by diversifying, entering new markets and attracting the business traveller. Not to respond, I felt, was not an option, for there was a danger that Virgin Blue would be squeezed out of the middle. Brett Godfrey disagreed and decided to step down. I felt sad to stop working so closely with my friend, but we remain close (and even co-own Makepeace Island together!) and he will always be a part of the Virgin family.

As we began searching for new blood to bring in, the top candidate emerged from the least likely source. John Borghetti was the number two guy at, of all places, Qantas. He had worked his way up at the company for thirty-six years and was widely expected to become the new CEO. Instead, he was passed over for the job in favour of Alan Joyce. As soon as I met John I realised that he understood the power of people and the importance of brand. He was largely self-educated, had built his career on hard graft and worked in his dad's coffee shop when he was struggling to make ends meet for his family. As well as the business market, he identified regional and charter flying as key focuses for us.

Our big challenge was turning Virgin Blue from a local player into a global force through international partnerships. We expanded existing codeshare agreements – where two or more airlines share the same flight – and built new ones with powerful partners including Etihad Airways, Delta, Air New Zealand, Singapore Airlines and Hawaiian Airlines, as well as Virgin Atlantic and Virgin America. Virgin Blue customers could now fly to 450 destinations around the globe. In effect, we created the world's first virtual international airline, a model every other airline has been trying to replicate since, which has transformed air travel. Some people suggested it was like turning from easyJet into BA. I didn't want us to turn into either, though – I wanted Virgin airlines to be unique.

I invited all three of our airline CEOs over to Houston, where I was speaking at a National Business Travel Association event. John flew from Sydney to present plans for a fresh logo, livery, cabin interior, rewards programme and, most importantly, a new name: Virgin Australia. The airline was unrecognisable from the one we launched just a few years earlier – all except for our superb staff and commitment to service. In six months, profits went up 118 per cent and corporate and government revenues – our key target – grew 81 per cent. We gained half a million frequent flyer programme members and 1,700 new members were signing up every day.

With the newly rebranded Virgin Australia competing hard as a contemporary business and leisure carrier, I told the team my clear aim: to become the country's number one airline. When our new full service offering began making inroads on Qantas's dominance, they very publicly drew a line in the sand and stated in the press they would not go below 65 per cent of the market. We already knew from our own numbers that we were pushing them below that figure. It was sheer arrogance on their part. Now they knew we were deadly serious about growing into the premium market, Qantas were determined to stop us whatever the cost. Battle lines were drawn and they pursued a loss-making strategy of doubling the capacity we introduced onto routes.

Then, on Australian Derby Day in October 2011, Qantas CEO Alan Joyce called an impromptu press conference. He announced they were immediately cancelling all domestic and international flights: 'I repeat: we are grounding the Qantas fleet now!' he told the assembled press.

The cancellations were over a union dispute about job losses and pay, and left more than 100,000 passengers in the lurch. It left Virgin Australia with a decision to make: we could pump up our prices and make a killing while Qantas was out of the picture – or we could help the public. I was incredulous that Qantas would be so ready to let their passengers down, and offer us a huge opportunity in the process. Reasoning it was better to do the right thing than make a quick buck, we sprang into action to help stranded passengers. We brought in extra capacity from our airline partners, asked staff on leave to return to work and got as many people as possible to where they needed to go. We even offered free flights for passengers who had emergencies. As a result, many previously loyal Qantas travellers got to see what Virgin could do up close and switched allegiances.

As Qantas continued to engage in some pretty aggressive tactics, we had an ace up our sleeve. We had long been planning a A$250 million capital drive that would see our partners Singapore Airlines (yes, our former competitors had come on board as investors by this point), Air New Zealand and Etihad increase their stakes in Virgin Australia, providing us with a cash injection to keep improving our service. Alan Joyce's reaction to this perfectly reasonable step was to file a complaint with the Australian federal and

New South Wales governments. He claimed this 'foreign investment' was 'predatory' and would 'distort' the Australian aviation market. What this really meant was Qantas didn't want the competition, couldn't accept that times had changed and wanted the government to support the old monopoly. Sensibly, the Takeovers Panel dismissed their complaint and we went ahead with the deal.

With its credit rating downgraded to junk and share prices dropping to a record low, Qantas campaigned hard for the Australian government to take the extraordinary measure of providing them with a debt guarantee or a A\$3 billion unsecured loan. I presumed Joe Hockey, the Federal Treasurer, would dismiss their pleas, but to my great surprise he seemed receptive. Bizarrely, he described Virgin Australia as a '2,000-pound gorilla', beating up poor little Qantas. But it wasn't as if Qantas was ever in serious financial trouble – they just didn't like their monopoly being shaken up. It was clear Qantas had dug its own grave through bad management. If a company is performing poorly, it is only right that another better-run business comes along to take its place. If the government was going to bail out Qantas, would they make the same guarantee available for all airlines?

With its historic position as Australia's national carrier, its market dominance and far larger fleet, did the Flying Kangaroo really need an extra leg up? I took out a full-page advertisement in News Corp Australia newspapers and argued our case: 'Business people worldwide should think twice about investing in Australia for fear of such intervention in their sectors. Qantas has gone to its shareholders on numerous occasions over the last few years to wage its capacity war against us. Now that shareholders have turned that tap off, the company is turning to the Australian taxpayer to try and bail it out.' Rather than hinting at a debt guarantee, the government should have been urging Qantas to get its own house in order.

It looked increasingly likely, however, that the government would side with Qantas. But Joe Hockey was starting to get frustrated with them. This came to a head when he was late for a press conference in Sydney after Qantas cancelled his flight. The *Sydney Morning Herald* said 'it could be the most costly non-flight in its history'.

'I want to apologise upfront for running late,' he told the media. 'I don't want to talk about airlines, particularly now that they are asking for guarantees and they might not get it after today, because they cancelled my plane!' Later on he added: 'Virgin's a terrific airline and, I'll tell you, my Qantas plane was cancelled this morning and I jumped on a Virgin plane, thankfully.' Of course, we had been more than happy to help!

The debate raged on and more and more of my time was spent fighting our corner. I was getting up in the middle of the night to do interviews with Australian press, writing letters to officials, drafting notes to John and the team and immersing myself in the facts and figures behind the issue. Finally, on 3 March, Prime Minister Tony Abbott was ready to announce his government's decision.

'I have enormous faith in the ability of Qantas to compete and to flourish,' Abbott announced, 'but I think it is best placed to compete and to flourish if it is unshackled, and unpropped up by government, I hasten to add.'

To my huge relief, they had seen sense and were not going to give the debt guarantee or A$3 billion unsecured loan. Rightly, Mr Abbott explained that it was not the role of governments to underwrite debts for airlines, or help one airline over another. All Qantas needed was effective management: 'If you look at the history of Qantas over the last decade or so, it was hugely profitable for most of that time. That demonstrates to me that a well-managed Qantas is more than capable of competing, and not just surviving, but of flourishing. I think this decision that we've made today also says something significant about this government. We do not believe in government by chequebook.'

It was also pleasing to hear Mr Abbott's view that Virgin Australia was just as Australian as Qantas. Yes, I am not Australian and nor are some of our partners (neither are many of Qantas's shareholders, by the way). But Virgin

Australia employs thousands of Australians, from the CEO down. There is no reason why one airline should get more support from the government than another.

I rather enjoyed Alan Joyce's response to the news: 'In the Australian aviation industry you can never be surprised about anything that happens,' he said. At last, there was something we could agree on!

*

Back at Virgin Atlantic, after BA/AA's effective merger had been allowed to go ahead, we had been thinking about how to respond. We needed our own '2,000-pound gorilla' in the States to create a more level playing field. Delta Air Lines was the biggest airline in the US, and on 11 December 2012, they bought Singapore Airlines' 49 per cent stake in Virgin Atlantic.

While Singapore had been great partners, we needed a wider network and greater feed in the US. In return we could offer our brand, customer service expertise, wonderful staff and spirit of innovation. Like us, Delta is built on the principle that staff and customers are the most important parts of the business – shareholders will succeed if staff and customers are happy. Delta wanted to improve its presence at Heathrow and compete more effectively with AA across the Atlantic. Plus, they valued our experience. The deal was nothing like BA/AA's, which was about maintaining a monopoly – this was about levelling the playing field. We finally had the network to compete with BA and other airline goliaths (and in July 2017 we agreed with Air France–KLM and Delta to form an enhanced joint venture.)

No prizes for guessing one person who wasn't pleased about it, though. Willie Walsh threw his toys out of the pram and suggested that Virgin Atlantic would be history within five years.

'I can't see Delta wanting to operate the Virgin brand, because if they do, what does that say about the Delta brand?' he said.

Willie's claim was absolute rubbish – I had no intention of letting Virgin Atlantic disappear, and neither did Delta. At our joint announcement, a journalist asked Delta CEO Richard Anderson if there was any validity to what Willie was saying.

'No!' he said. 'This makes my blood boil.' He had bought into Virgin *because* of the brand.

Willie then went on to attack me personally again, falsely insinuating I was preparing to retire: 'I just don't see that the guy has anything that stands out in terms of what he has achieved in the industry. I've said it publicly, I don't respect him in the way I respect other people in the industry and that's a personal view.'

While I usually laugh off criticism, when I see our competitors overstepping the line, I will protect my teams in every way I can. So I challenged Willie to a sporting bet: if Virgin Atlantic was still flying in five years' time, BA had to give £1 million to our staff. If we were no longer in the air, I would personally pay £1 million to BA's staff. His response to my wager was childish: rather than the loser giving the winner's staff £1 million, he suggested they should receive a knee in the groin.

'It seems a very painful and foolish thing for Willie Walsh to propose,' I wrote on my blog. 'But I would be happy to accept. We've got used to BA hitting below the belt over the years, but I'm confident it would be the other way around on this occasion.'

I urged Willie to get a move on if he was planning to have any more kids. I also called for the loser to donate £1 million to a good cause of the winner's choosing, so some good came out of this rather silly episode. Sadly, but predictably, when December 2017 came around and the wager was due, Willie refused to cough up. Since it seemed slightly childish, I decided it would be churlish to knee him in the groin. However, if you lose a bet you should do the honourable thing – here's hoping Willie agrees eventually.

With so much change, it felt like the perfect time for new blood at the top of Virgin Atlantic. After nine years of wonderful service Steve Ridgway was ready to pass the mantle, and we brought in Craig Kreeger, who had spent twenty-seven years with American Airlines. He got the brand, had the industry nous to get the Delta deal running smoothly, and oversee a transformation of our aircraft, routes and services.

Picking the right CEO is critical – the wrong person at the top can sink a business, no matter how long it's been running. Choosing the right partners is even harder, as trust and understanding takes so long to build up. One part of the Delta deal I initially saw as a negative was how long it took to go through – three and a half years from idea to rubber stamp. Perhaps if I was younger I would have got more impatient. Now, I saw the advantages – we had time to get to know our partners, and build the foundations for success. At one point, Delta discovered a weakness in the contract that meant fluctuating fuel prices benefited them more than us. Before we even mentioned it, they brought it up and we resolved it. This is the way for true partners to behave. I am confident the relationship will last my lifetime and beyond.

Crucially, for all the serious business there is humour in the relationship, too. On my first visit to Delta's base in Atlanta to meet the staff, I was onstage with Richard Anderson when I noticed he was wearing a truly ghastly polka-dot tie. With my trusty pair of scissors in my pocket, I crept up behind him and cut it clean off. As I held it aloft and called for the partnership to be a tie-free zone, Richard was laughing as much as I was.

When Richard joined us for Virgin Hotels Chicago's launch a few months later, he saw a huge display of cut-off ties decorating the wall of our diner, Miss Ricky's (an homage to my penchant for cross-dressing). This time, Richard was prepared. He walked into our meeting wearing a rather unique tie around his neck: it was made of chain-mail, like an Arthurian suit of armour. I tried in vain to cut it off, and vowed to bring a chainsaw to our next meeting.

22 Plain Sailing

'It's cold and will only get worse but at the moment it's bearable. Holly and Sam are coping well as are the rest of the crew.'

On 22 October 2008 at 18:23:03, I tweeted for the first time. I had no idea what I was doing and had yet to see the point of it. At that moment, I had more pressing concerns than the whys and wherefores of social media; we were in a boat in the middle of the ocean, attempting to break the world record for the fastest crossing of the Atlantic in a sailing boat, and I needed to keep my head together.

The idea behind the crossing had been to raise awareness about Virgin Money on both sides of the pond, as well as have another great adventure and, hopefully, another entry in Guinness's famous book. This was a record attempt with a difference, though, given the individuals who had come along to join me as fellow crew members. After they had kissed me goodbye and wished me luck on so many previous expeditions, I was very proud to have my children on board; we had always wanted to take on challenges together as a family and now we were.

But while I was delighted, this was the hardest adventure yet for Joan: it wasn't just her husband risking his life, it was her kids, too. As she had done before my round-the-world ballooning adventures, Joan told me: 'If you die, it's your fault, and I won't be coming to your funeral.' When the children were small and I went on hot-air balloon adventures, Joan had to stay strong for them and not show her concern. Her attitude for this trip, as always, was cautiously supportive.

'I don't think you can stop somebody doing what they want to do,' she told one of the team who asked how she felt about our trip. 'You have to trust the network behind the project that they will keep them safe. And just stay upbeat. Every time you have a negative thought, you have to have a positive one.' Unbeknown to us until we arrived back home, Joan had a panic attack worrying about losing all three of us while we were at sea.

None of us realised quite how dangerous the trip was. We had every confidence in our companions, who were the British America's Cup sailing crew TEAMORIGIN. Three of their number had won gold medals at the Beijing Olympics that summer, including Ben Ainslie, who would go on to become the first person to win medals at five consecutive Olympic Games in sailing. With such a crew, we not only felt safe, but had every confidence in breaking the record of 6 days, 17 hours, 52 minutes and 39 seconds, to become the undisputable fastest mono-hull sailing yacht to cross the Atlantic. As soon as they approached us, late the year before, I had jumped at the chance. Although I had already brought the Blue Riband trophy back to the UK by breaking the record for the fastest crossing of the Atlantic in any boat, this was a challenge I had never attempted, and the idea of doing it with my kids was very appealing.

As we waited in New York for a weather window, I didn't really think too much about the risk. When the weather window finally came, it arrived with a small but significant caveat – it had a hurricane coming up behind us. We reasoned that it would give us extremely strong winds to help us break the record, as long as it didn't break us first! During the first twenty-four hours the boat was absolutely screaming along, all the while making dreadful noises, as if it was going to capsize at any moment. The strain on the keel was enormous and the boat kept threatening to tip over. All the while, colossal waves were billowing over the boat. Although we were safety-lined into the boat, I still worried a wave could knock anyone overboard.

While the crossing was incredibly rough, spirits were high. Sam, in particular, got his sea legs almost immediately and loved every minute of the journey up on deck. The rest of us weren't faring so well. The organisers had underestimated how much water we needed to pack on board so were having to drink cans of fizzy, sugary pop, which gave almost everybody upset stomachs. Holly and I became dreadfully ill. I couldn't remember feeling so sick in my life and it was tremendously debilitating. I have been on many boats in tough situations and been fine, but on this occasion my body let me down. Meanwhile, Sam continued to happily wolf down packets of dried goods that tasted like dog food, while Holly threw up in the sink next to him. We persevered; the trick is to batten down the hatches emotionally, and take it one minute at a time.

As is so often the case at sea, circumstances change in a heartbeat. Just as I was feeling my worst, we had to abandon the record attempt. We were well ahead of target when huge waves crashed into our yacht from behind and took one of our life rafts. Olympic hero Ben Ainslie was bellowing instructions to us and adrenaline was pumping hard as the storm ripped through the mainsail. Very quickly I realised we were in serious danger. It was a scary moment as I looked around at Holly and Sam's worried faces.

Thankfully, the experienced crew swung into action and we managed to change course and get out in one piece. Rather than limping across the Atlantic and having the hurricane catch us up, we decided to head for Bermuda. For twelve hours, we got the most beautiful downwind sail. As the excellent sailing conditions continued, our sickness went away. I sat on top of the boat with my kids and we shared one of the nicest days of our lives. It made the whole trip worthwhile.

A couple of weeks later, I heard the terrible news that the Virgin Money boat had turned over in more dangerous weather at sea – the keel had snapped. It makes me shudder to think how easily that could have happened while we were in the middle of the Atlantic. In all likelihood, there would have been no more challenges for us; no Virgin Money, no grandchildren and you certainly wouldn't be reading this book.

*

When I asked Holly and Sam if they had enjoyed the experience, I could see that familiar yearning for more adventure reflecting back at me. That's the thing about taking on challenges – once you get a taste for them you can't let go. It's no surprise that both of my kids have a thirst for risk-taking, and some of my most treasured memories are from when we have embarked upon challenges together.

In 2014, I joined Sam on his 1,000-kilometre journey from London to the summit of the Matterhorn. The Virgin Strive Challenge was a new adventure Sam and my nephew Noah dreamed up on their way down Mont Blanc after we climbed the mountain in 2012: to run, row, cycle, hike and climb entirely under their own steam all the way from the UK to the top of one of the world's most formidable peaks, the Matterhorn. Noah and Sam pulled together a core team of ten to complete the whole trip, with 350 others joining en route, myself included. The challenge would raise more than £750,000 to invest in projects that offer alternative ways of supporting young people in the UK to thrive in life, not just in exams.

My mum acted as starting marshal as the Strivers set off on 20 April. By the time I joined them in Switzerland they had already completed three back-to-back marathons, been thwarted by Hurricane Bertha's aftershocks as they tried to row the Channel, and cycled over 100 kilometres from France into Switzerland. I surprised them by turning up in full cycling gear. The hills were turning into mountains as we made tracks for Verbier. It is a particularly tough climb, and, turning the tables on that record attempt across the Atlantic, Sam took me to one side and offered some support.

'I'll hold back with you today, Dad, and we'll help each other up the hills.'

He didn't know I had a surprise up my sleeve, though. 'I'll be fine, Sam,' I told him. 'I've been training. You go to the front and don't worry about your old man. I'll see you at the top.'

Sam was worried my old-fashioned bike – or, more importantly, my old-fashioned legs? – wouldn't be able to hack it. The locals told us the record for making it up the hill is twenty-five minutes, and we estimated it would take us an hour and a half. After ten minutes I was floundering towards the back of the group when suddenly I got an extreme burst of pace. Wimbledon champion Marion Bartoli had a look of pure shock on her face as I flew past her. Verbier's top fitness coach appeared equally confused as he struggled in vain to keep pace with me. Finally, I met Sam near the front and zoomed past him without comment, eventually getting up the hill in twenty-four minutes! When Sam reached the top the best part of an hour later, the only part of my body aching was my face, from grinning too much. Sam looked absolutely knackered, and flabbergasted that his dad had outdone him. After I got him to agree to get me a polka-dot jersey as honorary King of the Mountains, I decided to reveal my secret: I had a special battery-powered bike! With all the sneakiness of a Lance Armstrong, I had hidden it below the Strive branding under my seat.

'You bastard!' said Sam, with a giggle.

That night we gathered at Verbier for a very special occasion: I was going to propose to Marion Bartoli. We had got on swimmingly when she competed in the Necker Cup the previous November. But there was a sore moment when, playing beach tennis, Marion lost her Wimbledon winner's ring. I got out my trusty metal detector (there's plenty of buried treasure from the original pirates of the Caribbean) and began searching. We looked and looked to no avail. Six months later, we found it and now I was determined to put it back on Marion's fair hand. I gathered everyone around at the Lodge and got down on one knee. I'm not sure what Joan would have made of it – Marion's fiancé certainly looked perplexed.

We got back on the road the following morning for a seven-day hike to Zermatt. After a straightforward first day climbing to the Cabane du Mont-Fort and taking in the views of the Grand Combin, I was feeling fresh. But by day three it really got tough, with howling winds pushing against us and rain thundering relentlessly down. As visibility deteriorated, huge boulders were dislodged all around us and tumbled down the mountain. Torrential rain and the constant uphill terrain were getting to everyone and the tension only mounted as we tiptoed around rocks, fearful of starting an avalanche. All aching limbs were worth it, however, as we reached the top of the peak, turned the corner and the sun miraculously appeared. It was a moment I'll always treasure as we all fell silent and looked on in wonder. Once the sunshine returned things got a little easier and everyone was able to make it to Zermatt in one piece. From there, the mighty Matterhorn loomed ominously in the distance, one last challenge.

At the base of the Matterhorn there is a beautiful church; its graveyard is full of the remains of climbers who came to grief on the mountain in the past. It was 3 a.m. when the Strivers set out from the tiny lodge we were huddled in to begin the dangerous ascent. The stars were lighting the way for Sam, Noah and the team. The conditions were getting dire. Sam, among the fittest of everyone, was seriously ill with altitude sickness and was lying on the ground in the snow retching. But having got this far, he was fighting hard and determined to make it to the top with his cousin. His guide, mountaineer Kenton Cool, who's summited Everest eleven times, advised Sam to turn back with 200 metres to go. Being so close, Sam was determined to carry on.

As the drama was unfolding below, I circled above with the door to the helicopter open, very concerned for Sam. I couldn't believe that after surviving so many adventures myself, my son had followed in my footsteps but wasn't going to make it. We could barely see what was going on. But by 9 a.m., with every last drop of their energy, Noah, core team Striver Stephen Shanly and Sam took the final steps together and reached the summit of the Matterhorn. I cried with delight from above. It was a spectacular sight; I wished I could have been down in the snow with them.

Mostly, though, I was scared about Sam's condition, which was deteriorating fast. Noah and the others had to hold him up as they unfurled a flag on the summit. My helicopter was short on fuel, and as we veered away from the mountain a rescue helicopter was on its way up. It was unsettling, knowing I could do nothing to help Sam and worrying whether he would be able to make it down the mountain. After an anxious wait, the rescue team attached him to a winch and he held onto a rescuer as he was carried off the top. Sam opened his eyes, somewhat delirious and unsure where he was. Thankfully they got him into the helicopter and safely down the peak.

By that point I had landed and was waiting anxiously back at base with Sam's wife Bellie and Holly. When Sam arrived and staggered out of the helicopter to us, we gave him the biggest hug, wrapped him up and got him inside. Neither Sam nor I could stop laughing through our tears – him with pain, me with relief and happiness. We were fortunate to have him back.

Rather than relieved at being alive, Sam was just disappointed he hadn't been able to complete the climb down the mountain. His sister reassured him: 'The challenge was only from London to the top of the Matterhorn – nobody said anything about coming down again!' I felt so proud of Sam, Noah and the whole team for overcoming so much adversity and defying the odds to complete their journey. They had travelled thousands of miles in a month of body-breaking endurance tests, with the purpose of helping young people less fortunate than themselves. They had banded together as a family. That's part of what adventure is all about. I pledged to myself to clear my diary next time and join them on the whole trip.

*

Having saved our lives on the Atlantic with his quick thinking in 2008, I got the chance to return the favour to Ben – now Sir Ben – Ainslie in 2015.

That January, Ben was sailing around the BVI with his new wife Georgie Thompson. As we waved them by, it never crossed my mind that they would need any help from us. After all, Ben is the most successful sailor in Olympic history. His miraculous America's Cup exploits, when he inspired Oracle Team USA to victory from 8–1 down, will quite possibly go down as the greatest comeback of all time. He clearly knows what he is doing on a boat!

But Ben had a serious mechanical problem on board and was very quickly heading for a dangerous reef, a sunken ship and a very unromantic end to his honeymoon. He was forced to put out a distress call for assistance and our water sports team rushed out to meet him. The furling system broke on the mainsail and it became so twisted that the sail couldn't go in, out, up or down. Our team raced over and between them managed to climb the mast and cut the sail, just about avoiding a bigger calamity.

As they made it back to shore I skipped down to the beach to meet them.

'I thought you were the best sailor in the world,' I said cheekily.

Ben accepted my invitation to stay for a while and it was great to catch up with him.

The following year Ben invited me out to New York to be the sixth man in his Land Rover BAR team for the America's Cup World Series. I knew it would be an initiation of fire, but I was confident I could handle it as I took my position on the back of the catamaran. Soon we were absolutely screaming along in very rough waters.

'How are you doing back there?' shouted Ben.

'It feels like being in a washing machine!' I bellowed back.

After about twenty minutes, the extremely tough conditions got even worse. Ben turned to me and said: 'Richard,

I'm sorry but I can't have you on the boat any more, it's just too risky.'

I reluctantly agreed and went to the chase boat to watch the races. It was a day of constantly shifting and dying breezes, meaning that any team could have won – which is exactly what happened. The British team were superb, but had some bad luck. They had been in position for a race win, when the wind completely died and they began to drift off course. Then a series of unexpected wind changes catapulted Emirates Team New Zealand from dead last, to win both the race and the regatta. Land Rover BAR ended up coming fifth in the race and fifth overall in the event – a frustrating result after a succession of brilliant starts.

Afterwards, I said to Ben. 'If you'd kept me on board the whole time we would have won every race – I'm a jammy bastard!'

23 'Somebody mentioned the word "hurricane"'

After the accident in July 2007, Scaled's propulsion testing programme was shut down for about a year. Then, as there was no certainty that the propulsion system was completely safe, Scaled embarked upon a long programme to replace the carbon-fibre oxidiser tank with a unique aluminium-lined tank. It set Virgin Galactic's development back a long, long time, and cost a huge amount of money, but it was obviously the right thing to do. I urged patience from everyone involved and remained highly optimistic we were on the right track.

While the propulsion plans took a back seat, Scaled pushed on with the crucial work of testing the mothership and spaceship. At the same time, we debated when Virgin Galactic should start accepting reservations. I was keen to get the ball rolling as soon as humanly possible, but was reminded of the story of Pan Am's aborted space programme in the sixties. One of my favourite scenes in *2001: A Space Odyssey* is when the director Stanley Kubrick imagines guests flying on a Pan Am flight to a Hilton Hotel in space. I had always wanted to turn it into reality (with Virgin Galactic replacing Pan Am and Virgin Hotels replacing Hilton, of course) and wasn't the only one. After the moon landing, Pan Am began adding names to a waiting list for flights to the moon. Their conservative estimate on a flight date was the year 2000. Almost 100,000 people signed up to the list over two decades, and Pan Am handed out First

Moon Flights club membership cards. It was tremendously exciting and great for the brand, but enthusiasm for space travel slowed at the same time as Pan Am's profits dwindled. In 1991, nine years before their aspired space launch, the company went bankrupt. The First Moon Flights club never got close to becoming a reality: I didn't want Virgin Galactic to go the same way.

With the technical development plans back on track, however, Virgin Galactic's London team focused upon our sales strategy. I've always found the best market research is to ask the people closest to you for their opinion, and then steadily branch out. All my family wanted to go to space, with the notable exception of Joan. But they were used to the idea of adventure and exploration, not least from spending time around me on dozens of balloon and boating challenges. Would the general public – especially those with deep pockets – be willing to make such a big commitment? Back when we started taking deposits in 2005, we debated how much of a deposit we should ask from our first customers. My only real yardstick was that, years earlier, the Russian space programme quoted me an astronomical multi-million-dollar fee. In the end, we settled upon $200,000 per reservation. This was obviously far too high a price for most people to afford, but we viewed the first future astronauts as pioneers who would pave the way for cheaper, more frequent flights as the programme developed.

I was well aware that we were asking for a great deal of trust from our future astronauts. We couldn't give them a specific timeline for when they would go to space. We couldn't tell them exactly what the experience would be like. We couldn't show them what they would wear, or even who they would go with, let alone how they would feel. But we could promise them the adventure of a lifetime. For this, we required a deposit up front. We set up a website and waited to see if anybody would sign up. The demand was staggering. The website crashed from sheer traffic volume and people turned up at Virgin Management's doors, some even with the cash ready to go. Very soon, hundreds of people were able to join me in proudly calling themselves future astronauts.

With progress on the mothership and spaceship gathering speed, I began training for my own spaceflight. Just before Christmas 2007, I travelled over to the National Aerospace Training and Research Center in Southampton, Pennsylvania. I had heard all about some people being sick as they were thrown around during centrifuge training, or even passing out from the g-forces. But, having had several adventures in the sky, I was looking forward to it. My son Sam joined the course, too, along with Will and some of Virgin Galactic's future astronauts. They included Alan Watts, who earned a flight on SpaceShipTwo after cashing in his Virgin Atlantic frequent flyer miles – now that's what I call an upgrade!

The experience was an amazing adrenaline rush. It was also slightly tougher than I envisaged, and I was delighted my body held out. I was put through an STS-400 centrifuge ride, which created the kind of g-forces I could expect on the ride up to space. I was pinned back into my seat and could feel my cheeks vibrating as the pressure pushed them back against my ears. My vision came close to blurring at one stage, but I remembered the training from earlier in the day: you have to grip your bottom muscles tight and practise breathing techniques to avoid losing vision. I felt a little silly at first, but any such feelings disappeared when I realised how effective it was. Coupled with a flight simulator ride that recreated the different steps of the journey from take-off to rocket ignition to orbital entry to re-entry, I came out feeling that I was already much better prepared for launching into space.

*

By the end of January 2008 we were ready to unveil the designs of both SpaceShipTwo and WhiteKnightTwo. All the Galactic team and more than a hundred of our new future astronauts gathered in Mojave for the big reveal. I asked Mum to come out to the event, and told her I had a surprise in store for her. We had been calling WhiteKnightTwo the mother-ship since its inception. Now I wanted to make it official. We pulled back the hangar doors to roll out the aeroplane that would carry our spaceship up to 50,000 feet. I loved watching Mum's eyes light up as she saw her name glistening proudly on the side of the vehicle – Virgin Mother Ship (VMS) *Eve*.

It was wonderful having my dad by my side that day, too. Both Mum and Dad have offered me constant support and guidance my whole life, which I have often felt most keenly ahead of big adventures. Whether preparing to fly a balloon over the Pacific or guide a boat across the Atlantic, they have always been there to cheer me on. Importantly, they have been metaphorically by my side when things have gone wrong, from boats sinking off the Scilly Isles to balloons crashing into the ocean. I told them all of this owed as much to their encouragement and sense of adventure as anything.

The testing continued. By March 2009, Scaled pilot Pete Siebold had taken WhiteKnightTwo up on her fastest and longest flight so far. They rose up to 20,000 feet and 140 knots during the two-and-a-half-hour flight, completing seven successful tests in the process including in-flight engine restarts and evaluating handling qualities. Back on the ground, the new rocket motor system passed its first tests successfully. After more successful test flights in June, space was beginning to feel a whole lot closer.

With each breakthrough, however, new costs arose, and we really needed an investment injection to maintain the momentum. I was worried, because without concrete results it would get tougher to convince Virgin's board to keep pumping in money, more difficult to keep public perception positive and harder to maintain team morale. The business was at a tipping point, and I felt we needed a substantial partner with hundreds of millions to invest in order to take it to the next level.

Months earlier I had had the idea of approaching Sheikh Mansour, Deputy Prime Minister of the United Arab

Emirates and one of the world's richest men. I knew he was fascinated by space travel, and wondered if he would be interested in investing in Virgin Galactic. Flying over Abu Dhabi, I decided to land and chance my arm. One of the advantages of being relatively well known is that I can often get through to very busy people at short notice. I managed to get an appointment to see the Mansour family the following day.

I spent the night creating a considered, detailed analysis of the investment opportunity. But as I walked into his beautiful home, all of that went out of the window. I was nervous. I did not know the Sheikh, and was slightly out of my comfort zone. As soon as I saw the half-dozen men gathered around the table and took a sip of water, I knew I needed to appeal to their imaginations. I used my hands a lot, illustrating my vision of a future Spaceport in Abu Dhabi, and the opportunity to be at the cutting edge of a whole new industry democratising space. They looked intrigued, but I still felt vulnerable – the future of Virgin Galactic, and my life's dreams, could possibly be at stake in this room. For a moment, I wasn't sure which way the meeting was going to go. But then the Sheikh broke into a smile. By the end of the day we had shaken hands on a deal for Aabar Investments to inject $280 million into Virgin Galactic.

When it comes to deals like this, or any negotiations really, the key is to display passion, know-how and determination. Get to the point quickly, be persistent and consistent, and don't rely too heavily on prompts, statistics, and certainly not PowerPoint slides. I went into the meeting with my notebook in my back pocket, armed with beautiful spaceship pictures, a lot of enthusiasm and belief in the project. Investors buy into people and ideas, not numbers alone.

The deal was a game-changer. Until this point the company had been wholly owned and funded by Virgin Group, which put a strain on our wider operations. With so much riding on our space programme, we had to control costs tightly elsewhere, manage our cash carefully and be very stringent with other investments. Patrick McCall and the Galactic team worked day and night ironing out the details, and did an unbelievable job to finalise the deal, with Aabar taking a 32 per cent stake. It valued the business at over $1 billion. We also agreed to later explore the additional development of systems to launch small satellites at unprecedentedly low costs, reliably and flexibly, and Aabar were particularly keen on the idea of research labs in space. Their commitment – and, of course, their willingness to put their money where their mouth was – gave us all a massive confidence boost. It was a really important moment for the company financially, and also for me personally. I had been taking more of a back seat when it came to investment deals around the Group, and this was a timely reminder that I still had a few surprises up my sleeve. When I called the Virgin Galactic team I was pleased to tell them, 'There's life in the old dog yet!'

*

It wasn't only financial issues that we needed to overcome. As we prepared to unveil SpaceShipTwo in Mojave that December, the weather wanted to play its part in blowing us off course.

We had decided to erect a huge tent in the desert and wait until nightfall to show off the spaceship under the stars. Governor Schwarzenegger of California and Governor Richardson of New Mexico, both enthusiastic supporters of the project, were on hand for the historic occasion. Arnie was his usual exuberant self, mixing with everyone. He was joined by many of our future astronauts, Holly, the Queen's granddaughters Princesses Beatrice and Eugenie, 800 journalists and VIPs.

As darkness descended, the silent shape of SpaceShipTwo – now officially named Virgin Space Ship (VSS) *Enterprise* – was carried down the runway by her mothership. Lights flashed, music blasted and, bizarrely, snow fell all around. It was a very proud moment, but one that very quickly turned into a truly terrifying night. A storm had been gathering around us and gale force winds began whipping the great tent. But no one seemed to mind: the party was flowing, we were enjoying ourselves peering through telescopes stargazing and admiring the spaceship.

Then somebody mentioned the word 'hurricane'. Jackie McQuillan, our press guru, rushed up to me and said the fire department wanted us to abandon everything, get in the buses and leave immediately.

'What a load of rubbish,' I said. 'Look how much fun everyone's having, there is no way we are going.'

I walked over to the fire chief, ready to tell him to calm down and enjoy the party. But I could see by the thunderous look on his face that I should climb down quickly. He meant business.

'If everyone hasn't evacuated the area in the next few minutes,' he told me, 'we could have a major disaster on our hands.'

As everybody rushed out to some hastily scrambled buses, I looked back out of the window to see the whole 200-foot marquee take off! It was a close-run thing: the last person had barely got out in time before scaffolding went crashing onto the ground, sound systems were smashed and anything not tied down flew up into the sky.

As the wind increased to 116mph, locals told me there hadn't been such a combination of high winds, rain and freezing temperatures in Mojave for over thirty years. I was worried the spaceship would disappear into the desert along with the tent, or at least be badly damaged, but the team got six buses and RVs to surround SpaceShipTwo, and then we very slowly edged it towards the hangar. Remarkably, the team managed to get her back indoors unscathed, and everyone was OK. I turned to the flushed, astonished faces on the bus.

'If there was ever an example of how something can pick up your dreams and throw them up into thin air, this is it!'

*

In 2010, we saw SpaceShipTwo fly for the first time. Scaled Composites planned a 'captive carry' test, where VSS

Enterprise would fly attached to VMS *Eve*. Both spaceship and mothership looked magnificent against the deep blue Mojave backdrop and the test went perfectly.

Away from the runway we secured one of the most important deals in the spaceline's history: appointing our first chief executive. We pried George Whitesides, who was already a future Virgin Galactic astronaut, away from the prestigious role of chief of staff at NASA. Will Whitehorn had done a superb job as president, but George had the space industry know-how to move the company into a commercially operational business. What's more, he was already deeply committed to our mission. George had met his wife Loretta at a UN space conference. When he heard about Virgin Galactic he knew he had found the ultimate wedding present, and bought two tickets to enable them to be among the first astronauts to fly on SpaceShipTwo. They still intend to be the first couple to honeymoon in space. It was also important to have an American at the helm to navigate the business, policy, licensing and regulations that govern the space industry in the US. What's more, George could help attract even more talent to the team as we looked to begin building and testing spaceships ourselves. It was a real challenge finding people skilled enough – and Virgin enough – to grow the Galactic team further.

The Scaled test flights came thick and fast after George's appointment; WhiteKnightTwo had now flown forty times, including four captive carry tests with the mothership and spaceship mated together. The fourth of these was SpaceShipTwo's first crewed flight. This was swiftly followed by the first manned glide flight in commercial space history, on 10/10/10. The perfect score date turned out to be spot on. I looked on from the desert below as VMS *Eve* dropped VSS *Enterprise* into the clear sky from 45,000 feet. From that great height, Scaled's test pilots glided her serenely down to the desert floor. It felt overwhelming and humbling watching such a powerful, beautiful vehicle glide so gracefully, touching back down to earth as light as a feather.

After watching our spaceship glide down to earth so elegantly on a number of further occasions I thought it was time my kids and I got in on the act. On a boiling hot day in New Mexico in October 2011, 800 guests watched us jump off the spectacular structure of Spaceport America. Unlike my last leap off a building in Las Vegas, it all went smoothly.

'I trust that will be the first of many safe landings!' I shouted as we touched down.

Most of the future astronauts gathered with us in New Mexico were not celebrities; they were simply people who had always wanted to go to space and were fortunate enough to be able to afford it. We welcome people from all walks of life, people who will be amongst their countries' first ever astronauts, families eager to share the experience of a lifetime together, individuals who have looked longingly at the stars since they were kids – anyone who shares our passion for space. We made a point of offering no discounts, whoever was asking, and have only ever offered one free ticket: Professor Stephen Hawking, who is one of my heroes and was also a pioneer of scientific theory and among the smartest people in history, happily accepted our invitation.

'I wouldn't mind dying in space, surrounded by the stars. It would be a good way to go!' he told me.

We have not pursued people in the public eye to pay for a reservation, though, of course, some have done so and we've welcomed them into the community with everyone else. Every now and then one of them is keen to tell the world about their planned space adventures, and I'm always happy to help. This was the case when Ashton Kutcher became our 500th astronaut. I phoned Ashton to congratulate him.

'I can't wait to hear your own vision for crossing the final frontier and going to space with us,' I said.

'And returning!' Ashton came back.

Not long afterwards, Justin Bieber and his manager Scooter Braun signed up, too. I got an enormous number of tweets pleading with me to make Justin's ticket one way! I thought they were quite harsh. Justin is a big talent, and with his success has come constant pressure to grow up in the public eye. Like any young lad, he's made mistakes and acted up. But with Scooter's friendship, a wonderful mentor as well as a very astute businessman, I'm sure Justin will go on to do even greater things.

*

While Scaled continued testing the human spaceflight vehicles in Mojave, we were also working behind the scenes on another transformational space business: satellites.

As plans developed for a privately funded satellite launcher system, I quickly realised this business had the potential to change the world. We had already partnered with NASA to provide opportunities for engineers, technologists and scientific researchers to fly technology payloads into space on SpaceShipTwo – the first time NASA had contracted with a commercial partner to provide flights into space on a suborbital spacecraft. With SpaceShipTwo developing well, some of the Virgin Galactic team turned their attention to LauncherOne, our new air-launched rocket specifically designed to deliver small satellites into orbit. We had been working on it in the background since 2008, but by 2012 our strategy was taking shape and I decided to share the idea at the Farnborough International Air Show.

Standing beside a full-size replica of SpaceShipTwo, and surrounded by aviation experts and enthusiasts, I revealed a prototype for LauncherOne, a two-stage vehicle that would be launched from 50,000 feet by Virgin Galactic's mothership WhiteKnightTwo, and which was capable of carrying up to 500 pounds to orbit for prices below $10 million. Because of the flexibility provided by air launch, infrastructure costs would be low and launch locations would be tailored to individual mission requirements and weather conditions. Virgin Galactic's partner Aabar Investments was on board to help fund the development of frequent and dedicated launches at the world's lowest prices. We even had our first LauncherOne customers, with four private companies, including an asteroid mining venture, putting down deposits and expressing intent to purchase several dozen launches.

'LauncherOne is bringing the price of satellite launch into the realm of affordability for innovators everywhere, from start-ups and schools to established companies and national space agencies,' I told the audience. 'It will be a critical new tool for the global research community, enabling us all to learn about our home planet more quickly and affordably.'

There were lots of questions about whether developing LauncherOne meant we were taking our eye off the ball with human spaceflight, but we had recruited a dedicated team to design and build LauncherOne (and by 2017 the team had grown into a new company, Virgin Orbit).

'I see the two as mutually beneficial,' I continued. 'This way we can make the most of our resources and knowledge. Launching small satellites is an area ripe for enormous disruption, and we have the team, the technology and the expertise to shake up the whole industry and make it far more affordable.'

While the trend, from mobile phones to chocolate bars, has been for things to get smaller and smaller, satellites have gone in the opposite direction. They are doing more amazing things, but getting more expensive. We wanted to reduce the size and thus cut the cost, opening up the market for many more people. We hoped the satellites could help enable projects from space-based solar power to more efficient food production and transportation; more effective disaster management to humanitarian assistance. Perhaps most importantly, we hoped to connect many of the billions of people who are still unconnected.

As we moved into satellites, increasingly excitable pieces began to appear in the press more frequently. Many declared a new 'space race' between me and some fellow entrepreneurs, namely Tesla and SpaceX founder Elon Musk and Jeff Bezos, the Amazon and Blue Origin founder. 'The Space Race is back in full swing – only this time with tech titans taking on the roles of aeronautic adversaries,' wrote *Fortune*, while CNBC described the industry as 'a game of thrones among three billionaires'. There is certainly professional rivalry between us, but also enormous respect and a shared desire to shake up the space industry. When governments stopped investing and NASA funding was cut, space exploration largely dried up. Now a new generation of entrepreneurs is trying to bring innovation back to the stars.

I'm proud that Virgin Galactic's pioneering programme has helped pave the way for more private companies to enter the market. Space is not out of reach any more and we have really kick-started a multi-billion-dollar industry, creating innumerable jobs and dreams in the process. Rather than Elon, Jeff and me being direct rivals, the reality is that we are all looking at the industry from slightly different angles and in different businesses. They intersect at the edges but are not on top of each other, and there is healthy competition to keep everybody going. In the human spaceflight field, we are just ahead, and in small satellites we are operating in various exciting niches. Elon, by contrast, is focused upon the goal of sending people to Mars, an admirable if extremely expensive goal.

I knew there was certainly a market for this, from an experiment I dreamed up with Larry Page and Google in 2008. During a long night in the beach house on Necker, we devised a plan to launch a new joint venture called Virgle: The Adventure of Many Lifetimes. The company was launched to take humans to Mars, and was accepting candidates for one-way tickets to colonise the Red Planet. Thousands of people applied, and very few thought to consider the carefully chosen date of our launch: 1 April. I think getting to Mars will be possible in the future, but I also believe that Virgin Galactic, The Spaceship Company and Virgin Orbit's approach of manufacturing vehicles of the future, offering human spaceflight and small satellite launches, is the best way to open space for the benefit of humanity and the earth itself.

*

The countdown was finally on for SpaceShipTwo's first powered flight. After completing another glide flight test with the rocket motor components installed, more successful feathered tests and nitrous vent tests, our breath was blown away by a 'cold vent' test. This meant completing the profile of the fast-approaching milestone flight in the air, apart from actually igniting the rocket. Instead, oxidiser flowed through the propulsion system and out through the nozzle at the rear of the vehicle. A spectacular trail spurted out from SpaceShipTwo and I got my first taste of what SpaceShipTwo will look like as it takes us to space.

A few weeks later, on 29 April 2013, I got more than a taste, when we were back out in Mojave for what would be Scaled's first attempt to break the sound barrier with the spacecraft. I had the same butterflies in my stomach I felt before my ballooning adventures, that feeling where time slows right down to a crawl, even though you know it will soon speed up beyond comprehension. The atmosphere was electric as we made our way over to the hangar, abuzz with last-minute preparations.

As the clock struck 7 a.m. we gathered on the tarmac and waved Scaled's test pilot Mark Stucky and co-pilot Mike Alsbury into the SpaceShipTwo cockpit. Virgin Galactic's chief pilot Dave Mackay was clambering into his seat in WhiteKnightTwo, assisted by Scaled co-pilot Clint Nichols and flight test engineer Brian Maisler. With little fanfare, SpaceShipTwo took off mated to WhiteKnightTwo. As they flew up to the release point, we waited 47,000 feet below, with a few quiet words being exchanged to ease the tension, all eyes fixed on the sky above.

Forty-five minutes into the flight, WhiteKnightTwo dropped SpaceShipTwo to fly freely alone. Then, with a flash of fire, Mark triggered the rocket motor. Whoosh! The main oxidiser valve opened and the rocket ignited. I could see a magnificent plume of flames coming out of the back of the spaceship, and pointed in awe. SpaceShipTwo shot forward ferociously, rising upwards in a rapid ascent to 55,000 feet. With the engine burning, the spaceship's speed rose and rose, going supersonic with an audible pop, and achieving Mach 1.2.

Before we could take this all in, it was over. The burn lasted the planned sixteen seconds, and the pilots began their descent back to earth. I turned to Burt and gripped him in a tight embrace, before turning to my right to hug George and getting caught up in a mass of arms and grins. As the vehicles landed, less than an hour after they had taken off, my first feeling was one of overwhelming relief. But this was quickly succeeded by sheer joy, and I could barely get my words out. I was able to spend a brief moment congratulating the pilots, and simply told them how proud I was of them all.

'You just made history,' I told them.

But I still had my eye on the future. I emailed the Galactic management team, telling them, 'We should invest in increasing the size of the initial fleet of spaceships from two to three, and put a team at work on beginning the second SpaceShipTwo as soon as possible.' I didn't know then how prudent that would prove to be.

24 A Lost Night in Melbourne

It was like a scene from the film *The Hangover*, except with more of a thumping headache. I woke up feeling extremely dehydrated and somewhat the worse for wear. Where was I? I was in a hotel room, but which hotel, which city, even which country I wasn't completely clear about.

As I stood up and staggered over to the window, I tried to pull back the curtains. Bad idea. I squinted in the sunlight, before closing them again, but at least now I knew where I was. Melbourne. Slowly, in the back of my mind, a memory began to stir. Motor racing, that was it: I was here for the Grand Prix. But then other less good memories began to surface. Jenson Button's girlfriend. A baby in a restaurant. A man shouting at me in the urinals. I sat back down on the edge of the bed and tried to piece together what had happened ...

*

The chain of events had started in March 2009, when I got an early-morning call from Ross Brawn on Necker. The celebrated Formula One maestro had started his own team, Brawn GP, and Ross felt they had a real chance of winning the championship. But Honda had pulled funding from their outfit and unless they got investment – fast – there would be no team at all. As I sat there in the morning sunshine, I listened as Ross explained they had an experienced driving duo of Jenson Button and Rubens Barrichello, and Ross was confident he had built a title-worthy car.

'So what can I do for you?' I asked.

'We're short on cash,' Ross explained. 'We need a sponsor to come on board if we are even going to make it to the start-line at the first race in Melbourne.'

I didn't know much about motor racing but I knew a man who did: Sam's friend James Rossiter, who just happened to be in Japan test-driving Brawn's car. I tracked him down and spoke to him about what Ross was saying: Sam's friend backed him up, saying the car was a winner, the fastest he had ever driven. On hearing that, I rang Ross straight back and said we were happy to back the team. We went through forty-eight hours of heavy negotiations, with Alex Tai securing a deal to get Brawn through the first race, with the understanding that, should they win it, we'd have our brand on both cars for the whole season for a nominal sum. We got extra branding space on the car and Virgin Atlantic provided tickets for the team and drivers, too.

With race qualifying just hours away, I packed my bag and dug out my passport. We managed to get some Virgin stickers printed up, which I shoved in my bag, and jumped on the first plane to Australia. I arrived in Melbourne on Friday, and hurried to the track to stick the logos on the sides of the cars. They had got a little crumpled on the flight, but looked great as Button and Barrichello went zooming around the track. Their cars weren't quite as impressive, though, mustering only the sixth and fourth fastest times in the first practice session. However, in qualifying the next day they were transformed. Jenson just beat his teammate to pole position for a Brawn/Virgin one-two.

Slightly giddy from the team's performance, the sun and the jetlag, we headed into town for dinner and a couple of drinks at Nobu. Ross and Alex came along, too. We were in understandably jubilant form and the drinks were flowing freely: because of the excitement of the day, we felt as if we'd won already, and had to keep reminding ourselves that we had only qualified first, not yet sealed the Grand Prix.

Jenson and his girlfriend were sitting at the next table, enjoying a far quieter evening as he had to race the next morning. By contrast, through a mixture of tiredness, jetlag and drink, I soon found myself very, very inebriated. This wasn't like me: I can't remember ever getting that drunk, before or since. Fuelled by alcohol, I went over to Jenson's table and sat down next to his girlfriend. I may have been slightly blurry-eyed, but was still able to realise how gorgeous she was. Foolishly, I then told her as much. Jenson understandably took offence and I decided to retreat quickly from the table (thankfully, we smoothed it out).

Meanwhile, a delightful couple came up to me with their baby and asked for a photograph. Happy to oblige, I took the baby in my arms and stood up to smile at the camera. The next moment, so I'm told (I didn't find out until the next day), I was on the other side of the restaurant and the parents were chasing me – I had wandered off with their baby! Perhaps I was getting some early practice in for my own grandchildren. After finally reuniting the child with his mum and dad, it was high time I visited the bathroom: surely I couldn't mess that up? But as I stood at the urinal, I realised a man had followed me into the toilet.

'Richard, it's great to meet you, can I have your autograph?' he asked, sidling up next to me.

'Of course,' I said, turning to face him, completely forgetting that I was still relieving myself. Before I knew what was happening, I had managed to piss all over the guy's trousers – not exactly the memento of meeting me he had been hoping for. After that debacle, I'm afraid the rest of the night is a complete blur, which is probably for the best.

As I recalled each of these incidents, my embarrassment increased. I was incredibly thankful – and lucky in this day and age – that none of my antics had made it onto social media. Sobering up as best I could, I made my way back to the Grand Prix circuit for the race. There were cameras pointing at me from every angle and I felt even more self-conscious.

'That's it,' I said. 'I'm giving up alcohol for six months.' I stuck to it, too.

I managed a smile for the press, but it felt like an F1 engine was revving inside my brain. Inside the circuit, it seemed as if all 80,000 spectators were screaming at us as we walked down to the pits. Thankfully, the talent of our drivers took the edge off my headache. Jenson, the model professional and a seriously talented driver, was ready for his big moment on the starting line and led the race from start to finish: to cheers from the crowd he pumped his fist in delight as he took the chequered flag. Rubens followed close behind in second place for an unbelievable one-two. I was stunned: this was a team that had gone from the brink of folding to the top of the world in a matter of days. While the drivers got ready for the presentation, I charged down past the finishing line high-fiving fans as they chanted: 'Richard! Richard! Richard!' For a minute, I felt like one of the rock stars we'd signed for Virgin Records. It really was a miraculous performance from Ross and the team, going from rank outsiders to title favourites. I was delighted to be part of it, though waved away the celebratory champagne!

I joined Brawn for several more races during the season, most memorably in Bahrain, where we added Virgin Galactic branding to build awareness of our spaceline in a new market. As I watched the car speeding around the track, I was concerned the logo just didn't stand out.

'Has anybody got a pen?' I asked, racing round the pit. 'I need a black marker.'

Just before the race was about to start, a helpful lady pulled a Sharpie out of her handbag. I grabbed the marker, jumped onto the track and coloured in the logo more – now it shone out as Button cruised through the field to take the chequered flag.

It was a hot day as always in Bahrain, but made doubly so by the heat from the engines. We were all dripping with sweat as the race ended and TV crews started swarming around the pit lane. Realising I was going to be interviewed, I whipped my drenched shirt off to replace it with a dry one. But the TV crew chose that moment to begin their interview, leaving me half-naked while broadcasting to millions, but with a huge smile on my face after a wonderful Grand Prix.

Jenson went on to win six races and claim the World Drivers' Championship, while Rubens won two and helped the team cruise to the Constructors' title. Brawn GP was rebranded and sold at the end of the season, thus becoming the only team ever to achieve a 100 per cent championship success rate. It just goes to show what you can achieve with a talented team, the willingness to take risks, belief in what you are doing and a healthy helping of luck.

'Today was as high a day as I can remember,' I told the press after that first race in Melbourne. While it was true in a sporting sense, too, they had no idea what I'd got up to the night before. For that matter, sadly neither had I!

*

Strange as it might seem, that night in Melbourne wasn't the craziest experience during my involvement with Formula One. That came a few years later when I found myself sitting in a packed Perth bar in my pants, having my legs shaved. I should probably explain.

After such an amazing experience in Formula 1 sponsoring Brawn to the world championship, we were keen for more – this time as part of the Virgin brand outright. But we quickly discovered we didn't have the financial clout to compete with the big boys like Ferrari and McLaren, who spent hundreds of million on their cars. Instead of going for the title, Virgin Racing had fun battling another new team, Lotus Racing. Their owner, Tony Fernandes, is an old friend who used to work at Virgin Atlantic and Virgin Records. He has done a superb job building up AirAsia, an airline we took a 20 per cent stake in, and it was he who suggested our own competition.

'Richard, our teams are never going to get onto the podium. Let's start a competition of our own. If my team finishes higher than yours, you have to serve as cabin crew on an AirAsia flight. If your team beats mine, I'll serve on one of your flights.'

'On one condition,' I agreed, confident we'd win. 'The loser has to dress in a *stewardess's* uniform.'

It seemed a good idea at the time, but I regretted that at the end of the season, when we lost the bet. Back in Perth, Tony had a massive grin on his face as he ordered me to take off my trousers.

'I'm going to enjoy this,' he smiled, razor in hand.

'I'm not!' I yelped.

Duly humiliated, I headed back to the hotel for some rest before the early flight to Kuala Lumpur – and my crew debut. As I left my hotel for the airport at 4 a.m., Tony was only just returning from a casino, looking slightly the worse for wear.

'Hurry up, Tony,' I joked, 'or you'll miss the plane!'

We made it to the airport, where a make-up artist ordered me to sit still as she tried to apply some bright red lipstick to me. It was a tough job because I couldn't stop laughing. I soon mastered the pout, though, and emerged from the dressing room resplendent in drag. I had a vibrant matching red jacket and skirt, as well as tied-back hair and fishnet stockings. I was most proud of my red shoes, though. Unable to find red high heels to fit my feet, we picked some up from a drag queen shop. I carried them around in hand luggage all week before the flight – and got one or two strange looks from airport security along the way!

When Tony saw me, he couldn't help but laugh. 'Richard, you look far too pretty, despite the beard,' he said.

'Well, you took terrible,' I replied. 'Come on, let's have some fun.'

Flashbulbs lit up my mascara-enhanced eyes as we entered the airport lobby. I planted a kiss on Tony's face, smearing lipstick all over him. He hoisted me up (it made a change from me lifting ladies on our own airline launches!) and we headed onto the flight. After the exertion of picking me up, and with a mammoth hangover to nurse, Tony settled down into his seat to enjoy my service. Armed with a tray full of smoothies, I sneaked up on him.

'Should I do it?' I shouted to the other passengers, the tray balanced precariously in one hand.

'Don't you dare!' exclaimed Tony.

But I couldn't resist, soaking him from head to toe. 'I guess I'm not good at taking orders,' I smiled.

'Damn you,' laughed Tony, as he stripped off and wandered around the plane in a daze, wearing only his pants.

Then it was down to work, carrying out the safety instructions, serving drinks (without too many more spillages), and helping the other passengers. 'Coffee, tea, or me?' read the crews' t-shirts, in a nod to the famously lascivious fictional memoir of Trudy Baker and Rachel Jones, two sixties stewardesses. Thankfully, none of the AirAsia customers chose the third option.

'I've looked up to you for years,' one Aussie passenger quipped, 'now I've looked up your skirt!' I laughed, but when he started talking about me having the whole package, I moved my trolley swiftly along the aisle.

'Why haven't you shaved your beard off, too?' asked another flyer.

'The only time I did that was to launch Virgin Brides,' I explained, 'but Joan didn't like it – I've never been tempted to go clean-shaven since.'

The flight became even more surreal. I was soon spoon-feeding Tony dinner and then listening to some business pitches from budding entrepreneurs. We managed to raise more than $300,000 for the Starlight Foundation from that flight. It was odd sitting in full drag giving serious business advice to people on everything from solar panels to internet start-ups, but it seemed to work.

Finally, we arrived in Malaysia and all got well and truly soaked in champagne. As I removed my make-up in the bathroom, Tony popped his head through the door as I turned on the shower.

'Thanks for being such a good sport, Richard. And just to confirm: you are sacked.'

25 Shoes

One quiet December evening I was sitting on Necker browsing through my iPad when a tweet from a young lady in the US called Shannon Smith jumped out from my screen. She simply said she would like to spend a day in my shoes.

'Will send shoes,' I replied.

Without hesitation, I took my shoes off, walked over to the office and set about sending her my size elevens. We flew the shoes from Necker to the UK, then from London to New York. From there, Virgin America flew the shoes (and a book and t-shirt as Christmas presents for Shannon) to the West Coast. Then some of our Virgin America teammates hand-delivered my shoes to Shannon's door.

'You can keep the shoes on one condition,' I told her. 'You have to wear them for a whole day, or I want them back! Happy holidays.'

Shannon was more than up for the challenge, and upped the ante, too. Not only did she wear the shoes for twenty-four hours, she did it on Christmas Eve while performing her day job, then going on to volunteer at the Ascencia Winter Shelter in Glendale, California. She shuffled around in my too-big trainers while serving homeless people Christmas dinner, handed out gift bags and I'm sure put a huge smile on the faces of many people in need. She even made a video of her day, and doubtless collected some blisters and funny looks.

I was so impressed that I wanted to take the challenge further. Youth homelessness is an issue close to all our hearts at Virgin, and we have worked to tackle it through campaigns like Virgin Mobile's RE*Generation. So, we called on everyone online to tweet the #shoeathon hashtag, and donated to the Ascencia Winter Shelter on behalf of those who did so.

This story, in a nutshell, encapsulates the power of social media: a journey that started with a single tweet read on my iPad ended up making a tangible difference to people's lives.

*

Two of the big changes over the twenty years since I wrote my first autobiography have been the rise of social media and the way the internet has changed the way we consume information.

When I open my mouth I'm never completely sure what is going to happen next. However, 'Joan, have you seen my iPad?' is something I regularly come out with these days. I read every day on my iPad. There will always be a place for the printed word, but it will be increasingly niche as even better tablets and phones are released. I did an interview with the *New York Times* on Valentine's Day 2000, which they headlined 'Taking Virgin's Brand into Internet Territory'. 'Richard Branson says the web is ready for his style of business,' ran the sub-heading. The web may have been ready, but I definitely wasn't, in many ways Virgin wasn't, and this cost us a lot of time and money.

One of the biggest mistakes Virgin ever made was not being fast enough off the mark to become a digital leader. In the past few years one of my focuses has been putting our brand at the forefront of new technology. We put a lot of the errors to bed in the UK with the growth of Virgin Media and its unique business model. From our adverts with Usain Bolt to our WiFi offering on the Tube, it has become one of the main ways the brand is known in Britain.

However, there have been many episodes along the way to learn from.

To begin with, we were extremely quick off the mark when it came to the iPad, and decided to launch the world's first iPad-only magazine, called Project. I joined the team outside Apple's flagship New York store, covered head to toe in newspaper – another one of Jackie McQuillan's arresting outfits. The magazine was great fun, pioneering a new way for people to digest stories. Running Project became even more enjoyable when Rupert Murdoch launched The Daily – his own iPad publication – and we got some friendly competition.

'This is not a battle,' I said at the launch. 'This is not a war. It's the future of publishing. If you'd like to call it a battle, then call it a battle on quality. I think when you see the competition, you might agree that our team win hands-down.' However, as both Rupert and I quickly realised, we had completely misjudged the market and we were publishing into a void. The critical reception was positive, but there weren't enough people with iPads, and certainly not enough willing to pay to read a magazine. Within less than a year, both publications were dead.

I was disappointed that Project didn't work because journalism was where I'd begun all those years before. I started *Student* magazine because I had a passion for making a positive difference in the world, and thought one of the best ways to do so was by spreading the word in print about injustices, as well as sharing new breakthroughs and innovations in arts, culture and politics. While I disliked school, I always loved writing and often posted letters home, published comment pieces in the Stowe School newspaper, and thought about becoming a journalist.

As *Student* took off, I rapidly entered a surreal world of interviewing the likes of Mick Jagger and John Lennon, and commissioning pieces by Jean-Paul Sartre and David Hockney. In 1969, I even wrote an article in the *Daily Mirror* headlined 'Enter The Peaceful Drop-Out'. Aged nineteen, filled with the optimism of youth, I ruminated on the power of individuals to stimulate positive change. But as well as realising my journalistic ambitions through *Student*, I was trying to make ends meet, calling up potential advertisers and organising distribution. Without even knowing what the word meant, I was becoming an entrepreneur. Then, as we struggled to balance our books, the mail order records business we had started in the back of the magazine took off. Simultaneously, we were running the Student Advisory Centre, our non-profit organisation helping more than 500 young people each week cope with issues ranging from loneliness to contraceptive advice to sexuality. With these projects taking up lots of time and effort, *Student* went on the back-burner. Soon Virgin Records' shops and later record label superseded everything and my journalism career was parked.

But while Project wasn't a success, I like to think *Student*'s spirit of outspoken thought and heady fun is revived through a different way of connecting with people: my blog and my Twitter account. In the same way I try to highlight causes we care passionately about, and I hope we've made a difference by campaigning online about global issues ranging from boardroom diversity to ocean conservation. We've basically started our own in-house, online publishing operation, and thanks to social media I'm back in the editor's chair.

To begin with, I was unsure about its benefits. But 20,000 tweets, scores of social networks, forty million followers and a world record for the most LinkedIn followers later, I'm happy to be proved wrong about social media not being here to stay. When Bob Fear and Christine Choi at Virgin HQ first set up my blog and Twitter account, I was surprised when lots of people started asking me questions online. There were random ones like 'How do you make a fig roll?' alongside people with genuine queries about Virgin. It was fun, and I started to realise how powerful Twitter could be. I called Jonno Elliott, my personal investment manager, and we soon ironed out a deal to take part in Twitter's next funding round. It was the start of a new series of investments into technology that I've become keen on pursuing.

As well as the novelty factor, I could see how important social networks could become for customer service, something that has always set Virgin apart. When I was running companies hands on, I always made a point of personally handwriting replies to people who had complaints. Since I didn't enjoy this, I made sure the problems were solved and not repeated. At the end of 2008 I received what is commonly referred to as the funniest complaint letter of all time. The author hadn't enjoyed his meal on a Virgin Atlantic flight from London to Mumbai, and let me know in, frankly, hilarious terms. 'Well, answer me this, Richard, what sort of animal would serve a dessert with peas in?' he wrote about our Indian meal option. 'How can you live like this? I can't imagine what dinner round your house is like; it must be like something out of a nature documentary.' As soon as I read the letter I called the Virgin Atlantic team to ensure our meals were back up to top standard. Then I phoned the unhappy customer, apologised for his below par experience and thanked him for his constructive, if tongue-in-cheek, letter. 'I'm very sorry about this. On the bright side, you really made me laugh, which always helps to get my attention!' Even in social media's early days, it spread like wildfire. Those companies who haven't reacted to the expectations of swift, useful online service will see their customers move to their rivals quicker than you can type 140 characters.

*

People also often question how I find the time to write so regularly; whether notes, letters, blogs, op-eds, or even books like this. But the reality is I'm always getting my thoughts down on paper. The trick is to make it part of your daily routine. You have time to eat, drink, brush your teeth and do dozens of other things every day – just add writing to the list. I jot down ideas, thoughts, requests, reminders and doodles every single day; if I didn't, I would forget them before I could ever put them into action. It doesn't matter if you use a notebook and pen like me, or a shiny new tablet like Holly – the key is making writing a welcome habit. But keep a little pad in your back pocket just in case – you never have to charge a notebook.

Making lists is both a way of remembering things and of ticking off achievements to mark progress. Without notes and follow-ups, chances are nothing would get done. I have met one particular government minister many times who never takes notes; he agrees on things and nothing happens. Another minister I know always takes notes, follows up and gets things done. If somebody works for me and doesn't take notes, I ask them: 'Are you too important? Note taking isn't beneath anyone.' I take notes in every meeting, to keep the frame of mind to learn. I edit as I go along, and follow up with dates and tasks in order of importance. I couldn't have written two autobiographies without them.

Virgin has a note-taking culture and I'm certain it wouldn't be the success it is today without it. The same goes for my assistants. I couldn't get through the work day without Helen. She is my memory, travels the world with me and knows what I am thinking before I ask. Sometimes I feel that assistants work harder than the people they are working for. All of mine over the years – including Helen, Nicki Elliott, Penni Pike, Sue Hale, Saskia Dornan, Sam Cox, Alexia Hargrave, Sarah Ireland, Louella Faria, Emma Dona and Caroline Gold – have shown unbelievable diligence. They really do become part of the family, and are among my greatest friends, too.

My first widely read blog, in early 2010, was about the art of delegation. It was an appropriate theme since delegation has been a secret of my success for five decades. Asking for support is a strength, not a weakness. If you try to do everything yourself, you won't succeed and will make yourself miserable along the way. As a dyslexic, things like spelling and grammar have never come naturally to me. Rather than waste time pondering the difference between 'there', 'they're' and 'their', I find talented people to collaborate with and delegate to. I now work with Greg Rose and our content team on around 600 blogs per year, and call the team several times a day (and night!). If you think that sounds too time-consuming, think of all the things you do that take lots of time and are not productive. Rather than slave over a spreadsheet, why not write a blog and turn your pitch into a story? Humans communicate through stories; it's how we make sense of our surroundings, ourselves and our place in the world. As the writer Lawrence Weschler said in *The New New Journalism*: 'Human beings have glands that secrete all sorts of things. But the human mind secretes stories. We live narratives. That is the only way we know how to experience anything, and it is our glory.'

In 2013 an IMB study found that only 16 per cent of 1,700 CEOs were participating in social media and just one had their own blog. Yet social media is fast becoming the number one way to share stories and engage with customers on a global basis, with no restrictions from media partners, territories or anything else. Every CEO should be online, representing their business, letting their customers as well as their staff into their world, and learning in real time the feedback that could make all the difference to their companies' fortunes. Some organisations still spend tens of thousands of pounds doing surveys hardly anybody bothers filling in, in the hope of finding out what their teams and clients really think. If they just logged online, they could find out a whole lot faster, and have an instant platform to reply, sympathise, share and – as importantly – say thank you.

As I discovered from my dad, nobody ever learned anything by listening to themselves speak. I try to reply to as many people as possible, at least a few every day. If it were a one-way street, there wouldn't be many people walking down it. The whole point is to spark conversation and initiate debate. In fact, put down this book (for a moment!) and tweet me a question using #askrichard – I'll try to answer it. (Thanks for all the brilliant questions so far and I hope my replies have been useful and raised a smile.)

I was sitting in Soho House in New York one September and decided to answer some questions from Facebook over breakfast. There were lots of business queries, and one man asked: 'What was your first big opportunity?' Underneath his question, somebody else asked: 'Who did you lose your virginity with?' I glanced at my screen, took another sip of tea, then chose to tackle the second question. It turned out I had just been in touch with my first girlfriend, a delightful Dutch girl called Rudi. She'd contacted me after half a century to say she'd found some of my old love letters. (We met up later with our families in Amsterdam to reminisce about old times and laugh over my high-on-hormones teenage compositions.) The guy who asked the first question saw my answer and commented: 'Richard, you ignored my serious request and instead answered a silly question about sex. I'm not even disappointed.' In a roundabout fashion I had answered his first question, though – in many ways, losing my virginity was my first big opportunity!

26 Revealing Character

'Sports do not build character,' American journalist Heywood Broun once wrote, 'they reveal it.' I've always found the second half of this statement to be true, and often find out more about potential business partners on the tennis court than in the boardroom. But the first half I am less sure about from my own personal experience: when I first began playing sport, it was the only thing I had to build my own character around.

I was seven years old when I was sent away from my family to boarding school in Sussex. Scaitcliffe Preparatory School was not a happy home for me, as my dyslexia was not diagnosed and the teachers just thought I was simple. I was repeatedly caned for giving wrong answers, failing tests and even walking across the wrong patch of grass. To add insult to injury I had to say: 'Thank you, sir' every time the headmaster caned my backside. I was, like many kids, unhappy, miserable, lonely and longing for escape.

This escape came in sport, when I discovered I had a talent for games. I quickly became the captain of cricket, football and rugby. Being good at sport automatically meant that being bullied by older boys was out of the question, and even the schoolmasters went easier on me. After winning trophies every sports day in my first few years at Scaitcliffe, I had a day to remember just before my eleventh birthday: I won every event I entered. As well as the sprints and distance runs, I triumphed in the long jump on my first ever attempt, breaking a long-held school record in the process. I even learned my first (and probably last) bit of Latin,

'Victor ludorum', which means 'The winner of the games' – another prize I got that day. When I met my sister Lindy and parents in a big white marquee afterwards, I said, 'I've decided I'm going to be a professional sportsman.'

But my sporting career was ended before it really began. The very next term we were playing a football match against a rival school and, after I scored the first goal, the game turned dirty. As I latched onto a through ball and prepared to shoot, the defender marking me slid in to tackle me from behind. He fell across me and my legs buckled, horribly twisting my knee. I let out a bloodcurdling scream, and the next thing I knew the school matron was driving me to hospital. I had badly torn the cartilage in my right knee, and, after injections and an operation, the doctor said it was unlikely I'd play contact sport again. I was distraught.

School took a turn for the worse as I didn't have any athletic achievements to detract from my appalling academic record. Before I even had the chance to fail the Common Entrance exam, I was moved from Scaitcliffe to a 'crammer' school called Cliff View House. There, other than eerie early morning runs on the freezing Sussex coast, there was no sport to distract me. Instead, I found a new diversion in the form of the headmaster's beautiful eighteen-year-old daughter. As an impressionable thirteen-year-old, I was overjoyed that she took a shine to me, and we quickly arranged some late-night liaisons. I was promptly expelled when the headmaster caught me sneaking back through my dormitory window. When he asked what I was doing I replied: 'I was on my way back from your daughter's room, sir.' I only escaped expulsion after pretending I was suicidal and being dragged back from the cliff known as Lovers' Leap. Many years later I was mentioned in the divorce proceedings for the headmaster's daughter, her husband claiming our schoolboy fling forty years earlier had contributed to the end of their marriage. I can't see how, but wish them both all the best.

*

While my dreams of becoming a professional sportsman were never fulfilled, it didn't mean that I couldn't still enjoy the benefits of exercise, and even raise some money for good causes in the process. That opportunity came up in 2010, when my friend Andy Swain called me up to let me know that the sponsorship of the London Marathon was up for grabs.

I'd watched the London Marathon from afar for years, and had always been tempted to give it a go. But I knew it wasn't the kind of event you could just turn up to and perform in – it takes months of preparation. The sponsorship deal seemed just the prod I needed to take part. As soon as I spoke to Andy, I thought it would be perfect for Virgin Money, and got Alex Tai and Jayne-Anne to look into it.

'It's a perfect fit for Virgin,' I told them. 'A great British event that brings all kinds of different people together and gets them active, having fun and pushing each other to their limits.'

The event was already a huge success, but we felt we could shake up its fundraising strategy and raise lots more money for good causes. We set up not-for-profit website Virgin Money Giving to boost online fundraising, making sure all donations went directly to where they were needed most – the charities people train, fundraise and run so hard to support. In each of our first six years the Virgin Money London Marathon broke the fundraising record and the race is now the largest annual single-day charity fundraising event worldwide, with £830 million raised since it began in 1981.

If we were going to sponsor the marathon, I knew at some point I was going to have to put my trainers on. When the call came asking if I would run, I immediately said yes – then forgot about it for a few months. It was a busy time, and I didn't have much chance to add running to my schedule. Since injuring my knee as a child I hadn't done any serious running and I wasn't sure if my cartilage would cope. My regular kitesurfing and tennis would surely keep my fitness ticking over, and I'd worry about the running part later, or so my logic went. In the meantime, my kids went about rallying their own amazing team to tackle the marathon. They set up a charity to accelerate change for young people in the UK, and convinced their friends to join in an audacious fancy-dress record attempt to mark the launch. Big Change was born, and soon thirty-four friends could be seen tied together on training runs around west London. They challenged themselves to become the most people joined together ever to complete the 26.2-mile marathon course – all while dressed as a giant caterpillar. Perhaps it was all those Eric Carle bedtime stories I had read Sam and Holly while they were growing up? When I heard how hard they were training, I realised I needed to shape up. I began running around Necker each morning and stopped eating my favourite chocolate digestives. By the time the day came, I felt confident I could make it around the course.

It was a roasting hot day in London that Sunday morning in late April 2010. The crowds were hot, never mind the runners at the start line: I, meanwhile, was the hottest of the lot, dressed as a gigantic butterfly at the head of Team Caterpillar, sweating out of fear about what I'd let myself in for. But as the miles started ticking by, the crowd seemed to get louder and louder. To my surprise I found that, though my legs ached like never before, the enthusiasm and support of both the crowd and my fellow competitors kept me going. Fellow runners kept stopping to shake my hand, and the atmosphere was one of pure delight. It was great running with such a strong team, with Kenyan athletics legend Tegla Loroupe and my friend Natalie Imbruglia among them.

It was tough going dressed as a butterfly: the fabric was heavier than it looked and really slowed me up running into the wind. But soon I had bigger problems. I was advised to take some energy gel when I felt tired, and Nick passed it to me around the fifteen-mile mark, as we passed News International's HQ. I immediately felt my stomach grumble, and began groaning. I started to panic that I was going to shit myself, dressed as a giant butterfly, in front of thousands of people – what a way to launch the Virgin London Marathon! Thankfully, Tegla saw what was going on and quickly gave me a pill to settle my stomach. It was a close call!

As we turned into the home straight, I looked across at the union flags flying in the breeze and my kids just behind with beaming smiles on their faces. It was one of the proudest moments of my life. Team Caterpillar broke the Guinness World Record, while Princess Beatrice, one part of the caterpillar, became the first member of the royal family to complete the marathon. Somehow, I made it round in 5 hours, 2 minutes and 24 seconds. If you want advice on how to tackle a marathon, I can tell you from experience that it's simple: don't worry if you fall flat on your face – at least you're still moving forward!

After the marathon, I had a taste for trying more sporting challenges with my children, and getting Virgin involved, too. In 2012 Virgin Active began sponsoring the London Triathlon, the largest of its kind in the world. I joined up with my kids again to take part in a relay team including David Hasselhoff, who I had last seen when making a guest appearance on *Baywatch*. The Hoff gave me some unusual advice in case I got myself in a spot where I didn't want to get recognised.

'I always carry a mask of my own face in my back pocket,' he told me, rather bizarrely. 'Think about it. If people are looking for you, the last place they expect to find you is behind a mask of your own face.'

Mask-free, we enjoyed a great day swimming, running and cycling around the capital alongside 14,000 other triathlon enthusiasts.

*

Marathons and triathlons aside, sport and exercise have long formed part of my daily routine. I start every day on Necker with a walk around the island, before heading down to the tennis courts for a game. We're fortunate to have a tennis professional on the island to put me through my paces as well as to help guests improve their games.

One of the first coaches we hired was Arthur Hicks, who had impressed Sam while giving him lessons at Virgin Active in London.

'He sounds perfect,' I told Sam. 'Offer him the job right away.'

Sam called Arthur up while he was driving home from the local supermarket in his banged-up 1972 VW Beetle, struggling to see through the torrential rain. He was approaching a roundabout as Sam phoned, and upon seeing his name on the screen, chose the only suitable option available to him if he didn't want to miss the call: he drove straight onto the roundabout and parked. Rustling Sainsbury's bags, driving rain on his metal roof, blaring horns and curses from passing motorists were just some of the things he had to contend with as he began a life-changing conversation.

'I was wondering if you have ever heard of Necker?' Sam asked him.

'Um ... yes, I believe Muslims pilgrimage across the Sahara Desert to get there, don't they?'

'Ha, ha! Yeah, sure they do! Well, would you be interested in working there?'

'Working there as what?'

'As a tennis coach.'

Arthur was confused. He had never been to the Middle East, and didn't really know much about the region. However, leaving the wet London winter for the roasting desert sounded attractive. 'Yeah, OK,' he told Sam. 'I'll do it!'

That evening, Arthur related his tale to his dad, who listened all the way through with a look of utter confusion on his face. With fatherly wisdom, he opened his laptop and typed 'Richard Branson, Mecca' into the search engine.

'You, my son, are an idiot,' he laughed, showing him the screen where Google had asked 'Do you mean "Richard Branson, Necker?"'

Arthur did a great job coaching tennis on Necker for our guests, as well as improving my own baseline game. He kindly described it as 'the best tennis-coaching job in the world'. Thanks in part to Arthur and his successors Mike and Josh, I'm still yet to lose a match to either Holly or Sam, despite their best efforts. I made a friendly bet in 1995 that they wouldn't beat me before I turned sixty-five. Winning the bet was an especially happy birthday present. One day, kids, one day!

I love going to watch the world's greatest tennis players battle it out on major occasions like Wimbledon and the US Open. I always look forward to visiting SW19, though usually fall foul of their rule-making. I had to borrow a tie a few years ago just to get into the Royal Box (since being knighted I am invited every year). As I've mentioned, as a rule I always avoid ties, but as I was Martina Navratilova's guest on this occasion I had to tie the dreaded knot around my neck.

The UK has greatly benefited in recent years from the superb example set by Andy Murray, who has inspired so many people to pick up a racket. The past decade has been a golden age of tennis, and for a Brit to be fighting toe to toe – and reaching world number one – against all-time greats Roger Federer, Novak Djokovic and Rafael Nadal is incredible. But, watching him, I find myself recalling one huge opportunity that got away from us.

Eleven years earlier, I got a phone call from Peter Norris. A fellow tennis fanatic, he excitedly told me how he had just watched the best young player he'd ever seen. His name was Andy Murray, he was sixteen and he was convinced he would one day win Wimbledon. I immediately got in touch with Andy's mum, Judy, and arranged to meet them both for lunch, with a view to Virgin Active sponsoring him. We went to a small restaurant we owned at the time in Oxfordshire called Le Petit Blanc and talked over Andy's prospects over a delightful meal. He was quiet, respectful and very polite. I also had a quiet word with his mum at the end of the meal. I asked about Andy's injuries – he had a lengthy lay-off with a split patella – but Judy assured me they were simply growing pains. We got on very well and I went away determined to sign him up. I called up

Matthew and Frank right away and urged them to do the deal. Somehow, as sometimes happens in these situations, it didn't work out. However, it's no surprise Peter went on to become Virgin Group chairman. If anyone can spot a future Wimbledon champion a decade earlier, his business intuition is fine with me.

I got a taste of what it's like to be on the receiving end of Andy's serves when I was invited to play a charity match at Queen's Club alongside him, Tomáš Berdych, Tim Henman and Jonathan Ross. The then Mayor of London Boris Johnson was even on the court, dressed like a player from the 1920s, with a wooden racket to match! It whetted my appetite for more competition between the best players in the world and amateurs keen to take them on. However, rather than in the austere settings of professional sporting institutions, why not hold a tournament with a party atmosphere? I've always believed that if you see a way to improve on something, go ahead and do it yourself. With that in mind, we set up our own tennis tournament. While it wouldn't have the ranking points or prestige of Flushing Meadows or Roland Garros (just yet!) it would have a few subtle differences: lemurs on the sidelines, parrots flying overhead and shots of tequila for the players!

The idea for our very own tennis cup on Necker came from Mike Richards, another former tennis pro on the island. 'We can turn the idea of a tennis tournament completely on its head,' he explained, when pitching me his plan. 'It will be a serious sporting contest, a family festival and a week-long party rolled into one. We'll play by different rules on and off the court. Plus, we'll raise lots of money for Virgin Unite and other great causes.'

Mike is the kind of entrepreneur I often gravitate towards – one who doesn't even realise he is one until he starts a project. He was untried, or, as I like to think of it, uninhibited by too much experience, and full of fresh ideas. Mike told me he'd get ten top current pros and tennis legends signed up, but by the time the US Open came around in September we hadn't secured any big names. At

Flushing Meadows, I shared the idea with Novak Djokovic and his delightful wife Jelena; thankfully they loved it immediately. They kindly agreed to auction a package at the Djokovic Foundation's New York event to play with Novak at the Necker Cup. One down, but we needed to sell another nine to cover our costs.

As we arrived at the Capitale Gala, we were (in Mike's immortal words) 'shitting a brick'. We needn't have worried. Plenty of offers came in to play with Novak, and also to take me on.

'I'll pay £140,000 to play with McEnroe!' shouted a guy at the back.

John McEnroe? We didn't even know if he was there. Suddenly, the spotlight was on Mac, who nodded his head and said, 'Sure, why not?'

The auctioneer kept it going, and I could hear excited yelps coming from Mike's pocket, where his fellow organisers were listening in on speakerphone. 'I think I'm melting into my chair,' he whispered.

I'm not sure what the likes of Novak Djokovic and Rafael Nadal were hoping for when they arrived for the Necker Cup, but I'm pretty sure we surpassed their expectations. The first night of the 2013 tournament started the day after the professional tour's last event ended, so the players could let their hair down. I found myself standing at the bar with Boris Becker on my right and Rafa on my left. Before we'd dispensed with any pleasantries, tequila shots were being poured.

'So this how they do it on the ATP Tour?' We laughed before taking another shot.

One of the unique features of the tournament is pitting members of the public, including Virgin Active competition winners, against the stars. The pros know just how to go easy enough to make it fun, but still keep it ultra-competitive. In my heart of hearts, I know the top players could swat me aside if they really had to, but I love competing with them on as level a footing as possible, and doing my best to hold my own.

After losing the first Necker Cup (I must admit, that Djokovic is a very handy player), I was determined to win out in the second year. Jimmy Buffet challenged me to a special doubles exhibition match, with the loser donating a big sum to charity.

'Fine,' I told him. 'Plus, if I win, you have to play a free concert here tonight. If you win, I'll send you to space.'

Jimmy snapped up my offer. 'One thing,' he added. 'I'm picking my own partner.'

Jimmy brought in world number one doubles player Mike Bryan as his partner. I was worrying how I could compete, when I spotted Rafa Nadal walking down the beach. After I convinced the then world number one singles player to join me, I was more confident. The stage was set for an epic match. It was going well, with Boris Becker and the Cuban Brothers compering, much to the crowd's amusement. The lemurs were hollering and the parrots squawking. I'm trying to get the macaws to say 'great shot, Richard' rather than simply 'hello', but haven't quite managed it yet.

On court, Jimmy and Mike had the upper hand, but we dug in. As with any great tennis match, it all came down to the final game. The ball dropped to my left, and for some unknown reason I tried a backhand volleyed drop shot. To my amazement and delight, it dropped against the line to win the match. If sport does reveal character, as Heywood Broun suggested, then I guess the fact I took a risk-taking shot at such a crucial moment tells you plenty about who I am. That it went in tells you I really am a jammy bastard. The music was good that night!

27 Dad

However important business is, family always comes first. Which is why, in early March 2011, I arranged my schedule so as to be able to fly from New York to England, to be there in time for my father's ninety-third birthday.

The whole family were there for the celebrations at his house in Cakeham, Sussex. And while the weather made for an absolutely beautiful few days down by the sea, what I really remember is sitting around the fire in the evening as Dad regaled us with stories from his youth. He has always been a terrific storyteller, much like my Uncle Charlie, and could send me off to faraway places in my mind within a matter of moments through his wonderful wordplay. Whether it was thrilling me with accounts of landing on the beaches of Salerno during the Second World War, amusing me with tales of his early romances, or moving me with anecdotes about his own childhood, I'm sure I got my own love for sharing stories from him.

Dad's life, like that of so many, had been shaped by the events of the day. He had a passion for swimming, representing Cambridge University in the pool, and was in line to swim for England when the Second World War broke out. Joining up, he was sent straight to North Africa, later seeing action in tanks in the Middle East, Italy and Germany. When he returned to England, Dad found it tough to get through his studies, but dutifully followed his own father and many generations of Branson men into the legal profession. What he really wanted to do was become an archaeologist: while in North Africa he spent a lot of his time collecting fossils in the desert, hiding them before he shipped out for Salerno. Years later, we went back and collected them and I still treasure them.

Given how much he'd supported me over the years in pursuing my own dreams, I was delighted when I got the opportunity to return the favour. One day I got a call from a balloonist in Egypt, where we had launched the first hot-air balloon company flying over the Valley of the Kings.

'I've been flying across the Valley,' the balloonist shouted down the line, sounding incredibly excited. 'I was about a hundred yards from the bottom, when I saw a ledge. There was a big stone blocking something and I think I could make out hieroglyphics on the wall. Richard, I think it might be an undiscovered tomb!'

I thought he was pulling my leg, but he assured me it wasn't a joke.

'Get out here quick,' he insisted, 'and I'll show you.'

I immediately made two phone calls. The first was to the British Museum to speak to an expert in ancient Egyptian history. She assured me it was very possible there were undiscovered tombs in the area our balloonist was navigating:

'It could well be Ramesses VIII's tomb,' she told me. 'If so, it could make Tutankhamen's look like Woolworths.'

The next call I made was to my dad. 'Pack your bags,' I told him. 'We're going to Egypt.'

As we flew to Luxor together, we decided we weren't going to let anybody know what we were doing. We met up with the balloonist and he gave us rough coordinates of where he had seen the site. Getting there was extremely tough – hot-air balloons tend to go where the weather takes them. After five days, we found absolutely nothing. Although I was disappointed, Dad was in his element. He was researching legends, finding more artefacts and looked the part in his wide-brimmed hat and khakis, too. It was the closest he ever came to becoming an archaeologist.

Back in Cakeham, I sat up with Dad late into the night, telling stories and laughing together. Now into his nineties,

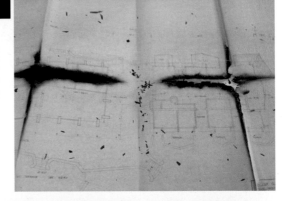

August 2011
Terrifying moment watching the Necker fire burn the Great House down

August 2011
The original Necker Island blueprints, rescued from the Great House fire

August 2011
Kate Winslet recreating her rescue of Mum from the Great House fire, the morning after on Necker Island

2011
Rebranding Virgin
Australia with
John Borghetti
and the team

October 2011
The out-of-
this-world view
from Spaceport
America in New
Mexico

December 2011
Toasting Holly and Freddie's wedding on Necker, exactly 22 years after I married Joan

February 2012
Jumping into freezing
water on a climate
change fact-finding
mission in Antarctica

February 2012
With Kim Kardashian
and Britney Spears at
the pre-GRAMMY
Gala in LA

September 2012
Preparing to climb
Mont Blanc with my
kids and friends

Chamonix-Mont-Blanc France: 1036 m - 4809 m

October 2012
Hugs with the Virgin Trains team after we won back the West Coast Main Line franchise

November 2012
Introducing tennis great Novak Djokovic to Necker's thriving ring-tailed lemurs

November 2012
It's only rock 'n' roll but I like it! With The Rolling Stones in London. Left to right: Promotor Paul Dainty, Charlie Watts, Keith Richards, me, Mick Jagger, Ronnie Wood

November 2012
Swimming (and posing!) with tiger sharks
and lemon sharks in the Bahamas

December 2012
Proud of Sam's film documenting
the global war on drugs

February 2013
Talking business with Jayne-Anne
Gadhia at Virgin Money in Newcastle

March 2013
Sam and I with
some of our
Guinness World
Records
(I have seven
and counting!)

March 2013
Leading the way uphill at the Cape
Argus Cycle Race in South Africa

May 2013
Coffee, tea or me? Serving Tony
Fernandes while working as Air Asia
cabin crew after losing a bet

Circa 2013
Looking out at the Great Migration from Mahali Mzuri, Kenya

September 2013
Breaking the Taboo with the Global Commission on Drug Policy in Geneva, Switzerland. Left to right: me, Kofi Annan, Ernesto Zedillo, Fernando Henrique Cardoso, César Gaviria, Ruth Dreifuss, Michel Kazatchkine, Jorge Sampaio, Thorvald Stoltenberg

November 2013
Freddie, Holly, Sam and Bellie pushing me into the pool at the Temple on Necker Island

November 2013
Welcome to our home

November 2013
The closest siblings any parents could wish for, Sam and Holly all smiles on Necker

Circa 2013
I love relaxing at the Lodge, our stunning ski resort in Verbier, Switzerland

Circa 2013
The Roof Gardens in London, scene of some of the best Virgin parties

Circa 2013
Rock lodge at Ulusaba, our incredible safari hideaway in South Africa

November 2013
Celebrating Rafa Nadal and my win over Jimmy Buffett and Mike Bryan at the Necker Cup

December 2013
Launching a new Virgin Active health club in Madrid

2014
One of my 20 cups of tea per day, looking out to sea on Necker

January 2014
Fun, fast filming with Usain Bolt in Jamaica

February 2014
Floating on a zero gravity
flight with some of the Virgin
Galactic family

March 2014
Meeting the inspirational
Malala

May 2014
Kisses for Love Field after winning Virgin America's battle for slots

May 2014
Another tie bites the dust!

June 2014
Sharing a joke at Virgin HQ in London with our chairman – and Holly's mentor – Peter Norris

July 2014
Happy 90th birthday, Mum! Celebrating with the family on Necker Island

Circa 2014
Over the moon with SpaceShipTwo's supersonic test flight

2014
Space is Virgin territory: WhiteKnightTwo and SpaceShipTwo on a test flight above Mojave skies

August 2014
Getting animated on
The Simpsons

September 2014
Selfie time with Virgin Atlantic

September 2014
Sam retching on top of the Matterhorn,
before I watched a helicopter rescue him.
Left to right: Stephen Shanly, Sam, my
nephew Noah

September 2014
Sam and Noah on top of the Matterhorn –
just before Sam was rescued from the
peak by helicopter

Pete Siebold lifts his right fist
to signal he is alive after being
thrown out of SpaceShipTwo in
mid-air. He was one of the first
people in history to walk away
from a supersonic accident

October 2014
SpaceShipTwo's test flight accident

October 2014
Whole team
hug after
SpaceShipTwo's test
flight accident

2014
With the B Team in
New York in 2014

January 2015
Proud
grand-dude!
Joan and I
babysitting
newborn
grandkids
Etta, Artie
and Eva-Deia

his brain remained as sharp as ever, though he'd had to slow down a little; he had a really bad hip that couldn't be operated on because of sores on his legs, so he couldn't travel as much as he once had. The conversation came around to Holly and Freddie's upcoming wedding. A few months earlier, I'd been sitting on the balcony up at Rock Lodge, Ulusaba, looking over the plains as elephants roamed below, when Freddie had rung. He was the young man Holly had met at school, and had been by her side ever since. Freddie is a smart operator – after a sterling career in shipping he joined Virgin's investment team. He has been instrumental in creating and helping build Virgin Sport, our new business creating festivals of sport that combine running and fitness challenges with community celebrations. But, far more importantly, he has loved and respected my daughter unreservedly from day one. So it was no surprise that I was getting the call; and after pretending I was too busy to arrange to see him, I put Freddie out of his misery and offered him my blessing and congratulations.

A week or so after the party, I rang Dad up to talk about the arrangements for the big day: Holly and Freddie had decided they wanted to get married on the same date and in the same place as Joan and I had: 20 December, on Necker Island. Dad listened carefully, and then stopped me in my tracks with his reply.

'I really hope you all have a wonderful time,' he said simply.

As he spoke, I understood what he meant. It was like an arrow through the heart. I think he must have known he only had a few hours left. That night, 19 March 2011, he died peacefully in his sleep.

I was devastated. However far away we had been from each other in terms of distance, we had always remained extremely close. Dad felt as constant a part of my life as the sun rising and setting each day. He had lived as full a life as anybody could wish. Like Joan, Dad never embraced celebrity, but he was by my side in the quietest, gentlest, most loving way possible, since the day I was born. I thought back to the day he walked me up and down the garden in Shamley Green when I was thinking about quitting school. He told me he wanted me to qualify as a barrister, as his father had told him a generation earlier. Then, acknowledging the parallels with his own life and realising he wanted me to do whatever would make me happiest, we did another lap of the lawn: 'Richard, forget everything I just said. Do whatever you want to do. Your mum and I will be right behind you, all the way.' He was true to his word.

Thinking of Dad, my mind transported me back to Mrs Avenall's sweet shop, near our home when I was six years old. My little sister Lindy and I had climbed onto a chair to 'borrow' five shillings from Dad's top drawer, where he kept his change. We walked to the shop and exchanged our five shillings for piles of wonderful sweets. Before Mrs Avenall handed them over she rang my dad. He rushed straight over. 'I think your children must have stolen some money from you, Mr Branson.' My father looked her straight in the eye: 'How dare you accuse my children of stealing!' We left the shop, Dad never said anything about it again – and we never stole again. That was Dad: wise, kind and fiercely loyal.

Dad had always loved spending time on Necker and enjoyed studying the animals, often wandering off on an island walk with his trusty binoculars in hand. He also appreciated Necker as the place where he had spent so much time making memories with his family. So it was no surprise that, before he died, he asked me to have his ashes brought to Necker Island when the time came. He wanted them scattered at the far end of the island, where he could be among his loved ones in the beautiful natural habitat he revered so much.

I was the only one in the family who didn't attend the service at the crematorium. I stayed away, not because I was so upset to lose him, but because I wanted to remember him as he was in life. I have never for a moment regretted that decision. As Joan put it best: 'Everybody grieves in different ways, and we should all accept that.' But I was there for the wonderful get-together we had later on Necker to scatter the ashes, full of love, laughter and joy – just like Dad. All of his family and friends came to celebrate his incredible life, which had been his greatest adventure of all.

Dad died a happy man. The only way you can do that is by filling your life with purpose and love: what you give, what you do, how you treat people and how you make them feel. Whenever Dad is brought up in conversation, it isn't long before everyone is rolling around laughing, recalling one of his many anecdotes, adventures and 'Ted-isms'. He taught me how to get people's attention and affection through stories, how to see the humour in everything, how to wear my heart on my sleeve. Most of all, he taught me what it means to be a father and a man. Together with my mum, he showed me why it is so important to put others before yourself, and why it is crucial to live every day as if it is your last.

A few years later, my friend Suhail Rizvi's father passed away, and he sent me a lovely note that also reflects how I feel about my dad. 'As a child he taught me how to live, as an adult he taught me how to parent. When I thought he had nothing left to teach me, he taught me how to die with grace and dignity.' After Dad's death, it did make me think about my own mortality a bit more, about Joan, about Holly and Sam and my family. I'm sixty-seven, my wife has turned seventy and our children are in their thirties. I vividly remember thinking when Holly was born that when she reached her thirties I really would be old. So, although I hope to live into my nineties, like my parents, it is natural to think about the end a little more.

We all have to accept our own vulnerability – one fact of life is that it doesn't go on forever. While I don't think it is important where one's physical remains are put, I will take up a little piece of the place I love most – Necker. I would be pleased to be buried at the remote, far end of the island under a few stones, with wildlife all around. But I wouldn't want everybody to gather sombrely when it happens. In fact, I would recommend people turn up in swimming costumes, with colour blazing, drums beating, humour abounding and love surrounding all. I would like a joyful celebration of my life, not a sad mourning of my death. I think the most pleasing thing for myself and Joan is that we have two fantastic kids who have found two wonderful partners. I'd be very surprised if they aren't married for life, as Joan and I have stayed together. I am happy my legacy will live on with my family, and making a difference like Dad did. He had a kind word for everyone, an infectious laugh, a cheeky streak and a thirst for exploration that I am immensely proud to have inherited. His favourite phrase was: 'Isn't life wonderful?' It truly is, though a little less wonderful without him.

*

A few years before his death, my father had passed on some sage advice to my nephew, Jack Brockway. They'd been together on a boat, and Jack had told Dad how he'd heard a sound in the night, decided it was probably nothing and ignored it. Although on that occasion, there had been no problem, my father had chided him for not checking.

'You should always take a look if you hear something unusual at night,' he told him, 'especially if there are older people with you. It only takes a minute to check, and it could make all the difference'.

On 22 August 2011, Dad's advice saved our family's lives. It was four in the morning and I was asleep in my bed on Necker Island. Outside, torrential rain was lashing against our bedroom window, but tropical storms are relatively common in these parts, so when I woke up and stole a glance at Joan sleeping soundly beside me, I just turned over and closed my eyes again. A few hundred yards away, twenty of our closest friends and family, including Mum, Holly, Sam, Jack, Kate Winslet and my nephew Ned Rocknroll, were sleeping soundly in the Great House.

The danger, however, was greater than anyone realised, with wild winds whipping the palm trees and blowing in an

almighty lightning storm: one of those huge bolts of lightning had hit the roof and set it on fire. When Jack woke up,
having once again heard a strange noise, he remembered
my dad's advice and got out of bed to look. What he saw was
200-foot-high flames engulfing the Great House and ran to
raise the alarm. Sam, who was staying in the house next to
ours, heard the commotion, too. He opened his door and
saw a blood-red sky before his eyes. He ran to my bedroom
and banged his fist against the window.

'Fire at the Great House!' he shouted. 'Fire! Fire! Fire!
Fire!'

It was one of those stomach-wrenching moments you
hope you will never experience. Jack ran right into the
flaming house with no hesitation. I charged out of my home
stark naked, running to catch Sam as fast as I could. With the
hurricane-speed wind rushing around me in the darkness,
all I could see was the fire. It was at this moment that I fell,
family jewels first, into a cactus. That was excruciatingly
painful, but nothing compared with the horrible feeling in
my stomach knowing Holly and Mum were inside the house.
I disentangled myself and rushed to help, my heart racing.

It was like a scene from a horror movie. Jack was already
in the house, leaping from room to room hollering, helping
half-asleep kids, grandparents and adults out of the building
as it collapsed around them. Fear struck my heart as I
arrived at the house when I saw nobody had emerged. Then
out of the smoke came Kate carrying my mum, followed by
her kids and all my nephews and nieces. As the wind was
howling and the rain was screaming down, one thought
dominated my mind: where was Holly? Had she woken up?
Was she still alive? Then there she was, running towards me
and hugging me as we retreated from the house. In a matter
of minutes, but what seemed like hours, everyone got out
before the fumes overcame them.

As I stood staring in disbelief as the fire raged, I suddenly
remembered my notebooks. Not thinking, I dived back
into the house to try to rescue them, along with my personal photographs. I could see the fire coming down the

corridor – my office was halfway down and I made a run for it. As I threw open my office door I could smell burning wood. The roof and one of the walls were on fire. But the brown cabinet where the notebooks and photographs were kept was not yet alight. I hesitated for a moment in the doorway, saying to myself: how important are these things? Do I really want to risk diving in there and trying to save them, at the risk I could get trapped myself?

Common sense prevailed.

It's not worth it, I realised.

Get out.

It was the right decision. As I shut the door, I flinched at the sudden pain and realised the handle was already white-hot. I ran back down the burning corridor and out into the pouring rain to join the others. We huddled together in shock as our home burnt before our eyes. I turned to see Kate's fearless young children, ten-year-old Mia and seven-year-old Joe, clinging tightly to their mother.

'Everything's gone,' I heard someone say.

I thought of the lifetime of diaries and photographs disappearing up in smoke and I turned to Mia and Joe.

'Remember, it's not material things that matter in life,' I told them. 'Things aren't important, people are. All that matters is that everyone is safe.'

The torrential rain mingled with tears running down my face, but as soon as we were certain everyone had escaped unharmed, all I felt was overwhelming relief. There was nothing we could do for the building: being on a remote island in the middle of a tropical storm, it was no easy task for the fire service to make the dangerous crossing to Necker. Plus, with so much of the Great House built of wood, the fire rapidly consumed it.

The fire burnt on long into the morning and we began to think about what we had lost, and what we were so lucky to have clung onto. I counted my lucky stars that everyone was OK. We all gave lots of hugs to Mia and Joe, who are among the bravest children I've ever met. Kate couldn't remember as dramatic a scene in any of her Hollywood films.

'I was wondering when a director was going to shout CUT,' she said.

Humour is usually the best way to deal with a crisis, and we must have looked funny clustered together on the beach, the flames still flickering in the background like the end of a summer blockbuster. I stared into the whites of my family's eyes, shining bright out of their soot-covered faces, and couldn't help but smile. Joan and I told stories about the kids growing up in the house. I remembered teaching Sam how to play chess, sitting in my favourite spot with Joan on the balcony looking out at the sunset, smelling the sea, and many nights dancing on the tables. After this bittersweet reminiscing, we pulled out a large blank sheet of paper and began talking about how we could rebuild the house as soon as possible, making it bigger and better than before. I was determined that our wonderful team would stay in the jobs they loved while we did so.

The guests were all scheduled to leave that day, but every single one of them stayed on in solidarity, sleeping on floors and helping to clean up. I was very touched by the way they pitched in. It was surreal watching the sun rise over the island, as the storm continued to rage around us. The next morning two policemen came over to inspect the blaze. I stood with Joan, Ned and Holly near the foot of the Great House, and saw the policemen gazing up at the house. Then they went to the poolside bar, opened the fridge and pulled out two cans of Red Stripe. We looked at them, they looked back at us and we all smiled. What else could we do?

The fire continued to burn for three days. I began walking in the ruins of the house, feeling haunted and lost, but thankful it was only material possessions lying in the rubble around my feet. I could smell the cinders of my treasured notebooks and our family photos, burnt to a crisp, decades of ideas and memories gone forever. Then, as I looked down, I saw another survivor of the fire – Esio Trot, our favourite red-footed tortoise. His stunning rosy feet and beautifully patterned shell were horribly scorched and he was making his way precariously out of the still burning wreckage. I picked him up and rushed him over to Vaman, Necker's conservation manager, for some emergency treatment. A few years on, Esio has fully recovered and gone on to successfully breed – though his feet and shell still bear the scars of the fire.

There was another happy consequence of the disaster, too. As Kate and her kids stayed on to help clean up, she fell head over heels in love with my nephew Ned. The day before the fire Kate and I had re-enacted a classic scene from *Titanic*, recreating her iconic pose on the bow of my boat *Necker Belle*. I happily took on Leo DiCaprio's role. With arms outstretched, she whispered, 'I'm flying, Richard!' A day later she was escaping a burning building. A day after that, she fell in love. Within a year, she and Ned were married and now have a beautiful baby boy together named Bear Blaze. Meanwhile, Mum – stubborn and independent as ever in her ninetieth year – was already beginning to deny receiving any help whatsoever to escape the fire.

I kept thinking back to my dad. If he hadn't had that conversation with Jack, it's quite likely everybody would have died. He was certainly watching over us. I don't believe that everything happens for a reason. But I do believe that, whatever happens, you can learn from it and create something really positive. Better things can come out of adversity. Like a phoenix from the flames, I was sure the Great House would rise up again even more beautiful than before.

*

Even though the fire took place less than six months before Holly and Freddie were planning on getting married, we were all determined the wedding should go ahead. As we discussed different options, it was Holly who came up with a great idea as to how to proceed.

'Why not get married in the ruins of the Great House?' she suggested.

We all loved the plan, and set about making something wonderful out of the wreckage. It would make it unique as, with the builders moving in the following day, it was a spot on which nobody else could ever again get married. It also meant that the venue was open to the skies, so a marquee had been erected in case of rain. This I wasn't so sure about.

'Don't you think it would look more beautiful without the tent?' I asked Joan and Holly.

Their stony looks quickly told me I should keep out of it and let the ladies decide – the marquee stayed. It was the right call: when I woke up on the morning of the wedding, for the first few hours it rained like I hadn't seen since the Great House fire. The sea became incredibly rough and guests couldn't make it over to the island for the ceremony. Some hardy souls did manage to swim to the shore, but things weren't exactly going to plan. I turned to Joan in bed as we watched the rain hammer down.

'I'm worried we're going to have to cancel the wedding,' I said.

But as Holly came rushing in to see us, throwing an umbrella aside, we gave her the biggest hug in the world and I knew it was all going to work out. I couldn't believe how beautiful and grown up she looked in her sparkling white dress.

'I'm so, so proud of you,' I told her.

By the time of the ceremony, the weather had transformed into a beautiful day and all of our guests made it to the celebration. As Holly took hold of my arm to walk up to the special altar, I savoured every step, even though inside I was more nervous than I could ever remember being. I tried to hold back the tears, but then caught the eye of Sam sitting in the front row. He was crying with joy during the ceremony, while I hung on tightly to Joan's arm and smiled with pure happiness.

For Holly and Freddie's first dance, we had covered over part of the swimming pool. For the music, their favourite singer Ed Sheeran played (he'd become a superstar since agreeing to perform, but being one of the nicest people one could hope to meet, he stuck to his promise and turned up).

I found myself remembering the words of my father, shortly before he died. 'I really hope you all have a wonderful time', he'd said. Looking around at friends and family enjoying themselves, it was clear that everyone was following his wishes. I took Joan's hand and joined the others in dancing the night away.

28 Like a Rolling Stone

Towards the end of the 1990s, I began to get that creeping feeling that modern music was passing me by. More and more regularly I would find myself reverting to my old favourites – The Sex Pistols, Peter Gabriel, Pink Floyd and Bob Marley – when playing records. There was a period when I spun Mike Oldfield's wonderful *Ommadawn* album on repeat.

'I genuinely can't think of a new artist I want to hear,' I told Joan. I was sounding like a stereotypical grumpy old man, and knew that something needed to change.

A few years earlier, I had sold Virgin Records to Thorn EMI in order to give Virgin Atlantic the financial clout to compete with British Airways. Having signed a contract agreeing not to start another record company for at least five years, I had to watch from the sidelines as Virgin Records continued in its new form without me. There was too much talent for it to fail: one of my original partners, Ken Berry, was still at the helm, and new artists like Massive Attack, Soul II Soul, Daft Punk and The Chemical Brothers pushed the label forward. Virgin Records maintained our brand in the market and I was still proud to see acts like The Spice Girls bringing girl power to the mainstream at the BRITS in 1997, and The Verve setting the tone for guitar music as Britpop came and went. Even so, it hurt not to be involved.

As soon as I was legally allowed to start a new label, I put my Mike Oldfield records away and got back into the game by launching V2 Records. Our first signing, The Stereophonics, were soon climbing up the bills at festivals and won the Best Newcomers award at the 1998 BRITS. Now there were new artists I really wanted to hear. We went on to nurture the likes of Moby, Elbow and The White Stripes and I loved being back in the business I used to live and breathe.

But even as we were building this new wave of success, the writing was on the wall for the old way of running a record label. In 1999 Sean Parker launched Napster, the innovative peer-to-peer file-sharing site. It started to change the way consumers thought about music, from a physical object they could purchase and cherish into a virtual product they could consume for free. While Napster was gone by 2002, Steve Jobs had in the meantime revolutionised the music business all over again. In October 2001, around eight months after launching iTunes, Apple released the first iPod. Now there was a slick service for people to download music on cheaply, and a stylish device to play it on.

When I spoke to Steve about the iPod, he told me he had got his inspiration from an idea I'd had back in the eighties. I gave an interview to *Music Week* on 1 April 1986 revealing we were secretly developing a Music Box, which could store every song in the world, and allow people to download any music they wanted for a small fee. 'BRANSON'S BOMBSHELL' ran the headline. Four giant computers around Britain would store all the music and it would spell 'the end of the music industry as we know it'. Scientists at a top-secret location I couldn't reveal 'due to fears of industrial espionage' had designed the technology, I claimed. That afternoon, my phone was ringing off the hook with nervous record company CEOs who begged us to cancel the idea. At noon, we put them out of their misery and let them know it was an April Fool.

When I met Steve in San Francisco many years later, he smiled at me and said: 'Loved the article, by the way.'

'Which article?'

'The Music Box – I loved the concept. Always thought it was a good idea.'

When the technology caught up with his imagination, the result was the iPod. So it's entirely possible I had inadvertently played a small part in killing my own business.

Too late, we tried to react and launched our own online music store, Virgin Digital, on 2 September 2005, and our own MP3 player. We had one of the world's biggest music libraries, with more than 2.5 million songs available to download. But after spending £20 million developing Virgin Digital, we realised our products just didn't have the simplicity, or the scale of production, to compete with Apple. We had to take it on the chin, and wrote off big losses as we shut down Virgin Digital two years later.

But while the way people were consuming music was changing, the quality of the music I'd been involved with over the years remained undimmed. I was reminded of that a few years later on a warm July evening in 2012, as I watched (and listened to) the opening ceremony of the London Olympics. Danny Boyle had turned what can be a stale affair into Isles of Wonder, an extravaganza celebrating everything that makes Britain Great. Suddenly we viewers were cruising along the Thames on a wild rock 'n' roll boat ride, down a route I had taken thirty-five years earlier with The Sex Pistols. It was electrifying.

As the ceremony continued into the Olympic Stadium (there was no police raid of the boat on this occasion!) I was waiting for an appearance from another old friend. Mike Oldfield had let me know he was performing, but I had no idea how special it would be. A huge set of tubular bells hung behind Mike as this famously shy performer created the most astonishing wall of noise while dancers and actors transfixed the billion or so people looking on. Then, before the athletes paraded their national flags, a young Virgin artist from Scotland took to the stage. Emeli Sandé had a look of fierce determination on her face as she kicked into a stripped-back rendition of the traditional hymn 'Abide

With Me', given a modern twist through some subtle electronic backing rhythms.

A joyous combination of old and new that melted hearts and stirred souls, it was everything music should be. I felt incredibly proud looking on, seeing Virgin Records at the heart of this uniting moment.

*

It wasn't only record labels that were being hit by the deadly digital combination of Apple and illegal downloading: their influence also caused enormous trouble for the record shops, Virgin Megastores included.

At its peak in the 1990s we had more than a hundred retail outlets across the UK and dozens more in over twenty countries worldwide. The Virgin Megastore in Paris was the biggest tourist attraction in France – incredibly, it had more visitors than the Louvre. Over in New York, we had opened our Times Square store at a time when the area was riddled with crime and dilapidation; our popularity helped transform the area into a hotspot. Megastores were places young people could be themselves, relax and socialise.

But by 2005, footfall was dropping and profits were falling. And it wasn't just the online revolution doing the damage: the big supermarkets also had a huge impact by cherry-picking the most popular albums and massively discounting them. We couldn't compete, and, with more people moving their record collections online, Virgin Megastores' days looked numbered. The Virgin board tried to convince me we should sell Megastores before things got worse and I remember sitting in a rare board meeting getting increasingly frustrated.

'I know we're losing money, but you can't put a price on keeping our brand in music and visible on the high street.'

I continued to look for a way to save the chain. When a prime retail spot on Oxford Street came on the market in August 2007, just a few hundred yards from our original Virgin Records location above a shoe shop, I sensed an opportunity for a Virgin Megastores revival. But our biggest traditional rival, HMV, beat us to the punch by a matter of hours.

Several deals to sell – with Fopp, private equity groups and HMV themselves – got close without going through. Finally, the Megastores' management team of Simon Douglas and Steve Peckham approached us. They felt they could turn it around and wanted to buy the business. I ummed and ahhed. The Megastores had played a huge role in my life, and been a massive part of the Virgin brand. They had kept Virgin young and created a real emotional connection. I was worried that a lot of the heart would be cut out of the brand. But at the same I came to the conclusion that we no longer needed our Megastores brand in Britain: Virgin Mobile was growing fast and Virgin Media was bringing the brand right into people's homes: the writing was on the wall for high street music retail, and we had to get out. It hurt me to admit it, but I realised I had probably hung on to the stores for too long already.

As we signed over the company, I couldn't help reminiscing about the times I'd spent in the first Virgin store, sitting on pillows smoking joints, having fun. We sold the company without the branding to Simon and Steve in September 2007. They launched Zavvi, an entertainment retailer operating out of our old Virgin Megastores premises, and got off to a decent start. But then the global financial crisis hit towards the end of 2008, and Woolworth's went bust. On paper, this sounds like a good thing for a company in direct competition with Woolworth's. But Zavvi's main supplier of stock, from CDs to DVDs to games, was a company called Entertainment UK – they had inherited the contract from Virgin Megastores. Entertainment UK was a subsidiary of Woolworth's; when their parent company closed down they went bust, too, and stopped supplying Zavvi. It was right before Christmas, the most important period for any retailer, and Zavvi simply could not get stock on their shelves. Zavvi shut down as well. If we hadn't sold Virgin Megastores, it might have been us.

*

But while the traditional way of selling records might have been drying up, the music industry was learning to make money in different ways: at the same time as digital music was taking hold, the live scene was beginning to flourish in a really lucrative way: here was an experience you had to be there to appreciate, and people were prepared to pay for the privilege.

While I don't get to as many gigs as I used to, I still love going to festivals. In the mid-nineties I was pondering the idea of creating a new Virgin music event. There was no point launching just another festival; it had to be different. Then, over a few drinks, Jarvis Cocker from Pulp and Jackie McQuillan came up with the idea for V Festival.

'Jarvis wondered why Virgin didn't have a festival already,' Jackie told me.

'Well, why don't we? That's a great idea. We'd have to make it different, though – I don't want to make something unless it's unique.'

'Well, the idea is that we put the same festival on two different sites on the same weekend, with half of the bill playing at each venue on alternate days.'

'Sounds good. Let's give it a go!'

A few months later, we pitched up at Chelmsford and Stafford for the first ever V Festival. I bumped into Jarvis backstage – at least I think it was him. He was dressed up as a giant gorilla, keen to avoid being recognised as he stumbled around the fields. The festival remained one of the staples of the music calendar until 2017. I was tempted up onstage a few times, mainly to introduce artists like Paul Weller and The Stereophonics. But whenever I'm stood up in front of thousands of people like that, it always reminds me that I'm happier behind the scenes than in front of a huge crowd.

What I really like at festivals is strolling around the grounds and hearing what the fans are enjoying. This was especially the case at FreeFest, a festival we put on with Virgin Mobile USA to support youth homelessness charities. As the name suggests, the festival was absolutely free to anybody who volunteered to help people living on the streets, with VIP upgrades for doing thirteen hours' community service. With donations from the festival we built the RE*Generation House in Washington, DC, to provide shelter for homeless youths.

At the festival, which was held at the famous Merriweather Post Pavilion in Maryland, the atmosphere was always extra special because the crowds had really earned their place by caring for others. But that doesn't mean there wasn't room for fun. You could find me behind the bar serving drinks with Flavor Flav, or above the main stage spraying bubbly onto the crowd below, while parachutists landed on the tiny roof alongside me.

Emboldened by the success of V and FreeFest, in late 2012 we were at work on a deal to bring The Rolling Stones back to the stage. I have always loved Mick Jagger and the boys for their attitude as much as their music. Our histories have often overlapped. I was a very nervous sixteen-year-old when I first interviewed Mick for *Student* magazine. I can vividly remember walking to his home at 48 Cheyne Walk, my hands shaking as I carried a primitive tape recorder two feet by two wide to record the encounter. He rarely did interviews and seemed to have agreed to do it out of respect for the audacity of a spotty teenager daring to ask in the first place. It wasn't my finest piece of journalism, but it made me love The Stones even more.

When Virgin Records got off the ground my number one target was always The Stones, and we got close to signing them on several occasions. In 1975 the band's manager, Prince Rupert Loewenstein, tried to fob me off by demanding $3 million. I called his bluff by saying we would offer $4 million. After rushing across Europe and calling every distributor I had ever come across, I cobbled the money together. Prince Rupert was impressed, but we had started a bidding war and eventually lost out to EMI, who upped their bid to $5 million.

It put me on the band's radar, though, and they started to record at our Manor Studio in Oxfordshire. On one memorable occasion there I had to cover for Keith Richards as he ran naked across the lawn with somebody else's (equally naked) wife, followed closely by her gun-toting husband, who was demanding entry at my front door! When Keith decided to go solo, we brought him to Virgin to release his albums *Talk Is Cheap* and *Main Offender*.

When The Stones came back on the market in 1991, I was determined not to miss out again. There were rumours in the industry that they were past it, but I was convinced they had a good ten years left in them – even that guess has proved to underestimate Mick and co.'s longevity. We worked out a deal that gave us rights to their formidable back catalogue as well as releasing their fantastic album *Voodoo Lounge*. At the signing party above Mossiman's restaurant, I couldn't stop grinning, and Mick looked pretty pleased, too.

'I wouldn't fancy being an apple between those two sets of gnashers,' said The Stones' bassist Bill Wyman.

Letting go of The Rolling Stones so soon after signing them was one of the toughest parts of my decision to sell Virgin Records in March 1992. But my relationship with Mick and Prince Rupert remained strong even after the deal – they were savvy businessmen who understood why I had sold, and it did little harm to The Stones, whose next world tour went on to become the highest grossing tour of all time.

Fast-forward twenty years and it had been a long time since The Rolling Stones had played live together. Mick and Keith's tumultuous partnership seemed to be at one of its low points after Keith mocked Mick's manhood in his autobiography, *Life*. But 2012 was after all the fiftieth anniversary of the band, and surely they wouldn't let the milestone pass uncelebrated? We were approached by Paul Dainty, a promoter who had worked with The Stones since their first shows. He was trying to get the band back together and wanted to partner with Virgin to do it. I was excited about the prospect of seeing them playing live again after so many years, let alone the idea of putting the gigs on. We launched a new company, Virgin Live, to promote a special series of four shows. Two would be in London and two in New York. Who would have thought that a relationship that had started in the Swinging Sixties would still be going strong five decades later?

November the 29th came round and I travelled to England for the show. I met my kids and went backstage at the O2 Arena to find the band. I felt very nostalgic seeing them together again after all those years. 'Keith, you are looking more and more like a pirate,' I laughed – thankfully he did, too. Charlie looked as unfazed about all of the fuss as ever, while Mick's toothy grin was going strong. Ronnie, meanwhile, was reminiscing about Necker: he had recently been out to the island with his delightful new bride for their honeymoon and we had enjoyed a few games of pool together.

'It must be twenty years since I've seen you all together,' I said.

'No walks down memory lane now, Ricky,' said Mick.

You could sense the excitement in the room as we posed for a few photos. We said our goodbyes as they had to get ready for the show, and I headed up to our box to watch. As the minutes ticked by until the band came onstage I stood looking out at the huge crowd and decided I wanted to get among them. We made our way through the audience and got close enough to the front just in time to see Mick take the stage in a silver snakeskin jacket and begin his trademark moves. 'Paint It Black', 'Jumpin' Jack Flash', 'Satisfaction' and 'It's Only Rock 'n' Roll' all zipped past, while Javier Bardem pulled out some outrageous dancing in the next row and Penelope Cruz looked on, highly amused. After dancing to 'The Last Time' and hoping the lyrics wouldn't be too portentous, I went to take my seat for a breather. I promptly fell flat on my arse, which only reminded me there is never a right time to sit down during a Stones gig!

*

The Rolling Stones' anniversary in 2012 was swiftly followed by a musical milestone of my own. As the fortieth anniversary of Virgin Records came around in 2013, I was kindly honoured with an Outstanding Contribution to Music GRAMMY. In a pre-awards bash the night before, I accepted on behalf of all the people who had helped build our company. It felt strange being in Los Angeles among the industry bigwigs again after so long, and not just because I had to wear a tuxedo. Tom Hanks told me he could remember listening to some of our bands from the seventies.

'You always had the coolest album sleeves,' he said.

The likes of P Diddy and Dr Dre were quick to cite the influence of Virgin Records, too.

'Now here's a real entrepreneur,' said Dr Dre.

'You're doing pretty well with Beats!' I said. He went on to sell his headphones business to Apple in a $3 billion deal. It was quite a surreal evening.

But then the night took a tragic turn. I was wrestling with my tux back in my hotel room when there was a knock on the door. It was the police, asking that I stay in my room while they investigated an incident a few doors down. It turned out Whitney Houston was staying on the same floor, and had sadly passed away in her bathtub. Whitney was a supreme talent and a kind, friendly presence whenever I came across her. Her heart-breaking death reminded us all that business and awards don't mean that much. There is nothing more important than the health of you and your loved ones.

Life is certainly too short not to appreciate people who have been significant in it. So when somebody suggested getting all of the old Virgin Records gang together one last time, I decided the moment was right. If not now, when? I travelled over to the UK, wondering how we would get on after all these years. When I walked into a little café in Notting Hill, the others were already there.

'Jesus, you lot look old,' I said.

'I was going to say the same thing!' chimed in Nik Powell, my childhood best friend and co-founder of Virgin Records.

After a cup of coffee we decided to take a walk around some of our old haunts. First off, Nik and I crept into the crypt where we started *Student* magazine and the Student Advisory Centre. To my amazement I found a tattered old leaflet for *Student* on the floor near one of the tombs.

'OK, who planted this?' I asked. But everyone assured me it was genuine.

'They haven't cleaned down here in forty years,' chuckled Nik. 'Well, we never did when we were here.'

We quickly fell back into the old rhythm. Nik went on to build a wonderful education programme as director of the National Film and Television School, after producing Oscar-winning films including one of my favourites, *The Crying Game*. I loved hearing what he and the rest of the boys were up to, and was pleased but not surprised by how well they were all doing.

We headed to the original Virgin Records store in Notting Hill, which is now a Holland & Barrett shop.

'This is as anti-rock 'n' roll as you can get,' I said, looking up at the health vitamins and supplements.

'Stop moaning and get into the window,' came the response.

I duly obliged, recreating a pose I once made in the display as a policeman walked past. The young manager of the shop was far from impressed, and had no idea why I was clambering over his pills and protein shakes: 'Sorry,' I said. 'I'd explain what we're doing but you wouldn't believe me anyway.'

Over lunch we shared some jokes with Tom Newman, the record producer who helped create *Tubular Bells*. He looks even more like a bohemian bandit these days, but his mind is as quick as ever.

'Remember that song we recorded in the toilet at the Manor?' he asked.

I groaned. 'How could you forget recording a band's bowel movements in the bog?!'

Roger Dean, the designer who drew the original Virgin Records logo, came along looking as pristine as usual, while

John Varnom, the PR genius who came up with so many iconic campaigns for us, was still sharp as a tack. We walked over to Vernon Yard next, where our original offices were, and Steve Lewis, our deputy managing director, remembered who sat in which room back in the day.

'You always had the best office, Richard,' he laughed.

'Well, I was paying for it, after all!'

Phil Newell, our technical director, remembered every single incident like it was yesterday, while Stephen Navin, the lawyer who (mostly) kept us out of court, ensured we stayed out of trouble forty years on.

'It's been wonderful to catch up with you all,' I said as we sat down for a quick drink in Little Venice. 'Let's not leave it another forty years.'

'Richard, I'm not sure any of us have that long left!' said Nik.

I find all reunions strange. When you haven't seen people for thirty years you quickly realise they are fundamentally the same but look a lot different. I'm sure it's what they're thinking about me, too. The difference is they've seen my ugly mug in the press so aren't as shocked by how I look. Will we see each other more often now? I don't think so; our lives are spread around the world, and there's no need to spend too long looking back. But it makes me happy knowing we have managed to remain friends for so long and can still enjoy each other's company.

Later, we went to officially celebrate with a special Virgin Records exhibition at Victoria House. I took my mum and the family along for a real walk down memory lane, from Geri Halliwell's union flag dress to Phil Collins and me posing as suited and booted businessmen. But we were looking to the future, too, with Naughty Boy, Professor Green and Jake Bugg there to keep me on my toes.

'It looks like we've got the same leather jacket on,' I beamed at Jake. I suspect that pleased me more than him!

29 Necker

It had been back in 2005 that Joan and I decided to move to the BVI permanently. By this point in our lives, we had found ourselves on Necker Island more and more. Holly and Sam spent all their holidays with us in the BVI, so although they would continue to work in the UK, we decided to take that step. The kids were very chilled about it, and so were we. Our lives have always been quite nomadic anyway, particularly as the Virgin businesses started to become more global, so moving to the place we most loved came naturally to us. The move was so gradual that there was little reaction at Virgin, especially as technology made it increasingly simple to work remotely. Some inaccurate commentators claimed I left Britain for tax reasons. This could not be further from the truth. I spent forty years working around the clock in the UK to build businesses that have transformed industries, created greater competition and choice for consumers, and, hopefully, put a smile on people's faces along the way. These companies have created tens of thousands of jobs, paid hundreds of millions in tax – and will continue to do so. Whilst I do travel to the UK on business from time to time, I now live in the place that brings most joy to those around me. The BVI is our home; it is where we can live life to the full, work hard, play hard, and look forward to spending the rest of our days.

After the 2011 Necker fire, it took two years of hard work to redesign and rebuild the Great House. Finally, in 2013, our home was our home again, and we were ready to reopen it. We decided to invite the same people who were there when the fire happened, including Mum, Sam, Holly, my nephew Ned and his now wife Kate Winslet, and my nephew Jack, who had raised the alarm that night. As fate would have it, the very evening we returned to the Great House we were welcomed by the biggest, most spectacular lightning storm to hit the island since the fire. As an enormous clap of thunder above the house rang around my ears, I smiled.

'Well, the gods are welcoming us back!' I shouted over the noise.

We had fitted the largest lightning rods imaginable to the roof, so we are well protected from future storms. I like to think of the rebuilt Great House as being like the old house, with its breathtaking views and Balinese inspiration, but on steroids. It is the place where people come together on Necker, so making it open, welcoming and unpretentious – but still spectacular – was what we had in mind. My favourite spot on the balcony, where I always go to sit and think upon returning to the island, was recreated exactly as it was before.

One feature I couldn't resist adding to the Great House was a crow's nest on the roof – complete with a Jacuzzi (more on that later!). It was the perfect place to enjoy the view, gaze at the stars, relax and think things over, perhaps with a glass in hand and a loved one by your side. When it was installed, I joked that there have already been lots of Necker babies – the favourite name for girls conceived here is Annecker – and the Jacuzzi will probably contribute to lots more! As we have so many younger guests visiting – and young-at-heart guests, too – we also added a zip-line for an exciting way to travel from the house to the white sandy beach below. It's not bad for a morning commute.

*

I had originally envisaged Necker as a place for musicians to come, hang out and record. I found the fire-charred remains of the original blueprints for Necker's very own studios when

I was searching through the ruins after the fire on the island in 2012. While the recording studio never came to fruition, the idea of creating a sanctuary for musicians and others certainly did. Everyone from Ronnie Wood to Bono, Kanye West to Mariah Carey – who popped up in my Jacuzzi while I was showing the MTV *Cribs* film crew around the island – comes to stay.

Another guest who certainly enjoyed his visit was Harry Styles. The One Direction boys are decent young lads who'd suddenly had the spotlight thrown on them. They were handling it extremely well and so-called scandals like smoking the odd spliff are certainly nothing for parents to worry about. In time-honoured tradition, Harry was having a little girl trouble when he came to stay. He was visiting the BVI with Taylor Swift, another extremely talented young performer, when they had a falling out. I invited him over to take a break from everything, and we got talking in the Jacuzzi one night.

'Remember to have fun amongst all the chaos,' I advised him.

'I'm trying to,' he said.

'And look after yourself, or you'll burn out by the time you're twenty-five. When I was working with Boy George, he was in a similar position to you, in demand everywhere he went, and he struggled to deal with it. Make time for yourself, because nobody else will.'

I came away with the impression of a fun-loving, sensible young man with a smart head on his shoulders and the world at his feet.

As well as the visits to Necker of assorted stars, my role in the music scene continued to enjoy something of a renaissance. After the success of The Rolling Stones' comeback, I found myself with plenty more offers for us to get involved with other music legends. In March 2014, we were approached to sponsor a Led Zeppelin reunion tour. I was very surprised that such a tour was a possibility – Robert Plant had made it clear on numerous occasions that he was happy with his solo career and had no wish to re-form the band. However, the promoters claimed the potential was genuine for a fifty-concert tour, with twenty-five stadium shows and twenty-five arena gigs everywhere from New York to Tokyo, Los Angeles to London. They said it would start in August, go through to December and we would have to stump up £15 million to get involved.

After considering the offer, we politely declined, so I was somewhat surprised to see headlines appear in the newspapers, stating that Robert had turned down a £500 million offer from me and ripped up the contract in front of my face. Apparently Virgin Atlantic was even renaming one of our planes *Stairway to Heaven*! I called up Robert.

'Just to let you know,' I told him, 'this rubbish isn't coming from us.'

'Don't worry, I never thought it was,' he replied. 'I'm proud of Led Zeppelin's history, but I want to move forward with my own life and solo career. In fact, I'm about to go on tour again.'

'That's wonderful. It's disrespectful to your solo projects for people to keep banging on about the past. Anyway, really look forward to seeing you on tour.'

It's great to see so many other artists of my generation still thinking of the future with new ideas and inspiration, whether it is Robert, his old bandmates Jimmy Page and John Paul Jones, or my friends Peter Gabriel and Mike Oldfield.

'I just do things because I love them and I want to do more new things that I love,' Robert had explained. As usual, he had found just the right words.

Speaking of Mike Oldfield, not long after I saw him onstage at the Olympics, he invited me over to his home in the Bahamas. I luckily timed the visit with another special performance of *Tubular Bells*. This venue was far removed from the Olympic Stadium, though. It was Mike's son's school, and all the kids had learned their parts to give a very sweet rendition of the signature track. It was beautiful, innocent and very powerful – all the qualities I see in Mike.

Back at his house, we got talking and Mike was more open than I could ever remember him being. He has always been a fiercely private, somewhat introverted individual, but I sometimes manage to draw him out a little. This time, he was doing more talking than I was. He had a stunning new album, *Man On The Rocks*, coming out on Virgin Records and was clearly on top of the world, surrounded by his loved ones.

'You seem really well,' I told him. 'I can't remember seeing you look so content.'

'I am, Richard. I'm happy, the happiest I've been in a long time.'

Mike's genius was the reason Virgin had got off the ground all those years ago. Now, after many years in the doldrums, I was delighted to welcome Virgin Records back into the family, fittingly in the company's fortieth year. After some typically complicated and long-winded horse trading between the labels, Virgin moved to Universal HQ and in 2012 joined with Mercury to form Virgin EMI. It was a tumultuous time that ended with Ted Cockle taking over as CEO, joining from Island Records.

As soon as we met I could see Ted genuinely cared about Virgin Records' heritage, as well as its future. He recognised that the Virgin name still held a lot of sway and began revitalising his team behind the brand. They have brought together some of the most exciting new acts around, including James Bay, Bastille and Emeli Sandé, an incredible talent and warm soul I've been fortunate to see perform on Necker and get to know. The masterstroke was enticing the biggest international artists, from Rihanna to Katy Perry, Lorde to Taylor Swift, to release their records in the UK through Virgin. Suddenly we were combining home-grown talents like Jamie T and Laura Marling with stadium-shaking superstars. We jumped to the front of the global dance movement, too, as deadmau5, Tiesto and Swedish House Mafia all signed on.

Within the Universal system, Virgin had become a honeypot and was named the number one singles and albums company in the UK five years running. A Virgin brand I once thought was going to disappear is revitalised, re-energised and rejuvenated. In the past few years, Emeli Sandé has sold more than two million copies of her record *Our Version Of Events*. But that's nothing sales-wise compared to twenty years earlier. For some context, in 1993 I convinced Janet Jackson to join Virgin Records by taking her up in a hot-air balloon above Oxford and jokingly saying that I would use her as ballast unless she signed. Her next album, *Janet*, sold more than fifteen million records worldwide. Although the industry has since gone through a rough time, artists and labels are now beginning to benefit from people paying for streaming subscriptions.

I would love to have time to listen to more records and go to more concerts, read more books and see more plays. Because I keep so busy, I think there is a cultural hole in my life. I argue to myself that I'll be able to do lots of the things I don't have time for when I am old or unwell. I have a cold at the moment, so started watching David Attenborough's *Planet Earth II*. I do everything to the extreme, so I devoured the whole series in quick succession. Usually I work on flights, but I recently waded through the whole *House of Cards* boxset in a matter of days. If I do get into a good non-fiction book, I can't put it down and can become quite unsociable. Even so, it is a perennial New Year's resolution to read more and listen to more albums again.

*

While she has only dipped her toes into the music world, there are few people more rock 'n' roll than Kate Moss. Her weeks on Necker always go with a bang, including when she stayed in 2014 to celebrate her fortieth birthday.

I have known Kate since she was fifteen, when she walked through an airport and her life changed forever. It was a journey that had started when my sister called me up one day and said that her best friend, Sarah Doukas, had an idea for a company. I agreed to meet Sarah at her home, and she pitched her vision of a new kind of modelling agency run in a more entrepreneurial way. Rather than joining the treadmill of competing agencies, she would focus upon nurturing young talent, managing them all the way through the trials and tribulations of a tough industry and helping them move into other exciting areas after modelling. Sarah was smart, savvy and clearly knew what she was doing. It also helped her cause that I was young enough to be attracted by the concept of owning a modelling agency! I liked Sarah's attitude and could empathise with somebody running a business out of their home. A former model herself, Sarah told me she used to sell antiques from a market stall on the King's Road when she wasn't strutting down the catwalk. I said yes there and then to her pitch and became her partner in Storm.

After the meeting Sarah flew off to Miami to get the business off the ground. It was while walking through the airport that she caught sight of the most striking fifteen-year-old girl she had ever seen, holding hands with her mum. Sarah approached them and asked the mum if she had ever thought about her daughter modelling. The mother, Linda, passed on her details and thought that would be the end of it. But Sarah followed up and the young lady ended up becoming Storm's first model. Her name? Kate Moss.

The rest, as they say, is history. Sarah and Storm have gone from strength to strength, helping the likes of Alexa Chung, Lily Cole and Sophie Dahl build careers on and off the red carpet. As for Kate, she became the iconic face of a generation. She's been good enough to join me for many wing-walks launching Virgin Atlantic routes. When she was hounded by the tabloids after a storm in a teacup scandal in 2005, I suggested we team up once again. With rumours that she was losing all her sponsorship deals, Kate starred in a

Virgin Mobile advert where she landed the mother of all contracts. She quickly bounced back to her rightful place as modelling's top girl.

Part and parcel of the supermodel territory is having to put up with a lot of press intrusion. I got an insight into Kate's world when I took a call one Friday morning from the *News of the World*. The reporter told me they were running a front-page splash that I had a cocaine-fuelled threesome with Kate and Keith Richards in the master bedroom on Necker Island.

'We've got this on very good authority,' the journalist assured me.

My first thought was: what a great story – do I really have to set them straight?! But Jackie grabbed the phone as the journalist repeated that they had 'got the story straight from the horse's mouth'.

'Which horse?' asked Jackie. 'Shergar?'

I took the phone back, laughing. 'Well, I'm very flattered,' I joked with them. 'But I'm afraid Keith has never visited Necker. Sorry to ruin your splash.'

Common sense prevailed and they didn't run the story. I don't think Joan would have been too pleased if they had. Plus, it wouldn't have helped Kate's image – although it might have helped mine and Keith's!

When Kate is on Necker she can usually be seen on top of the Great House table, dancing away day and night. I've rarely seen anyone work so hard and play even harder. She surrounds herself with friends she trusts, who have been around for a long time, and are very loyal. It's a model that works for Virgin, too.

*

People often ask me what it is really like living on Necker, and I have never been shy about sharing. For the first time, I decided to open up Necker to the BBC for a special documentary, *Billionaire's Paradise: Inside Necker Island*. While I try to share what life is like here every day, the programme promised to open up more about our staff and guests' experiences. The crew had complete access to all areas of the island and we had no editorial control.

The filming happened to take place during one of our 'Celebration Weeks', when guests book individual rooms on the island. It makes for a great mix of people, and a very different atmosphere from the weeks when guests book out almost the whole island, or we just have the family here. Necker is an inimitable destination where our guests, very often highly driven, hard-working people, come to relax and recharge.

Not surprisingly, certain elements of the press went into overdrive attempting to paint the island as more outrageous than it really is. With typical sensationalism, the *Daily Mail* even compared me to Hugh Hefner, rather overlooking the fact that I have been happy with the same woman for four decades.

'Well, you did both get your start in business running magazines,' said Joan.

'True, but *Student* was a very different publication from *Playboy*!'

Anyway, no harm was done, the island was depicted beautifully and we had a good laugh sitting around the big screen with all our staff watching the documentary. Necker received a huge amount of interest, even more than usual, after the programme had aired. Bookings went through the roof, and I'm looking forward to welcoming many more guests to Necker in the years to come. It is the wonderful mixture of guests and staff that ensures my family and I never feel cut off here, rather, feeling a freedom I find nowhere else.

I also love surprising some of our employees who have really gone the extra mile by flying them to Necker, hosting them for a few days and saying thank you in person. Some years ago, all of Virgin's senior management were over for a working break deciding our strategy for the coming year. They were talking about being more adventurous, which I wholeheartedly agreed with.

'Let's see you put your money where your mouth is,' I told them. 'We're going on a little boat ride.'

We sailed over to nearby Moskito, where I took the team for a walk along the cliffs. As we were looking out at the horizon, they slowly grasped what we had come for.

'Right, here's the cliff,' I pointed. 'It's time for us all to jump off. Who's going first?'

Some looked aghast, staring down at jagged rocks and stormy seas below.

'My family and I have made the jump many times before,' I reassured them. 'Now, if I told you to jump off a cliff, would you do it – literally?'

Leading from the front, I went first, to show it was relatively safe. One by one, the team started diving off the cliff, in various stages of undress. However, that day I hadn't taken the strength of the ocean into account. The jumps went fine, but the current was threatening to sweep my entire senior management team away. We frantically called for a rescue boat, while bobbing helplessly in the Caribbean. Thankfully, the boat arrived and we got back to Necker safe and sound. After enduring that experience, the CEOs would perhaps be a little more ready to take calculated risks back at their businesses – after jumping off a cliff, making the odd change in the boardroom won't seem so scary!

*

I fell in love with Necker when I was twenty-nine years old. Now, nearly four decades on, I adore it even more. We have managed to turn it from an uninhabited island into a sustainable, productive place where my family and I will be able to thrive for the rest of our lives. We aren't getting any younger so looking after our health is a priority. I want to continue my active, creative lifestyle, where I can work, play tennis, kitesurf, swim and relax. I've travelled all over the world, from Mallorca to Australia, Tahiti to Bali, Bora Bora to Hawaii, and never found anything remotely as magical as Necker Island.

As a Monopoly player, the last thing I would ever part with is Necker. But even if I had to, I would somehow keep a right to camp on the beach.

30 Weddings

Ayear on from their wedding, Holly and Freddie were happier together than ever, and Joan and I were becoming increasingly unsubtle in our hints about grandchildren. While our daughter was happily married, Sam also had his eye on settling down with the woman he had fallen in love with.

'I've just met the most beautiful woman I have ever seen,' he told me – something I was quick to agree on when he introduced me to Isabella. While everyone calls her Bellie for short, I enjoy teasing her about having what must be the longest name of anyone in the world – Isabella Amaryllis Charlotte Anstruther-Gough-Calthorpe – but she is worth every one of those fifty letters.

When Sam had decided Bellie was the woman he wanted to spend the rest of his life with, we were on a conservation trip to Madagascar. We were keen to learn more about lemurs, the critically endangered primates. Dr Russ Mittermeier, a world-leading lemur expert, took us deep into the heart of the country to see these beautiful creatures in their natural habitat. Helen and my nephew Ludo also joined us on the trip, and we learned a huge amount about lemurs and how we could help protect them.

We now have a thriving conspiracy of lemurs (I love that collective noun!) on Necker and Moskito Island. We've successfully raised some of the rarest breeds, including panda lemurs, red-ruffed lemur triplets and ring-tailed lemur twins. As well as lemurs, scarlet and white ibis and stout iguanas, one of the things I'm most proud of about Necker is the reintroduction of flamingos to the region. I love going down to the smaller flamingo pond where they breed. They may be courting, strutting up and down with their heads going back and forth, showing off, much like humans. They may be starting to build nests of mud eighteen inches off the ground, so their eggs are safe. They may be learning to fly. Watching the young trying to land is like watching a plane miss the runway time and again. Every now and then we have to help them out of a bush when they crash-land. Just seeing the beautiful scarlet body and the black wing-tips as they fly in the sun mesmerises me. The wildlife of Necker spurs me on to support the conservation of all species. My definition of a sin is for humans to allow a species to die out. Animals cannot speak for themselves – it is up to all of us to protect them and their habitats. This is why we've tried to make Necker a real Garden of Eden. Our house is surrounded by huge iguanas, which are very friendly, but sometimes terrify the guests. I have to make it clear they are vegetarian. I get into traffic jams with giant tortoises and have to abandon my golf buggy and wait for them to cross the road. There is nowhere you can stand without marvelling; it is a microcosm of what earth was like before man set foot on it, and of what we all have to fight to get the world back to. Madagascar, I believe, used to be the same, but is now enormously damaged by defor-estation, agricultural fires and habitat destruction.

As we wandered through the Madagascan bush, we chanced upon another person keen to learn more about the importance of protecting the lemurs: Professor Brian Cox. 'Small world!' I exclaimed. 'Of all the people to meet in the middle of a tropical jungle,' he smiled. We decided to combine forces. Later that afternoon we found the extremely rare and – to most observers anyway – rather strange looking aye-aye lemur together. I was honoured to take a photo with Brian and a baby aye-aye.

'This is the only way I'm not going to be the ugliest member of a photo with you!' I joked.

Brian became fast friends with the family. We enjoyed a fine stay at the beautiful Anjajavy L'Hotel on the shore, where lemurs played up in the trees all around us. It was here that Sam took me to one side and told me he was planning to pop the question to Bellie that night. I was thrilled.

'That's the most wonderful news I've heard since Freddie rang me about Holly,' I said.

Sam sneaked off and built a big, beautiful love heart on a quiet beach further down the cove, and picked out a stunning, secluded cave. To my delight, Bellie said yes.

*

When I was a young man I never thought about getting married. Then, before I knew it, I was saying 'I do' to Kristen, far too young. A couple of years later we went our separate ways. I never thought I would find the true love of my life, but Joan came along and true happiness followed. While I didn't exactly walk down the aisle when I married Joan (I flew into the wedding in a white suit and top hat, hanging from the bottom of a helicopter), our marriage has been an amazing partnership. All of which made the events a few years ago so frightening.

I had woken up very early on Easter Sunday 2010 on Necker, looking forward to spending the day with my family after an early morning tennis match. I got back from the courts, went to kiss Joan good morning, and was immediately shaken to the core. As I pulled back the covers, I saw that one of her legs had swollen to twice its usual size. We immediately knew this was extremely serious. I called for help, as Joan stayed reassuringly calm. Fortunately, Holly, Sam and the whole family were on Necker with us, and we quickly gathered around the bedside to support Joan. Even more luckily, our friend Tim Evans, who just happens to be the Queen's doctor, was on the island, too, and he managed to stabilise the situation.

We got Joan helicoptered over to the hospital in the British Virgin Islands immediately. The doctors told us she had developed an enormous blood clot, which is very frightening because you know that the slightest movement can send one of those clots to the brain, lungs or heart. Initially, they planned to do nothing except give Joan some stabilising drugs. Holly, Sam and I got on the phone to every expert we could find and sought second, third, fourth and fifth opinions. It helped that Holly is a trained doctor and was able to offer an educated view. We learned there were some superb specialists, Dr Katzen and Dr Powell, at a hospital in Miami that used a very new procedure and it sounded like they could help Joan. Another specialist, Dr Woolf, said to me: 'If she were my mother, I'd take her to Miami.' But we would have to move fast – the procedure would only potentially work if done within a few days of the problem developing.

I have spent a lifetime making decisions, but this was potentially a life or death choice for my wife. Did we move her to a specialist and risk the journey causing more problems? We decided to go for it and Joan was medevacked to Miami, where we also have family. The specialist carried out the procedure and, to my huge relief, it was a complete success. Without it, Joan could have been dragging her leg around for the rest of her life, or worse. Instead, she was able to make a full recovery and walked out of hospital after a week. We discovered she had an undiagnosed blood disorder that could have killed her at any time. Now she has the proper medication and thankfully the problem has not resurfaced.

Having my wife in trouble was a far more harrowing experience than any of my own brushes with death. I find any time when my family is suffering excruciating. Making life or death decisions for family requires the same skills as making crucial business decisions, but, of course, it feels so much more intense. As an entrepreneur you are better equipped than anyone to question things, listen and learn and ultimately make a call. But there is always another company – there is not another wife, son or daughter. It doesn't matter how much money you earn; nothing is worth more than your family's health.

The horrible feeling that I could have lost my partner made me realise, if I ever needed reminding, how much I love her and how much I appreciate having her around. We have always been a very, very close family. But scares like Joan's illness pull us even closer together. With Joan and me going strong after more than four decades by each other's side, it is no surprise that people often ask us what our secret is. It would be presumptuous to say that there is a secret. So many relationships don't work out – more than half of marriages don't. You are extraordinarily lucky if the chemistry works and it lasts forever. But Joan and I have loved each other unreservedly for all these years because we understand how each other thinks, respect what each other wants and needs. I've seen many other people who have decided to change their partners: they don't generally end up happier in the long run. The feeling that the grass is greener can often be a mistake. They might unearth some extra passion for a while, but that is unlikely to last forever.

Relationships need to have a lot of give and take. If there are any little niggling things you don't like about each other, confront and address them. Last night, for example, I couldn't sleep; every time I got back into bed I woke Joan. Her being able to gently let me know, sure in the knowledge I would understand, means that tonight if I can't sleep I will make an extra effort to be quiet. Sometimes you don't realise. Often tiny little things make all the difference. Life is made up of a series of small moments; we simply must try to cherish each one. Whether that is watching a film curled up on the sofa, going out to dinner, or spending time with our family, we try to make our time together count.

For Joan, this does not mean living exactly the same life that I enjoy. While she loves people, she doesn't particularly relish being the life and soul of the party. I am always keen to spend time with new groups on Necker, while Joan will stay in the background – we don't begrudge each other that. I travel a lot, so we are not smothering each other. I don't drag her away on business trips, or out to business dinners very often. In the early days she did come along, but we quickly realised she didn't enjoy it so we changed things. She is a wonderful reader, has a tremendous love of music and films, and is a fine judge of character. As she is now past seventy, I always urge Joan to take it easier (while completely contradicting that advice myself). She keeps me grounded and makes me giggle. Upon seeing whatever scruffy clothes I have thrown on in the morning, she will tell me with a smile: 'You are the poorest rich man anyone has ever met.'

I think the key to lasting love is listening, making sure you act upon your feelings and giving your partner the enormous respect they deserve. Experience plays a huge role, too. I made a lot of mistakes when I was younger. When I married my first wife, Kristen, we were just kids; we thought we knew it all, but we knew next to nothing. It was destined never to last. Joan and I have solid foundations, respect and understanding. That's not to say there aren't rare occasions when we have a little tiff, or I am sad about something else. If I get down, whether about business or an argument with a friend, I try to remind myself that time heals and it will pass. Even if you've messed up big time, share what you've done with people who love you and they will help. When I mess up, Joan is that person. As I wrote this I asked her what she thought was the key to our lasting love: 'Oh, I don't know, Richard, we just work. You're silly; you make me laugh a lot. Some people are just meant to be together.'

*

As well as enjoying my own special relationship, I am also in a position to help other couples to tie the knot. Since I got my Universal Life Church ordainment, I can often be found on Necker standing in front of a husband and wife-to-be on Turtle Beach, or the Sandspit, or Bali Hi, and uttering the words, 'You may now kiss the bride.' They aren't exactly traditional ceremonies, but they're always memorable!

One that really stands out is the wedding of Google founder Larry Page and his wife Lucy on 7 December 2007.

I was flattered to be asked to officiate at the wedding. Larry and I have been good friends ever since he visited Necker several years earlier. We are sort of opposites. He comes from the tech world and is a bit of a boffin, but in the most normal, approachable way. There is a bit of an age difference, but we get on really well together. He comes up with dozens of new ideas every day, and we never know which direction our conversations will take. Lucy is as bright and beautiful as anyone, and gets on wonderfully with Joan and all the family, too.

I was determined to do a good job officiating at their wedding, and neatly hand-wrote all my words for the ceremony on some nice paper. Twenty minutes before the wedding started they blew out of my hand and disappeared. I was in an absolute panic trying to remember the words, and just about managed to bluff my way through it. Both Larry and Lucy are keen kitesurfers, and decided to kite around the island after the ceremony, wearing beautiful matching white gear and boards emblazoned with 'L Loves L'. We watched them enjoy a beautiful kite, before they headed back towards the beach.

Then: 'Look out! Shark!'

As they reached the shallows, shouts went up as the guests saw a huge tiger shark fin appear. The guests were screaming, Larry and Lucy's mothers were shouting, people were waving at them to go back out to sea. Larry's security guard grabbed a knife and bravely ran into the sea to take the shark on.

'No!' I screamed to the guy with the knife and ran towards him. At this stage, our island manager Keny climbed out of the incredibly realistic shark outfit we had specially constructed for the wedding. Everybody burst into fits of laughter – even the security guard! I think Larry and Lucy may have just about forgiven me.

Six years on, there were no sharks, real or otherwise, to disrupt Bellie and Sam's wedding. Both of them adore the natural world, so after their engagement took place amid the wildlife of Madagascar, it seemed fitting that their wedding would be at Ulusaba. Family and friends flew out to the bush ahead of the big day on 5 March, and we created the most beautiful space for the ceremony. Animals roamed freely all around us, and I was amazed how the couple managed to create something completely different from Holly and Freddie's wedding, but equally as perfect.

I was delighted that Brian Cox was there, and he gave a humbling speech about the power of love and the universe around us; then Bellie's remarkable, unrehearsed words left everybody fumbling for tissues. After a spectacular ceremony, I looked up to the skies to see another enormous thunderstorm on the horizon. We scrambled for the cover of Rock Lodge and all watched together as nature put on the finest fireworks display one could ever wish to see.

Seeing my children get married were really special moments for all the family. It also really made me take stock of where I was in my own life now I was in my sixties. Virgin had grown beyond my wildest dreams. The strategy of consolidating our businesses into the key areas in which we knew the brand worked best – travel, finance, health and wellness, telecoms – was paying dividends, but I still felt like there was so much to do. Whether it was expanding our non-profit efforts or getting to space with Virgin Galactic, I believed my biggest challenges were still ahead of me. I felt restless, I felt energised, and eager to work hard and play harder.

But there was something else always in the back of my mind, too. I was missing my father. I was so used to asking his opinion on everything from business decisions to holiday ideas, sharing stories and jokes. I really missed calling him up for a chat. But Mum was coping wonderfully, keeping extraordinarily busy and living life to the full. I was determined to do the same. Perhaps it was realising I was advancing in years, but I began to be really eager for grandchildren. Dad had doted on Holly and Sam, and I was keen to do the same with my own grandkids if I got the chance.

31 Start-ups

One day in the late sixties my mum saw a necklace lying in the road near Shamley Green and took it to the police station. After three months nobody had claimed it so the police told her she could keep it. She came up to London, sold the necklace and gave me the money. Without that £100, I may never have started Virgin. We paid the bills, expanded our advertising and kick-started what would go on to become a brand employing more than 75,000 people. Mighty oaks from little acorns grow ...

In 2011, in my hammock back on Necker I was handed a report. Opening reports usually fills me with as much dread as opening my mouth at the dentist, but on this occasion it felt different. Control: Shift had been put together by Virgin Media Pioneers, our online community of enterprising people. Through the report, we had tried to give a voice to young entrepreneurs who are vital to the economy, but are not being heard. I asked young people directly: what changes would make it more likely that young entrepreneurs will thrive and prosper? I wanted to know what barriers they believed were blocking their path.

This was following a summer when riots across the UK had led to some very lazy generalisations that young people are all disillusioned, disenfranchised and disconnected from their communities. When the riots happened, I was saddened, but not all that surprised. They made me think back to my own days protesting in the sixties. When young people feel they are not being listened to, their reactions can spill out into the streets. However, the reality is that there are thousands of young people out there building exciting futures for themselves and others. They just need a little help along the way, from each other, from enterprises large and small and from the government.

One suggestion was to change the way entrepreneurship is taught in schools, with business training starting younger and being more adaptable. I talked to my daughter Holly about it. While she was at university, she felt she could have learned just as much in a shorter period and believed students should be given the option for more flexible learning. If you want to fit a degree into three years instead of four, or two years instead of three, you should be able to. I started asking everyone I met: 'Why did you go to university? What did you learn, and could you have spent the time more productively?' The majority felt it hadn't been the best use of their time and, at the very least, it could be improved.

Another idea from Control: Shift was about fostering a culture of collaboration, recalculating the way society invests in young people and encouraging young people to do it for themselves. The new generation felt their elders did not respect them. This resonated with me from my days running *Student* magazine. I would go into meetings and not be taken seriously because of my age, my clothes, even my voice. Too many potential entrepreneurs were discouraged back then by the snobbery of their elders – and it seemed this was still a problem in the twenty-first century. If entrepreneurs who had been there, done it and got the t-shirt could support rather than shun new talent, this problem could be reversed. I thought the solution was simple: mentorship, which had been essential for me, from my mum's support to Freddie Laker's. Getting advice on how best to achieve goals, overcome obstacles and outmanoeuvre competition is often the missing link between a promising business person and a successful one. Plus, it's always good to have someone to talk to.

I had been lobbying for entrepreneurial loans and more support for young entrepreneurs for years, writing letters to various governments and bringing it up in one meeting after another. But now our research put down in hard data a hunch I'd had for decades: young people need more access to finance at the most important point in their business careers – the start. Here was the solution down on paper: the British government happily grants £30,000 loans to put students through university. Why not give loans to young people who want to start their own business rather than enter higher education, or after they've entered it? As Virgin Media Pioneer Abdul Khan put it: 'I could get a loan to do a two-year degree in enterprise – but not a loan to start my own business.' I empathised with this, having struggled to raise the small amount needed to start my own first business. Banks would never have supported a magazine for students with a fifteen-year-old founder, and the idea of the government helping new businesses was unheard of.

But, as with the necklace my mother had found on the street, it doesn't always take big investments. In March 2012, I was speaking in Liverpool at the Global Entrepreneurship Congress when sixteen-year-old Aaron Booth stood up and told me how he felt there was a big gap between large businesses and the young generation. I agreed and asked about his own entrepreneurial idea – he had a dream to start his own baking company. Within five minutes of hearing his vision, I made a £200 investment to kick-start his business.

Moments like these really got me interested in microfinance, and how just giving people a little bit of a leg-up can make a huge difference. I have long admired Dr Muhammad Yunus, my fellow B Team member who created the Grameen Bank in Bangladesh, which offers small loans to impoverished people without the need for collateral. Since it started in 1979, it has been the ultimate example of business changing people's lives for good, and has helped to raise millions of Bangladeshis out of poverty. Dr Yunus is a spritely, energetic man who always has a glint in his eye and a brainwave at the ready. Inspired by his example, we began exploring what models could work elsewhere. The Branson Centres of Entrepreneurship, based in the Caribbean and online, are a great example. We give entrepreneurs guidance, connections and opportunities through our peer and partnership network and have helped thousands of entrepreneurs to become a force for good and stand on their own feet.

Another example was on my doorstep in the British Virgin Islands. I was kitesurfing between Necker and Moskito Island with Larry Page when we got talking about the young entrepreneurs we knew and how shocking the rate of failure is.

'It was the same for us before Google got off the ground,' he said. 'We had this exciting idea we thought could make the internet so much more valuable, but were scraping around to get enough money to rent a garage.'

After drying off, we sat at the bar discussing what we could do to help more young entrepreneurs get a foot on the ladder in the British Virgin Islands.

'I've been lobbying British MPs for years to give start-up loans to young entrepreneurs,' I said. 'Why don't we just do it ourselves here?'

We agreed there was a role for small, targeted start-up loans for BVI entrepreneurs with exciting ideas and sound business models and set about creating a joint fund between us.

'If anybody manages to pay their loan back, all that money will go to another entrepreneur,' I suggested. 'The pressure for them to pay it back is that they are depriving another entrepreneur of the opportunity.'

The chance to put this idea into action came one Friday night when the team was heading over to Jumbies, a beach bar in nearby Leverick Bay where the music is loud, the food is good and the characters are as colourful as the cocktails. Eager for a dance to let off some steam, I hopped into the driver's seat of the speedboat and drove us over. While tucking into dinner, a local Rastafarian guy called Gumption chattered away in my ear. Gumption was the regular life and soul of the party, winning the limbo contest and dancing with anyone and everyone nearby. But it turned out he had a serious side, too, and a smart business head on his shoulders.

'I want to start a glass-bottom-boat business,' he said. 'I just need the boat.'

He explained to me how he wanted to share his local knowledge of the surrounding ocean and its magnificent species, while giving tourists a taste of the true personality of the BVI. Importantly, he also understood the need for purpose within his business, and was keen to support the conservation of sea turtles in the area as part of his business plan.

'There's definitely a market for tourists who love nature here. If you're serious,' I told him, 'we'll look into it.'

I went back and talked it over with Larry and Lucy. We all agreed it sounded a fine investment. The concept involved modest financial support – all Gumption needed was a few thousand dollars to buy a boat – with lots of mentoring and access to support. Quickly, Gumption became our first BVI start-up loan recipient. Within six months, he had paid back his loan in full. Mind you, with a name like Gumption there was no way he was going to fail!

*

Over in the UK the moment seemed right to launch a similar scheme: the economy was floundering and young people were struggling to pay university fees, let alone start new businesses, while the Virgin companies in the UK were in a strong position to make a difference on the issue. I sent out letters to scores of MPs hammering home the idea for start-up loans.

I mentioned our ideas in a letter to David Cameron. 'With more than one million 16–24-year-olds out of work and the numbers rising, I am sure you are looking for every way to tackle this problem and prevent the creation of a jobless generation,' I wrote. 'Too many young entrepreneurs struggle to get small amounts of money to start a business, and yet young people can access loans to study a degree in Business Studies.

'Together with Virgin Media Pioneers, I think Government should re-purpose part of the Student Loans as the Youth

Investment Fund, and make lower rate loans available as start-up capital for young entrepreneurs. It does not need to be big amounts to kick-start an idea; but Government could also look to banks and business to provide matching capital, discounted services and help assess the viability of the business plans. My team has more information on the ideas in this letter and would be happy to follow up with your office.'

While we built up a real groundswell of support behind the scenes quite quickly, the press continued to ignore the issue. I was determined to get it in front of the public and in January 2012 had the ideal opportunity. I was in Parliament for a Home Affairs Committee debate on drugs policy, so brought along three of the Virgin Media Pioneers, Zoe Jackson, Abdul Khan and Ronke Ige, to lobby the politicians. As we handed out the Control: Shift report outside the House of Commons, we were immediately surrounded by several dozen MPs, seeing an opportunity to support young entrepreneurs (and get their faces in the papers!). Before they knew it, journalists were reporting that the MPs were backing drug reform, too. That was fine with me – it was win-win. Plus, I'm convinced that in a few years' time those same MPs will be brave enough to admit their true views and support drug policy changes as well.

Despite this breakthrough, we still needed the backing of the government top brass to really get things moving for start-up loans. We got Zoe, Ronke and Abdul into the crowd for a PM-Direct session in Maidenhead and I urged them to question David Cameron about the idea. Political debates can be very intimidating places, so full of bellowing and bellyaching that it is hard to get a word in. Thankfully, Ernestina Hall from our comms team kept digging Zoe in the ribs until she plucked up the courage to ask her question about start-up loans. The Prime Minister's response was perfect: 'Oh, yes, I have read Richard Branson's letter. It's very sensible, a brilliant idea,' he said. The clip ran on the BBC news that evening and start-up loans moved one step closer to reality.

The team went in for a meeting with Mr Cameron's office the next day and pulled our industry-wide working group back together. The result was the development of the non-profit StartUp Loans Company, which began with a pilot in Cumbria and the North East of England. Lord Young, whom the government put in charge of the scheme, estimated that it could help create 900,000 more jobs across the country by stimulating entrepreneurship, a figure I thought was achievable. I started casting around the Virgin Group trying to work out how best we could help. After Virgin Media had done lots of the groundwork with the initial research, Virgin Unite and Virgin Money now partnered with the Northern Rock Foundation and Project North East to form a consortium in the delivery of StartUp Loans. As a Delivery Partner for the scheme, we began handing out loans to young entrepreneurs in sectors ranging from tech to textiles.

In August 2013, I headed to Virgin Money's Gosforth headquarters to meet some of the first entrepreneurs who had been given loans. I met Andy Stephenson, who typified the new entrepreneurs the scheme could help. He used a start-up loan to launch Weekend Box, which delivers brilliant activity boxes to parents' doors. Within five months the company was growing fast and Andy was on his way to Downing Street to tell the Prime Minister his story. Andy reminded me of my younger self, starting a company in response to a problem he came across in his day-to-day life and thought he could solve: 'The inspiration for starting Weekend Box was both personal ambition and necessity: it began when I was buying gifts for my niece and nephew who are both five years old. I wanted to buy something educational yet fun. I couldn't find anything, so I quit my job and started developing Weekend Box.'

The trial was going well with more than a hundred talented business persons like Andy signing up, but not enough new entrepreneurs were being attracted. In its first six months, the scheme had only loaned £1.5 million and the government, understandably, wanted to make a big splash with some headline-making numbers to justify making the trial more permanent and expanding it nationally. We realised, however, that it would take time to build partnerships, nurture talents and spread the word. I needed to make sure David Cameron wasn't about to pull the plug on a project that could massively boost the economy, as well as thousands of people's lives and aspirations.

I got my chance when I was in London to speak about entrepreneurship and innovation at the G8 Innovation Conference. Onstage, I commended the government on their continuing support of start-up loans: backstage, I grabbed five minutes to discuss it with the Prime Minister. We sat down in a little room in the bowels of the Excel Centre, and over a cup of tea I reiterated my vision for supporting new entrepreneurs. He didn't really have much choice but to agree, but thankfully he was courteous, listened intently and remained firmly behind the idea. The Prime Minister explained how he saw start-up loans as a key legacy that could grow into a landmark policy in years to come, and also clearly understood why partnerships between business and government in these early days are needed to make a difference.

We treated the whole project exactly as if it was any other start-up company. As a non-profit, budgets were minimal but we had plenty of imagination. The energy and enthusiasm surrounding the idea reminded me of the early days of Virgin Records. We knew that by thinking big, while not forgetting the little details, we could find a winning formula. For example, to come up with a nationally successful model we needed to think regionally. What specific gaps in the market were there in Norwich? What new opportunities did young people in London want? Was there a shortage of tech firms in Newcastle? Whenever you are setting up a new project, the most important thing is to surround yourself with people who are better than yourself, have different skills and a healthy combination of enthusiasm and experience. For this business, we found Sir Tom Shebbeare as chairman and Mei Shui as managing director. I told them I wanted to see a full plan within the next few months – and I'd be back over in October to launch the company.

*

The development of Virgin StartUp Loans wasn't my only attempt to help budding entrepreneurs. The previous year, we had set up Pitch To Rich, our annual competition to find the best and most innovative entrepreneurs in the UK. Thousands of people sent in one-minute video pitches, the best became finalists and were invited to my children's home in Oxford. Sam and Holly set up a big tent full of foldaway chairs in the back garden, where they also hosted the *Sunday Times* Fast Track 100 awards, bringing together the year's fastest growing British businesses. There's a real entrepreneurial spirit to the day, with everyone mingling on the lawn and discussing their ideas.

In Pitch To Rich, entrants have the chance to win investment from us, plus mentoring, legal, branding, networking and marketing advice. It was born out of Virgin Media Pioneers, which helped to kick-start, among others, Jamal Edwards' career. Jamal's mum gave him a video camera for Christmas when he was fifteen and he began posting clips of his musician friends in London. By the age of sixteen, his YouTube channel SB.TV had become a phenomenon, helping to launch artists including Ed Sheeran. I'm happy to give Jamal the odd tip when we meet up at Virgin events and he gives me plenty of fashion advice back! I saw SB.TV as a digital cross between *Student* magazine and Virgin Records, so it's wonderful how Jamal uses his voice to highlight important youth issues like voting and drug reform, too.

At Pitch To Rich 2012, I offered the finalists some advice: 'If it can't fit onto the back of an envelope, it's probably a bad idea. Keep it short, sharp and picture-perfect.' Dan Watson won with his potentially revolutionary SafetyNet invention. It supports sustainable fishing by allowing unmarketable fish to escape fishermen's nets. Since then, Dan has gone on to win the annual James Dyson Award for inventors. By 2016, Pitch To Rich had morphed into VOOM, the UK and Ireland's biggest and most valuable pitch competition, with more than £1 million of prizes on offer. As the posters said: 'I've got 99 problems but a pitch ain't one!'

When I'm travelling I get about three to five serious pitches a day. In the past twenty years I would estimate I have heard 25,000 pitches. As Doctor Yes, people do have an expectation when they pitch to me that I will always say yes. Of course, many of these ideas are not up to scratch. One technique I use if that's the case is to politely not respond and change the subject. Likewise, in a business meeting, if somebody is saying something I completely disagree with, I will keep quiet. If people don't respond to me as I suggest something, I know immediately they disagree. When this happens, I say, 'I can tell by the fact you haven't responded that you see it differently. What do you think?'

Too many people presume they are right and don't listen to other points of view. They speak categorically and then close their ears. I consider myself a good listener and apportion a good deal of my success – not to mention my marriage – to this. Some entrepreneurs surround themselves with brilliant people and then ignore them. Most people who behave in this autocratic way get their comeuppance. You need to be a genius, like Steve Jobs, for that to work. I know I am not better than anyone else, so I take a different road.

I try to keep up with the entrepreneur community's exploits online, usually bump into them a few times a year and send personal letters of encouragement. There are many, many positives about the rise of social media, but I am also an old-fashioned believer in the humble written letter. Making the extra effort to say thanks in a genuine, personal manner is pleasurable and goes a long way. In an age where most of us are staring at screens for much of the day, putting a pen to paper and really thinking about what you have to be thankful for can be therapeutic, too. From Princess Diana to Elton John to Barack Obama, each has taken the trouble to send me handwritten letters (which I've obviously responded to by hand) – they mean so much more than emails.

I was reminded of the difference a letter can make when I was giving a talk to hundreds of students in Ukraine – a country that at the time was in a continuing state of political turmoil – in 2014. A young girl stood up and said: 'You were in Kiev four years ago and you met my friend. She was really struggling and you said you would help her get back on her feet ...' My heart jumped into my mouth; I didn't remember the girl and couldn't be certain I'd followed through with my promise. Standing here in front of these wide-eyed students, eager for some positivity and hope in a country suffering after months of painful conflict, I had been talking about the need for collaboration and kindness. If I hadn't helped this girl's friend, they would have been empty words.

'I just wanted to thank you for sending my friend a letter and helping her,' the girl continued. 'She's now in college and starting her own business. You walk the walk as well as talk the talk.' I breathed a sigh of relief. It was a good example of the value of sending personal letters. However small a difference my letter made, it had been worth writing.

Another good example came from Olivia Hill, a twelve-year-old schoolgirl who sent me a wonderful note about her own entrepreneurial dreams. In 2014 she was a year-eight student at Aylsham High School in Norfolk, which specialises in business and enterprise. She was beginning her first GCSE in Business Studies and wrote to me asking about the key skills I used when first starting out. I swiftly replied. The advice might be useful for other young business students, too, so here it is:

Dear Olivia,

Many thanks for getting in touch. I'm honoured you have chosen yours truly as the subject of your business studies project. As somebody who did not particularly enjoy school, I hope you have some fun finding out about Virgin's adventures! As you pointed out, my life in business started with *Student* magazine when I was a few years older than you are now. We set up *Student* to give a voice to people like me who wanted to protest against the Vietnam War and the establishment. I didn't have a career in business in mind, we just wanted to make a positive difference to people's lives. I soon learned one of the best ways to do that is to become an entrepreneur. The key enterprising skills I used when first starting out are the very same ones I use today: the art of delegation, risk-taking, surrounding yourself with a great team and working on projects you really believe in.

As you mentioned in your letter, I suffer from dyslexia but was able to turn this to my advantage. I delegated the areas I struggled with to people who also believed in the project. This freed up my time to focus on what I was good at – the strategy of the magazine, making contacts and developing marketing. We had very little money so had to take risks to get our magazine on the map. I approached to be in *Student* people like Mick Jagger and David Hockney, whom somebody with more experience may have been too intimidated to contact. For some reason, they said yes! I secured advertising by calling up big brands from the school phone box, telling them their rivals were already advertising with us and playing them off against each other.

It was all great fun, and we learned so much about business by taking chances, getting things wrong and getting up to give it another go. Back then, people who were interested in starting their own businesses were not encouraged in school. Nowadays, while I still think much more could be done to encourage entrepreneurship in education, there are lots of tools and mentors to help you get started in business. If your GCSE studies spark your interest too, then that's brilliant. If you don't get top grades, remember there's a lot more to life than some letters on a piece of paper. Have you thought about your own first business idea yet? When you do, be sure to let me know.

Which reminds me: I must write back to Olivia and find out how her business plans are going.

*

Back in autumn 2013, the day had come to launch Virgin StartUp. There was only one place that seemed fitting to do so: the entrepreneurial hotspot of Silicon Roundabout.

When I lived in London, most of the innovations coming out of the city were attached to people with west London postcodes. Now, east London has become the cultural centre of the city, with artists, musicians and, most notably, start-up businesses flocking to Shoreditch, Hackney and beyond. There is great value in working within a community of people with shared mindsets and goals, all striving to achieve new things. It certainly helped being surrounded by our competition when most of the record labels worked within a few streets of each other. I see the same benefits in the way that Virgin Galactic and their fellow space companies are pushing each other to new heights.

The best-known example of this groupthink competitive advantage is in Silicon Valley, where most of the world's brightest tech talents have gathered for the past decade. With companies from Google to Apple and Facebook to Twitter all operating within the same geographical boundaries, the atmosphere of innovation on the West Coast is tangible. I have long believed the UK is floundering behind the US and elsewhere when it comes to technology, and the lack of a principal hub to nurture the undoubted British talent is one of the main reasons why.

So it's great to see Silicon Roundabout filling this role. Some people think it's a silly label, but it's memorable and plenty of people thought Virgin was a ridiculous name, too! The entrepreneurial spirit is thriving in the UK, especially when it comes to technological breakthroughs. By 2014, 16,000 new businesses had registered at Silicon Roundabout and the tech sector accounted for more than a quarter of all new jobs nationwide. While the UK is still definitely missing its own Google or Facebook-esque global powerhouse, it's catching up.

We pulled into Shoreditch, and went inside Boxpark to discover a flurry of activity; entrepreneurs were swapping stories and contact details, caterers were handing out croissants and I went hunting for a cup of tea. A couple of young lads grabbed me, said they were in business together and asked: 'Have you got any inspirational words for us?' It's not easy to be 'inspirational' on demand, but thankfully I had a Dr Muhammad Yunus quote stuck in my head: 'All human beings are born as entrepreneurs. But unfortunately, many of us never had the opportunity to unwrap that part of our life, so it remains hidden.' Now, as you do have the opportunity, don't waste it.

I think entrepreneurship is our natural state – a big adult word that probably boils down to something much more obvious like playfulness. When we are young, before we have our childlike wonder beaten out of us by adult life, we are at our most inventive and ambitious in our actions. I've always tried to keep that youthful spirit. Running a business with your mates is the best thing in the world, but it can quickly turn sour. The important thing is to remember you were friends before business partners, and can remain friends afterwards. I had differences with my Virgin Records co-founder Nik Powell, even though we had been best friends since we were three years old. I can't even recall the details of what we quarrelled about, but I can remember climbing trees together when we were kids in Shamley Green. Now we're good friends again. Life's too short, and if everyone could befriend their enemies the world would be a better place.

It may be controversial to say it but there is no job more important than being an entrepreneur. When you analyse everything about the world and all the improvements that get made, almost without exception it is an entrepreneur that has made them. It might be an entrepreneurial doctor, or architect, or artist – anything. The world is improving day by day, week by week and year by year at an extraordinary rate, thanks to entrepreneurs in every single profession. The number of people being pulled out of poverty globally is amazing, fewer people are starving and more people are working. Fortunately, that means even if there are rotten governments in place; yes, they can do harm, but this is considerably less in a world made up of hundreds of thousands of entrepreneurs.

As the launch day progressed, I grew even more convinced we were doing the right thing in providing assistance for new entrepreneurs. Too many young people are still held back by a lack of support, a lack of genuinely useful, practical training – and, of course, the lack of readily available start-up capital. But we are trying to change that, and meeting with some success. By summer 2018, Virgin StartUp had provided more than 2,500 loans to up-and-coming entrepreneurs in England and Scotland in less than five years. What does 2,500 loans look like? Over £33 million in funding, tens of thousands of hours of mentoring, hundreds of brilliant ideas turned into reality and a new generation of thriving entrepreneurs. Plus research indicates every £1 loaned to a start-up business is worth £3 to the economy. A huge positive of the scheme is that 41 per cent of our recipients are female, which is great news when you consider that only 19 per cent of UK entrepreneurs are women. Virgin StartUp is also proving an excellent channel for previously unemployed people – nearly 20 per cent were not working before they launched their businesses with our loans.

Getting a loan isn't the endgame, though. It helps fund the building of prototypes, market research and proof of concept. This can then enable entrepreneurs to go to angel investors or secure further funds from the bank – it can be a stepping stone to scaling a business. For others, it could be all that is needed to turn a one-man operation into a thriving small business. It is vital to be flexible, treat each case on its merits and each applicant as an individual. As ever in business, it is all about people. Some need their hands holding before they are in a position to receive a cash injection – there would be little point in giving out loans then forgetting about the people you have invested in. That's why we maintain such strong ties with the loan recipients, holding regular catch-ups, regional StartUp events for networking and inspiration, and ensuring their mentor relationships progress well.

As I left the Virgin StartUp launch with all the energy and ideas flowing through me, it made me think back to nearly five decades earlier. The words of my old Stowe School headmaster, Mr Drayson, popped into my head: 'Branson, I predict you will either go to prison or become a millionaire.' In the end I did both: years later I met up with Mr Drayson and he brought along a 'humble pie' to eat. The world has changed a lot since I set out in business, but until now a lack of support for young people with bright ideas has been ever-present. Now, everyone wants to be an entrepreneur, and there are a lot more options available to make it happen. Economies will rise and fall upon the creativity and ingenuity of entrepreneurs, and big companies and governments are beginning to realise that start-ups are the job creators of the future. We're trying to encourage other countries, from Canada to Australia to the US, to adopt start-up loans. I've said it before, but there really has never been a better time to start a business.

32 Calculated Risks

At the start of 2014 I spent time taking stock of how the Virgin Group was developing. We redefined our focus on changing business for good, investing in five core consumer sectors: travel and leisure, telecoms and media, music and entertainment, financial services and health and wellness. With Josh Bayliss as CEO, it was the most defined strategy we had ever put down on paper and it was working. New Virgin Mobile companies and Virgin Radio stations were spreading the brand further afield, in South America, Asia and the Middle East; the brand had the global feel I had always wanted. But there was still room for improvement. Looking over the figures, I pulled out some that caught my eye: more than sixty active Virgin businesses serving over sixty million customers worldwide, making over $24 billion in annual revenue. I rarely sit back and think about the sheer scale of the business, but this brought it home. I sent a note to Josh and our senior management – the V Team, as we call them. 'These figures are great. Now, 60 companies, 60 million customers – can we make it $60 billion revenue?'

One of our businesses in which the figures were moving in the right direction was Virgin Money. As a result, we began to think about floating the bank on the stock market. Behind the scenes, however, trouble was stirring. CEO Jayne-Anne Gadhia felt the board was not behind her. This wasn't a good sign: every company needs strong, united leadership, especially when preparing to float. My instinct, though, was that the issues were probably being blown out of proportion. But within a few days things had escalated to the point that I thought Jayne-Anne might go. When a board meeting was scheduled for the Sunday evening, I rang Jayne-Anne.

'I don't understand everything that's going on,' I told her, 'but I want to. Could you get on the next plane to Necker? We'll talk it over.'

Jayne-Anne flew out the same day. As soon as she arrived and dropped off her bags, it was obvious she was very agitated and highly charged.

'Why don't you come for a walk on the beach?' I suggested. 'I often find the sand between one's toes helps to calm things down.'

So that's what we did. With the warmth of the sun on our backs and the coolness of the water on our feet, we strolled along the coastline, taking in the view, looking out at the reef, listening to the sounds of the birds overhead and the waves gently crashing. As we walked and talked, Jayne-Anne told me she didn't feel supported. I listened to her for a couple of hours and accepted what she said.

'Some people think you're being a pain in the arse,' I said, 'but you've been at the centre of Virgin Money since it was just an idea in an attic. You're a great leader, you've done some extraordinary things, and the last thing we need is to lose you. You will have my full support.'

I appreciated her honesty and her heart, as well as her business acumen. She had a strong vision for Virgin Money and wanted to see it through. I wanted exactly the same thing. Following our conversations, Jayne-Anne wrote to me outlining her vision for floating the company and making positive changes for the future: 'The business is growing fast, our projects are delivering and our hard-working team is loyal and motivated. I will stop talking about the past and look forward positively to finishing the job I started many years ago to the benefit of the staff and shareholders who put their trust in me. Thanks for everything.'

I wrote a letter to Wilbur Ross, Virgin Money's other biggest shareholder, attaching Jayne-Anne's note and explaining my view: 'Have spent many constructive hours with Jayne-Anne. I really believe we have cleared the air. She's been grateful for the frank discussion, is humbled and apologetic that there was a need for a trip to the sun, and I believe will move forward reinvigorated and determined to finish the job she started to the benefit of the shareholders.'

At a meeting the next day, the board decided to go ahead with the flotation in September. Viewing situations from afar is sometimes clearer than being on the front line. In the UK they couldn't see the wood for the trees – with a bit of distance and perspective, which I had from Necker, I could see the wider picture. It is worth remembering that people who run businesses see them as their children. As shareholders you've got to be very careful to give them the freedom and support to look after their children. If Jayne-Anne had left it would have put the IPO back several years, caused the company huge disruption, demoralised staff and damaged the brand (and an excellent one at that!), not to mention removed one of the far too few female CEOs at top companies. And all for what?

Back in the UK, Jayne-Anne was a force of nature. The team worked relentlessly to an unforgiving schedule and, by September, Virgin Money were ready to float. But the markets were proving particularly volatile, and another unexpected issue was also presenting challenges: Scottish independence. A referendum had been called for 18 September, and, as the date neared, polls suggested the outcome was too close to call. With Virgin Money based in Edinburgh, we were among many companies which would have been negatively affected by Scotland leaving Great Britain. Jayne-Anne believed independence would put the IPO back more than a year, and was worried we would need to relocate south.

I hoped Scotland would stay, for personal as much as business reasons. My wife and her family are Scottish, I have Scottish heritage and it is one of our favourite places in the world. I believed its people would be best off remaining a part of the union. But I thought it was sensible to remain neutral publicly, as it was a vote for the Scottish people. A couple of days before the vote, I was in Ukraine trying to encourage more business leaders to call for an end to the conflict there. The atmosphere in Kiev was extremely tense – it was only a matter of months since revolutionary scenes on Maidan Nezalezhnosti, and the east was still under siege from Russia. I held a public discussion at the Yalta Summit about the need to bring Russia back into the international fold, and the role business persons can play in reconciliation. As I came out of the meeting I was surrounded by Ukrainian journalists, confusing me with questions. The issue of Scottish Independence was furthest from my mind, when a journalist from Bloomberg brought up the vote. I replied without thinking: 'If Scotland left Great Britain it would be an absolute disaster.' So much for staying neutral!

I used my blog to try and explain my views more thoughtfully: 'As a businessman, considering Scotland's economy, prosperity and security, I think it is imperative it stays in the union. It is clear that the people of Scotland want change. And whatever the outcome of the referendum, change is on the cards. If the vote stays as close as the polls suggest, there won't be a mandate to separate, or to keep the union exactly as it is. Keeping the status quo is no longer an option and the Scottish Parliament needs greater powers.' Thankfully, the Scottish people opted to stay, with Westminster promising to devolve more power. It was one of the few times I've been happy about the answer 'No'. With markets stabilising, we decided the time was right to make an Initial Public Offering.

*

Two of my favourite things are taking calculated risks and helping to grow businesses. I've built my career on these pillars with Virgin, but I have always made targeted investments outside the Group, too, such as the Twitter stake I mentioned earlier. More recently, these have developed into a full-blown venture capital strategy. Jonno Elliott and our investment team find innovative businesses at early stages and we take relatively small stakes to support their growth. The portfolio of more than thirty-five companies is always growing in areas ranging from health to education, technology to financial services. I am as inquisitive as ever, and believe if you have resources you should use them well.

Our investment policy is to support businesses we feel can make a positive difference. It's foolish to do something just for financial gain – that usually ends in failure. Every household name today, from Pinterest to Slack (a couple of my other investments), had to start somewhere. The best, most purposeful start-ups are living, breathing examples to new generations that creativity, innovation and good honest hard work really can change the world for the better.

Whenever I speak to young people, or whenever I write on my blog, I'm determined to help turn more of those people looking for inspiration into the leaders who inspire the entrepreneurs of the future. My prominence online has other benefits, too, proving useful for discovering the most exciting start-ups for us to invest in. There is now a long line of ambitious entrepreneurs with bright ideas itching to share them with us. I am always more than happy to hear them out and do so on Necker, while travelling or online.

One question people ask me a lot is what I would do today if I lost all my money and had to start from scratch. My answer? To begin with, I'd have to make sure I went bust in the most spectacular, exciting failure in history. Then I'd autograph lots of £10 notes and sell them (hopefully for more!). Next, I'd go through all my notebooks, find the best ideas that had fallen through the cracks and start them up. While business may have changed from when I started out, the principles are the same and still fit what I am good at: finding markets that need shaking up, coming up with ways to make people's lives better, then finding brilliant people to bring it to life. Once an entrepreneur, always an entrepreneur. I know I'd find a gap in the market somewhere.

How successful I'd be in that market is open to debate. My friend Elon Musk notoriously told *Management Today* in 2014 (though he's since assured me he was misquoted!) that I lack practical technological skills: 'I like Richard and I think he's doing some cool things. But technology is not really his whack.' To a degree, he was right. We have very different brains, which is part of the reason we get on so well. He has a lot more technical knowledge than me and is very detail-focused, while I think in broader strokes. We'd probably make a good team. As I once joked while he was holidaying on Necker: 'If you don't have your own ventures one day, you're welcome to come and run one of mine – just brush up on your people skills.'

What I am good at is coming up with interesting ideas and then finding amazing people to turn them into reality. I see investing in start-ups in the same way. I'm not always caught up in the details of what a particular app will or won't do; I'm more interested in the personalities behind the companies, and the purpose within their visions. I'd happily invest in a company that ends up failing in order to find a young entrepreneur who will go on to change the world. Entrepreneurs are the job creators and innovators of the future; it's up to those of us who have been fortunate enough to have some success to give them all the support we can. It's a privilege to see so many entrepreneurs taking their start-ups to the next level and transforming the way the world lives, thinks and does business.

When I meet entrepreneurs, especially in tech, I am often struck by how young they are. But then, when I started out, I was a teenager. The only other entrepreneur people had heard of (though nobody used the word 'entrepreneur') was Body Shop founder Anita Roddick. There was British Airways, British Steel, British Telecom, British Coal, British Gas, British Rail – the government ran everything, and poorly. Entrepreneurship wasn't something 'proper' people did. It was seen as a dirty business, as if the idea of creating and making money from it was beneath people.

Over the last fifty years, thankfully, that has changed and there are new, exciting breakthroughs all the time. Today I wore a pair of Snapchat Spectacles on the tennis court to film my game, then took an update call about M-Kopa, the East Africa solar energy provider we have invested in. Tomorrow there will be another breakthrough. Entrepreneurs are now everywhere, and society is benefiting.

There is a popular sentiment that if you haven't made it in tech by the age of twenty-seven, it's unlikely you'll make it at all. The same used to be true in music, though, of course, many artists haven't made it past the age of twenty-seven. It is wonderful that so many young people are succeeding in business and I hope they will have progressive attitudes and use their wealth and influence for good. One has to hope they have the maturity to look after their companies and, most importantly, their people well. In my experience, some have that, some haven't. Like lottery winners, entrepreneurs who make huge amounts of money overnight can be slightly confused about what to do with it. I met the WhatsApp founder Jan Koum in San Francisco after Facebook bought his app for $19 billion. He was so rich so young and hadn't given much thought about how it was going to change his life. But, thankfully, he did want to look after his team and use his money as a force for good – I'm sure he will. After five decades, I have much experience in how to use my wealth, know what I want and have more understanding about what causes to focus on.

Does this focus on non-Virgin companies mean I'm less focused on my own brand? Not at all. When I wrote *Losing*

My Virginity we were still fighting to survive and that book documented all the struggles. In the last twenty years it would have been extremely stupid of me to let the Virgin Group go under, as we've built up such a strong brand to play off. I've been able to spend a lot more time speaking out on issues I care about and encouraging others to do the same. But I do worry about Virgin not continuing to take risks in the way we used to. We now have the resources to do things with a long-term perspective for the first time. We can consider building hotels, cruise ships and space-lines that will take years to come to fruition, rather than needing to get records sold each week to balance the books, or an airline up and flying in six weeks to stay in business. Now, it's absolutely critical to keep that early hunger I had. I mustn't get complacent; I've still got to be fleet of foot and quick to jump upon opportunities. There is a danger Virgin could become too risk-averse without me. It is easier for me, as the founder, to be risky. When you're CEO or a board member it is more difficult, as you are playing with somebody else's money. But I have every confidence the adventurous streak that Virgin was built on runs deep, alongside the shrewd business sense. With a sound investment strategy and a great team, our success rate should keep going up – but only if we keep sticking our necks out.

*

At the same time as we were preparing our flotation of Virgin Money, similar plans were also in line for Virgin America. While Scotland had proved to be an issue for the former, for the latter our challenge was epitomised by the second largest state in the Union: Texas.

The first time we'd landed in Dallas in December 2010 on our inaugural flight from Los Angeles, I'd thrown on some leather, spurs and cowboy hat to wrangle a herd of Texas longhorns. After a few attempts I was cow-herding like John Wayne (or so I thought).

'This is the most unique airline inaugural Dallas has ever seen,' the airport manager told me, which you could take both ways.

'I don't know if you mean that as a compliment,' I smiled, 'but I'm certainly going to take it as one!'

Still wearing my cowboy gear, I was introduced to Willie Nelson, who was fresh from being arrested for having marijuana on his tour bus. He was performing for us at the Dallas Opera House that night (our Free Willy party!) and invited me onto his tour bus. Let's just say that by the time his set began we were both very, very relaxed!

While we were proud to be serving Dallas/Fort Worth, we also wanted to fly into Love Field, a downtown airport more convenient for business travellers. Love Field had not been open for business for many years. In 1979, the Wright Amendment was enacted, heavily restricting air traffic at Love Field and allowing hometown business Southwest Airlines a monopoly. The result was that, with a lack of choice, consumers were quickly being ripped off. Fares rose 37 per cent over five years, the largest increase anywhere for an airport of its size.

When the Wright Amendment was lifted in October 2014 we seized the opportunity to bring fair competition to the market. We weren't asking for much – just two gates. We got approval to fly from the Department of Justice but, as ever in the airline industry, it wasn't that simple. Southwest wanted to keep their monopoly and, as the hometown airline, wielded a lot of power. To get round this, we hatched a plan to take Dallas by surprise, holding an impromptu landing and press conference. I raced over from Necker and tried to liven up the political debate going on behind the scenes for control of the gates. We started selling tickets to destinations we planned to service, from New York to DC, San Francisco to LA. Sure, we didn't actually have the slots to fly them yet, but why let that get in the way? Our event turned into a heady mix between a political rally and a party, falling on the same day as Cinco de Mayo celebrations. In total, more than 28,000 people signed our petition to support free-market competition. Our message was getting out there.

Not everyone was as impressed, though. Jennifer Gates, one of Dallas council's key decision-makers, emailed us saying she was horrified, particularly by my behaviour at the party: 'I have to tell you I am appalled watching the news tonight that Virgin believes they can win the gates with tequila shots and Branson body-surfing the crowd. It is belittling to the process, which I believe should be governed by our legal advice and what is best for Dallas.'

I replied graciously, reminding her she was missing the bigger picture: 'Really sorry if the news coverage of our event last night – and my crowd-surfing – offended you,' I replied. 'At the event, we were celebrating with our supporters and we'd just let the KIPP Dallas school know we had raised $55,000 for their college trips based on our first day of Love Field sales, and I asked the crowd if we should top it off with a drink – and they agreed (perhaps, not surprisingly!). In the same way that [Southwest Airlines founder] Herb Kelleher taught us 30 years ago to drive more competition and lower fares in the States. We wanted to raise awareness and I hoped we were doing it in a way that made people smile. The last thing I wanted to do was offend. I am very sorry if I did so. We respect the City's process – and hope to have the opportunity to bring lower fares and a bit of competition to Dallas flyers.'

Behind the scenes, powerful local interests were putting the pressure on city leaders. We fought back with humour: on the day of Dallas City Council's decision, we leaked a tongue-in-cheek love letter I wrote to Love Field. The accompanying video of me pining over my unrequited love spread rapidly: 'My dearest Love. From the moment I knew I had a shot at you, you were all that I could think of. Others would keep you all to themselves. I invite competition for your affections. Nay, I demand it. After all, no one should have a monopoly on your love. My virile, young planes are yearning for your runways. You make my heart soar to the highest heights, and my fares drop to the lowest lows. You have the window seat to my heart, kitten. It's time to let our love take flight, no matter how hard they try to keep us apart. Your sweetheart, Richard.'

The following day, due to public pressure, hard work from the team and common sense from the authorities, we were finally awarded the gates. I was proud that our efforts to win the hearts and minds of the public had not gone unnoticed. It proved once again that having the facts on your side is one thing, but telling a great story with just enough charm and chutzpah can make all the difference.

33 The Accident

A few weeks before the next planned powered test flight in Mojave in October 2014, I travelled over to see the Virgin Galactic team for some training even closer to the real thing – a thrilling g-force training flight.

Virgin Galactic chief pilot Dave Mackay took me up in an Extra 300L plane, a small but ultra-fast and reliable aircraft trainer. It reminded me of the time I went up in the back of a Spitfire for a UK TV show. I was arguing that the Spitfire was the greatest plane ever built, so had to keep talking up what a beautiful machine it was and how smooth it handled. I got the chance to prove my point by taking it for a spin. With perfect timing, however, I was hit with a horrible wave of sickness. It doesn't matter how fit you are, sometimes sickness can overwhelm even the best prepared body. You can train to try to avoid these things and overcome the fear of the unknown that can cause sickness – but it can still happen. I put my hand over the camera pointing at my face and promptly threw up, managing to direct it into a paper bag and avoid the plane's vintage interior.

I was keen not to repeat this when Dave took me up in the Extra 300L, and remembered a trick my mum had taught me from her stewardess days, when plane rides were a lot more bumpy than they are today. She recommended a few swigs of prune juice to settle the stomach, so I gulped down a glass before strapping myself into the plane. Not a good idea! I forgot my mum was dyslexic, too – prunes help with constipation, they don't settle stomachs. The main reason for undertaking the flight was to become more confident and comfortable in handling elevated levels of g-force in a real-life situation. I would also be able to experience micro-gravity and enjoy a landing very similar to a typical SpaceShipTwo approach onto the Mojave strip.

The Extra 300L is an in-line two-seater aircraft in which the pilot sits in the rear seat and the co-pilot (me) sits in the front. In other words, I had the best view in the house. The arid landscape looked stunning from above, and eerie when we circled over the famous aircraft graveyard where dozens of old commercial planes are lined up, rusting away more slowly in the desert. As I was looking down, Dave gradually built up the g-force as we climbed higher and higher. We went up from 2 g to 2.5 g, to 3 g then 3.5 g, with gradual building up, then easing off. I practised the anti-g straining manoeuvre I had learned in my training and, thankfully, felt fine the whole time, having got rid of the prune juice before we took off.

'Can we do a few loop the loops?' I asked, growing in confidence and unable to resist having a little extra fun. Dave is a born flyer and was happy to oblige. We did a few loops before he surprised me with a barrel roll. I even got to try out flying the plane. It was a magical experience and I felt more ready for my spaceflight than ever. When we landed, Dave turned to me.

'Have you ever thought of being a pilot yourself?' he asked.

I considered it for a moment. 'I don't think I've ever really wanted to be a pilot. I wouldn't trust myself, my mind wanders too much. It's different in a hot-air balloon. The balloon wanders all by itself!'

That afternoon, we had a grand reunion of everyone involved in winning the XPRIZE. Burt was there, full of terrific tales and homespun wisdom. I loved swapping stories with Brian Binnie, Anousheh Ansari, Peter Diamandis and the gang, and we all wondered where the past decade had gone.

I then hot-footed it back over to the FAITH hangar for a sneak peek at the uniforms we will wear to space. I had been told they were quite daring and dark.

I felt a small thrill as I pulled on an all-in-one navy flight suit. The designer explained how it was made from a heat-resistant synthetic material called Nomex® Meta-Aramid, and that it was woven using a 3D-engineered pattern. Most importantly, it looked and felt great.

Burt had kept his pyramid house in the desert. After the fitting, I took a group of our future astronauts over there to share our latest plans. It had been a while since I had been there, and the beautiful alien murals and remarkable aeroplane designs inside the great pyramid structure had been updated. It couldn't have been more Burt if it had had a pair of mutton-chop whiskers on the walls. I kept looking around the room, seeing my own excitement reflected on everybody else's faces.

As I departed, I had no idea that the next time I would return to Mojave would be the most difficult journey of my life.

*

From: George Whitesides
To: Richard Branson
10/31/2014 7:07 AM
Weather trend unfavorable. Will keep you updated.

Early in the morning on 31 October 2014 I was sitting at home on Necker Island with a feeling of schoolboy excitement. Around me, Halloween decorations were being hung up all around the house and kids were trying on their costumes. But my mind was elsewhere: I was waiting for historic news from the Mojave Desert, where Scaled Composites was intending to carry out the fourth powered flight test of SpaceShipTwo. To add to the tension, the weather was delaying take-off. It left me on tenterhooks, as I waited for CEO George Whitesides and the Virgin Galactic team monitoring the situation to update me.

From: George Whitesides
To: Richard Branson
10/31/2014 9:22 AM
Take-off. So far winds are holding.

This was it. I could feel my fingers tingling with anticipation. If this test flight was successful, SpaceShip Two would be flying faster than ever before, going supersonic, soaring through the skies to the edge of space, travelling higher than any commercial vehicle in history and making another giant leap towards commercial space travel.

Back on Necker Island I was conducting an interview about Virgin Galactic to the Sundog Pictures team, who were making a documentary about my ballooning activities. I spoke excitedly about the flight test and shared my hopes of flying to space myself in the next year, with more powered flight tests provisionally scheduled for the coming months.

From: George Whitesides
To: Richard Branson
10/31/2014 9:57 AM
Update: if we drop, probably around 10 minutes past hour.

Over at the Mojave Air and Space Port in California, optimism was high, buoyed by the previous three successful powered test flights. The wind was just about holding off and it looked as if SpaceShipTwo would get up in the air. The team from Scaled Composites were in the control room and many of the Virgin Galactic team were out on the tarmac, having downed tools to watch the test.

At 12.20 p.m. local time, WhiteKnightTwo took off, with SpaceShipTwo secured to its underbelly. The mothership flew smoothly off the runway and began its climb to an altitude of 50,000 feet. Dave Mackay was at the controls of the mothership, with Pete Siebold and Mike Alsbury from Scaled in the spaceship.

At 1.10 p.m., WhiteKnightTwo released the spaceship as planned and it flew freely into the clear blue sky. The pilots experienced a split-second drop through the air, before igniting the rocket. They were pushed back into their seats by the sheer force of the rocket and began their planned ascent up towards the edge of space.

Back on Necker my eyes were glued to my iPad, waiting for George Whitesides to email through the next live update on the test. I got a call from Sam, who was in Philadelphia, carrying out centrifuge training and medical examinations in preparation for our future spaceflight together. There wasn't a date in place, but it was moving ever closer with each successful test. As Sam phoned from inside the test centre, I marvelled at his timing.

'Sam,' I said proudly, 'at this very minute WhiteKnightTwo is soaring sixty thousand feet in the air above Mojave, waiting to release SpaceShipTwo. If this test goes well, it could be us in that spaceship very soon.'

The phone signal crackled as another email from George flashed up on my iPad.

'Dad?' As I stopped speaking, Sam sensed something was wrong.

'Sam? Sam, I've got to go. Something's happened. I love you.'

From: George Whitesides
To: Richard Branson
10/31/2014 10:17 AM
Bad day. The spaceship seems to be lost. I don't know status of pilots. I will report more when I get more information.

I felt a sickening sensation. I was overwhelmed by different feelings: sadness, confusion and adrenaline took over. After staring at the screen for what seemed an eternity, but must have been just a few seconds, I made a decision and punched in my reply.

From: Richard Branson
To: George Whitesides
10/31/2014 10:18 AM
So so sorry. Will be with you as soon as I can. On my way.

'There's been an accident in Mojave,' I shouted to Helen, rushing out of the Temple. 'We've got to go right away.' Ducking through Halloween party decorations as I went, we scrambled for our bags and passports and jumped in a speedboat in a matter of minutes. I promised to phone on the way to Mojave to find out what more information the team had managed to gather, so I could prepare for what I would be confronted with when I arrived.

I didn't know what had happened, but I knew I needed to be there. We didn't know what we were facing, but I knew we would face it together.

About two minutes after SpaceShipTwo was released, it had broken apart in mid-air, travelling at supersonic speeds. At this point we did not know if Scaled's pilots were alive or dead. We also had no idea what it meant for Virgin Galactic and our space programme. All I knew was that I needed to be with our team. As our plane took off from Tortola, I sent out a message: 'Thoughts with all @virgingalactic & Scaled, thanks for all your messages of support. I'm flying to Mojave immediately to be with the team.'

As I raced over to the US, George was already bringing the Virgin Galactic staff together in Mojave: he showed extraordinary leadership to rally the shattered morale and broken hearts of hundreds of staff who had seen the incident. At the same time, the National Transportation Safety Board (NTSB) was also on their way to begin their investigation into the incident. I wondered what I could possibly say or do to help in this desperate situation. As I landed on the way in Miami to refuel, I was desperate for more information and keen to gather my thoughts before arriving at the Spaceport. Mike Moses, the Head of Operations, was being drip-fed details from emergency responders and Scaled in Mission Control, as well as from Dave Mackay in

WhiteKnightTwo. At one point when the team was huddled together, the good news came through that Dave and WhiteKnightTwo were OK. From the window the team could see the mothership landing – it was like a long-lost friend coming home. Mike ran out of the room and gave Dave an emotional welcome back to earth.

As we entered the Mojave airspace, I was all too aware we were flying through the same area SpaceShipTwo had flown for the last time just hours before. I stepped off the plane a few metres from our FAITH hangar, while the press already hovered nearby. George and Christine ran out to meet us, and before my feet touched the ground Helen and I hugged them tight: the first tears of the day.

When I walked into FAITH I immediately went to spend time with the Virgin Galactic and Scaled teams, who were watching on.

Rick 'CJ' Sturckow had been in the chase plane following the spaceship. He had the best view of SpaceShipTwo's break-up, but couldn't be certain what had happened. He told us that one pilot's parachute had definitely opened – later we learned it was Pete Siebold's – and he had followed it down, praying the pilot was alive. Pete had been thrown out of the spaceship still strapped to his seat as it broke up around him, and somehow floated free of the falling debris. He fell for 25,000 feet, unconscious as he tumbled through the sky. Shaking himself awake, he had the presence of mind to unstrap himself, flying free of the seat, which automatically opened his parachute.

CJ's main priority was to be able to give the coordinates of the landing, so any potential rescue could take place as quickly as possible. However, knowing that nobody had ever survived an incident like this at such speed and height, he was far from hopeful. He watched the figure falling, falling through the air underneath a bright red parachute, a tiny dot on the blue horizon. But then, miraculously, he saw Pete lift his right fist in the air, signalling that, against all expectations, he was still breathing, still moving and still fighting to live. Pete landed with an almighty bump: his shoulder was broken and he was badly shaken, but, unbelievably, he was alive. First responders raced to the scene using CJ's coordinates, and Pete was rushed to Antelope Valley Hospital. Pete was one of the first people in history to walk away from a supersonic accident. To be involved in an in-air vehicle break-up at those speeds and that height, and live to tell the tale, is nothing short of a miracle. He is a true survivor.

We would have to wait for the large amount of footage recorded from inside the cockpit to fully determine exactly what had happened. I went over to see the NTSB team in a neighbouring hangar. They told us what the ground rules were, how they would behave and how we should behave, what we could say and what we couldn't say. We agreed we would open up very clear communications channels on both sides and cooperate fully with the investigation, which could take up to a year.

I spoke to the NTSB chairman Christopher A. Hart and told him: 'From our point of view, all that matters is we do everything we can for the pilots and their families. Then it is obviously crucial we get to the bottom of what happened so we can learn from it – the sooner the better.'

By now, first responders were on the site where the spaceship had crashed, with news helicopters flying overhead beaming the wreckage into millions of homes around the world. It quickly became clear that our worst fears had been realised – co-pilot Mike Alsbury had not survived the accident. It was believed he had been killed instantly inside the spaceship as it broke apart, and was still strapped into his seat when he was found on the desert floor. Everyone looked around at each other, inconsolable at the news.

I stepped away from FAITH for a little while and met Sam, who had arrived from Philadelphia.

'I'm so sorry, Dad,' he said, as I clung to him for a big hug. It was so, so good to have him there.

'Thanks for coming. I don't know what we can do to help, but let's do whatever we can.'

We went back into FAITH to visit the Virgin Galactic team and I could see on people's faces that some of them were really struggling, mourning the loss of Mike Alsbury, as well as the loss of the spaceship. They had all stood outside in the morning sun with high hopes for the test, and watched as their dreams had seemingly broken up before their eyes.

The NTSB showed us the first photo of SpaceShipTwo's engine and fuel tanks intact on the ground. Based on that, we knew for certain that the engine, rocket and fuel tanks had not blown up. Contrary to already surfacing, highly unsavoury media reports, there was no explosion – the rocket motor had nothing to do with the accident.

I went back in to see the Virgin Galactic staff. I knew my job was to lift morale and thank them for everything that they had achieved so far. Sometimes being calm and strong is the only choice. In situations like this I am always worried how my body is going to react. In critical moments such as the one in Mojave, the crucial thing is to hold yourself together and try to avoid breaking down. Fortunately, I managed to stay relatively composed in front of the team. The thing is to not think selfishly, put yourself in other people's shoes and try to do your best for them. Sometimes you have to rely on sheer emotion.

'I think we all need to have the biggest hug in the world,' I said.

Some people are religious, some people are spiritual and some are neither. But a hug is something that everybody can appreciate. We stood there in the middle of the hangar, where SpaceShipTwo had been mere hours before, and had a massive group hug. It served its purpose, lifting everybody's spirits just enough to get us through the rest of the day.

But even as I could feel the warmth and release of tension in the hangar, I couldn't switch off the question that was nagging away in the back of my mind. Catching the eye of some of the others, I knew I wasn't alone in having the same thought.

What next?

What happens now?

34 Moving On

I needed to let the world know as much as I could possibly share about what had happened to SpaceShipTwo, although we were constrained by the NTSB investigation. Nonetheless, I felt the need to call a press conference to address the incident. That was easier said than done, as there wasn't a free room for the session to take place. Then Sam went into the back of the hangar and found a small podium. He and Tom Westray from Galactic picked it up and carried it over to the gravel car park. The media quickly stuck their recorders on top, and, with the desert as a backdrop, the press conference began.

The NTSB gave their first statement, presenting their initial findings and clearly stating that the rocket motor had been found intact on the ground. Then George Whitesides stood up and put our feelings across perfectly: 'Space is hard, and today was a tough day. We are going to be supporting the investigation as we figure out what happened today, and we're going to get through it. The future rests, in many ways, on hard days like this. But we believe we owe it to the folks who were flying these vehicles as well as the folks who have been working so hard on them to understand this and to move forward, which is what we'll do.'

Next it was my turn and I took a piece of paper with my scribbled notes on it up to the podium. Normally I ad-lib, but on this occasion I wanted to get my words exactly right, especially considering the rules the NTSB had understandably laid down. I echoed George's thoughts and also shared my own, determined that we would learn from what had happened. 'In testing the boundaries of human capabilities and technologies, we are standing on the shoulders of giants. Yesterday, we fell short. I truly believe that humanity's greatest achievements come out of our greatest pain. This team is a group of the bravest, brightest, most determined and most resilient people I have ever had the privilege of knowing. We are determined to honour the bravery of the pilots and teams here by learning from this tragedy. Only then can we move forwards, united behind a collective desire to push the boundaries of human endeavour.'

After the first press conference, and in the following days, we were still not permitted to share details of what had caused the accident, due to the continuing NTSB investigation. The people who knew weren't able to talk. The people who didn't know, meanwhile, were talking wildly: certain sections of the media sprang into action with all kinds of false and irresponsible reporting. We were astonished how a few people with no information at all on the subject could be repeatedly wheeled out as supposed experts across all major media.

I felt hurt, though I'm old enough and ugly enough to handle it. But I was devastated for our dedicated team who had to deal with all manner of sensationalist and unfounded accusations, while they grieved the loss of Mike Alsbury and tried to make sense of losing SpaceShipTwo. Before there was even time for Virgin Galactic to provide a statement with the information we had so far, a local blogger falsely claimed to have seen SpaceShipTwo's engine sputter and fail to perform. This was completely untrue, but contributed to a growing story that the rocket technology was to blame.

Many of the press swallowed this whole, with this widely shared Associated Press tweet a typical example: 'BREAKING: Witness reports SpaceShipTwo exploded in flight after ignition of rocket, crashed in desert.' Fantastical accusations grew to a crescendo in the coming days, and I was disgusted at the way a test flight accident turned into open season for desultory cheap shots. Some of the press even claimed Scaled had 'no licence' and 'no rocket' to operate with, which were clearly false, as Scaled had been granted an experimental permit from the FAA and completed a series of successful rocket-powered test flights. Journalists got many details wrong, such as claiming the vehicle was made out of metal rather than carbon composite.

Most galling was the attempt by some in the press to cast doubt on Virgin Galactic's absolute commitment to safety. One journalist insinuated all of our engineers had told him the project was dangerous and claimed many of the team had walked out. He said the crash that caused Mike Alsbury's tragic death was 'predictable and inevitable'; it was neither.

In my opinion, 99 per cent of the press are very good, research their stories well, check facts and serve an incredibly important purpose for society. They keep people honest, hold them to account, let the public know about exciting new innovations and protect freedom of speech. On this occasion, a few armchair critics who had no first-hand knowledge of the accident made baseless, defamatory and malicious claims. I perhaps wouldn't have minded so much if these falsehoods were well written or well argued. Instead, rather than approaching Queen's Counsel to sue, some of the articles seemed to me to warrant a complaint to the Society for the Protection of the English Language! But my time and energy were much better spent supporting the Virgin Galactic team through this most difficult period.

Rushing back home to Necker from Mojave to host a fundraising event for Virgin Unite, I broke out of the discussions to do a series of press interviews regarding the future of Virgin Galactic and the nature of the accident. The UK press, in particular, continued to be extremely hostile – it felt like open season for anybody who wanted to get in some cheap shots. Jon Snow attacked me live on Channel 4 for being back on Necker and was incredibly antagonistic in his questioning.

'I find it very insulting, the whole tone of your questions,' I said, as Jon seemed to be ignoring the NTSB's evidence by continuing to cross-examine me about the rocket motor and engine. 'I respect you enormously normally. I have no respect at all for the way you are conducting this interview. But anyway, I will answer your questions.'

I was fully transparent, repeating again and again how Virgin Galactic was an extraordinary company trying to do things no business had done before.

*

In the days and weeks after the accident we used our social media channels to act as an instant press release service, effectively getting our side of the story across to millions of people. Even so, I opened up my iPad several times a day to see articles and hear interviews of increasing unpleasantness. *TIME* magazine wrote it was 'angry, even disgusted' with me personally and claimed that 'a Virgin crash always seemed troublingly likely'. They called me 'a man driven by too much hubris, too much hucksterism and too little knowledge of the head-crackingly complex business of engineering'. (I'm no rocket scientist and have never pretended to be – but I have hired the world's finest.)

A month earlier, the *Daily Mail* proudly displayed the headline 'The only thing Branson has fired into space is his ego'; now they really went for the jugular. One of the problems with this coverage was that, even as new evidence emerged, the initial falsities remained in the public consciousness.

The investigators were very angry about the standards of reporting and called a press conference to make clear that the rocket had not exploded and the engine and fuel tanks were intact on the ground. When they concluded their initial investigations, their findings confirmed that Scaled co-pilot Mike Alsbury had unlocked the feathering system lever too early. By design, at the appropriate point when the spaceship was travelling at Mach 1.4 on its ascent towards space, the co-pilot would pull a handle that unlocked the tail. As Scaled's previous tests had shown, aerodynamic pressures would push down on the tail and maintain its usual position aligned with the wings. Later, once the rocket burn was over and the spaceship was floating in space at very low speeds, another handle would be pulled by the pilots to move the feathering system into play. This would move the tail into its feathered position and allow the spaceship to glide down to earth as smoothly as a shuttlecock. It had to be deployed when the spaceship reached the correct speed, height and angle; otherwise it had the opposite effect of destroying the vehicle rather than keeping it safe.

On this occasion, however, Mike had unlocked the tail well before the spaceship was at the correct vertical angle. Rather than aerodynamic forces pressing down to keep the tail in position, they pushed up and made the tail fly upwards. This caused SpaceShipTwo to flip violently over backwards and break apart in mid-air: reading the findings, it was desperately sad to think that Mike's mistake had contributed to his death, and the loss of SpaceShipTwo. As this information spread to the press, it was amazing how it was dismissed in some quarters in favour of the more sensational angle of an explosion, which would be more damaging to Virgin Galactic's credibility.

Having realised that they had made a mistake about exploding rockets and engines, some of the press tried a new angle: they falsely wrote that I faced a serious investigation into spending the deposits of future astronauts. Some of the press also claimed the majority of our customers would want a refund. The *Daily Mail*, meanwhile, reported that I was facing 'a backlash' from restless customers. In fact, we had not spent any of our future astronauts' deposits. They are deliberately held separately from operating funds; any customer is entitled to a full refund at any time. Only a tiny fraction of our more than 700 customers have ever asked for a refund – those who have done so received their money back immediately. In the days after the SpaceShipTwo incident, we expected a number of future astronauts to get cold feet. On the contrary, very few people have cancelled their tickets. In fact, on the very day of the accident, two individuals actually signed up for tickets to space as a gesture of goodwill – it was a huge confidence boost for us all.

That wasn't the only boost. While some of the press were highly critical, the response of our community and the wider public was unbelievably supportive. The thousands of messages of goodwill that flooded in from people who believed in Virgin Galactic and our mission overwhelmed me. At Mojave, the Galactic team covered an entire wall with supportive messages for the Scaled Composites pilots and their families. They came from everywhere, from social media to Virgin Galactic customers, from close friends to people I had never met, from Bono to my own dear mum.

'I wish you guys that your program will recover from this and get even stronger afterwards!' wrote the astronauts living on the International Space Station. 'To strive, to seek, to find, and not to yield!'

Graça Machel got in touch to say: 'Sadness yes, but much more encouragement to honour the journey covered so far, and embrace the way ahead with the same courage, determination and optimism.'

June Scobee Rodgers, the widow of Space Shuttle *Challenger* commander Dick Scobee, wrote: 'This setback is tragic, but the courage and commitment of your fellow team will soon help you all to recover, and from the energy of grief, the phoenix will arise with even more resolve and commitment.' Messages such as these brought real solace at a time of darkness.

I was very grateful that some of the press began to report more responsibly, and recognise that Virgin Galactic had dealt very well with an extremely difficult situation. They interviewed genuine experts who understood Virgin Galactic's purpose and expertise.

Astronaut Mark Kelly did a series of interviews providing context around the challenges of space travel and the professionalism of Virgin Galactic. Professor Brian Cox kindly dedicated an episode of *The Human Universe* on BBC1 to the memory of Mike Alsbury. It focused movingly on the development of Virgin Galactic and the importance of commercial space travel to the development of humanity. Brian somehow made time to record an additional segment that paid tribute to Mike and the bravery of all test pilots. I watched it with tears streaming down my face. I wrote in my notebook: 'We owe it to all of those who have risked and given so much to stay the course and deliver on the promise of creating the first commercial spaceline.'

*

For all the frustrations with the press coverage, by far the hardest part of the tragic accident remained the loss of one of SpaceShipTwo's test pilots, Michael Alsbury. Mike had worked for Scaled Composites for thirteen years and was a dear friend and inspiring colleague to the many, many loved ones he left behind. My heart went out to his parents, his wife and children, his sister and the rest of his family and friends. A fund was set up to honour Mike and hundreds of thousands of dollars were quickly raised.

I flew back to Mojave to attend and speak at Mike's memorial service a few days later, and was honoured to spend a short time with his family. They were understandably distraught at Mike's passing, but have conducted themselves with incredible strength and compassion at all times. As Ralph Waldo Emerson said: 'It is not length of life, but depth of life.'

There are no words to express our grief at the loss of such a wonderful young man. But there are actions we can all take to honour his memory. We will continue our programme with Mike forever at the forefront of our minds, for his commitment, his passion and his sacrifice. The team gave a nickname to the new SpaceShipTwo we were building: 'Hope'. It is Mike who has given us this hope, and we hope to achieve in Mike's name the dream he had pursued so bravely.

*

The NTSB, meanwhile, had completed the on-scene part of their investigation. They had taken away the SpaceShipTwo debris for further examination, and begun processing the vast amount of video evidence available. They had also interviewed Pete Siebold, whose account of the vehicle's motion was consistent with other data the NTSB had gathered. Pete described how he had been thrown from the spaceship, as it broke up in mid-air, and unbuckled from his seat before his parachute deployed automatically. He was unaware of his co-pilot pulling the lever to begin the feathering system.

There was lots of debate, both inside and outside Virgin, about what the setback meant for our future. We got a taste of what some of the media would have been like if there had been a technical problem. NASA suffered fatal accidents during their development, but it didn't stop them persevering. Could Virgin Galactic have withstood the onslaught if SpaceShipTwo's engine had exploded? Would we have been able to pick ourselves up from that and continue?

I sat down with George to discuss going forward. We knew we had all the support of our astronauts, of our team, by and large of the public (though not some elements of the press).

'We've been crucified in the last few days for an accident that wasn't our fault,' I said. 'It was a test flight, we lost a test pilot. If we carry on, we're going to have to go through a lot of test flights again with the next spaceship. Because they are test flights, there is the possibility it will happen again. Are we going to be able to look in the mirror if that happens a second time? What will happen to our reputations? What will happen to the Virgin Group generally?'

George was very honest. 'We can't rule it out. NASA had a number of accidents while developing the space programme. We are in early days. There is a possibility it could happen again.'

I felt the company would be unlikely to survive another accident, from a financial standpoint. Some of the Virgin Group board were sceptical about continuing and I could see their logic. There are many safer ways to invest our money and there is no question that the Virgin Group would be better off financially in the short term if we invested the money we are spending on Virgin Galactic into other companies. If I hadn't owned the company, I think the programme would have been knocked on the head some years ago. On the day we started, if I'd known it was going to take twelve years I suspect I wouldn't have gone ahead with the project either – we simply couldn't afford it. Fortunately, over the past decade we have had successes elsewhere in Virgin, as well as outside investment from Aabar in Virgin Galactic, which has enabled us to continue our dream. Sometimes long-term investments like this can only happen in private companies where an owner has a vision. It may not make perfect sense financially in the short term, but I only have one life and if we can pull this off it will be extraordinary and make so much difference to so many people.

'If we can get through the test programme,' George continued, 'the chances of an accident happening with customers on board are extremely unlikely. Getting through the test programme is going to be tough, but I believe we can do it.'

'The only way we will know is to give it a go,' I agreed. 'Rather than continuing to work with Scaled, let's bring everything in-house and give it everything we've got.' The Spaceship Company, which is owned by Virgin Galactic and shares George as its CEO, had already been working on the new SpaceShipTwo for many months. Now, we took charge of all parts of the building, testing and developing process. We also took charge of our own test pilots. These were the major changes after the accident, giving us control over every aspect of the programme.

Back at Virgin HQ I knew I was in a minority in wanting to continue. But that didn't stop me – I believed in the project, believed in the team and believed in the vision. My instinct is if you create something extraordinary there will be a market in the end. Is it a vanity project? I don't think so. Elon Musk's desire to go to Mars, and our wish to put people into space, certainly can both be perceived as vanity projects. But if people didn't want to test themselves in an extreme way, progress wouldn't happen and the world would be a sadder, smaller place.

It's important in life to question one's motives. Am I doing it for the right reasons, or for egotistical reasons? This book has helped me to reflect on that. Does it justify the amount of money we're spending on it? Will it make a real difference to the world? Having asked all those questions, I came to the conclusion that I'm correct in sticking my neck out on this one. I take inspiration from the way President Kennedy invested in the Apollo programme; people questioned the benefits to mankind, but the moon landing ended up doing more for mankind than almost anything else. The information, the connectivity, the sheer awe of young kids like me marvelling at that incredible trip, has burnt brightly for generations. It is worth the risks and the expense to make other people's dreams become a reality, as well as our own. With the *Virgin Atlantic Challenger* we sank the first time. We rebuilt it and succeeded the next time. With attempts to cross the Pacific in a balloon, we failed, learned from it, then did it the next time. I'm confident Virgin Galactic will succeed eventually, too.

We continued our work. The Galactic team inside FAITH were already back working around the clock on our next spaceship. One of my better decisions had been to push starting development of another SpaceShipTwo around eighteen months earlier. It was already about 50 per cent structurally complete. My vision was always for a spaceline consisting of a series of spaceships, motherships and a spaceport, not just one spaceship. I was also concerned that if there was ever a problem with SpaceShipTwo, it would be foolish for the staff to have nothing to do. So the hard work went on and the team got back to the nuts and bolts of spaceship development and rocket science.

*

I have spent a lot of time thinking about what the Virgin Galactic brand means to the broader Virgin Group, and what it could go on to mean for the world. It has never been just a business to me. Virgin has always wanted to make a difference. We have gone into markets where others dare not tread, and shaken them up. We don't just provide services or products; we provide experiences that leave people changed, and wanting to create new world-changing experiences themselves.

The teamwork and entrepreneurial spirit of everyone involved, from the engineers to the marketers, the rocket scientists to the doctors, is unprecedented. Many of the team quit bigger aerospace companies to join Virgin Galactic and speak enthusiastically about being part of the larger purpose and the culture. Their opinions are valued, they are empowered to make smart decisions quickly and build and test revolutionary new systems. They are unbelievably bright and share an uncommon connection through working together on something truly extraordinary.

I am honoured to continue to be a part of the journey. It has been a lifetime's ambition to go to space, but this is born out of a personal desire to see space democratised and transform life back here on earth. By giving people the opportunity to experience the overview effect, I am convinced they will come back to earth determined to make a real difference. Aside from creating astronauts, developing the world's biggest satellite constellation could be transformative for the hundreds of millions of people who are still unconnected.

Just as the risks of space travel cannot be underestimated, so the benefits of commercial space exploration cannot be understated. As Joseph Baladi put in a *Singapore Business Times* piece titled *'Per ardua ad astra'* – Through adversity to the stars: 'Virgin Galactic is, in a real sense, on a mission that has the potential to change the course of human destiny. ... Virgin Galactic will surely one day take "tourists" into space. But this is a means to an end. The real contribution Virgin Galactic is making lies in breaking a frontier that will eventually reveal endless new possibilities and help transport humankind to the next level. It is a grand purpose.'

Yes, I believe that commercial space travel can become a profitable enterprise – but that is not the point. If I had merely wanted to make more money, I could have invested in far safer, more reliable sectors. I believe that putting our faith in space travel serves, quite literally, a higher purpose. We could expand our understanding of the universe, explore the great unknown and improve countless lives back on earth. In the decades to come, we could be a precursor to further space exploration, which could lead to the colonisation of other planets and the eventual endurance of the human race. There can be no greater challenge.

As we continue our space programme, I remain convinced we will be the first commercial company to fly people to space, for the benefit of everyone on our own planet. As Professor Stephen Hawking said, the team at Virgin Galactic 'has my utmost respect for enabling more of humanity to experience the true wonder of space. I have said in the past "Look up at the stars and not down at your feet", but I believe that "looking up" will no longer be a requirement to see the universe in all its glory.'

35 Floating

T he weeks following the SpaceShipTwo accident were an extraordinary time of conflicting emotions for everyone at Virgin. The tragic loss of Mike Alsbury was front and centre of my thoughts, but the Virgin America and Virgin Money teams had to get on with their own jobs at hand. For many, many months, we were preparing for two of the biggest decisions we had ever made: taking the companies public on the Stock Exchange. It was the hardest couple of weeks of my life, going back and forth from Mojave, dealing with the fallout from the accident and trying to keep on the ball with the IPOs.

We held a board meeting at Virgin Group and very quickly I realised there were very mixed views around the table about whether we should carry on with the floats. We had to ask tough questions, which it almost felt distasteful to discuss in the circumstances.

'Does anybody think it is disrespectful to carry on with these deals?' I asked.

But everyone agreed we had to keep moving forward with other Virgin businesses.

'Is the brand resilient enough to stand up to all of the extra scrutiny?' asked Josh, thinking aloud. 'I think it is, but what does anyone else think?'

As we talked it through, it became abundantly clear to me that the right thing to do was to persevere. Josh too argued very strongly that we should carry on.

'The only reason we shouldn't go ahead is if we don't think these companies are strong enough,' he said. 'I'm absolutely convinced they stand on their own two feet, and this isn't affected by the Galactic incident.'

By the end of the meeting, everyone was on the same page. 'Let's truck on,' I said. I've no idea why that phrase came to mind.

With Virgin America's partner Cyrus Capital, we went through the exhaustive process of getting a successful listing ready for the Nasdaq Stock Exchange in New York. Over in the UK, meanwhile, Jayne-Anne was preparing Virgin Money for their IPO. What we were attempting was unprecedented: two public listings in two completely different sectors by one brand within twenty-four hours. But while I agreed with Josh that we should go ahead, and much as I regard my role as present, I didn't feel it was right for me to attend either IPO in person, out of respect for those affected by events in Mojave.

So often in life, timing is everything. On 13 November we announced Virgin Money's flotation on the London Stock Exchange. Another bank, Aldermore, announced its intention to list a month before us and had to pull out, as the market wasn't right. If we had been a week earlier we would also have had to pull. As it was, the IPO was priced at 283p a share, valuing Virgin Money at £1.25 billion. The market took to the flotation well; shares rose a little on the first day and kept rising in the ensuing months. We made a final £50 million payment regarding the sale of Northern Rock, making the total paid to the British government over £1 billion. When we announced our full-year results in March 2015, pre-tax profit had more than doubled to £121.2 million. All of the shareholders who had doubts earlier in the year were now satisfied.

'Is this really our bank?' I wrote to Jayne-Anne. 'I feel almost like a grown-up!' It felt a long way since I had been rejected by Coutts for being a hippy.

Since going public, our punk roots have come to the fore. What would be more fitting than to put the original counter-culture heroes and Virgin Records rebels The Sex Pistols on our credit cards? We were celebrating our heritage and marking ourselves out as being a completely different challenger bank from our rivals. As we sent around the advertising copy to newspapers, I was amazed that, four decades since we had been arrested for using the word 'bollocks' on the album cover, and winning the court case, they still refused to run the adverts!

I wasn't worried, though; it was another occasion for us to say bollocks to normal banking. Since day one Virgin Money has done things differently to make everyone better off. The original fourteen people Jayne-Anne brought across with her to launch Virgin Money have now been joined by thousands more staff, serving 2.8 million customers across seventy-five stores and five Lounges.

'It turns out banking without the bollocks wasn't such a bad idea after all,' I wrote to her. 'And I'm more than happy for you to call me an absolute banker.'

The very next morning after the Virgin Money flotation, David Cush and the team gathered in New York to ring the bell and officially make Virgin America a public company. From an IPO price of $23 a share, prices soared 25 per cent, making the airline worth over $1 billion. As I look back on Virgin America's progress, it is one of the businesses I am most proud of. One of the Virgin Group's partners, Evan Lovell, reminded me his first ever call as a Virgin America board member was with a bankruptcy counsel. We reported a $270 million loss from the start of operations to midway through 2010. At the end of 2013 we announced a full-year profit of more than $10 million. As 2014 came to a close we had more than twenty destinations across the US and Mexico and thousands of industrious staff and fervent fans.

As with The Sex Pistols credit card, there was a musical link for Virgin America, too. On the same day we went public on the Nasdaq Stock Exchange, we also reached the magnificent milestone of one million hours of commercial flying. The historic journey went to one of our very first planes, when she flew from San Francisco to Newark. Fittingly, she was called *California Dreaming*.

*

When people wonder whether we are stretching ourselves too thinly, across too many different sectors, they are forgetting one of the traits of the Virgin brand – its ability constantly to adapt. We have gone through countless inventions and reinventions, and will continue to do so. After fifty years, our brand has a freshness others don't have. We are still more human, more adventurous and exciting and have added trustworthiness to that.

It will be interesting to see what Virgin is like thirty years after I've gone. That's going to be a really interesting challenge for the team and my children. I think it will be quite a different company – the danger is, will it be too professional without me? We need to keep our risk-taking attitude and stick our necks out when the time is right. I have seen so many companies come and go, largely because they didn't reinvent themselves. They stayed in a sector that had died, whereas Virgin was always one step ahead of the game. I learned that from the great musicians as much as anyone else. David Bowie, Prince, Madonna – their careers are lessons in the power of transformation. Most people think: know your onions, then stick to them. My worry is that people will get bored of onions and move on to carrots instead, putting your onions out of business. So I enjoy trying to be the person selling carrots before anybody else does.

I have always thought I should only go into businesses I have a genuine passion and interest in. It's why I started with a magazine, then went into music as a young man. As I started travelling more, it made sense to branch out into airlines, holidays and hotels. As somebody constantly on the move, mobile phones and connectivity were a good fit next. When I got a little older, I became more health-conscious and our health and wellness businesses followed. Now, I find myself running banks and even, in South Africa – I recently learned – launching funeral insurance. Talk about a birth-to-death way-of-life brand! We have carried out research showing our brand is the favourite among three generations. If we hadn't evolved and turned it into a way-of-life brand, that could never have happened.

I'm not the same man I was in my twenties, and the brand isn't the same either, but we have the same core values we always had. One of the keys to this is local knowledge, and altering our approach to suit the market. A great example of this is Virgin Active, a global brand that maintains a common purpose while containing unique characteristics in each country. In 2015, I was in Melbourne, hanging upside down from a piece of rubber in a class I am reliably informed is called Anti-Gravity Yoga – if you say so. The new clubs were very different from the ones I went on to visit in Singapore and Bangkok, and different again back in England, where we were expanding further. It would be impossible to spread to so many markets with so many different offerings if it wasn't for the power of the Virgin brand. As Matthew readily admits: 'There's a reason it says Virgin Active above the door, not Matt and Frank's Fitness Factory!'

When you go into new territories it is helpful if you already have brand recognition, but crucial to have local knowledge and adapt to the environment. In Singapore, I asked why we weren't calling Virgin Active 'health clubs' as we were everywhere else. The local manager explained to me that the phrase had a connection with brothels, which was certainly not the impression we wanted to make – especially with Virgin in our name! Similarly, in our clubs with a predominantly Chinese demographic we don't use any black colours on our branding, as it has connotations of death – the very opposite of our full-of-life philosophy. If we had gone in with a cookie-cutter approach and replicated what worked elsewhere, we would have fallen flat on our face. It was a useful lesson in looking out for holes in the road before they materialise. If you stop mistakes before they happen, life gets a lot easier.

Virgin Active is one company that closely mirrors my vision for the whole Virgin brand. It is all about improving people's lives, has a spirit of fun and entrepreneurship at its heart, and is committed to giving staff and customers the best possible time. The way it has been run, from a bootstrap start-up into a global business, is the perfect example of delegation and trust. By letting them make their own mistakes and enjoy their own triumphs – chipping in whenever necessary, instead of being on the phone every day second-guessing their decisions – Matthew, Frank and the team have grown a worldwide brand people love.

By 2015 Virgin Active had grown profits for eleven consecutive years and employed more than 20,000 staff. The question now was whether we should follow in the footsteps of Virgin Money and Virgin America, and think about a flotation. But after looking at an IPO with our partners CVC, we decided instead to sell 29 per cent of our stake to Brait for £230 million, retaining 20 per cent of the business and the branding rights. The deal valued Virgin Active at £1.3 billion – not bad for a company that started with one gym in Preston burnt to the ground.

It was a fitting figure, too, as we now had 1.3 million members across our 267 clubs in nine countries and four continents. The deal was a perfect example of our investment strategy for the new business landscape: building companies to scale, then accessing external capital to build them further through sales of stakes to partners or through the public markets. I called Matthew and reminded him of the promise he and Frank had made at our first meeting sixteen years earlier.

'You said we would build a billion-dollar company,' I recalled. 'Well, today you've done it. Well done!'

*

The danger with going public, of course, is that the company you've developed is open to the possibility of a takeover. In 2016, just eighteen months after we'd made it public, that was the threat that faced Virgin America.

Throughout the previous months, rumours had been growing that bigger airlines were queuing up to buy Virgin America. The rumours were true: while we continued to expand our routes and services – adding Hawaii, improving our touch-screen entertainment – behind the scenes a bidding war was raging. I had no desire to sell: indeed, my instinct was to defend the business we had grown from nothing to become the most-loved airline in the US. Sadly, there was nothing I could do to stop it. Because I'm not American, the US Department of Transportation required that I hold a large part of my interest in Virgin America through non-voting shares, which severely limited my influence over any takeover.

Although a few Asian airlines had expressed an interest, the battle for control was shaping up between JetBlue Airways and Alaska Air. I decided to meet separately with JetBlue CEO Robin Hayes and Alaska CEO Brad Tilden. They were eager to get my support and hear more about Virgin America and the history of the brand. I came away with the instinct that Alaska seemed to understand our purpose and spirit more intuitively. Having said that, we had history with Alaska: along with most other US airlines, they had been among the companies trying to block us getting off the ground. I still remember standing at an airport gate in 2009 after we'd finally got permission to fly and cheekily mooning the Alaska team on the next gate!

I had started Virgin America out of frustration at poor service and a belief we could do it better – the same reasons we had launched Virgin Atlantic and Virgin Australia. One of the best explanations for these poor standards was consolidation, and, as time has passed, American aviation has only got more consolidated. By 2016 the four biggest airlines in the US – American, United, Southwest and Virgin Atlantic's partner Delta – controlled around 80 per cent of the market. Ten years earlier, by contrast, there had been nine major airlines in the States. Into this shrinking market, Virgin America had won people's hearts and fierce loyalty. I wanted to make sure that whoever won the race to buy us didn't throw all that we'd worked for away. As the bidding continued, Alaska came out with a spectacular offer and JetBlue decided they couldn't go any further.

On 4 April 2016, Virgin America's board of directors unanimously approved a merger agreement for Alaska Air to acquire Virgin America for $57.00 per share – approximately $2.6 billion. This was an enormous return, especially considering the hundreds of million we had lost in the early days of the airline. But I was heartbroken and spoke out about how sad the deal made me feel. People loved this airline. I believed we had so much more to do, more places to go and more friends to make along the way. I would love to have seen the directors be braver and grow it into the fifth major airline in the US.

I wasn't the only one to feel disappointed. Virgin America's loyal customers were absolutely furious, and I could understand why. One Elevate Club member wrote an expletive-filled rant that illustrated the strength of feeling about the deal. 'Go to Hell ... I loved Virgin America. Now, this merger means that you'll just be another bullshit airline. Can't wait to see how the customers get fucked over. Go ahead and blow some more sunshine up my ass. I read all of the crap listed about the merger. Smells like bullshit to me. Thanks, but fuck you.' Mike Brophy tweeted me: '@VirginAmerica being acquired by @AlaskaAir is like Apple being acquired by Microsoft. There went the last great airline.'

It was the feedback of our staff that hurt the most. I spoke to several of the team I have got to know well, and they were all gutted. It felt like the shareholders had sold our people – brilliant, passionate, unique people. When I asked a few of the team, 'Hypothetically, if we were to start another airline, would you join us?' the answer was a unanimous 'Yes'.

I build companies because I love creating things that make a difference – Virgin America is a perfect example. I'm not motivated by more money in my bank account, other than to use it to create more things I'm proud of. I went to San Francisco and spoke to more of the team. 'A cheque in the bank is honestly not that exciting a thing,' I told them. 'A living, breathing, heart of an airline with all its people, all that it is achieving and the difference it is making to lives is an enormously satisfying thing. You should always be very proud of that.'

We had to move on fast, and concentrate on the battle to keep the Virgin America brand and team flying. I emailed back and forth with Brad, urging him to explore the possibility of Alaska using the Virgin name, or at least a two-branded option and keeping our wonderful team together. It would be madness for Alaska to buy Virgin America, then simply strip it of everything that had made it great in the first place.

Brad invited me up to Seattle to meet their team and get to know their people. After we completed a lively Q&A with the staff, I got the feeling that they were as eager as we were to find a productive way forward. Brad told me if he dropped the Alaska brand and just used Virgin America he would lose his job. I understood; Alaska held a lot of emotional weight in Seattle. Our teams put our heads together: Evan, Christine and Nick from Virgin Group, along with David Cush, Luanne Calvert, Abby Lunardini and the Virgin America team, did sterling work making the case for our fantastic team and brand. We pointed to the example of Virgin Atlantic and Delta, two airlines working seamlessly together while growing both brands strongly.

'We're going to take some time over the next several months to learn more about their brand,' said Alaska's spokesperson Joe Sprague. 'The Virgin brand is popular globally. We want to respect that.' That turned out not to be true. In mid-March 2017, Alaska informed us that they would retire the Virgin brand in 2019 and lay off a lot of people. I was angry, but helpless to stop the decision. I penned a heartfelt letter to Virgin America, our people and our customers.

Dear Virgin America,
    With a lot of things in life, there is a point where we have to let go and appreciate the fact that we had this ride at all ...
    We went through a lot together. And you were worth every minute, every penny, every battle. We earned every loyal guest and fan. Every market was hard-won. It was a long and hard journey but in the end you are the best consumer airline in America.
    To each of your brilliant Teammates, I know that you will continue to do great things, whether you stay on with Alaska or pursue a different path ... To our wonderful guests, I speak for everyone at Virgin America when I say we are eternally thankful. For believing in the little airline that could ...
    Businesses come and go but beloved brands make lasting impressions and remain in your heart. As an entrepreneur's brand, Virgin is always starting new businesses. And we will not stop ...
    George Harrison once said 'All Things Must Pass'. This was the ride and love of a lifetime. I feel very lucky to have been on it with all of you. I'm told some people at Virgin America are calling today 'the day the music died'. It is a sad (and some would say baffling) day. But I'd like to assure them that the music never dies.

As fate would have it, I found myself in Seattle, Alaska Airlines' hometown, soon after. Virgin Atlantic was starting a new route to the city, but reporters wanted to know about Virgin America. I leaned back in my chair, paused, then let rip. 'I thought I'd be polite, but I've decided not to be,' I said. 'They spent $2.6 billion buying it. Sadly, it seems, they have decided to rip the heart out of the airline. It just seems such a waste. I wonder what it was that Alaska bought, and why did they bother?'

Alaska failed to meet earnings and revenue expectations as the deal pressed on, leading CNBC to suggest that the airline had 'lost its mojo'. Mergers are never easy, but they are particularly hard when the brand that customers love is being lost. In January 2018, Condé Nast's Cynthia Drescher even wrote a loving obituary to our airline:

> Next time you log on to in-flight Wi-Fi, score an affordable airfare to Hawaii, sip a surprisingly sophisticated cocktail at altitude, or notice new tech or accessibility enhancements to the in-flight entertainment, spare a thought for Virgin America and its people, who succeeded in their impossible goal to better air travel. Virgin America is survived by cousins Virgin Atlantic, Virgin Australia, Virgin Holidays, Virgin Hotels, Virgin Trains, Virgin Vacations, Virgin Galactic, Virgin Voyages, and father Sir Richard Branson.

But most moving were the scores of messages from our teammates as they left their jobs. One wrote saying that her time at Virgin America had been 'the highlight of my 30-year airline career and my life to be honest'. I agreed with her that Alaska had got 'much more than an airline, they bought a truly unique culture that changed the airline industry'. She continued: 'I can't believe that a company bought us with no regard to what we built or any effort to try and keep us. I have a feeling that they are already regretting that poor decision. The Virgin America brand is a feeling that Teammates embrace daily on a personal level and it becomes who we are in work and life. I'm a Virgin at heart forever.' It's feedback like this that makes all the hard work worthwhile, but the loss even more heart-breaking.

We have the option of starting a new airline in America. The rules still make it tough for me to own much of a US airline. But we could always work with an existing US airline to create something magical again – now that would be an exciting challenge.

36 Audacious Ideas

On New Year's Eve 2013 I was welcoming in the new year by dancing on the bar on Moskito Island with Larry and Lucy Page, and Jeff Skoll (a wonderfully generous individual who helped start eBay). As the party started to wind down, we clambered down onto our seats and began pondering one last drink. After I had rustled up some ill-advised cocktails, we decided we should see the new year in by doing something together that year that would really make a positive difference. By the time we had recovered the following day, I suspect the four of us had forgotten the conversation. But I always have my trusty notebook – even on New Year's Eve – and there were some very scrappy notes in there, one of which was just two words long: Audacious Ideas.

A few months later I was in a Hobie Cat sailing from Necker to Moskito with Jean Oelwang, Holly, Sam and Chris Anderson, the founder of the brilliant TED Talks, when I suddenly remembered our New Year's Eve pledge.

'I know what Audacious Ideas is,' I realised. 'Well, kind of.'

Coincidentally, Chris and I had previously discussed holding a TED summit on Necker for CEOs to drive a more purpose-driven way forward for business, and do something bigger than we could ever do on our own. He too had been talking to Jeff about igniting large-scale philanthropic funds. We decided to merge the ideas and agreed that we should do this together. Audacious Ideas was conceived on a bar and born on a Hobie Cat! We slowed up the boat, circled Necker and spent the trip thinking up the most audacious ideas we could all come up with. By the time we pulled ashore, we had agreed to hold an 'Audacious Ideas' gathering to tackle the most important issues in the world with people with financial firepower who want to make a real difference in the world. Chris volunteered his wonderful TED team to lead the project, which we all agreed to, with Virgin Unite in full support.

'Where will we hold it?' asked Holly.

'Here, of course,' I waved towards Moskito.

Chris hosted a number of meetings with us and other donors to help shape the idea further, and in May 2015, I was back on Moskito with a group of wealthy philanthropists (who have asked to remain anonymous). We had decided in advance upon a shortlist of organisations to potentially support, who would pitch their ideas via video and live link. Successful pitches included: Kawisafi, a group focused on bringing solar power to people living in poverty in Africa; RMI, focused on integrated energy planning in Africa; and The War on Methane, an ambitious EDF project working with the oil and gas industry to stop methane leakage. We had lots of questions, and debated each pitch long and hard. People generally do their own thing in philanthropy – but over those few days I think people learned what fun it can be to work with others.

The pitch that stood out for me was from Andrew Youn. Andrew runs One Acre, a remarkable non-profit organisation that supplies hundreds of thousands of smallholder farmers in East Africa with financing and training to reduce hunger and poverty by dramatically improving the productivity of their small pieces of land. It was clear immediately there was a lot of interest in supporting this idea. We all huddled together in the living room on Moskito as Andrew gave his pitch on the screen, ending by asking for $100 million in funding. We walked out into the corridor, had a chat, agreeing what we could each put into the pot. Then I came back in alone to see a very nervous-looking Andrew staring back at me on the TV.

'First of all, Andrew, we all love your idea. But I'm sorry; we can't get you all the money you need. But we can get you $1 million.'

He said how very grateful he was, but I could tell he was a little disappointed.

'Only joking!' As everyone came rushing back into the room, I told him he had his $100 million. 'Now get out there and transform many, many, many more lives in many, many more countries.' There was much laughter and even tears among those who'd gathered and been so incredibly generous.

In two days, over $150 million was committed to some great projects and many new partnership ideas were formed. One project that could have the most lasting effect on our globe started with a conversation about the need to get the pension industry to switch their trillions of investments to tackle the Global Goals – a series of ambitious targets to end extreme poverty and tackle climate change. If $2 trillion could be invested (for profit) most of the Goals could be reached. TPG founder Bill McGlashan, Bono, Jeff Skoll, myself and others agreed to show the pension industry how it could be done. We agreed to set up Rise, a social impact fund to invest in companies that purposefully would make a real difference in the world. Within months Bill and the team had raised $2 billion to kick it off. It had indeed been an incredible few days! We all agreed that Audacious Ideas would become an ongoing event.

'We can't have it too regularly, though,' I whispered to Jean. 'I want to fund all of these ideas – but I'll soon be bankrupt!'

However, in July 2017 we gathered again, on Necker this time. Quite unbelievably, it even surpassed the first event.

Seven projects got pledges of support. Sightsavers, whose challenge is to eliminate trachoma (an absolutely horrible blindness that affects millions in Africa), asked for $50 million, so they could use that pledge to raise another $100 million from governments. They are planning to eliminate trachoma in ten countries, deliver 61 million treatments for trachoma and other neglected diseases and perform over 127,000 surgeries.

Two other wonderful organisations, Living Goods and Last Mile Health, wanted to take on 50,000 female community healthcare workers, to provide on-call home help to over 50 million people in Africa over four years. Using mobile telephony and a smart health app, these women will be able to diagnose and treat deadly diseases that are entirely treatable. Child deaths alone will be reduced by 25 per cent.

The Bronx Defenders Bail Project is yet another wonderful organisation that presented. Rich people in the US can afford bail, poor people can't. So they go to prison whether they are guilty or not. Bronx Defenders asked the Audacious Ideas group to put up a sum of money that could be used to help people pay for their bail. They believed they could help 160,000 people over five years, many of whom are innocent.

GirlTrek wanted to recruit and train an army of 10,000 health activists in the States. The goal is to get one million black women walking regularly in the US, a solution to obesity, diabetes and heart disease. The project will also have multiple long-term benefits, revitalising communities and promoting healthier and safer neighbourhoods.

An idea for free online educational degrees for 50,000 refugees was also well supported, as was an exploration plan for the Twilight Zone, the vast midwater layer of the deep ocean between 200 metres and 1,000 metres below the surface. This is currently a largely unexplored ecosystem and it may contain more fish resources than all other fisheries combined, with massive implications in sustaining the rest of the ocean. Norway, amongst other countries, has recently issued permits to fish these waters. Therefore, there is now a rush to explore this area before it is too late. Scientists, conservationists, policy makers and the public will be able to use the data from this research to understand these waters.

In just three days on Necker, well over $200 million was pledged, which when leveraged up with matching funds from government overseas development organisations, should equate to half a billion dollars. The money is going to organisations and entrepreneurial people who have been incredibly closely vetted. It will save numerous lives, avert numerous illnesses, prevent hundreds of thousands of people from unnecessarily becoming blind, cure many who are blind, help in the fight against climate change, keep many poor and innocent people out of prison, help protect the ocean, and empower black women in America. Although, as the host, I had to step forward more than I had budgeted for, it couldn't have been money better spent. We abided by the Necker rule – work hard in the day, play and get to know each other in the afternoon and evenings – and it had worked.

Paolo Nutini, Joan's favourite singer, was good enough to fly out to entertain everyone on the last night. We all danced into the night and everyone left the next day with the biggest smiles on their faces. After all those years of working hard to make money, for everyone there, giving was even more satisfying. How wonderful that all of our teams, such as the TED team, our Necker and Moskito staff and all the Virgin employees who work so hard, can feel they have made such a transformative difference too.

From the original New Year's Eve pledge and Hobie Cat brainstorming session, a lot of positive things came out of Audacious Ideas in a very short time. After the event I reflected on what had made it so special. I thought about the nature of ideas, and, looking up at my bookshelf at the Temple, was reminded of John Steinbeck's wonderful thought: 'Ideas are like rabbits. You get a couple and learn how to handle them, and pretty soon you have a dozen.' Ideas can be dazzling, indefinable and mysterious; they can strike at any moment, and can change the world. But they only change the world if they can be honed down into something understandable, relatable and definable – while not losing that little piece of magic that made them a great idea in the first place. They need the right setting, the right timing and most importantly the right people to turn them into reality.

Reflecting on Audacious Ideas, I thought once again about how governments and civil society cannot solve the world's problems alone. It is going to take everybody – especially those of us with the resources to make a wider impact. More than any other organisations, businesses have the resources to make change happen at scale. As companies grow larger and society's problems increase, this is truer than ever.

One of the ideas we practise with our people and companies is something I call 'Circles'. First of all, draw a small imaginary circle around yourself. Before you can do anything for others make sure you have the right balance and health in your own life. Only then can you draw a slightly larger circle around your home that incorporates family, friends and neighbours and even the street outside your home. See how you can make a difference to everyone within that circle. If you clean inside your house, do the same outside it and so on. If you have a bit of money or a small company, draw a circle around the whole street or as much of the local community as you feel you and your team can help. Draw up a list of things that need fixing and set about doing so. If you are a national company, draw a circle around your country and set about tackling some of the bigger issues and helping government get on top of them. If you are an international company, like Virgin, use your entrepreneurial skills to look at really big global problems and set out to address them. If every individual and every company draws circles, then soon they will overlap and we will together resolve most of the problems in the world. It's a simple idea, but I would suggest you try it and we can start a revolution of circles.

*

Echoing John Steinbeck's wise words, this was a period when business ideas and opportunities seemed to be coming in thick and fast. Some of these were new; others were the coming together of plans we'd had for years.

One of the people integral to Virgin's growth was Will Whitehorn, and I was telling him about some of my ideas over lunch in London: spaceships, hotels, cruise ships, conflict resolution, sports companies, trains, satellites, luxury resorts, drug reform, the list went on.

'I'm still keeping busy,' I said, laughing.

'You call that busy?' Will laughed. 'That's positively fucking comatose compared to what you used to be! Your houseboat was literally sinking under the weight of fax machines, notebooks, telephone lines and footfall.'

'Fair enough. But I'm still not keeping out of trouble.'

No matter what is happening in my business life, regardless of what situation my companies are in, somewhere in the back of my mind I will be mulling over a new idea. I like to think it is my curiosity and thirst for fresh inspiration. Will, however, has another view.

'Richard, you have ADHD.'

'Do I? No doctor's ever mentioned it.'

'OK, well, you have the attention span of a gnat.'

This is fair enough, in some cases. But being able to see the bigger picture is what has enabled me to move into so many different sectors. Most business leaders want to oversee every single part of their operation. I hone in on what is important. This can be tiny details, not just over-arching strategy.

Either way, I find brilliant people like Will, I delegate and let them get on with it. I am able to let go, when other people can't. As shareholder, I delegate to management teams who take strategic decisions to drive our business forward. But I can also be as stubborn as hell when I believe in an idea and those same brilliant people around me do not. I have learned that my mind works in different ways to many others. If I had to name a skill I possess, it would be lateral thinking. When all logic is pointing in one direction, but it just doesn't make sense to me, I question it. 'Forgive me, it's probably my dyslexia,' I will begin, or 'Sorry, I'm probably being foolish, but I don't quite follow you.' Then I will ask seemingly obvious questions, which don't always result in the answers I expect. Out of this inquisitiveness, companies are sometimes born.

*

A good example can be found in the hospitality sector. For many years Virgin had a small number of hotels, mostly in the UK, and a few in Europe, such as my beloved La Residencia in Mallorca. In the aftermath of 9/11, these were among the first things we sold off to help keep Virgin Atlantic and the Group afloat. I used to play Monopoly a lot as a kid. I played aggressively, always expanding when there was the chance to buy a new street or build a hotel. Occasionally I would have to turn hotels upside down when I ran out of cash. My adult life went on to imitate my childhood.

Hotels fitted the Virgin brand, however, and I always wanted to get back into the business. We slowly managed it through the development of Virgin Limited Edition, our luxury properties company. I love creating things, but hate the idea of them sitting empty when our family is not there. I am always keen to share in what we create. So why not let others come and enjoy our little slice of paradise, and pay the overheads at the same time?

One time I was in Morocco with my family, preparing for our transatlantic hot-air balloon challenge. My parents went exploring while we waited for the right weather conditions to launch. They found the beautiful Kasbah Tamadot in the Atlas Mountains and instantly fell in love with the area and the local community. Mum and Dad sat me down and told me they would not talk to me again if I didn't buy it there and then. I think they were joking, but it did the trick and now we have turned Kasbah Tamadot into an incomparably beautiful resort.

The list of locations continued to grow: our vineyard Mont Rochelle in South Africa welcomes keen wine tasters; The Lodge in Switzerland has become our regular New Year's escape and shelters keen skiers and hikers all year round; Mahali Mzuri, our equally stunning safari lodge in Kenya that sits slap bang in the middle of the Great Migration, has joined the collection, too. Most recently, we finally found a way to get back to our adored Mallorca coast, buying the stunning Son Bunyola to recreate the magical feel that La Residencia had in the early days. I absolutely love creating physical spaces out of bricks and mortar for people to enjoy. Somehow, the concept behind Necker, which started out of personal passion, had turned into a cohesive group of resorts, led ably by CEO Jon

Brown and thoroughly enjoyed by my family, as well as our thousands of guests.

While the luxury market remained strong, the experts told me this was an exception and there was no place for more mainstream hotels. I mentioned my admiration for sharing economy start-ups earlier. One that passed us by, despite me being keen to invest, was AirBnB. From the branding to the ethos of trusting your fellow man to look after you on your travels, I absolutely loved the idea and am delighted to see the entrepreneurs behind it thriving. However, I still felt there was space for more traditional hotels if they were reimagined with all the pain points removed.

Ever since we began Virgin Atlantic, people have often stopped me in flight and asked where our hotels are. We commissioned some research and it showed that most people thought we had city hotels already! Virgin Holidays has done a wonderful job creating vacations for travellers getting off Virgin Atlantic's flights, but we still fly people to cities all over the world every day and send them off the plane to other people's resorts. Surely it was time we created a group of beautiful city-based Virgin Hotels?

A crisis is often a good time to start a new business. When the 2007 economic downturn happened, I thought it would be the perfect moment to begin searching for suitable properties. The first hotel we found was in Chicago: a stunning, neoclassical building that briefly opened as the Old Dearborn Bank in 1928, then swiftly closed as the Great Depression hit. You can still see the huge safe downstairs – now the home of the spa! We saw how the iconic building could combine classic charm with contemporary style, and become the embodiment of what Virgin stands for, in hotel form. I was more excited about the team we were forming than any building, though. Raul Leal, a hospitality expert who understood the brand right away, came on board to run the company, and his team has followed in his footsteps of living and breathing the Virgin way. I visited the hotel for a hard-hat tour while it was still a dusty shell, with original fittings covered and carpets rolled up along the walls. But I could see the vision of what it could become, and see the team's eyes light up with enthusiasm.

While out for a pizza afterwards, I told Raul I was confident he would have our first hotel open for business by the time I returned. We talked about every annoying thing our rival hotels did – charged for WiFi, spiked prices for everyday items in the minibar, blasted infuriating muzak into your room – and we found ways to turn these problems into positives. We began pulling the tail of our rivals before we were even open. We turned up outside hotels that charged for internet access, like the W and the Marriott, and gave their guests our own free WiFi through a special Virgin Hotels truck. It caused a stir, annoyed the neighbours more than a little and made our mark on the city and its people. Soon job applications and pre-booking requests were overflowing in the office.

We asked women who travel a lot what they really want from their hotel rooms – they said two things: safety and convenience (which men want, too, of course). The team developed chambers, instead of rooms, which could be divided in half so guests can be separated from anyone entering the room with deliveries or luggage or room service. Then we added two dressing tables, beautiful lighting and mirrors, drawers for make-up, extra cupboard space and big shower benches to make shaving legs easier. The beds are unique designs that allow you to get into all sorts of positions, including being able to sit up and work, rather than squeezing behind a tiny coffee table with your laptop. We built an app to control everything from the room temperature to the room service.

Best of all, I insisted on a 'Yes!' button on every phone. Guests can press it, request anything their heart desires, and our team will deliver. My favourite request so far was for a singing performance – a few of the staff were quickly charging to the room and blasting out their best Beyoncé impressions. When I went to Chicago for the grand launch on 16 April 2015, we held a *Ferris Bueller's Day Off* parade, with me in the lead role. As tens of thousands of people shook their tails to 'Twist 'n' Shout', blocking off the street, the police issued us with a writ. As ever, ask forgiveness, not permission! While the authorities weren't happy, the guests certainly have been – within a year we were named Best Hotel in America by Condé Nast.

*

Another business idea that had long been dormant was moving the company into cruise ships. This time, the inspiration to pick this concept up came from an old drawing.

After the Necker fire, I had been eager to take stock of exactly what was not lost in the blaze. I waded through some boxes positively overflowing with memorabilia, old diaries, concept art and plain old junk collected over the past five decades.

I felt quite nostalgic rummaging through – not a regular sensation for me. There's nothing like sheer clutter to remind you of your past, but it always makes me want to bring order to it, then move forward again. Trying to reach a box of books, I almost stepped through an old drawing made for Virgin Atlantic showing what the brand could look like if it was expanded into cruises. I picked it up, dusted it off and saw an image of a very different type of cruise: glamorous, exciting, in dazzling colour. It felt like a sign.

As it happened, I had just been on the phone with our investment team, talking about the very same subject. We were looking seawards to see whether we could transform another established but stuffy sector: cruising. I had first thought about starting a cruise line when I was twenty-seven. At the time I wanted it to only be for under-thirties. Once I turned thirty myself, I decided that we'd have to add a clause that would still allow the owner aboard! I have never been a fan of modern-day cruises and can understand why they have the reputation for poor service and long, boring journeys. I have admiration for the golden age of cruising, however, when there was glamour and adventure attached to it. Surely it would be possible to recreate that faded grandeur and combine it with some modern excitement? How hard could it be to build a big – OK, very big – boat?

As it turns out, the answer is, very difficult. After long and detailed negotiations with Bain Capital, one of the world's leading private investment firms, we agreed one of the biggest deals in Virgin's history. In June 2015, I took a helicopter ride across Biscayne Bay and landed at Miami's Museum Park. I was in town to announce that PortMiami would be the home of Virgin Voyages' first cruise ship. Renowned Italian shipbuilders Fincantieri are building three mid-size ships for us, with the first ready to sail in 2020 and the next two following in 2021 and 2022.

One of the main concerns we had about getting into the cruise sector was sustainability. So we've partnered with clean energy start-up Climeon, an industry-first, to create ocean-friendly ships that will effectively turn heat waste into energy in order to save CO_2.

Wandering around the dock, surrounded by the great and good of this enormous industry, I still felt that the cruises sector was a bit stuffy. While I was skipping around in a red and white sailor's uniform, complete with captain's hat, there were ties everywhere I looked – even in the roasting Miami sunshine. So I offered the Mayor of Miami-Dade County, Carlos A. Giménez, a helping hand to cool him down, cutting his tie off, then repeating the trick with PortMiami CEO Juan M. Kuryla and Fincantieri chairman Vincenzo Petrone. Mayor Giménez thankfully saw the funny side and promised to 'pass an ordinance forbidding ties from now on'. Virgin Voyages' new CEO, Tom McAlpin, joined me to raise our flag in the dock and the company was officially launched.

The next major milestone in getting our ship together was in October 2017, when I travelled to Genoa, Italy, to lay the keel for Virgin Voyages' first vessel. Before we arrived, I met up with Boy George, who I hadn't seen since I had tried to get him off drugs many years earlier. Back then, things were looking very bleak for him; many of his close friends died from heroin overdoses (some in his home) and it was very likely he would be next. Having got to know him well since signing Culture Club to Virgin Records, I wanted to support him. Fortunately, having run the Student Advisory Centre for young people since I was sixteen, I knew what to do. I persuaded him to come to my house in the country, where I had arranged for a specialist doctor called Meg to come and help him get clean. He wanted to do it, and things began looking brighter for him. But, sadly, his manager arrived in his Rolls-Royce, so the press found out where Boy George was hiding out, and soon they were camping outside my front door. The *Sun* newspaper ran an editorial demanding his arrest, which was the last thing he or anyone needs while going through therapy. We decided to make a run for it. Well . . . more like a crawl. To evade the paparazzi, we sneaked out of my back door and crawled for three miles through fields of long grass to a graveyard outside a church, where we had a car waiting. We made it, but unfortunately Boy George was arrested not long afterwards and fell back into his addiction.

So it was a real pleasure to see him looking so fit and healthy so many years later in Italy. He has really turned things around and told me he hasn't touched drink or drugs in fifteen years.

'I'm so blessed that my life is so extraordinarily fun and I can actually enjoy it now,' he told me. As we walked through Genoa airport together, all the immigration officers welcomed George by jumping up onto the table to dance, while 'Do You Really Want to Hurt Me' blared out over the speakers! Later, Tom McAlpin and I climbed up a crane above the shipyard to make our entrance. As Boy George started being DJ, we dropped 200 feet to the base of the ship, where we welded a ceremonial coin into the keel. Formalities over, I joined Boy George to dance together to 'Karma Chameleon'. The shipyard owners told me it was the biggest party they'd ever seen.

'Just you wait until we actually set sail!' I replied.

*

One of the best ideas we developed during this time wasn't to do with a new product, but a new approach as to how we looked after our staff.

I was working from my hammock when Holly sent me an article from the *Daily Telegraph* all about the video streaming company Netflix and its revolutionary vacation policy.

'Dad, check this out,' Holly wrote. 'It's something I have been wanting to introduce for a long time; I believe it would be a very Virgin thing to do to not track people's holidays. I have a friend whose company has done the same thing and they've apparently experienced a marked upward spike in everything – morale, creativity and productivity have all gone through the roof.'

The idea was catching on with a few Silicon Valley start-ups, where teams were lean and HR departments usually non-existent. But I wondered if we could make it work for a bigger business, and encourage more companies to follow suit. I have never worked from an office and have always urged my teams to get away from their desks whenever possible. Nine to five has never applied to me – unless you count our early Virgin Records days, when our usual hours were closer to 9 p.m. to 5 a.m.!

Over the years, technology has revolutionised, for better or for worse, how we all work. While developments have allowed people more freedom in the way they work, it also means many people end up checking emails in the evenings, answering non-urgent messages and working up presentations while they should be relaxing at home. Urging people to stop this extra work is simply impractical. Allowing them to make up their lost time elsewhere is not only achievable, it's appealing in the independence it gives people.

We had already introduced a flexible working policy, whereby Virgin Group's head office staff can work from home and take time off when they need it. But what would it mean to go further, and give our employees 'unlimited leave'? Exactly that – leave without limits. You read that correctly: we decided to let all our head office team take as much holiday as they want, when they want, fully paid. There is no catch – all the employees have to do is get consent from their manager. It is based on trust, and the assumption that nobody will leave their colleagues in the lurch and only take holiday when they are up to date with their work.

There are times of the year, such as around the Christmas holidays, when it makes no sense to have an office full of understandably unproductive employees. They really want to be at home bingeing on festive films with their loved ones, so what's the point of keeping them chained to their desks? By giving them the freedom to make their own decisions, plan their own workloads and choose their own holidays, when they do work they are likely to be far more effective. It's a great recruitment tool. I'm sure many staff will see it as a reward, but I see it as a way to make us more efficient. It's simply about treating people as you yourself would wish to be treated. Many people have asked whether this idea has come about because I live on Necker, but I worked flexibly even when I lived in London, too. It isn't about age either – when I became a parent that was the real shift to me wanting to spend more time working from home. Put simply, it works. If I can work from a hammock, start work at 6 a.m. and take time out in the day to go kitesurfing, there is no reason why one of my team in London or New York can't take a Friday off to enjoy a long weekend away, or leave the office early to see their child in a school play. I put it down in writing: 'We should focus on what people get done, not on how many hours or days worked. Just as we don't have a nine to five policy, we don't need a vacation policy.'

Not everybody saw it that way, though. What I saw as a simple, sensible solution to a modern problem was met in some quarters as an invitation to anarchy. The phrase 'unlimited leave' seemed to scare people. I was doing a talk in Washington and I told the audience: 'As long as our staff get their work done well, they can take as much holiday as they want.' I had said the same thing at another talk the day before and got a round of applause. This time there was no clapping. Confused, after I left the stage I asked one of the people in the audience why this was. 'Our bosses were all sitting in the audience too. I was afraid that if I clapped they would hold it against me.' I told them this was sad. Any manager who punishes their staff for expressing an opinion hasn't got the faintest idea about leadership. People in charge should empower their employees, not scare them into silence.

Since unlimited leave was introduced, we have seen an upturn in productivity, morale and staff wellbeing. We've had more job applications than ever before, with people keen to join a company that treats them like the capable adults they are. I'm sure more companies will follow suit, inside and outside the Virgin Group, and unlimited leave will be the norm within a couple of decades. If you are open and flexible your employees will be, too. Choice empowers people to make great decisions.

This was also the reasoning behind another of our new policies: Virgin Management enabling its employees to have up to a year's paid parental leave. In 2015 the British government introduced new Shared Parental Leave legislation, recognising the unfairness of the old policy that meant one parent missed out on lots of the crucial early months of their child's life. I was well aware of what a magical time it is for parents – and how much hard work it is. So we decided to take the policy a step further by giving all employees with four years or more service enhanced shared parental leave pay up to 100 per cent of salary for fifty-two weeks. We've had so many people work here whilst raising their families that I wanted to ensure they got to spend as much time with their kids as possible. It's just another little way of putting wellbeing at the heart of everything we do. The more you support your staff, the healthier and happier your business will be.

37 Satellites

I was sitting down at the bar in the Temple on Necker, watching the flamingos and scarlet ibis fly overhead, when a guest came over and told me he had an idea I couldn't afford to miss out on. This sounded familiar – but when Greg Wyler began talking about OneWeb, the biggest satellite constellation in history, my eyes lit up.

'Hang on,' I said, turning away from the birds and giving him my full attention. 'Let's get a drink at the bar and you can tell me more.'

'Basically, we'll have a massive constellation of satellites in the sky. These will interlock with each other – so the whole planet, including the four billion people who don't currently get coverage, will be able to.'

My mind raced through the possibilities. 'Will it be fast enough for everyone to get online?'

'Yes. Because they will be closer to the earth than other satellites, the internet performance will be faster.'

'I see. And that's where we come in?'

Greg was talking to me because he needed my contacts, investment and Virgin Galactic's involvement to make this work. With our air-based launch system, we could replenish satellites much faster and more cheaply than land-based launches. We would increase safety, access, reliability and frequency, while reducing costs. OneWeb could use Virgin Galactic's small satellite launch system to its full potential. Together, we began sketching out a plan to bring internet access to those in the world who didn't have it.

Greg wanted to see if I could introduce him to Google, as we were talking about hundreds of satellites and billions of dollars. I emailed Larry. 'I don't usually pitch to you,' I wrote, 'but I know this project will interest you greatly. Attached is a plan for developing a huge constellation of satellites, which Virgin Galactic's LauncherOne could deliver into orbit. Let me know if you're keen and we'll follow up.' Larry, it turned out, was very interested: 'This company has the potential to be as big as Google one day,' he told me. 'It could make a massive difference to millions of people's lives.' Greg began working out of Google's offices in San Francisco while they negotiated their deal and he built his team. But then he got a call from Elon Musk, offering a deal that was substantially better than the one Google offered. Elon told Greg one of the reasons he wanted in was for SpaceX to get the launch rights for OneWeb, rather than Virgin Galactic. When I heard this, I was saddened that Elon didn't consider working with Larry and me. We could have achieved even more by working together and, after all, we are friends. It would have made better business sense. If our positions were reversed, I would have talked to him and tried to collaborate rather than sweep the deal from under him. Some people find it hard working with friends, but I have always found the opposite. As long as there is trust and understanding, I truly believe it can work. Regardless, Greg started negotiating a contract with Elon. But, before long, they had a disagreement. Elon thought he could get similar spectrum rights (the frequency through which you can transmit data) to the key ones Greg owned. Elon parted company just before signing the contract, instead wanting to start his own rival satellite venture. At this point, Greg came back to see me, obviously disappointed, and explained the situation. The more we looked at it, from a legal as well as technical perspective, the more we just didn't believe Elon could get the spectrum rights. Up until this point we hadn't offered to be financial partners with OneWeb, just offering Virgin Galactic's services as a launch provider. Now I decided this was such a huge opportunity that we should to help to fund OneWeb, who by now had Qualcomm lined up as investors too. I emailed Greg: 'I'm happy to invest, and will help bring in multiple other investors, if we can reach an agreement quickly.' Finally, things ran more smoothly. Virgin joined Qualcomm as lead investors (followed in the months to come by a formidable group of investors including Airbus, Coca-Cola and SoftBank – it was notable how companies not traditionally in the space industry were inspired to join us). OneWeb was officially live.

By January 2015, I heard a rumour that Elon was going to try to spike what we were doing by rushing out an announcement about his rival satellite network before us. It was the week before the World Economic Forum in Davos and I was determined to be first to the punch. I sent a note to the team: 'We need to announce it this week – if not, we risk being drowned out by Elon's press conference, even though our project has far greater scale and chance of success.'

We worked on the deal through the night and on the first morning of Davos we made our announcement. OneWeb would build, launch and operate the world's largest ever satellite network, making high-speed internet and telephony available to millions of people who didn't currently have access. Virgin Galactic's LauncherOne programme – which became a new company called Virgin Orbit in March 2017 – would help make it possible with frequent satellite launches at a much lower cost and with greater reliability. The result is that we had what was the biggest order in history for putting satellites into space.

There were so many reasons why I was so excited by this project. Budding entrepreneurs who wanted to start businesses would be able to connect with the rest of the world and create jobs. People who didn't currently have access to proper teaching would be able to receive education. There was no end of ways the constellation could transform people's lives and revitalise communities. The investment marked a strategy shift for Virgin, too. It makes a big difference that we now have the resources to afford a long-term perspective. OneWeb and Virgin Orbit are prime examples.

After the announcement at Davos, I crunched across the snow and headed to another event, this time on equality in business. It was being led by Sheryl Sandberg, the brilliant founder of Lean In and COO at Facebook. As business leaders shared their views on how to get more women into boardrooms, I listened carefully and made copious notes. Before long, my notebook was full and I began scribbling over my programme. When there was no room left in the margins, I wrote on my name tag. Afterwards, Sheryl came over.

'I'm amazed you were the only one taking notes in the whole room.'

'I always do – how else would I remember everything?'

I find her an incredibly sharp, warm leader. Knowing how passionate Mark Zuckerberg and Facebook are about opening up internet access for all, I talked to Sheryl about the OneWeb project.

'This sounds fascinating,' she said. 'Come to the office and talk to Mark about it, too.'

The next week, I went to Silicon Valley. My first appointment was to see Elon at Tesla. He welcomed me into his office and we shared the latest on some of our other ventures, before getting down to business. On the subject of satellites, I put my cards all out on the table.

'This is a massive project. Why don't we just work together? We've got the network, we can help replenish satellites as they fall out, you can help put them up. There is plenty of money to be made for all of us, and we can make a bigger difference together.'

Elon's response was to bring up his main goal – reaching Mars. 'If I can make enough money to fulfil my Mars mission, I'm happy to do something together,' he said.

When I left the meeting I couldn't work out whether he wanted to be a partner or not, though I suspected the latter. Elon is tremendously smart and even more driven. I admire his talent and willingness to take calculated risks. He has been inches from failure on many, many occasions and kept pushing. He's the Henry Ford of his generation. Whether we end up working together or not, we'll have to wait and see. Regardless, we'll remain friends.

Continuing my discussions, I went on to Facebook, to talk to Mark Zuckerberg about OneWeb. For someone with the power, reach and influence of Mark, I am impressed how understated he is: the main focus of the company is on the team, not on him. As I sat there, outlining OneWeb's vision, I could instantly sense his enthusiasm.

'Enabling people in poorer countries to get web access is one of the most important ways to pull people out of poverty,' said Mark. 'I completely agree. I think we have a way to do it.'

Mark is less gregarious than Sheryl, but extremely perceptive, and I could see his heart was in the right place.

'By the way,' I said, 'I loved what you said at your IPO. Along the lines of: "We don't build services to make money; we make money to build better services."'

'I can't remember if I said that,' Mark confessed, 'but I definitely believe it.'

After our meeting, I walked out with Mark, we shook hands and he went straight to a desk in the middle of the office and sat down among his team. I have always thought it refreshing, and sensible, for leaders to get right among their people. That way you get to know them, hear their ideas, build stronger ties and create relationships in a way you never can sealed off behind a closed door.

Later in 2015, Mark and his wife Priscilla Chan announced they are giving 99 per cent of their shares away to good causes, a gesture I have enormous respect for. Achieving business success, while also helping people and the planet, is a constant in my life too. Hopefully more young entrepreneurs will follow suit – as well as old ones. I've always had massive admiration for Ted Turner, for business triumphs like creating CNN and generosity like helping set up the UN Foundation. Sam, Bellie and I were fortunate enough to stay with him on his Avalon Plantation near Tallahassee, Florida. A local taxi driver came to pick us up and I started making small talk: 'Do you shoot pheasants around here?' He responded: 'No, we haven't shot *peasants* around here for a long time. We call them white trash here.' I could hear Sam and Bellie falling about with laughter in the back seat. I just nodded along and tried to keep a straight face. Ted's estate is magical. He is a keen conservationist, the largest bison herder in the world and has reintroduced species like the red-cockaded woodpecker and even wolves. When we went out riding one evening Ted howled like a wolf and the wolves responded. His talent for combining business with philanthropy is something we can all learn from.

We didn't end up working with Facebook this time around. They pursued their own plans for providing WiFi connectivity in sub-Saharan Africa using drones, while Google took another direction, using balloons. I could be completely wrong, and it would be fantastic if their approaches work, but found both ideas quite bizarre. Having said that, I wouldn't bet against Larry Page or Mark Zuckerberg. Larry has already proved me wrong with self-driving cars. I remember being at the bar on Necker about eight years ago, when he told me 'Self-driving cars are my new obsession. Within the next decade, they will be everywhere.' At the time, I didn't think it was one of his more plausible ideas. But the technology has since improved, just as Larry had predicted.

In any one conversation Larry will come up with five or six incredible ideas. If it was anybody else I would make my excuses and get up and leave after the first. But because it is Larry I sit and listen, take it in, absorb and try to find the substance. One of his ideas I love is using giant kites to generate electricity. If it works it would be fantastic. The idea of the world being full of beautiful, colourful kites generating energy is inspirational as well as practical.

I'm sure that was a spinoff from his love of kiting and our trips around the BVI. While Larry was kiting on his wedding day, I got talking to his university lecturer on the beach. He told me how Larry came to him at the end of the course and told him: 'I've got these three ideas, which should I pursue?' The professor thought 'that Google thing' sounded the best – but believed all three would have been successful. I find it curious how Larry and his co-founder Sergey Brin get criticised now for not sticking to their core products and increasingly spending time and money in experimental ventures. What they basically say to the market place is: 'If we don't do it, who will?' I love that attitude – hopefully it is something that has rubbed off on Larry from our nights on Necker! He certainly has respect for the Virgin brand. We were onstage in front of a large audience of tech experts in San Francisco when Larry said: 'Richard has got an incredible three hundred companies and we've only got one.' 'I'll swap,' I replied. 'Quick as a flash!'

While the Virgin brand punches massively above its weight, we are still small compared to Google or Facebook. This means we can't do too many moonshot ideas at the same time. The space industry is our moonshot at the moment – anything more than that would potentially bank-rupt us. For example, in 2011 we launched a company, Virgin Oceanic, to explore the bottom of the ocean. We built a submarine and I planned to dive nearly 11,000 metres down to the Mariana Trench, carrying out several test dives in the craft. It was tremendously exciting, but fraught with technical difficulties in developing a submarine that could withstand the pressures of the deepest parts of the ocean. We had to decide: could we afford the huge expense of this moonshot at the same time as our space programme? Or should we move these funds into ocean conservation, creat-ing Ocean Unite and spending my time as an Ocean Elder? We decided upon the latter. Sometimes it is necessary to pivot a business into a new idea, and wait for another opportunity.

*

In June 2015, I was at the Royal Society in London, a fitting venue as the UK's national science academy, to share our latest progress on OneWeb and the world's biggest ever satellite constellation. First formed way back in 1660, the society has promoted and celebrated scientific achievement ever since. In the grandeur of its Grade-I listed, Carlton House Terrace headquarters, I felt in the right place to let the world know about our exciting plans.

Virgin Galactic, I announced, had signed a contract with OneWeb to serve as one of its inaugural satellite launch providers. We agreed to perform an initial series of satellite launches for OneWeb, making the deal at that point the largest commercial procurement of launches ever. These satellites, creating an unprecedented global communications system dwarfing any previous commercial network in the skies by a factor of ten, could bring connectivity to millions of people.

'It's a project with purpose with the power to change the world,' I told the assembled guests. 'By connecting remote areas, we can raise living standards and prosperity in some of the poorest regions.'

I left it to OneWeb's Greg Wyler to make the launch date predictions: 'The dream of fully bridging the digital divide is on track to be a reality in 2019.'

The scale of the deal, which will enable affordable broadband access around the world, including in areas currently unserved or underserved by terrestrial providers, meant that Virgin Galactic and Virgin Orbit could expand further, too. Just as the human spaceflight project was all being done in-house, we wanted to build every aspect of our rocket launcher ourselves. We opened the perfect spot in February 2015: a 150,000-square-foot facility at Long Beach airport. We moved 120 of our engineers and technicians there, and they immediately got to work. It is now the home of Virgin Orbit. The team has made so much progress, building more reliable and cost-effective rockets to launch the small satellite revolution. The market has already responded positively to Virgin Orbit, whose early-

January 2015
Call yourself a sailor? Celebrating rescuing Sir Ben Ainslie
and his wife Georgie on Necker Island

April 2015
Richard Branson's Day Off!
Launching Virgin Hotels with a
street parade in Chicago

April 2015
Reading a bedtime story –
Where The Wild Things Are – to
Virgin Hotels Chicago guests

July 2015
My adorable grandchildren Etta and Artie with their mum and dad on my 65th birthday on Necker

July 2015
Celebrating Joan's 70th in Oxford with the family

July 2015
Giving Joan a birthday kiss as our kids look on

July 2015
With my sisters Vanessa and Lindi and our mum on my 65th birthday

August 2015
Astronaut Mark Kelly's photo of Necker from the International Space Station

September 2015
In my happy place, kitesurfing in the British Virgin Islands

October 2015
Magical moment in South Africa helping a young girl hear for the first time

October 2015
Sharing ideas with Virgin CEO Josh Bayliss in Sydney

October 2015
The UNODC
paper calling
for global drug
decriminalisation.
When the UN
wouldn't release
the document, I
leaked it

UNODC
United Nations Office on Drugs and Crime

Briefing paper: Decriminalisation of Drug Use and Possession for Personal Consumption

Decriminalising drug use and possession for personal consumption is permitted by the international drug control conventions and is a key element of the HIV response among people who use drugs

This document clarifies the position of UNODC to inform country responses to promote a health and human rights-based approach to drug policy. It explains that decriminalising drug use and possession for personal consumption is consistent with international drug control conventions and may be required to meet obligations under international human rights law.

Terms and definitions[1]

Decriminalisation of drug use for non-medical purposes and possession for personal consumption can be as a matter of law ("de jure") and as a matter of practice or policy ('de facto'). De jure decriminalisation is the removal of criminal sanctions with the optional use of civil or administrative sanctions, such as fines or education. De facto decriminalisation (sometimes called depenalisation) is the decision in practice or as policy to not apply criminal or administrative penalties for certain offenses. In de jure decriminalisation models, personal possession and use remain unlawful, but are not criminal. In de facto decriminalisation models, personal possession and use remain criminal but may be addressed with alternative sanctions for offenders who are drug dependent or have committed minor crimes.

Negative effects of criminalisation

Treating drug use for non-medical purposes and possession for personal consumption as criminal offences has contributed to public health problems and induced negative consequences for safety, security, and human rights.

- **Health consequences and drug-related deaths:** The threat of arrest and criminal sanctions have been widely shown to obstruct access to lifesaving health services like sterile needles and syringes, opioid substitution therapy, naloxone for overdose, fueling HIV and hepatitis C epidemics among people who use drugs, and contributing to preventable deaths from those blood borne viruses and drug overdose.

- **Discrimination, social exclusion and violence:** The heavy emphasis on criminalization has fueled high levels of discrimination against people who use drugs, including exclusion from workplace, from education, from child custody and from health care. People who use drugs, especially women who use drugs, are particularly vulnerable to sexual, physical and psychological abuse.

- **Detention in compulsory centres:** Large numbers of people who use and inject drugs are held in compulsory drug detention centres without their informed consent, often without proper judicial process, facing treatment interventions that are not evidence based,[ii] and in contradiction with medical ethics and human rights.[iii]

- **Incarceration:** Worldwide, millions of people are imprisoned for minor, non-violent drug-related offences, in spite of the international drug control conventions' provisions permitting to apply alternatives to conviction in cases of a 'minor nature'. In many countries, a disproportionate share of those incarcerated is from the most marginalized groups such as people who are poor, and racial or ethnic minorities, leading to prison overcrowding and related negative consequences, including pre-trial detention. Incarceration, in turn, fuels poverty and social exclusion, as having a criminal record can negatively affect access to future employment, education, housing, and child custody and also exercising civil rights such as voting. Poor conditions and lack of HIV services, including drug dependence treatment, in prisons can fuel HIV, viral hepatitis, and tuberculosis infections among people who use drugs, and increase overdose risk.

International law

Governments have a duty under international law to take steps to reduce supply of and demand for controlled drugs. In doing so, they must ensure that these efforts are balanced with obligations to ensure adequate availability of controlled drugs for medical and scientific purposes and that these steps are consistent with states' human rights obligations.

The international drug control system, underpinned by three international drug control conventions, recognizes the "health and welfare of mankind" as its overarching concern. It establishes a dual drug control obligation: "to ensure the availability of controlled substances for medical and scientific ends while preventing the illicit production of, trafficking in and abuse of such substances."[iv]

The purposes and principles of the United Nations, as set out in the UN Charter, are to "maintain international peace and security;" and to promote "solutions of international economic, social, health and related problems" (which includes drug control) and to promote "universal respect for, and observance of, human rights and fundamental freedoms."[v] These three policy pillars of the UN - security, development, and human rights – guide drug policy. Indeed, the Commentary to the 1988 international drug control conventions should be read in context of these provisions. This means that the international drug control conventions should be read in context of these provisions. Indeed, the Commentary to the 1988 international drug control convention states, "particular care must be taken to ensure compliance with relevant constitutional protections and applicable human rights norms."[vi]

States have obligations under the right to health to take all necessary steps for the "prevention, treatment and control of epidemic... diseases,"[vii] to ensure access to essential medicines, and to take affirmative steps to promote health and to refrain from conduct that limits people's abilities to safeguard their health.[viii]

January 2016
Discovering I'm part-Indian
while researching my family tree
on *Finding My Roots*

January 2016
Talking leadership with
Canadian Prime Minister
Justin Trudeau in Davos

February 2016
Moments before I was kissed by a stingray in the Cayman Islands

February 2016
The Virgin Galactic team in Mojave celebrating the rollout of VSS *Unity*, our new spaceship

February 2016
Unveiling VSS *Unity*, the new spaceship built by The Spaceship Company and Virgin Galactic

May 2016
Celebrating the first 1,000 loans handed out by Virgin StartUp to entrepreneurs in the UK

March 2016
Skiing in Verbier with the family

2016
Virgin eRacing team
– electric cars are the
future of motorsport

2016
My darling Joan.
Some people are just
meant to be together

June 2016
Going viral after
surprising a sleeping
Virgin Australia team
member

July 2016
Talking to David Cameron on the day he announced he was stepping down as Prime Minister

August 2016
Great honour sharing lunch with President Obama at the White House

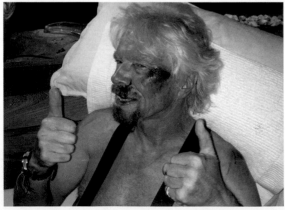

August 2016
Amazed I'm still alive after my bike fell off a cliff in the British Virgin Islands

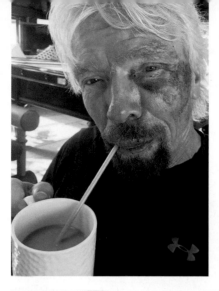

August 2016
Drinking tea through a straw after my
near-death cycling accident

September 2016
Climbing Mount Etna at the end of the
gruelling Virgin Strive Challenge

September 2016
Climbing to the summit of
Mount Etna with Holly and
Sam on the Virgin Strive
Challenge

September 2016
Tearful hug with Holly and
Sam after completing the
Virgin Strive Challenge

September 2016
If you want to go far, go together – cycling on the Virgin Strive Challenge

October 2016
With Bill Gates discussing philanthropy and clean energy in London

April 2017
Necker, the breathtaking island I bought in 1979. The BVI is now our home

December 2016
VSS *Unity*'s first test flight – I was watching on from below

2017
The thrilling moment when VSS *Unity* is released from WhiteKnightTwo and flies freely towards space

January 2017
Necker tennis tournament with the Obamas and friends

January 2017
Friendly
competition
with President
Obama out on
the water off
Necker

January 2017
Foilboarding
contest against
President
Obama on
Necker

February 2017
My view when I look up to the stars on Necker Island

March 2017
Working on Necker with Holly

March 2017
Introducing Etta and Artie to
Necker Island's flamingos

March 2017
Never too young to learn
the art of chess

April 2017
Diving the *Kodiak Queen*, a
WWII ship we sank in the
BVI to create a conservation
reef and dive site

April 2017
Marching in Washington with 200,000 people to call for ambitious action against climate change

April 2017
Eat your heart out, Usain Bolt! Fun at the first Virgin Sport Hackney Festival of Fitness

2017
The people who mean the most in the world to me

May 2017
How Virgin Orbit's adapted *Cosmic Girl* will look, with LauncherOne on the wing

May 2017
Making Ship Happen at the Virgin Voyages launch in Miami

May 2017
The Virgin Orbit team in front of one of our LauncherOne rockets in Long Beach

June 2017
A special hug with my son Sam and my newborn grandson Bluey

2017
All smiles with my first three grandchildren

adopter customers include government agencies like NASA and the US Air Force as well as commercial firms like OneWeb, GomSpace, and Spire Global.

The way we had pivoted the business was fairly typical of Virgin ventures – we have to be nimble, open to opportunities and ready for change.

Behind the scenes, I was thinking about how we could increase the efficiency and effectiveness of our satellites programme further. One big issue we had was that our mothership, WhiteKnightTwo, would be needed to transport both our human spaceflight programme and our satellite programme. While it is certainly capable, this is a lot of exertion for one aircraft. Plans to build further motherships were underway, but this would take a long time and cost a great deal, so we needed to think creatively.

I thought back to watching NASA's Shuttle Carrier Aircraft in action in the 1970s. They were two modified Boeing 747 jetliners, which were originally manufactured for commercial use before being heavily altered to ferry space shuttle orbiters. I remember first seeing the shuttle attached to the top of the 747 and thinking how peculiar it looked, then marvelling as they flew seamlessly as one. Could the same concept be applied for our spaceship? As the owner of three airlines, I had a good idea where we could source some second-hand 747s!

I got my notebook out and drew some little sketches of how this could work, before taking the idea to the Virgin Galactic team to drill down into the details. While putting our spaceship on top of the 747 didn't look workable right now (though it may in the future), we had another idea for our satellites. Perhaps we could modify the plane to attach LauncherOne to the wing? If the giant rocket could have enough clearance from the ground, it would free up WhiteKnightTwo, our mothership, to focus solely on commercial spaceflights.

Over at Virgin Atlantic, we were beginning to roll out our stunning new Dreamliners, so some of the older 747s were due to go out of commercial service. It just so happened that we had a plane that fitted the bill, with a perfect name: *Cosmic Girl*. Our engineers checked on the feasibility of attaching LauncherOne to its wing and gave it the go-ahead.

On 3 December, I travelled down to Texas to welcome *Cosmic Girl*, to Virgin Galactic's fleet. Boeing were also in Texas, already looking into the modification requirements for *Cosmic Girl*, and I asked their team leader a question we had been considering for a while.

'Do you think it would be possible for SpaceShipTwo to be launched from the top of a 747?'

'Based upon the success of the Shuttle Carrier Aircraft, I would say it is possible, with a lot of modification,' he said.

We started throwing around other ideas. Might it be possible to intercept a falling rocket fitted with a parachute, using a helicopter with a giant hook? If it worked, we could retrieve and reuse expensive equipment. For every twenty questions like this, there may be one that turns into a gem of an idea. It's important to look simplistically at everything – even the most complex problems could have answers staring you straight in the face. This attitude had also led to a small number of Virgin Galactic staff spending time pondering the question of point-to-point travel. This is the idea of hypersonic transportation from one place to another distant place via space. There is potential to fly from the US to Australia in two hours using this method and there's no reason why point-to-point travel can't be achieved (even if everyone might not enjoy the g-forces!). If I didn't have incentive enough, I was in Peru in April 2013 having breakfast outside our hotel when a young couple approached us. The man immediately asked:

'Is it true you could fly across the world in a couple of hours?'

'Well, not yet – but I believe we will one day.'

'How soon?'

'I'm not sure yet – but we're working on it. Why?'

'Well ...' He looked across at his girlfriend standing next to him, and she smiled. 'I live here in Lima,' she said. 'But he lives in Abu Dhabi. It takes so long to get to each other.'

'I see. Virgin Galactic are already working really hard on the problem. Now we've got an extra reason to make it happen!'

I think about technology intuitively. Piloting hot-air balloons around the world gave me a good practical understanding of aviation concepts, and I've picked up a lot from running our airlines. While I don't get involved in the nuts and bolts, or specifics like the inner workings of a rocket motor, it doesn't take me long to understand key structures and concepts. George is no longer surprised when I call him up three months after he has shown me a certain aspect of a fuel tank, and ask him how it is progressing. I'm not stuck in the weeds, and I trust that we have the world's best technical expert working on it, but I like to think I can add value by thinking about problems in a completely different way to the professionals.

As time ticked on from the OneWeb deal and development of our new spaceship and modification of *Cosmic Girl* continued, I thought about how we could keep momentum up. I'm a big believer in creating panic early. Too many leaders wait until deadlines are looming or a crisis is in full flow before injecting urgency into their team. By then it's too late. I like to shake things up in my teams and keep people motivated by pushing them to think as if it's a crisis, when everything is running on schedule. This way, innovations can be sparked, and future crises can be averted. Pondering this, I sent a note to the Virgin Galactic and Virgin Group management teams, trying to squeeze a little more momentum out.

Dear Galactic team,

Being dyslexic, I've never been one for spreadsheets. I need to simplify everything. It's how I've run companies for 50 years. So forgive the simplistic approach I've taken below, but I do think it's well worth a read. We need to urgently look into how we can reduce costs in the short term. For instance, can we bring any of the development in-house? Can we cut down other costs? [I then listed out costs based on items such as satellite amounts, labour, tanks, avionics, operations and propulsion.]

What if we decided to ramp up production quicker? What would that do to costs and profitability?

The benefits of speeding things up over the next three years are huge and all of this can be done in our Long Beach facility by utilising it fully. If no one can find fundamental flaws in these figures, we should have a serious discussion. It will mean upfront costs but on the face of it this would be money well spent. I'd like to arrange a phone call for tomorrow to have what I suspect will be a healthy debate on this! Obviously if I'm correct about the above this would be completely transformational, so let's put our thinking caps on and try to make something happen. Whatever else, we must move rapidly from TODAY.

We had a very productive phone call and the team began looking into the feasibility of making some of the changes. It isn't just big amounts and major deals I use this logic on; I try to simplify everything and apply this to every aspect of my life, however small or big. This means paying attention to detail. A good entrepreneur signs every cheque personally, say, every quarter. Doing so, they will pick up large and small discrepancies. We have used the same taxi firm in Miami for years. In checking the bill recently it was clear we were being ripped off. We called up and asked them to justify their new prices – they immediately apologised and cut their rates by 50 per cent. Then there are bigger amounts. Each year our banks required us to undertake a valuation exercise on some Virgin Group assets, apparently as part of their internal policies but for no clear reason, taking substantial time and costing us over $100,000 a year. One call and they agreed that they didn't actually need this. For every dollar you save today, the cumulative effect is enormous. Too often people only look into these details when times are tight and they are losing money. It is much easier to remove unnecessary over-complications and costs when business is doing well, keeping your company lean and mean.

*

In February 2016, I looked around the table at the Mariah Inn and saw four generations of my family surrounding me: Mum had flown out to the desert, along with Joan, Sam, Bellie and their first child – my granddaughter Eva-Deia (more about her soon!). The mood was celebratory: it was Eva-Deia's first birthday. But we were also in Mojave for another special occasion of a different sort: the unveiling of Virgin Galactic's new spaceship.

As we drove around the corner to FAITH, the hangar where the beautiful new SpaceShipTwo was waiting behind the scenes, I was eager for a sneak peek. As I popped my head into the spaceship, I was greeted with my first surprise on a day of surprises: the actor Harrison Ford! Dave Mackay was alongside him in the cockpit and only too happy to let Han Solo take the driving seat!

'How does it compare to the *Millennium Falcon*?' I asked.

'It's real life, it's fantastic,' he said.

We shook hands and I thanked him for coming. Later he told me all about his plane crash onto a golf course and how he had survived. It sounded hairy.

'You've had more close calls than me!' I told him.

'I don't know about that.'

'Well, you're welcome back here any time, and we'll get you to space one day.'

I was fascinated to see how this great actor, renowned for his *Star Wars* role, was eager to fly into space. David Bowie, who had sadly died the month before, was another who inspired us all to look to the cosmos with wonder through songs like 'Starman' and 'Life on Mars'. I was very fortunate to cross paths with David over the years (we did eventually sign him to Virgin Records) and he was truly unique. As a young man entranced by the moon landing in 1969, his breakthrough song 'Space Oddity' had a big impact upon me. It was interesting to hear in *The Last Five Years* documentary that he didn't want to go to space himself: 'It's an interior dialogue that you manifest physically,' he said. 'It's my little inner space, isn't it? Writ large. I wouldn't dream of getting on a spaceship – it would scare the shit out of me. I have absolutely no interest or ambition to go into space whatsoever. I'm scared going down the end of the garden.'

I empathised with his attitude of seeing space as a metaphor for internal exploration and expanding his state of mind. Space, as a symbol, is important to my own psyche, and how I see life as one wonderful, upward journey. But, unlike David, I was also very serious about physically visiting space. Rather than scary, I found the prospect exhilarating.

I rejoined my family in a neighbouring hangar, where they had met the assembled future astronauts and Virgin Galactic team for lunch. There was an atmosphere of impatience and excitement as we waited for the big reveal. 'What does it look like?' was the question on everybody's lips.

'You'll have to wait and see,' I teased.

Once everyone was inside FAITH, we ramped up the tension with a series of testimonials from Virgin Galactic's leaders, stressing the amazing teamwork that had gone into this journey. The spaceship's name, from our initial nickname 'Hope', had evolved to Virgin SpaceShip *Unity*. There was no other word to illustrate the togetherness that had defined the long months between the tragic accident of 31 October 2014 and this moment on 19 February 2016.

I lingered behind a curtain, atop a Land Rover in front of the spaceship, with the proud team of engineers that built her behind me. Malala Yousafzai shared some inspirational words about the role of women in science, and in particular in building VSS *Unity*. Her voice echoed around the hangar: 'My superpower is to speak for girls in a voice so loud that the whole world will listen. This spacecraft is such a great work, and it's a way that you are inspiring young people in this whole world to explore more, to go further and to have no boundaries.'

While I was itching to show off the spaceship, we had one more surprise: one of the most influential people in history and the only person with a free Virgin Galactic ticket to space, Professor Stephen Hawking. The hangar went pitch-black and silent, before the iconic sound of Professor Hawking's computerised voice began speaking.

'A man with the vision and persistence to open up space-flight for ordinary, Earth-bound citizens, Richard Branson made it his mission to make spaceflight a reality for those intrepid enough to venture beyond the boundaries of the Earth's atmosphere. I have had ALS for over 50 years now and while I have no fear of adventure, others do not always take the same view. If I am able to go – and if Richard will still take me – I would be very proud to fly on this spaceship.' Stephen's piercing blue eye was slowly beamed into the room from the UK – it was incredibly powerful. 'Space exploration has already been a great unifier – we seem able to cooperate between nations in space in a way we can only envy on Earth. We are entering a new space age and I hope this will help to create a new unity.'

Taking my cue, the curtain dropped and I arrived with VSS *Unity* to a stream of applause. Eyes widened at the striking new livery. Echoing what Stephen Hawking had said, I took the microphone: 'Together, we can make space accessible in a way that has only been dreamt of before now, and by doing so can bring positive change to life on Earth. Our beautiful new spaceship, with its stunning silver and white livery, is the embodiment of that goal and will provide us with an unprecedented body of experience which will in turn lay the foundations for Virgin Galactic's future. Her creation is also great testament to what can be achieved, when true teamwork, great skill and deep pride are combined with a common purpose.'

I wasn't going to let the occasion pass without marking Eva-Deia's big day in unique fashion, though. First, we smashed a baby bottle against the spaceship, the milk promptly splashing all over my face. Next, I cajoled Sarah

Brightman, one of our future astronauts, into kindly singing a touching happy birthday to my granddaughter. Then one of the most moving moments of the event took place, as Bellie shared some more of Professor Hawking's fitting wisdom on unity: 'When we see the Earth from space we see ourselves as a whole. We see the unity, but not the divisions. One planet, one human race. We are here together and we need to live together with tolerance and respect.'

Looking at the spaceship and then back to the people who had built it, I felt so proud of every single one of them, not only for their passion and commitment in a pioneering endeavour but also for their teamwork. I jotted down something one of the Galactic team said, and think it summed up the atmosphere perfectly: 'We think of the vehicles as almost our children, which makes us a family, and we are all so proud to see what they grow into.'

The word 'family' gets used too often by companies who treat their staff as anything but. I wish more businesses really did run like families. When things are going well, everyone has an even better time celebrating together. When things are tough you can rally around and help each other get through it. That's the way we work at Virgin Galactic, and the way we will continue to work. The new SpaceShipTwo is the first vehicle to be manufactured by The Spaceship Company, Virgin Galactic's wholly owned manufacturing arm, and is the second vehicle of its design ever constructed. It had been a long road. The team had started building the second SpaceShipTwo back in 2012, with each component part undergoing rigorous testing before assembly. Integrated systems verification, followed by ground and flight tests in Mojave and ground and air exercises at its future home in Spaceport America, New Mexico, were all to come. It took quite a long time between the roll out and flight tests beginning, simply because the team wanted to test everything in the most methodical way possible.

On 5 December 2016 I was back in Mojave pre-dawn to see VSS *Unity*'s fifth flight, and first time the spaceship had flown on her own. As Virgin Galactic's mated vehicles flew across the bright blue sky for about an hour, we mingled with the team and their families below, looking up in wonder. VSS *Unity* then detached and flew solo, gliding serenely to the ground and setting up more exciting tests in the months ahead. In February 2017 I was back for VSS *Unity*'s third glide flight (we have since completed successful feather flights and are gearing up for powered flights), watching on alongside Sam and Professor Brian Cox.

'People ask me, would you fly to space?' he told me, as we looked on at VSS *Unity*.

'Well, would you?'

'The moment I walked in this hangar and saw that spaceship, I thought: I want to get on that aircraft. So the answer is now yes – 100 per cent. In that!'

As we watched a pitch-perfect test, Brian became the latest person to be convinced he should join us when commercial flights begin. Hopefully that moment will come very, very soon.

38 Good Morning, Vietnam, Goodbye, Madiba

It is one of those quirks of life that, despite going on all those Vietnam marches back in the 1960s, it wasn't until 2015 that I visited the country myself. That September, after a whirlwind trip to Australia and an even swifter day visit to Bangkok to launch Virgin Radio Thailand, we landed tired and jetlagged in Ho Chi Minh City, or Saigon as it is still mostly known.

Within moments, however, I was wide awake. As we drove through the buzzing city streets, I saw entire families riding on single-seat motorbikes, propaganda posters peeling off the walls and people rushing past the gates of the Independence Palace. We were making our way to a speaking engagement, where I hoped to inspire Vietnam's rapidly developing young entrepreneurs to think about changing business for good. As we drove into the venue I could see it was going to be a busy event: people lining the streets outside and crowding the car as I got out. But, even so, I still wasn't prepared for the reaction when I took to the stage – I felt like the fifth Beatle! There was a roar as The Black Eyed Peas' 'I Got A Feeling' blared out of the speakers and I found myself in front of nearly 10,000 Vietnamese, most of them aged from sixteen to thirty.

As I discussed space travel, mentorship and my own connection to Vietnam, they listened politely but intently, bursting into applause at regular intervals. It felt strange being somewhere that felt so far away when I was young, and now being recognised so strongly: one of the effects of social media is that today I am recognised in most countries in the world. I felt a bit awkward onstage in Vietnam, and wanted to make more of a personal connection with the locals. There was a strong security presence, something I never like, and I felt a little too distant from the audience. I decided to sit on the edge of the stage and answer questions. It wasn't my greatest idea, as a crush forward started instantly, and I was quickly whisked into a waiting car while hundreds of people lined the streets. As dozens of scooters chased us in the heavy traffic, I high-fived the riders out of the window.

That evening I joined twenty-five of Vietnam's leading entrepreneurs for a dinner discussion about conservation. Vietnam has become the end point in the fight to save the magnificent rhino. In the past few years, the number of rhinos brutally killed for their horns has risen astronomically. More than 1,200 rhinos were killed in South Africa alone in 2014. The reason? Demand in Vietnam, China and the Middle East. As I sat around a huge table in an opulent Saigon hotel, I learned that many of my well-intentioned fellow diners used rhino horn. Whether as jewellery, or for non-existent medicinal properties, these sad superstitions and misinformation were leading to the slaughter of a majestic species.

Along with experts from WildAid and other conservation groups, I explained how rhino horn is nothing more than keratin, the same substance from which human hair and nails are made. I bit my nails, elaborating the point as I said: 'If you think that rhino horn is a magical substance that can cure disease, you may as well be chewing your toe nails.' As I listened to the entrepreneurs around the table, I realised how much the issue has already become part of a national conversation, and how much embarrassment it has caused for a country of ninety million people that is rapidly entering the global market.

More positively, I learned that younger Vietnamese seem to understand the seriousness of the problem and no longer wish to be associated with these harmful habits. By the end of the evening, several dozen business leaders signed a pledge to never again use rhino horn, and agreed to start a movement to end the use of rhino horn once and for all. Huge progress has happened elsewhere since, and in December 2016 China announced a ban on all ivory trade.

One of the people present at the dinner was a remarkable lady who had lived inside the Củ Chi tunnels during the Vietnam War, and had gone on to become one of Vietnam's most successful business people. The following morning she joined us for an adventure up the Saigon River by boat, heading up towards Cambodia. Once we were chugging past thick green vegetation into the Vietnamese forests, I thought of *Apocalypse Now* and Martin Sheen's journey upstream into the 'heart of darkness'. I reminded myself of Củ Chi's infamous history en route, reading about the site described as 'the most bombed, shelled, gassed, defoliated and generally devastated area in the history of warfare'.

As I stepped off the boat, I immediately felt the heat and humidity of the jungle. We were only forty kilometres from Saigon's centre, but the bustle of the city felt thousands of miles away. We made our way into the tunnels, when I heard the rattle of gunfire. Startled, we looked around at each other, only relaxing when our guide explained that an automatic weapon shooting range was now part of the forest.

We ventured further into the tunnels and I learned more about how and where the Việt Cộng lived and fought deep underground. I was amazed at the intricacy and sophistication of this half-century-old network of tunnels, which cover more than 250 kilometres. I looked at the snares used to physically and psychologically trap the US soldiers by the Việt Cộng, before we built up to venturing down into the tunnels ourselves. Even though the tunnels had been widened for tourists and lights had been added, I still felt claustrophobic, disoriented and very hot.

As I emerged from the tunnel I tore my shirt off. I'm glad no one seemed to believe that the bare-chested guy walking around the jungle was *really* Richard Branson. Standing there, cooling down, I thought about how this place had been where so many people had lived day-to-day, as well as fought and died. So much suffering had happened here, in such terrible conditions, for such futile reasons. By the time we left I had a new level of respect for the bravery of those on all sides who were forced to fight for their lives here. I also had an even more profound belief in the pointlessness of war, and the need to campaign for peace and conflict resolution everywhere on earth.

*

One person who was both badly and sadly missed in this regard was Nelson Mandela. Less than two years earlier, I had I woken up with the rest of the world to learn that Madiba had died. On one level, it wasn't a shock – Madiba had been ill for a long time – but it was a blow all the same. We had lost not only a great man; the world had lost one of its greatest leaders. Madiba had shown us what can be achieved by leading with integrity and empathy and the desire to help others. The act of forgiveness that Madiba gave his own captors who held him in prison for twenty-seven years will be remembered forever.

On a personal level, I had lost someone I looked to as a mentor and considered a friend. More than anything, Madiba had made me and many others smile, laugh and dance again and again. I remember the time he was travelling on one of our planes to New York, and found my young friend Peta-Lynn in the galley. He offered to make her a cup of tea and before long they were in cahoots, swapping stories. I have never known anybody transform rooms the way Madiba did, lighting them up with his humour, his humility and his wisdom. Whether it was asking me to help save South Africa's health club jobs or helping to create the Elders, unveiling a statue for Steve Biko or campaigning for HIV/AIDS sufferers, he was always working tirelessly for other people. Madiba made time for everyone, and had a magical skill for bringing the best out of people. I loved seeing how he interacted with his wife Graça Machel; their partnership was full of love and understanding and they weren't afraid to give each other time and space. Everyone could learn from that – I certainly have.

When Graça invited me to Madiba's funeral in his home village of Qunu, I dropped everything to be there. After landing in South Africa, I drove through the night to get to the funeral. As we entered the village, a breathtaking rainbow appeared on the horizon, which could not have been more appropriate in Madiba's rainbow nation. The old African adage 'You've not buried the person until you go to the village' also felt fitting. There had been a government-organised memorial service earlier in the week, which was a worthy commemoration of Madiba's life, but I'm sure he would have loved a little more dancing and singing!

After getting out of the car in Qunu, we were met by a few local people. I spoke to a sweet five-year-old girl called Jamie, who summed it up perfectly.

'It really makes my heart sore,' she said. 'I think I might cry.'

I was soon welling up, too. Before the burial several of Madiba's friends gave moving speeches, notably the President of Malawi, Joyce Banda. I wrote down her words: 'A leader is someone who falls in love with the people they serve and allows the people to fall in love with them.' I sat next to the delightful Oprah Winfrey and we shared some thoughts on how much comfort and hope Madiba had brought to us all.

After the funeral Madiba's family gave me the great honour of asking me to join them at the burial itself, which was a very poignant, private, traditional Xhosa ceremony. At one point I panicked when I saw that Madiba's grandson had fallen right into the grave. As I peered in, about to call out, three men pulled him out unhurt and he dusted off his suit. Then another grandson was pulled out of the grave. I hadn't realised that it was their tradition to go down onto the coffin and leave something that was a bond between them and the deceased.

It was fitting that the most moving moment came at the very end, from Madiba's dear friend Archbishop Tutu. Together the two of them have done so much to promote peace and reconciliation in South Africa and everywhere on earth. As Madiba's stone was being laid, Arch said: 'He does not need a stone for us to remember him; we carry him in our hearts.' Standing next to the grave, I knew this was not the end of Mandela's journey. The long walk to freedom continues for so many people around the world, and it is through us all that his legacy will prevail. The loss of Madiba hit me hard on my next birthday, which is the same date as his. Every 18 July he would find the time to call and wish me happy birthday. I missed not getting his call that day, just as I missed not getting a call from my father. I still get a lovely note each year from Graça Machel, who continues to do wonderful work in the world, particularly through the Elders.

Madiba, I cannot put into words what you meant to me but thank you for your leadership, inspiration, friendship and the joy you brought into all of our lives. You are, and will be, greatly missed.

*

At Madiba's funeral, one of the things that touched me was how often the Elders were brought up by different people, with many speakers taking solace in how Madiba's teachings will live on through their work.

When I look back upon my life, I believe and hope one of the most important things I have achieved is the creation of the Elders. The world needs the Elders more than anything right now. Getting that extraordinary group of people together, having them visit places others wouldn't, such as Russia, Darfur, Somalia, Palestine, North Korea, having them fight to stop conflicts, and succeeding on occasions, speaking out on issues like climate change and universal healthcare, is one of the things I am most proud of.

The Elders have already gone through a number of renditions. Before his death, Mandela led it in its early days with his assuredness and grace; then came Archbishop Tutu in the most wonderfully human, outspoken way. Now we have Kofi Annan, who is more of a diplomat but acutely focused on achieving the end goals. I've learned so much from the approaches of all three. Listening to them teaches me how to construct arguments, how to connect with people, how to lead from afar as well as with personal touches.

As advisers we handed over the keys to them once we'd set it up. That was very important to protect their integrity. The advisers can say what they think but all decisions are the Elders' alone. It can only last hundreds of years if it is completely independent of outside influence. The Elders are always challenging themselves to be more effective and considering how they can make a bigger difference. They are right to question in that way, and it is another thing I have picked up from them – ruthless self-analysis. As I write, the Elders are doing a complete review to see how to make the next ten years even more productive than the last. That's also what I try to do, every new year and every new decade.

While we as advisers do not interfere in the Elders' diplomacy, there are times when I feel I simply must speak out as an individual, regardless of the consequences. I have picked up a lot from watching the Elders' unique brand of quiet diplomacy, and know that much of the most effective advocacy goes on behind the scenes, in private, humble formats. The most common is simple written letters. Away from the public eye, I send dozens of private letters each year to politicians and organisations around the globe on issues ranging from LGBTQ rights to climate change, prison reform to drug reform. But sometimes these messages need to go public to have a wider impact. There have been, I hope, a few examples in this book, from the Iraq War to the HIV/AIDS crisis, where I have stuck my head above the parapet. In February 2016 I was honoured to join Amnesty International's Global Council. Salil Shetty, the human rights group's secretary general, kindly cited my 'consistent and very visible' advocacy on social justice issues. I was only too happy to spread their positive message and mobilise more people to stand up for human rights. As I get older, and spend more time focusing on philanthropic ventures, these moments are becoming more frequent.

There have been several times in the past few years when I have believed the business world could step in to help diffuse or improve certain situations. One of these was Ukraine, which has been in turmoil for several years. At Davos in 2014 we held a minute's silence for those dying on Maidan Nezalezhnosti. Two years later, more than 6,000 people had been killed, 1.3 million citizens had been displaced and the economy had nearly been crippled. And, after two years of fighting and international sanctions, many Russian people were suffering, too. The majority of Ukrainians and Russians just wanted to live in peace, and to have the opportunity to find prosperity for their families.

I visited Ukraine twice in 2014, meeting with people such as the Mayor of Kiev Vitali Klitschko and Yulia Marushevska, who had inspired many people with her online activism. I had a strong sense of optimism for and confidence in the country. 'There is hope, and it comes in the form of the next generation, and in business,' I wrote afterwards. 'Young Ukrainians are focusing on the problems that are currently damaging their country and are working for change.' I called for business to help stimulate large-scale investment and encourage cross-border trade: 'It's been proven time and time again that people that do business with one another are less likely to harm each other. Business can help to lift Ukraine out of conflict and set the tone for a prosperous future. And if the international business community encourages trade to flourish, young Ukrainians will be given great confidence to spur much-needed change.'

As the situation worsened, I worked with Advocacy Director Matthias Stausberg and Virgin Unite to assemble a group of sixteen concerned Russian, Ukrainian and international business leaders to speak out together in support of ending the conflict. We published an open letter offering to help: 'We as business leaders from Russia, Ukraine and the rest of the world urge our governments to work together to ensure we do not regress into the Cold War misery of the past. We call upon politicians to be bold and brave, so that our nations can end the painful suffering caused by war and once again collaborate for the greater good.'

*

While the danger in Ukraine was all too apparent on TV screens, other deeply troubling regions were receiving far less attention. One of these was the Maldives, a paradise archipelago in the Indian Ocean. I had first visited this stunning country in 2011 to attend the Slowlife Symposium, an event where everyone from Daryl Hannah to President Mohamed Nasheed had assembled to discuss the threat of climate change. Joan came along with me and we enjoyed fascinating discussions in an immaculate setting of achingly beautiful sunsets and sun-kissed beaches. I found the people even warmer than the weather, endlessly friendly and fundamentally entrepreneurial.

President Nasheed was the Maldives' first democratically elected leader. He had been imprisoned for five years by a dictatorship that had ruled for decades, before forcing the election he won. Once in power he inspired many with his calls for stronger global emissions targets. He even held an underwater cabinet meeting to illustrate the danger the Maldives faced from climate change, and called out fellow leaders for inaction: 'At the moment, every country arrives at climate negotiations seeking to keep their own emissions as high as possible. This is the logic of the madhouse, a recipe for collective suicide. We don't want a global suicide pact. We want a global survival pact.' We got on well and I found him an inquisitive, honest, driven leader. I told President Nasheed that I admired his stance, but joked that we all needed to be more positive in our language: 'Martin Luther King Jr. did not get his message across by saying "I have a nightmare!"'

The next time the country came across my radar was in February 2012, when a nightmare was exactly what Nasheed was having: 'Extremely concerned for my democratic friend Mohamed Nasheed, after coup against him in Maldives,' I tweeted. As we learned more, I discovered that Mohammed Waheed had seized power, but exactly what had happened was shrouded in mystery. Waheed got in touch and claimed he had taken control legitimately. I called Nasheed, who told me otherwise.

'I have been overthrown by a coup,' he told me. 'The confusion about what happened in the first two days came about because I was forced to remain in the Presidential Palace in order to be kept away from the press. I was therefore incommunicado and only managed to escape after a couple of days.'

Nasheed was concerned the new government was throwing out human rights and corruption cases. He called for new elections: 'Governments should only be changed through the ballot box and not by any other means. No military in the world should be allowed to take over a Government and hold on to it.' Having listened to both sides, I wrote on my blog calling for a free and fair election so the people of the Maldives could begin to put this ugly chapter behind them.

Sadly, peace did not come. While holiday-makers continued to visit the Maldives, oblivious to the human rights abuses going on, former President Nasheed was repeatedly threatened, culminating in a thirteen-year jail sentence in 2015 on a trumped-up terrorism charge.

Behind the scenes, a pro-bono legal team led by renowned human rights lawyer Amal Clooney was helping Nasheed to secure a thirty-day furlough to seek medical treatment in the UK. I sent letters to leaders in the US, UK and EU to help force through his release. 'In the spirit of democracy and the rule of law, we shouldn't rest until Mohamed Nasheed is a free man,' I wrote in my blog. It was still in the balance whether Nasheed would be allowed to leave the Maldives. Amal emailed me on 17 January: 'Dear Richard,

I wanted to let you know the latest. Nasheed was due to travel today. Then this morning, they suddenly imposed a new condition, seeking that Nasheed nominate a family member who would remain in Malé as a hostage – to be prosecuted and detained if Nasheed did not return within 30 days. Nasheed refused to agree to leave on that basis – his family is not involved in politics and he would never put them in a threatening situation. Will keep you posted.'

As I started to reply, the decision was reversed and Amal said they were on their way to the airport. 'That's wonderful news, if it happens,' I wrote back hurriedly. 'If we can help with flights let us know. Keeping fingers crossed.' Within the hour, she replied.

'It's wheels up!' said Amal. He was on his way to Britain.

*

It is strange how one collision in life can have such a positive impact. We have since worked with Amal Clooney on issues ranging from the refugee crisis to death penalty abolition. She and her husband George Clooney joined us for a Virgin Unite gathering on Necker Island where Amal gave a powerful talk on disrupting to protect human rights. There was time for lighter moments, too. I reminded George of the time he was asked who he would exchange places with for a day, given the chance. Very generously, he suggested he would happily swap with yours truly. My wife instantly replied: 'Deal!'

There was also much talk about the death penalty at that gathering, as a disturbing case was fresh in our memories.

I had heard about Richard Glossip, a prisoner languishing on Oklahoma's death row for seventeen years. A growing community of supporters, from Sister Helen Prejean to Susan Sarandon to Pope Francis, believed he was an innocent man. No physical evidence linked Richard to the crime for which he was convicted. Justin Sneed beat the victim to death with a baseball bat and only avoided the death penalty himself by claiming Richard had paid him to do it. Richard was convicted of first-degree murder and sentenced to death based on the sole testimony of Sneed, a man with every reason to lie. Others have since come forward to say that Sneed boasted he'd set Richard up. Despite this, Richard remained due to be executed on 30 September 2015.

As the efforts to free him fell on deaf ears, I decided upon a different approach. 'Why don't we take out a full-page ad in Oklahoma's biggest newspaper?' I said to my team on 29 September. 'The authorities might not listen online, or answer the phone, but they'll listen if their own citizens call for the execution to be stopped.' Within two hours the ad was sent over to the paper's editors. I appealed for this 'father, son and fellow human being' to be spared. 'This is not about the rights and wrongs of the death penalty. This is about every person deserving a fair trial.' I included the phone number of the state's governor, Mary Fallin, and urged people to call her demanding Richard Glossip's release.

For the second time, Glossip was served his last meal, all but certain that his final moment had come. Remarkably, he ordered pizza, and because of a two-for-one deal, offered to share it with his guards. On 30 September he was granted a last-minute stay of execution. The State of Oklahoma said there had been a mix-up involving the drugs needed according to its execution protocol. The very next day, the State went even further and issued an indefinite stay of all pending executions. For Richard, the stay has offered some relief in a seemingly never-ending ordeal that tells us so much about what is wrong with the US criminal justice system today. But it won't set him free. The fight for his full exoneration is far from over.

Just over a month later, I got to speak with Richard over the phone. We talked for nearly an hour.

'How are you holding up at the moment?' I asked him.

'I'm doing good,' he replied. 'You know. Fight every day to make sure this place doesn't bite me.'

'Well, you're a remarkable individual and I think what you've been through is barbaric. I don't know how any human being can cope with what you've been through.'

'I appreciate that.'

'I think that the death penalty itself is completely inhumane and dehumanises everybody,' I told him. 'But in your case you seem to have been sentenced to death in the interest of finality and not fairness, and your guilt has not been proven at all within any reasonable doubt. In fact, I think everything points to your innocence and that's why I think your case has mobilised so many people worldwide and not just in Oklahoma to take a stand. You should know you have a lot of supporters.'

'I do now ... One of the main things I wanted to do was to address the issue of the death penalty and make sure that this doesn't happen to anybody else. It's just ridiculous that this could happen that easily to somebody.'

It was a remarkable conversation. Somehow, despite everything, Richard was full of hope and optimism and without a trace of bitterness or fear. While continuing to call for Richard to be released, I was humbled to receive the Abolition Award from Death Penalty Focus in California. At the event, I shared my wider views on why I think the death penalty is a violation of human rights that has no place in a civilised society: 'Over the years, I have used my voice, my reach, and my resources to take a stand against the death penalty, in the US and elsewhere. Some countries – like Saudi Arabia, Iran, China and Pakistan – continue to execute people at an alarming rate, and convictions often follow legal proceedings that violate every standard of fairness and human decency. But there is a glimmer of hope,' I continued, to nods from around the room. 'For the first time ever, the majority of the world's countries – 102, to be precise – are abolitionist for all crimes. The Republic of Congo, Fiji, Madagascar and Suriname are the latest countries to join the growing list of those that abolished the death penalty for good. This is the moment to turn our attention to the US. Ending the death penalty in the US is no longer a pipe dream, but a growing movement that crosses partisan lines – a movement of those who understand it's not just the right thing to do, but also the sensible thing to do, no matter how you look at it. Less than ten years from now, I'm certain, the death penalty in the US will be history.'

We continue to campaign for the abolition of the death penalty and criminal justice reform in many different ways: some of our Virgin businesses have been working with and hiring ex-offenders for some time; in May 2014, I visited Ironwood Prison to learn more about the US criminal justice system at the first ever TEDx talk held in a California prison. Ahead of California's sadly defeated vote to repeal the barbaric law, we supported a series of hard-hitting films Sundog Pictures made called #DeathPenaltyFail.

How many innocent people have been killed? In total, 156 people have been freed from America's death rows in recent years. Who knows how many of those who remain locked up are innocent, too? As the wonderful Sister Helen Prejean said to me: 'We are worth more than the worst moment of our lives.'

There are obviously some people who remain a danger to others, who have done some truly horrific things and deserve to be imprisoned for life. But that is a tiny minority. The vast majority of prisoners deserve a second chance to become valuable members of society and need as much support as possible to get back on their feet again.

39 Brexit

On 10 May 2016, I was invited to attend a garden party at Buckingham Palace to celebrate the Queen's nine-tieth birthday. It was a magnificent occasion that even the light drizzle of the afternoon couldn't dampen: if anything the array of umbrellas only added to the colour of the occasion. Out on the lawn, I took the opportunity to congratulate Her Majesty for decades of remarkable service.

'You are the second incredible woman going stronger than ever in her nineties – you should meet my mother!' I said.

After she graciously passed on her regards to Mum, I spotted David Cameron across the grass. Earlier that day he had been caught on camera describing Nigeria and Afghanistan as 'fantastically corrupt countries'.

'Sorry to interrupt,' I said, deciding to have some fun, 'but this is urgent. David, I've just had a call from the Ambassador of Nigeria telling me that they have grounded Virgin Atlantic and BA planes. Apparently they're furious about some comment you made earlier today.'

As David went pale, I quickly put him out of his misery. 'Only joking!'

David's relief was palpable and we quickly got talking about the single issue that was dominating British politics: Brexit.

*

I have never had any desire to get involved in party politics in any country and I'm surprised when any businessperson does. I think it's invidious for businesspeople to get involved. If the party you've supported gets into power, any decisions they make that help your business will be viewed suspiciously. If the party you've rejected wins power, it's even less likely decisions will go in your favour! More importantly, I know I can have a bigger impact by remaining independent of political parties.

However, throughout the world I have got involved in campaigning on specific issues. In my home country, the British Virgin Islands, campaigning for laws to protect sharks, rays and turtles; in the US, trying to abolish the death penalty and reform drug laws; in Australia, campaigning to protect the barrier reef and stop new coal mines; in African countries, trying to change laws that discriminate against gay people (and so on!)

In 2016, Britain and Europe faced the most important decision to be made in my lifetime. A long-brewing storm reached a head when David Cameron announced an in-out referendum on Britain's European Union membership. Mr Cameron keenly wanted to remain in the EU, but the growing threat of the UK Independence Party (UKIP) and his own Conservative Party's disgruntled right wing convinced him to take an almighty gamble. He suspended 'collective responsibility' on the issue, allowing ministers to campaign on either side of the argument. Tories Boris Johnson and Michael Gove took their cue to join UKIP leader Nigel Farage in spearheading the Leave campaign. What followed will go down as one of the most unpleasant episodes in British history.

A few days after seeing David at Buckingham Palace, he sent me a handwritten note inviting me to come to dinner with him a week later, the night before the Brexit vote: 'On the referendum, I really appreciate all you have done,' he wrote. 'The nation really does look to you on this issue. So the more you feel you can do the better – it does make a big difference.'

It was already well known how strongly I felt that the UK staying in the EU was best for the British people, British business and Europe as a whole. But I bided my time for the right moment to throw my public support behind Remain. The Stronger In campaign wanted me to be a 'secret weapon', as the *Daily Telegraph*'s Jeremy Warner jestingly called me: 'Don't laugh ... Amid a sea of suits, he's a rock star player who manages to make business look like fun.' I decided I would speak out in the immediate lead-up to the vote, when swing voters were most likely to be swayed.

Our comms team pointed out that my intervention in this debate would risk me being reviled as a 'tax exile'. I clearly had no right to vote, so this was the only way in which I could possibly make a difference – but our team said that my commentary might result in public criticism that could affect my reputation and thus the Virgin brand. My response to them was the fact that I had clearly made the BVI my home for life some years ago doesn't mean:

(1) I don't care about a place where I lived for much of the earlier part of my life;
(2) I can ignore something that will have a material impact on my children and grandchildren who continue to live in the UK; and
(3) more importantly in a purely Virgin context, that I can't speak up as a long-term commercial investor in the UK economy. Whatever happened in the vote was likely to have a material impact on Virgin itself.

Over fifty years of business I have been happy to take all manner of chances, but I have always made sure I protected the downside. If Britain left the EU and the European Single Market, I believed it would be a catastrophe for both British and European people. My reputation is of being a risk-taker – the cat with nine lives – but leaving the European Union is not a risk I wanted the UK to take. Although these days I live in the British Virgin Islands, I didn't want to take a risk either as a major employer of people in both the UK and Europe and certainly not as a father and grandfather concerned about the world we leave to the next generation.

Memories of doing business before the EU was formed were still fresh in my mind. Moving my people between the UK and the Continent took months of negotiations, goods couldn't be moved without high taxes and higher bureaucracy and trading and travel were nightmarish. The EU has removed those barriers; helping UK companies big and small to expand abroad and trade without tariffs or taxes. What's more, people can live, travel, study and work wherever they please within the Common Market, creating a multicultural society that enriches all. Aside from economics, I recalled my father's horrific stories about fighting in North Africa, Italy and Germany during the Second World War, and my grandfather's ghastly tales about being gassed in the trenches of the First World War. If you work, play, learn together, and even marry each other, it is unthinkable you will ever go to war with each other. I lived in the UK for five decades and represent the first generation of my family not to fight on European battlefields. Instead I was able to become an entrepreneur, thanks to a new vision of peaceful partnership between Europe's nations – one built on trade, openness and collaboration. In fact, in 2012, the European Union received the Nobel Peace Prize for advancing the causes of peace, reconciliation, democracy and human rights.

The economic arguments carried weight, too. Up to three million British jobs are linked to the UK's membership in the world's largest single market – a market of more than 500 million consumers, offering unparalleled opportunities for investment and trade. Almost half of all British exports go to other EU countries. At Virgin alone, we employ nearly 50,000 people in the UK. I predicted Brexit would deal a devastating blow to the UK's economy, killing many jobs and hitting the strength of the pound. I wasn't saying the EU is perfect – far from it. But the UK needed to remain inside to have a seat at the table in reforming the

EU as a stalwart for peace against aggressors around it, and a beacon of democracy.

On the other side of the fence – at times it felt as if they were on the other side of the universe – the Leave campaign continued to peddle nonsense so outrageous it went beyond satire. A bright red 'battle bus' toured the country with an enormous lie plastered across the side of it: 'We send the EU £350 million a week. Let's fund our NHS instead.' The UK Statistics Authority stated this was misleading; the Institute for Fiscal Studies called it 'absurd'. Meanwhile, Boris Johnson was busy comparing the EU's aims to Hitler's, and Nigel Farage posed in front of a Nazi propaganda-mimicking poster showing a queue of mostly non-white refugees with the slogan 'Breaking point'. This was the tip of the iceberg.

I have always thought political campaigning should be subject to the same rules that we have to comply with when advertising commercially. It is just as important that politicians are held to account for the veracity of their claims. Post-referendum, the Electoral Reform Society reported that the campaign was full of 'glaring democratic deficiencies'. I agreed with its verdict that a public body should be formed to intervene when 'misleading' claims were made by campaigns, with a 'rule book' to govern campaign conduct. I think root and branch reform of the way referenda are run is needed. If this was the case, I am sure the vast majority of the Leave campaign's statements would have been banned. But, scarily, they seemed to be convincing people. I was disgusted by the xenophobia I saw. One of the problems was that key newspapers such as the *Daily Mail*, the *Sun*, the *Daily Express*, the *Daily Telegraph* and the *Sunday Times* were campaigning aggressively for Brexit. I suspect this was partly because the vast majority of people who read newspapers are over fifty-five, and it was these generations who were trying to bring Britain back to an imagined golden age. In my opinion they were being completely deluded. Britain is a far greater country today than it was sixty years ago. However, it was now a country teetering on the edge of disaster.

Events took a particularly dismaying turn on 16 June: Labour MP Jo Cox was killed in Birstall, West Yorkshire, after a constituency meeting. The murderer shouted 'Britain first!' as he shot and stabbed Jo – it was clear to me he had been riled by the hateful Leave campaign. This was a cruel and pointless death. I was moved watching Jo's husband Brendan act with such dignity as he said: 'She would have wanted two things above all else to happen now, one that our precious children are bathed in love and two, that we all unite to fight against the hatred that killed her.'

With opinion polls growing closer by the day, Virgin Group's London head office registered a campaign with the Electoral Commission to encourage the British public to vote to Remain in the EU. We wanted to get a positive message out about the benefits of the EU to counter the negative scaremongering. At the same time, we could have a little dig at the newspapers. We took out full pages in every paper, not disclosing the pro-Remain content until the ads were placed. Upon receipt, the *Sun* promptly doubled the price of the slot. We ran it anyway, along with social media advertising, concluding: 'June 23rd will determine if voters would rather live in Little England or in Great Britain. And Great Britain has always stood for democracy, compassion, justice and inclusion. Let the arguments of the day not diminish its place in the world. If you agree with me I'd urge you to vote Remain.'

In the days before the election, the opinion polls seemed to indicate that Brexit would not happen. Virgin Group carried on campaigning, giving a series of interviews and holding a joint event on 20 June with Virgin Money's Jayne-Anne Gadhia, where we declared we were 'VirgIN' for Europe. 'Hands up who is voting Remain?' I asked to the packed room of staff and reporters. The vast majority raised their hands. 'It's so important that everybody goes out and votes – unless, of course, you haven't got your hand up!'

That evening I went to Downing Street along with Jayne-Anne and Nick Fox to meet with David Cameron.

We shared what was generally a very upbeat dinner. With Brexit dominating so much work and conversation for months, we tried to talk about a range of other topics, from drug reform to entrepreneurial loans. After around ninety minutes, I said to David, 'Thank you very much for inviting us over, it's been a delightful evening. Look, you've got young children; you should go off and spend some quality time with them.'

Little did any of us know that he would soon have plenty more spare time.

The next morning I awoke back on Necker to a huge amount of personal vitriol thrown at me in the press and on social media. As I scrolled through scores of four-letter insults on my Twitter timeline, I got a taste of what it must be like to be a politician.

'I feel pretty sorry for MPs who have to deal with this every day,' I said to Joan at breakfast. 'What a horrible way to spend your time, throwing insults at others.'

But this was nothing compared to what was about to happen.

*

I was glued to the television as the results started rolling in around midnight. To my horror, and contrary to the polls, Leave narrowly won by 52 per cent to 48 per cent. My first reaction was shock. I couldn't comprehend that the British people really believed they were better off out of Europe. I felt so sad a country proud of its openness and inclusiveness was swinging away from that. It made me fearful for wider Europe, too.

I was convinced voters had been tricked by the misinformation of the Leave campaign. A top Google search after the result was announced – 'What is the EU?' – backed that up. Searches for 'What happens if we leave the EU' more than tripled. The Brexiteers began backtracking on most of the promises they had made. Nigel Farage admitted his NHS claims were untrue, while Boris Johnson and Michael

Gove squabbled and David Cameron resigned. Chaos abounded. Global share prices plummeted; the pound collapsed to its worst day in history against other major currencies; while the UK stock market dropped to its worst level since 2009. London house prices fell; flights to and from the UK were cut; the Bank of England predicted a slowdown, and leading experts warned of recession should the UK leave the Single Market.

Scotland and Northern Ireland hinted strongly they would take further moves towards independence. Whitehall estimated it would cost half a billion in lawyer and consultancy fees to negotiate Brexit, with *The Times* stating 'the bill could reach £5 billion over a decade'. Billions were wiped off company values; I received emails from US-based business leaders who told me they were cancelling plans to create UK-based offices and expanding their businesses elsewhere in Europe instead. Leaders in Britain admitted they may be forced to relocate abroad. Virgin was, of course, among the businesses affected. Sales dropped across the board while costs soared. Most notably, Virgin Money shares collapsed by 45 per cent and Virgin Atlantic went from forecasting a healthy profit to a loss. I thought people simply had not been told enough about what they had voted for and deserved the chance to be better informed. Rushing into Brexit without looking at all the options – legal, moral and political – seemed crazy. You don't arrange your divorce the day after you've stormed out of the house!

I flew to the UK from Necker on 27 June ready for the finale of Virgin Media Business VOOM, the UK and Ireland's biggest pitching competition. The following morning I went onto the *Good Morning Britain* couch with the intention of discussing how VOOM was supporting Britain's best new businesses with over £1 million in prizes. But instead, all they asked me about was Brexit. I told host Piers Morgan that I estimated Virgin had lost a third of its value overnight.

'Look at bank shares, some of them have gone down by as much as 50 per cent,' I said, adding that the pound had collapsed to its lowest level in thirty years.

On reflection, it probably wasn't prudent to share these details, but I was confident Virgin was strong enough to survive and thrive, whatever the market conditions. But this wasn't about my business – it was about getting across the sheer scale of calamity Brexit was unleashing on Britain and Europe. After VOOM later that morning, I raced off to the first of a series of hastily arranged meetings. I felt that Virgin had to do something to encourage Westminster to act, before the country was irrevocably damaged.

We arranged to see Home Secretary Theresa May. But when we left ITV Studios and hit the road, we found ourselves stuck in heavy afternoon traffic. My sense of urgency was killing me. 'Now or never,' I thought and jumped out of the car. I flew across Lambeth Bridge in my shiny red Under Armour trainers, surprising dozens of onlookers. We reached the Home Office just in time and were led into the Home Secretary's sparse, frugal office – breathless, sweaty and frustrated. Trying to collect my thoughts, I explained that I was speaking on behalf of the international business community, but also from my own personal experience of fifty years in business.

'This will be a painful experience, not just for Virgin, but for many businesses. The biggest companies are protected because they have lots of earnings in dollars and in the short term their shares should rebound. It is small and medium-sized companies that will suffer. Jobs and wages will drop and the very people who voted for Brexit will be hit worst.' With the collapse in the pound, overnight everyone was considerably worse off. I also shared legal advice Virgin had received: 'One of the top QCs in the country has told us Article 50 can only be invoked through an Act of Parliament. I have sent the legal advice we got to the Prime Minister and the Attorney General too. It would be worth you taking this into account if you become Prime Minister.'

The Home Secretary listened, nodded, but remained quiet. She kept her cards close to her chest, as she had throughout the campaign. Obviously she didn't want to make any commitments either way. She was widely expected to announce her leadership candidacy later that day. I believe good leaders need to be good listeners. She was certainly listening. Whether she was agreeing or not, she didn't give away.

'What do you think government should do to calm business concerns?' she asked.

'Call the whole damn thing off!' I wanted to shout. Instead, I said that it was critical she made it clear she would negotiate a deal that, at a minimum, gave businesses full access to the Single Market. Then I wished her luck in her leadership bid.

Next, I went on to Number 11 to see Britain's Chancellor of the Exchequer, George Osborne. As we sat down in the plush office, I couldn't help but think how strange life can be. Only a few days before it had seemed extremely likely that Mr Osborne would be the next Prime Minister when David Cameron stepped down. Now it looked like he would be out of a job (and, as it turned out, into a new one as the *Evening Standard* editor before long).

'I suppose politicians are used to these massive shocks,' I said.

'That doesn't make it any easier,' he admitted.

We left much as we had arrived: with a growing sense that absolutely no one in Westminster had any plan. They simply hadn't imagined Leave would win.

I travelled up to Holly and Sam's home in Oxford, and spent a couple of blissful hours of playtime with my grandchildren. But I still couldn't put Brexit out of my mind.

'It's my kids' generation that is going to suffer,' Holly said to me. 'Last week these kids had the option of living and working in twenty-eight European countries. Now they have one.'

The following morning I joined business leaders from across the UK for the annual Fast Track 100. The mood was sombre – their companies were already hurting. I ducked out of proceedings at 3 p.m. to call David Cameron and repeat the legal advice Virgin had received.

'We consulted with a top constitution lawyer, who made it clear the referendum was advisory, not legally binding. Under the British constitution, the Prime Minister cannot invoke Article 50 without going to the House of Commons for ratification.'

He said no one had mentioned it to him, and asked us to send on our information to the Attorney General.

I found it strange that the government's lawyers didn't seem to be on top of the legal ramifications of what they had got themselves into.

That night I had dinner with a group of young people and we got talking about Brexit. The results showed that the UK's younger generations were strongly in support of remaining in the EU: 73 per cent of eighteen to twenty-four-year-olds voted for Remain. However, the decision was toppled by much older generations – who make up a larger chunk of the voting population.

One young girl said: 'It really makes me want to weep. These people over sixty, who will be dead before long, have ruined our opportunities and lives. There's all this debate about letting sixteen-year-olds vote. They should be allowed – it's over sixties who shouldn't be allowed to vote.'

She caught my eye as she said it, and only then realised that I was over sixty myself.

'It's OK,' I said. 'I happen to agree with you that sixteen-year-olds should have the right to vote. They should have as much of a say as sixty-year-olds, and perhaps know more about the real world.'

Sadly, this issue has divided families like no other, with many kids feeling their parents really let them down. Like everybody, I met people who voted for Brexit, such as my father-in-law, who I have always got on well with. After some pretty ferocious arguments we called a truce on the subject and decided not to speak about it. I suspect we weren't alone in that.

*

In the aftermath, we were determined to keep moving. Whatever else is happening, I can always focus my mind upon business, make time for my family and prioritise the important things in life. I joined a board meeting on Moskito, where we covered everything from agreeing new financing for Virgin Australia and Virgin Galactic to changes in our royalty portfolio. Virgin America picked up the Condé Nast award for best domestic airline in the US for a record ninth consecutive year, and Usain Bolt joined Virgin Media's latest ad ahead of the Olympics. We signed off on an investment in a company I believed in passionately, smart doorbell service Ring.

On Necker, I completely cleaned out our home. It had needed doing for years. I went through everything, chucking out stuff that had piled up over the years – old t-shirts, files, trainers. I wanted to reorganise my life, and this was a good start. Everything was a jumble in the cupboards, so I created separate compartments for swimming, tennis, cycling, travelling. My mindset is 'if in doubt throw it out', but Joan is a collector, so when it comes to spring cleaning there can be battles (fortunately she wasn't at home!). It was a really worthwhile exercise and I felt more organised.

Over in the UK, post-referendum chaos continued, with unpleasant, racist incidents on the rise and a complete lack of leadership when Britain needed statesmanlike behaviour from its politicians. I was surprised to see news of my meeting with Theresa May had leaked.

'I suppose I wasn't exactly inconspicuous running into Westminster,' I said, looking at the headlines about our 'Secret Brexit Talks'.

As Boris Johnson and Michael Gove's Machiavellian tactics backfired horribly, Mrs May was emerging as the leading candidate to become Prime Minister. Meanwhile, David Cameron continued his duties as PM while the leadership campaign rumbled on. We had an appointment to meet at Farnborough Air Show on 11 July.

When I arrived at Gatwick from the Bahamas, there were other exciting plans to reveal. We were introducing Virgin Atlantic's new A350-1000 aircraft to our fleet. The $4.4 billion order was a real investment in the future of our airline. The A350 is 30 per cent more fuel- and carbon-efficient than the aircraft it replaces in the fleet and is reducing the airline's noise footprint at its airports by more than half. As Virgin Atlantic CEO Craig Kreeger put it, we were creating 'one of the youngest, cleanest, greenest fleets in the sky'.

We landed at the Farnborough Air Show, where David Cameron was on hand to celebrate the UK jobs the new planes would create.

'The fantastic Airbus A350 is part-built in the UK with Rolls Royce engines and other suppliers across the country,' he announced. 'It's an investment in the UK itself, and our world-beating aerospace industry.'

Afterwards, we stood on the veranda looking at the Red Arrows as they performed a stunning display in the blue skies above. There were pictures of me putting my hand on his arm, leaning over and speaking. The first word I said to him was: 'Bugger.' He agreed, and told me he expected to be in office for another two months, and was as busy as ever.

We then departed, and within ten minutes the news came through that Theresa May's main rival Andrea Leadsom had pulled out of the Tory leadership contest. I watched on as Mr Cameron made the correct and only decision in stepping down, allowing Theresa May to become Prime Minister. How fast things change. Brexit had cost him his job and his legacy, and was costing most companies and the country a whole lot more. Having said that, in my opinion he was a decent person who, Brexit aside, had done a pretty good job in tough circumstances.

The Brexit debate rumbled on, and the UK is still no closer to knowing how it will end up. In retrospect I shouldn't have spoken out immediately after the referendum; keeping my powder dry for two years would have been more effective. But it was a horrible feeling seeing companies we loved being damaged and knowing millions of people would suffer. I continued reading the views of experts, historians and politicians, eager to learn more. But the one that summed up Brexit best came from Groucho Marx: 'Politics is the art of looking for trouble, finding it everywhere, diagnosing it incorrectly, and applying the wrong remedies.'

Reflecting on my own forays in politics in 2016, I had broken my own rules. I don't regret it. I was – and remain – so genuinely worried that I would have kicked myself more for not speaking out than for speaking out. There may be Brexit or Donald Trump supporters boycotting Virgin because I say what I believe in. Knowing Trump, there could be situations where Virgin loses out in America. But we'll take that risk. Regretting not doing something is worse than regretting doing something. It means I can sleep with a clear conscience. We all have to fight for our values and protect the things that matter to us, but also appreciate the joys life brings us. I fully intend to continue doing both.

40 Traingate

To me, August means holidays with the family. It means Sam's birthday and all of our friends and loved ones joining us on Necker Island. But for the media, August has always meant one thing: silly season. And August 2016 ended up being particularly silly, after the Leader of the Opposition in the UK decided to take a Virgin Train up to Newcastle.

When Jeremy Corbyn boarded the 11 a.m. Virgin Trains East Coast service from London King's Cross to Newcastle, he walked past empty, unreserved seats in coach H, before strolling through the rest of the train to the far end. Once there, he decided to sit on the floor. The cameraman who was travelling with him then started filming.

'This is a problem that many passengers face every day on the trains, commuters and long-distance travellers,' said Mr Corbyn. 'Today this train is completely "ram-packed".'

Five days later, on 16 August, the video was uploaded online and soon received thousands of views on the *Guardian*. Watching the clip on my iPad on Necker, I thought the whole thing looked rather odd.

'Isn't the term "jam-packed", not "ram-packed?"' asked Joan.

'Either way, I'm not sure either applies in this case,' I said.

It was easy enough to check: Virgin Trains track how many empty seats are on each service, and estimated that 140 were free on this particular service. So why hadn't Mr

Corbyn sat in one of them? It seems he had more on his mind than comfort when sitting on the floor. One of his key policy pledges is for the railways to be renationalised. By taking part in his one-man sit-down protest, he was trying to make a contrived point with all the finesse of a sledge-hammer.

As the story, dubbed #traingate, spread like wildfire, the team painstakingly checked all the footage from the train's on-board cameras, as well as staff reports from on board. Rather than spending the entire journey on the floor, we found Mr Corbyn returned to coach H and took a seat after about forty-five minutes.

On 24 August, Virgin Trains released the footage. 'We have to take issue with the idea that Mr Corbyn wasn't able to be seated on the service, as this clearly wasn't the case,' our spokesperson stated. 'We'd encourage Jeremy to book ahead next time he travels with us, both to reserve a seat and to ensure he gets our lowest fares, and we look forward to welcoming him on board again.' To his great credit, Mr Corbyn was back on Virgin Trains just days later. He took the criticism he received in the press and online very well, and has travelled with Virgin Trains many times since while campaigning for the Labour Party across the UK.

All this fuss about a Virgin berth! After all this silliness had calmed down, I thought about the positive that had come out of it – the issue of much-needed railway reform in the UK being in the public eye. There is no question that some Virgin Trains services are very busy, and finding a seat can be tough unless you have booked in advance. This usually happens in particular circumstances, like the first off-peak train from London, or when major sporting events are being held. We have tried for two decades to discuss fare regulations with the government and are eager for ministers to sit down and talk with us, particularly regarding long-distance services. Simon Calder talked sense in the *Independent* when he said: 'Some fares need to rise to manage demand; that antiquated working practices must be modernised and that fare regulations need to be changed to stop the scandalous waste of peak-time trains leaving with too few passengers.'

There is also no question that we need to introduce more trains on the route. We are introducing a fleet of sixty-five brand new Azuma trains, increasing seating capacity on the route Mr Corbyn travelled by 28 per cent at peak times. We've also converted a first-class carriage to standard on our twenty-one nine-carriage trains on the West Coast route, providing thousands more seats each day. But the fact that the trains are extremely popular only highlights further the success of privatised rail. Under nationalisation, trains were a declining mode of transport in the UK, with terrible service, poor trains and unreliable timings. Now, rail travel is booming – passenger numbers have nearly tripled since we took over the network. Privatisation has brought with it better quality products, a focus on customer service and high standards to be held to. British railways are now definitively the safest in Europe and probably the safest in the world. Trains are cleaner, more frequent and with better service than ever before. Private companies are adding capacity and growing services to cope with the surge in demand.

*

As the Traingate story was unfolding, I was continuing to train harder than ever for the Virgin Strive Challenge, which was fast approaching. Two years on from Sam's hair-raising rescue off the summit of the Matterhorn, we were planning another adventure. This time I would join Holly, Sam, my nephew Noah and hundreds of others to travel more than 2,000 kilometres from the base of the Matterhorn to the summit of Mount Etna in Sicily. We would hike across the Alps of northern Italy, cycle to the southern tip of Italy, swim to Sicily, mountain-bike to the foothills of Etna, complete a half-marathon run up the volcano, and then hike to the top – all within the space of a month.

We hoped to raise £1.5 million for Big Change to support innovative projects that arm young people with the necessary tools they need to thrive in life, not just the class-room. It's a cause close to all of our family's hearts. Physically, this was no small challenge, and I was training accordingly. I'd been doing punishing cycles up steep hills on Necker's neighbouring island Virgin Gorda, tough swims around Necker Island's reefs, and increasing my tennis sessions to three hours per day. By the time I hopped on my bike on Virgin Gorda on 22 August, I was in the best shape I'd been in for over a decade – I had lost a stone within a couple of months.

'It's five years since the Necker fire today,' Sam said as we looked up at the first incline on Virgin Gorda, ready for another day's training.

'Well, time flies when you're having fun – not that this hill is going to be fun!'

A couple of hours later, the sweat was pouring off me as we circled our second lap. We were really pushing ourselves and the afternoon quickly disappeared. Before we knew it, night had fallen. I'd been so focused on the cycling that I'd barely noticed the darkness creeping in: as I was heading down a hill towards Leverick Bay with my sunglasses still on, I didn't see the 'sleeping policeman' – one of those wretched humps in the road – and hit it head on. The next thing I knew, I was being hurled over the handlebars towards the concrete road.

After dozens of near-death experiences (see the Appendix for a full list), for the first time my life flashed before my eyes. Perhaps it is because I am getting older, or because I have been reflecting more on my life through writing this book, but I saw a blur of images shutter across my brain from childhood to the present day, my family constant among them. I saw myself climbing trees with my sisters, kissing Joan, cradling Holly, holding Sam, hugging my parents. Strangely, a lot can happen in half a second. Everything was heightened. It is incredible what the brain is capable of. Not that I was thinking *that* at the time: as I went flying through the air head-first, my overwhelming thought was that I was going to die. My face hit the concrete road as my bike hurtled forward, dropped off the cliff and disappeared.

As I lay on the concrete, it took me a few seconds to realise I wasn't dead. Slowly I started to test out my movement in each limb. I could lift my neck. 'OK, you're not paralysed, that's good,' I thought to huge relief. My legs, too, seemed to be moving all right. I lifted my right arm; that also felt OK. But when I tried to move my left arm, I winced as stabbing pains shot through my shoulder. Then I put my fingers to my face and felt hot blood: as I looked at my hand, it glistened red. It turned out that my shoulder and cheek had borne the brunt of the impact: the fact that I was wearing a helmet saved my life.

The first person to arrive on the scene was Helen, who had just got back from holiday. She was wondering who it was lying prostrate on the road. I was so glad to be alive that my sense of humour was intact.

'Don't worry, I'm alive,' I laughed and winced at the same time. 'You've still got a job!'

As I was put on a stretcher and made it back to Necker, my bike was recovered from the bottom of the cliff, destroyed. I could have been down there with it, I thought, looking at the crumpled frame. I got patched up: as well as my cheek being badly damaged, my knee, chin, shoulder and torso were all severely cut. The next day I flew to hospital in Miami for scans and X-rays, which showed a cracked cheek and torn knee and shoulder ligaments. I'm usually quite a good patient, and don't like moaning too much, but one thing was annoying me as I put my feet up back on Necker.

'I can't believe I have to drink tea out of a straw!' I complained.

As I sat there trying to sip my cuppa, one of our guests had a six-year-old child with them, who looked aghast as he stared at my bloodied face.

'You look like the Elephant Man,' he said.

'Thanks,' I laughed. 'That's just what I needed.'

Over the next few days messages of support flooded in across my inbox and social media, which really did make a difference in keeping me positive. One came from David Tait, who used to run Virgin Atlantic in the US: 'I read your life flashed before your eyes,' he said. 'You must have been in the air for a very long time.' My sister Lindy sent her best wishes: 'Oh no! Poor you, Ricky. Reminded me of when we went to the dentist in Guildford and Mum wouldn't let us have any painkillers for our fillings.'

'Don't tell me there was an option for a painkiller?' I replied. 'Mum always told me it wasn't possible. Pure torture!'

Did my near-death experience make me think about the end more? A little. Nobody ever thinks they are going to die, but as more and more people I have known and loved have passed away, it does cross one's mind a little more frequently. The accident also made me think about my legacy again, a word I've never really liked. Whenever somebody introduces me as 'a legend in his own lifetime' I always think, 'Fuck, if I'm a legend then I must be dead already!' In the end, I've realised that legacy is not that important except to your children and family and friends. When I am on my deathbed, I just want to feel as if I have loved and been loved, done some good in the world and made a difference here and there.

One thing I have noticed is slightly more forgetfulness than when I was younger, especially short-term memory loss. I was onstage in Las Vegas recently and asked the host 'What's the biggest sporting event in America?' He told me: 'The Super Bowl.' The audience thought I was making a joke, but I had genuinely forgotten. That night, in bed, I desperately tried to think of the name again. In the end I got up, opened my iPad and Googled 'biggest sporting event in America' to track it down. My dyslexia has always meant I'm bad with names and terms, but I do worry it is getting worse. I have been tested for dementia and, thankfully, I'm clear, but it is a frightening thing. I'll be in a conversation sometimes and forget the third thing I was going to say.

It could be I have a very full brain with lots going on; it could be that I'm sixty-seven and these things happen. My mum, well into her nineties, is still incredibly active physically and mentally, and I'm hopeful I can be the same. Though Mum's memory is sadly beginning to wane, she lives with the same zest for life as she always has. Nessie and her friend Sally popped in to visit her recently, and she had forgotten they had arranged to have lunch.

'You've definitely got it in your diary,' said Ness.

'Have I?' asked Eve and got up from the sofa to find the appointment in the precious diary through which her life is organised.

'And what else have you got planned for this week, Mum?' asked Ness.

'Well ... I know I'm doing something with Maggie Magee on Monday.'

'What are you doing with her?' queried Ness.

'I can't remember. But I'm being picked up at 3 p.m.'

'Well you must know what you're doing with her and where you're going, surely?'

'I don't. But I must have written it down somewhere.' She began flicking through to her notes page in the diary.

'Ah yes,' she said, very matter-of-fact. 'It's her funeral.'

Ness and Sally cracked up in peals of laughter, although Mum didn't seem to think it was in any way funny or unusual.

'Oh dear, Mum,' said Ness. 'Poor Maggie Magee. Who is she anyway?'

'I don't know,' said Mum. 'But I'm going to the funeral.'

I can just hear my father roaring with laughter. When it was Dad's hundredth birthday, Mum (aged ninety-three) suddenly said: 'I don't understand why Ted went. He was far too young to go, and he shouldn't have left when he did!' She wrote to me too: 'Rick, old darling! As the swans drift past on the lake beyond, I can but think of our beloved Ted. Isn't life wonderful? Every hour, every minute, must be lived to the full. Only regret, you're not both here with us to share.'

If I thought too much about the idea that we are all walking to the edge of a cliff we will one day fall off, it would mess up my mind. We are protected by not giving it too much thought. The reality that it is a fact of life also makes me still think I must live life to the full. It actively gives me purpose to not waste a minute of the life I lead, to make a difference and have a blast in the process. If I leave early as a result, at least I will leave doing what I love. Sam had some fitting words for the situation, from Hunter S. Thompson: 'Life should not be a journey to the grave with the intention of arriving safely in a pretty and well preserved body, but rather to skid in broadside in a cloud of smoke, thoroughly used up, totally worn out, and loudly proclaiming "Wow! What a ride!"'

*

A few days later, on 1 September, I was over in the Alps, undergoing a last series of health checks before the Strive Challenge. The doctor advised me that the best course of action for my recovery was to rest up, but for me that was not an option.

'Will I do permanent damage?' I asked her.

'It's unlikely.'

'Great, I'm giving it a go then.'

As we began hiking from the foot of the Matterhorn with the team, my body was holding up surprisingly well. The weather did, too, and the views across the Alpine peaks were spectacular. When we came across a freezing lake, I decided to aide my recovery with the ultimate ice bath: Sam and I jumped out as quickly as we jumped in! The downhill trekking was harder on my knee, but easier on my lungs. I was getting through the miles, but going quite slowly, taking about thirteen hours each day and finishing last. Very sweetly, when I arrived at our hut, all the Strivers came out to clap me in. It was the first time in my life I've had a round of applause for being last – one of the advantages of being the oldest!

On the final leg of the hike into northern Italy I decided to leave early an hour before everyone else so I didn't hold them up. My legs had recovered well, were no longer feeling like jelly, and I covered the ground quickly. Near the end, I thought: 'I was last yesterday, I'll try to be first today!' I soon realised Sam was not far behind. While he could see me I just ambled along, but when I turned a corner I put on a spurt and raced ahead! Sam caught me, but we graciously crossed the finishing line together (a well-brought-up son!). That night everyone gathered around talking about the journey, the humour, the hurt, the heart-warming tales, the strains, the stories and the smiles. Joan stood listening to it all and then said: 'Small steps make big strives.' I think that makes a perfect slogan for what the Virgin Strive Challenge is all about.

After five days, seventy-six kilometres and 6,000 metres of ascent, it was time to get back on the bike. After my accident I felt a certain trepidation, but the only way to get over it was to start cycling again. We began making our way south towards Sicily. When I began, still weak from my injuries, I knew Strive wasn't going be an easy journey through the Italian countryside, sipping lattes and admiring the view. However, I wasn't prepared for it to be the most gruelling physical and mental test of our lives. Every leg was harder than the last, with people collapsing over the finish lines, too exhausted to walk or even smile. There were times when I wanted to give up. But every night the smiles had resurfaced, and so had the laughter, the high fives and the stories from the road.

Back on the bike, I felt shooting pains up my leg. 'Have I got this in me?' I thought. 'Can I really make it?' But each and every day, I pushed through. It's amazing what you can achieve with the right mindset; around me, people were visibly growing in confidence and strength and I tried to keep spirits high. Towards the end of the second leg, I left camp in darkness and pouring rain at 5 a.m. and laid down a challenge to my fellow Strivers: I would donate £1,000 to the fundraiser of the first person to catch me. The others left two hours behind me, and seven hours in I felt what it must be like to be a fox, as eight cyclists raced to overtake me. I was nearly wiped out by the lead cyclist, who just happened to be my son-in-law, Freddie!

The wet conditions, with heavy rain and landslides, were becoming a serious issue. In the space of a few fateful hours, one person crashed into a car and five people, including Sam, flew off their bikes, suffering nasty cuts. They hit oil on a blind bend in the road and were seconds away from going under an oncoming car.

On the toughest day of the whole challenge, I woke up in the pitch black to begin at 4.45 a.m. – and was surprised to find that my daughter, Holly, was up and ready to ride with me. She had sensed I was near breaking point, and she and Freddie put their own tiredness aside to help me along. I could have wept with gratitude. We rode for almost 200 kilometres that day, climbing steep mountains. After fourteen hours, darkness fell, and about half an hour from the end the organisers told us that we couldn't carry on. On three separate occasions, they had set up roadblocks to stop us, but each time we broke through them, yelling that we wanted to continue and singing 'We Shall Overcome' together. We felt like naughty schoolchildren! In the end, we made it together.

The next day we got back on the saddle for the final stretch of the cycling leg: riding to the toe of Italy. It was a fascinating and picturesque journey, which, thankfully, wasn't as physically gruelling as the day before. However, having already hiked seventy kilometres and ridden nearly 2,000 kilometres, my body felt fit but completely worn out. With just two hours to go to the finish line, Sam overtook me. As he passed, something stirred inside me and I got a burst of energy. For the rest of the leg I rode flat-out as fast as I could, whooping like a schoolboy. Developing mental toughness isn't just about being resilient – it's about accessing your reserve tank when you think you just can't go any further. At that moment, so close to the end and challenged by my son, I felt my reserve kick in. It's something that I've relied on a lot in life, and have had to access on many occasions in business. In the dark moments we all have the power to pull ourselves up to keep going.

After the cycling, it was time to get into the water. To celebrate World Oceans Day, I had challenged the actor Adrian Grenier to join me in raising awareness about ocean conservation by swimming 3.3 kilometres across the Strait of Messina. The weather conditions were relatively benign and the sun glistened off the waves as we dived in. But we went off too quickly, and I struggled with my breathing wearing a snorkel. Holly was worried I was having a heart attack. I assured her I was fine and switched to backstroke, while Holly positioned herself between me and Adrian to make sure we both survived the choppy water. After what seemed like an age, we made it to the other side.

Having completed a whole month of gruelling days testing us to our limits, we should have been ready for the final day of our journey, climbing Mount Etna. We were so fit by this stage, I thought it would be quite easy. How wrong I was. The day began with a half-marathon trail run to the halfway point of Mount Etna. I've finished the London Marathon, but this was tough going, with a constant steep incline and huge boulders to navigate. After several hours, we reached the hiking stage, leaning on each other through rough lava fields. By now, I needed all the help I could get, mentally more than physically, to overcome the exhaustion. Having Holly and Sam beside me helped so much to keep putting one foot in front of the other.

Finally, we made it! All the way from the Matterhorn to Mount Etna, under human power. Hiking, cycling, swimming, running, climbing, Striving. When we got to the top it was spectacular. I could see the lava that had spilled out, the beautiful shrubbery growing around and ladybirds in the stones. The best view, though, was seeing the jubilant faces of my fellow strivers, dancing and singing on the top of the volcano. It was the most exhilarating, extreme, fulfilling achievement.

Somebody said to me after Strive that there are three stages to life: youth, middle age, and 'you're looking well'! Sadly, it's probably true. I found myself getting more 'you're looking well' comments than usual after Strive. But the adventures we do as a family help keep me young, and give me another reason to stay fit and healthy. Will Strive continue? Of course. We're already planning the next one. During the first Virgin Strive Challenge, Sam and Bellie had told us the most happy news that they were expecting Eva-Deia, who was born after the first Challenge. Before the second, they told us they were expecting their second. Another Branson was going to embark upon the greatest adventure of all. I hope I am there every step of the way.

41 'We're free!'

'This is going to hurt for a while,' the dentist said to me. 'I could give you an injection to prevent pain, but you might end up drooling over lunch. Do you have an important lunch?'

'You could say that.'

The day before I had been playing tennis on Necker and slammed my racket into my front teeth for the second time in two months. 'I really am in the wars this year!' I'd said to Joan. The first time I had to get a new tennis racket after leaving such a dent in the frame. This time, my teeth fared worse than the racket. Looking in the mirror, I knew I needed a visit to the dentist. I had been invited by President Obama to join him for lunch in the Oval Office – an opportunity I wasn't about to turn down.

I chose pain over drooling and visited a dentist in Washington. One hour later, I was outside the West Wing, remembering when I first heard of President Obama. It had been at a dinner on Necker with investor Suhail Rizvi in 2004.

'I met the first black president of America this week,' he said. 'He's a senator in Illinois and he's probably the brightest person I've ever met.'

'Really?' I was dubious – I've heard a few people incorrectly predict future presidents over the years.

'Absolutely. He was president of the *Harvard Law Review* and he's just an extraordinary individual. His name is Barack Obama.'

Although I had massive respect for Suhail, I took his prediction with a pinch of salt. But three years later, I had been completely captivated by this young man's campaign for change at a time of real strife for America and the world. Now, as Obama's time as president drew towards its close, I found myself being escorted into the Oval Office. President Obama gave me a warm welcome and suggested we do a picture together in front of the infamous desk. To break the ice I commented on the pretty ivy growing on the mantelpiece.

'Thank you,' he said. 'It was there when JFK was shot and it has been kept alive ever since.'

The two of us then sat down to lunch. He started by telling me that he'd kept a close eye on the various not-for-profit initiatives we were involved in such as tackling climate change, conflict resolution, ocean conservation, prison and drug reform, ending capital punishment and inspiring young entrepreneurs. He said he felt we were closely aligned on almost every issue. We then went on to discuss kitesurfing and personal challenges.

'How do you manage to keep the balance between work and play so well?' he asked.

'I make sure to treat them as equal priorities – it's all just living. But then I'm not as busy as you, Mr President!'

'Well, I hope to keep a better balance when I leave office.'

President Obama cited John Kerry, his Secretary of State, as a person in his seventies who 'eats a lot' but manages to keep extraordinarily fit.

'Funny you should mention that,' I said. 'Secretary Kerry and I are planning to kitesurf the English Channel together soon with your ambassador to Britain. There's always room for one more,' I added.

I mentioned the incredible work that Jimmy Carter and Bill Clinton had achieved since leaving office. 'I think you're in a position to achieve even more since you're still young and leaving at the height of your popularity.'

President Obama agreed that at only fifty-five – that very day – he felt he had the time to devote to a lot of causes that we both felt passionate about. We spoke of climate change and he agreed it could be a very exciting challenge for companies to help overcome if the right framework was put in place by governments. He was proud of the fact that solar power had increased sixteenfold since he took office and excited about how cheap it was now. He said, with a smile, that he had a personal reason to fix climate change: 'I've got my eye on a plot on a beach in Hawaii and I don't want it underwater.'

Obama cited climate change and weapons of mass destruction falling into terrorist hands as the two biggest threats to the world. Otherwise, we agreed that the world was in the best position it had ever been and that between us all in the years to come it could only get better. Having spoken in this optimistic way, he went on to contrast it by mentioning how most of the problems of the world get dumped on his desk every morning in what Michelle calls his 'death book'.

He asked about Virgin Galactic, saying, 'I'd be excited to go up one day.'

'We'd be delighted to have you!' I replied. I told him about our Virgin Orbit satellite plans, too, and he was very interested.

As we spoke about prison and drug reform, he said he'd continue working on all these out of office: 'Using a sledgehammer doesn't work as President. Doing things step-by-step is more effective.' He explained he'd done that with cannabis reform and believed that, because of positive feedback from Washington State and Colorado, hopefully more than 50 per cent of states would follow and legalise over the next few years. On harder drugs he thought it would be more difficult. I cited Portugal and the excellent results they'd had by treating all drugs as a health issue, not a criminal problem. He agreed that if society could be educated better on such issues, reform would be that much easier: 'The problem is the public are not getting balanced, unbiased information.' It was one of the areas he wanted to look at when leaving office.

'There have to be better ways to educate people with real facts on issues,' he said. 'I think I'm the third most followed person on Twitter [behind Katy Perry and Justin Bieber!] – I don't want to waste that following and hope I can put it to use as part of our education efforts.'

We spoke about the death penalty and Equal Justice Initiative founder Bryan Stevenson's work.

'Would you consider using Presidential Decree to remove the death penalty for the sixty people under federal jurisdiction on death row?' I asked. 'Or at least five of the sixty that Bryan feels have particularly strong evidence for pardoning?'

Obama said that he'd read up on all of the cases and agreed that, for America to move forward, the death penalty should be abolished.

'I don't think you can truly be a civilised country until it is gone. Europe successfully abolished it many years ago,' I added.

He said that he was more inclined to pardon all sixty than make a judgment on five. He felt that was the morally correct path, since he disagreed with the death penalty on principle. I got the impression that he'd do it if Hillary Clinton was elected, and before he stepped down, to make sure it didn't damage her chances.

Turning to family life, Obama spoke of how he'd been looking forward to spending more time with Michelle and his children.

'The only problem is that now we're finally stepping down they are no longer children and will soon be leaving home. It's going to be slightly strange for us both, to be ending our jobs and "losing" our kids at roughly the same time.'

'You'll have plenty to keep you busy, I'm sure.'

He spoke passionately about wanting to help young people generally and in particular in Africa. I mentioned an organisation of rising leaders we were setting up called The NewNow.

'A younger version of the Elders?' he replied. 'Love the idea and would love to see how what we are both doing can overlap in the years to come.'

Obama mentioned how sad it must feel for young people in Britain after Brexit. He said he knew of young Brits who were so upset that older people had let them down. I agreed wholeheartedly and mentioned they were particularly sad they could no longer work and live in twenty-eight countries but were restricted to one. I almost hoped that I could go through lunch without talking about Donald Trump. But we spoke about him, too. I told President Obama of the time Trump had invited me to lunch and spent the entire two hours talking about his determination to get revenge on people who hadn't helped him when he went bankrupt.

Although he was confident the American people would elect Hillary Clinton, he did speak about the risks of reality TV shows, and how dangerous fake news on the internet could be in shaping people's views. On election night, watching in disbelief as Trump was elected, his words echoed in my head.

The lunch was coming to an end. I handed him a document that Bryan Stevenson and our team had prepared on the death penalty, which he promised to read. There were plenty of other things that I'd have loved to touch on with him (refugees, short-termism in business, biodiversity – the list goes on) but those would have to wait.

As we stood up to leave I noticed the red buttons on his desk. Obama saw me looking at them.

'They used to be there for emergencies, but now I use them for ordering tea for my guests.'

'I'd be pressing them all the time,' I joked. 'I drink over twenty cups a day!'

As we left the Oval Office, I carefully avoided walking into the bulletproof glass more than a foot thick.

'I look forward to seeing you again tonight at my birthday party,' he said. 'We've asked Stevie Wonder to play for an hour. I have to warn you it's likely to be two hours!'

Assuming all the ladies would be dressed to the hilt, I wore a suit (no tie). Then I saw Obama in jeans. It was the first time in my life I felt overdressed and I was at the White House! As the party got going after Stevie had sung 'Happy Birthday' to the President, to my horror Michelle Obama came over and pulled me to the front of the stage for a dance. I quickly retreated into the crowd, but look forward to telling my grandchildren one day that I once danced with the First Lady! I arrived back on Necker early the next morning to be greeted by my daughter's words: 'Welcome home. Sorry, Dad, would you mind changing Artie and Etta's nappies?' I was truly back in reality – or my ego had truly landed!

I came away with my views about President Obama strengthened. I believe he was instrumental in saving the world from an economic crash even more catastrophic than 1929. Obamacare, while by no means perfect, is an amazing achievement considering the difficulties posed by the Senate. Major progress has been made on climate change, criminal justice reform, legalising same-sex marriage and protecting natural resources. He has brought Iran and Cuba back into the fold. Could he have handled Syria and Isis differently? Who's to know? He comes across very naturally, which is very important. He doesn't use his huge intellectual prowess to talk down to people; quite the reverse. I know some people reading this book will disagree, but I think Barack Obama will go down as one of the greatest presidents of America.

*

That lunch wasn't my only visit to the Obama White House. A few months later, I told Joan that she should pick out a beautiful dress, get her hair and make-up done and prepare for a special evening. As she knows me so well, she detected something was up. She started pestering me to tell her where we were going, but I held firm. Eventually, just before the do, she convinced me and I let the secret out: we were going to the White House Christmas party.

It was a great honour to be invited back to the White House again, along with Virgin Produced founder and White House entertainment adviser Jason Felts. The Obamas addressed the crowd with the kind of warm, wonderful words we all got used to from the President and the First Lady. Later, Joan and I were fortunate to spend some time alone with both Barack and Michelle away from the hustle and bustle of the party in their private chambers for a nightcap.

Since we had last seen each other, Donald Trump had been elected and the world had changed.

'When we met, you said Trump had very little chance of getting into the White House,' I reminded Barack.

He grimaced, but added that he fully intended to offer as smooth a transition as possible. Once out of office, he said he would hold the new administration to account as best he could. I invited them to visit the British Virgin Islands, and they kindly accepted. Joan and I left dreaming of a White House Christmas, and looking forward to seeing them again.

*

'We're free!'

The first words out of Michelle Obama's mouth as we greeted them on Moskito were full of delight and happiness. Since I'd last seen Barack and Michelle Obama, Donald Trump had been inaugurated as the new US President. Getting away from the madness of Washington, they'd accepted our invitation to come and visit the BVI.

I've never been one for reserve and Barack and Michelle were eager to do away with formalities, too. When one of our team asked how to address the former First Lady, she gleefully shouted: 'Michelle!'

'It's so nice to have my name back after eight years,' she smiled.

As well as relaxing, the Obamas were also eager to get active. One of the first stories Barack told me when they arrived was how, just before he became President, he had been surfing on a dangerous break in Hawaii. When he came in after an exhilarating session, the new head of his security team turned to him and said: 'That will be the last time you surf for at least four years.' During his presidency, he didn't have the chance to get out onto the water. Now, he was itching to get back in.

At Necker, we have the perfect conditions and team to help anyone learn, and so I gave Barack a challenge. I had wanted to learn foilboard surfing for some time: could Barack learn to kitesurf before I learned to foilboard? We agreed that on the final day of the holiday we'd battle to see who could stay up the longest. Barack started learning to kitesurf on the beach on Necker for two days solid, picking up the basics and flying a kite as if going back to being a child again. Then he went into the water, standing up and getting a feel for the kite. Finally, he put the board at his feet and gave it a go.

On the next stretch of water, I soon learned that foil-boarding, even if you can kitesurf, is a completely new sport. You come shooting out of the water, crashing down at high speed, and very much need a helmet and body armour for safety. But I slowly got the hang of it. Barack and I both fell many times, but we kept trying again and again and made progress. We were neck and neck until the last run on the last day, when I got up on the foilboard and screamed along for over fifty metres, three feet above the water. I was feeling very pleased with myself, only to look over and see Barack go 100 metres on his kiteboard! I had to doff my cap to him and celebrate his victory. At the end of the thrilling kitesurfing session, he was standing shirtless at the back of the boat with an invigorated look on his face, muscles bulging and eyes beaming. I looked at him and thought: 'Eat your heart out, Putin!' On his next visit, we plan to do the long kite over to Anegada together – and I intend to get my revenge and win.

We also played competitive doubles tennis, pool and snooker, as well as once going over to Virgin Gorda for a few holes of golf. I quickly realised Barack is a superb natural sportsman, and I suspect he'll be beating us all on the tennis court on their next visit. I'm proud to say I won our chess duel, though! When we weren't playing sport, Barack and Michelle simply enjoyed Moskito, Necker and everything they have to offer. We took them to Anegada to see the remarkable Horseshoe Reef, the third largest in the world. Afterwards, we enjoyed a nice lunch at Cow Wreck, where somehow about 300 people also turned up at the usually quiet bar. It was lovely to see the esteem in which everybody held the Obamas, and the warmth they gave back.

Barack told me about his meetings with Nelson Mandela, Desmond Tutu, the Dalai Lama and the Queen, four of the people he admires most in the world. He said how, when he met them, they were even more impressive in real life than from afar. I asked how hopeful he was for the future, and he told me Michelle has more of a glass half-empty attitude, whereas he is a more glass half-full type of person. While all the news coming out of the US was about Trump trying to dismantle all Barack had worked so hard for, his attitude was just to get on with his life, have a well-deserved holiday and recharge ready to work – I'm sure, tirelessly – when he returned to the US. I was very excited to learn about the Obama Foundation, and they were equally keen to hear more about our efforts combating climate change, promoting ocean conservation and helping young people through entrepreneurial programmes. Our values match theirs, and we're all sure we will work together in the future.

Over the ten days they stayed we had a lot of fun, a lot of laughs and became good friends. On the last night they had the delightful idea of holding a party for all the staff on Necker and Moskito they had come into contact with. Alongside Holly and myself, they were the first up onto the bar dancing with us, getting the party going, making everybody feel at home and welcome. There were a couple of local women who looked a bit lonely on the sidelines, watching other people enjoying themselves. Barack and Michelle made a point of going over to them, inviting them into the group and dancing with them. They made time for everybody. When they left, Michelle told us it was the first time she had felt teary at the end of a holiday.

'Can we just bottle this up and keep this vibe?' she asked.

We went down to the dock and all the staff and I threw ourselves into the ocean as we waved them goodbye. They are just the most genuine, decent, wonderful people, and I can't wait to see what brilliant things they go on to do next and, if I can, support them along the way.

42 Grand-dude

'Richard, would you like to learn about your ancestors?'

Of all the questions I found in my inbox this was one of the more unusual. I know just about everything there is to know about my living relatives, but couldn't say the same about those who came before my great-grandparents. So I responded to Christine Choi right away: 'Of course, what do I need to do?' She set me up to appear on US TV show *Finding Your Roots* and I gave a saliva sample for their research team to look into my forefathers.

A few months later I sat down with historian and journalist Henry Louis Gates Jr to trace my roots. It was a real eye-opener. My father's family left a paper trail that could be traced back to Madras (now Chennai), India, in the 1700s. In 1793, my 3rd great-grandfather, John Edward Branson, set sail from Britain to India. After a gruelling six-month journey, in which his ship rounded the Cape of Good Hope and crossed the Indian Ocean, he reached south-east India, a trading hub of the fast-growing British Empire. He was eventually joined by his father, my 4th great-grandfather, Harry Wilkins Branson; and by 1808 three generations of my ancestors were living in Madras.

'Why do you think they made the journey?' asked Henry.

'Well, I would hope it was for the love of adventure, and maybe in search of a better life.'

It turned out that could well be right. The paper trail showed that they moved in search of fortune, and within ten years became successful businessmen – my 3rd great-grandfather, John, a shopkeeper and my 4th great-grandfather, Harry, an auctioneer.

'So I'm not the first entrepreneur in the family?' I asked.

I was fascinated to find out where I inherited my love of adventure, discovery and entrepreneurship, characteristics that define me. What was even more exciting was that the Madras archives uncovered a very surprising family secret. Strangely, the baptismal record of my 2nd great-grandmother Eliza Reddy didn't list her mother. Analysis of my DNA revealed that the reason for this was because my 3rd great-grandmother was Indian.

'So I'm part Indian?' I asked, beaming. Indeed I was.

'I wish my father had got to see these records,' I told Henry. 'He would have been captivated.'

A keen student of history, my mother loved the most surprising piece of information discovered on her side of the family: I'm related to Charlemagne, the 'Father of Europe'. It turns out that he is my 40th great-grandfather! Like my paternal ancestors, it appears that my maternal side also embraced the spirit of adventure. While probing Mum's family lineage something odd happened: my mother's great-grandparents, Henry and Fanny Flindt, disappeared from English census records. They appeared to completely vanish after 1861, but luckily showed up in Melbourne, Australia, sometime later.

'No wonder I have always loved Australia – it's in the blood!'

'It didn't go so well for them there though, Richard,' said Henry. 'Soon after arriving they were forced to file for bankruptcy. And in 1867 both Henry and Fanny died from dysentery, leaving their four children – including your great-grandfather, Sydney Flindt – orphaned . . .'

Ah. Not so good.

' . . . Fortunately, your 3rd great-grandfather, Julius Emanuel Flindt, brought the children back to England, and made them his heirs.'

The story of my 3rd great grandfather's altruism affected me deeply. Thanks to the generosity and kindness of one man, my ancestors managed to get back on their feet and find success and happiness. I hope that when my great-great-grandchildren look at our family tree they look at my name and think: Richard Branson was a cool grand-dude who made a difference. I'm going to work even harder now to make sure.

*

I'm the sort of person who looks forward rather than back, but being involved in the TV programme and thinking about my ancestry seemed well timed. When I was involved in the negotiations with Alaska Air over the sale of Virgin America, Joan had given me some helpful perspective: 'Well, it's not life and death, Richard.' She was right. While it was very important, and many people were being affected, life would go on.

I was reminded of how far my life had gone on when I flew to New York in April 2016. I was in town to attend the premiere of *Don't Look Down*, Sundog Pictures' documentary about my attempts to cross the Atlantic and Pacific in the world's biggest hot-air balloon. Now those *were* a matter of life and death. The idea for the film had begun to take shape when I mentioned my ballooning adventures in passing to Greg Rose, and added: 'I'm sure you know all the details about that.'

'Not really,' he replied. 'It was a long time ago now, Richard.'

It had indeed been many years since my ballooning expeditions with Per Lindstrand, and the younger generation are no longer so familiar with them.

'Perhaps it's time we bring those stories back to life,' I suggested.

I knew Sam had found a lot of unseen footage in storage, and I began sketching out an outline of what a documentary could include. I sent those notes to Sam and his partner at Sundog, Johnny Webb, on 19 April 2013. Three years later, to the day, I was standing on the red carpet at the Tribeca Film Festival, preparing to watch the film they had created with director Daniel Gordon.

Ahead of the premiere, I enjoyed a quiet dinner at Soho House with my co-pilot Per: it was the first time we had seen each other in eighteen years. Per and I have always been chalk and cheese, but he has a wicked sense of humour, a kind heart and is the greatest balloonist of all time. We eased back into our old rapport easily enough, and it was terrific to catch up.

'You don't look that much older,' he said, kindly.

'Well, you certainly do!' I joked.

To be honest, I never thought I'd get old. I know it happens to all of us, but I never thought it would happen to me. Watching my younger self in *Don't Look Down*, I had to confront the fact that I had aged. I went to the mirror afterwards, put my hand to the crevices in my face and realised I am starting to look like my dad. What happened to the young man in the film? Where did these lines come from? Up to now it hasn't bothered me. I still feel as fit as when I was in my early thirties and believe I can keep it up for a few years yet. I'm making the most of playing full-on singles tennis, kitesurfing, skiing, cycling, you name it. But, as I enter my seventies, it is inevitable I will slow up. I'll have to play doubles tennis and only kitesurf with two ladies on my back rather than three!

*

The other reason the *Finding Your Roots* programme felt so timely was because of the arrival in recent years of the next generation of Bransons.

One of the most wonderful, binding parts of any successful relationship is children. Back in 1979, Joan and I sadly lost our daughter Clare Sarah, who was born prematurely and died when she was only four days old. We were heartbroken, and I will never forget that feeling, but it brought us even closer together, and we were lucky to be able to raise two fine children in Holly and Sam. For a long time, I had been pestering them both about the future possibility of grandchildren.

After Holly and Freddie got married she went through a really difficult time trying to conceive. She confided they were beginning to wonder if they would ever become parents. So we were all overjoyed when Holly told us the amazing news in 2014 that she and Freddie were expecting twins.

After lots of hugs and tears, Joan turned to me and said: 'Twins? Great. That's one each, so we won't fight over them.'

'I'm having the girl,' I replied.

Not long after, Bellie and Sam decided the time was right to tell us their own happy news: Bellie was expecting a child, too. It was a joy being around Holly and Bellie as their pregnancies progressed, with the two girls able to support each other along the way.

All seemed to be going to plan until that December, about two months before Holly was due to give birth. I visited her in the UK on my way to the airport and, I don't know, call it fatherly instinct, but I felt something was wrong. Yes, she was having twins, but she just didn't look well. Back home on Necker at one o'clock the following morning I sat bolt upright in bed, with beads of sweat forming on my forehead. I still had the horrible feeling that something wasn't quite right. I picked up my iPad and wrote her a note. 'Dear Holly. All that matters is your health. You can always have other children if anything goes wrong on this occasion. If there is any doubt whatsoever about your health, you must put yourself first. Please don't take any risks.' The next day she went to see the doctor. Her blood pressure had gone soaring through the roof. They did a test and found she had pre-eclampsia, one of the biggest causes of death for mothers in pregnancy.

Holly was rushed into hospital, while Joan and I jumped on a plane to the UK. By the time we landed on 20 December, the doctors had decided to go ahead with a caesarean section, and we made it to the hospital just after two beautiful, perfectly healthy babies were born. We became proud grandparents to a handsome boy named Artie and a gorgeous girl called Etta – I only say it in that order because that is how they came out.

I was amazed to realise their birth coincided with both Holly and Freddie's anniversary, and Joan and my wedding day. What a magical coincidence. Holly was absolutely fine, and back on her feet in no time. It seems miracles sometimes come in pairs. All the family got together with the babies back at Holly's house and quickly adjusted to a delightful schedule of nappy changing and naps. Joan said to me: 'I can't describe how happy I feel, it's almost like falling in love all over again.'

As the days passed following the birth of the twins, we all got ready for the arrival of Sam and Bellie's baby. The birth wasn't due for a few weeks, but, with the instinct I seemed to have developed for these things, Joan and I decided to go over to England for the weekend just in case. We arrived the next day to find Bellie had been taken into hospital. While Holly, Freddie, Joan, Sam and Bellie's family waited with her there, I looked after the twins. We went shopping in Notting Hill and Joan and I popped into a children's shop to buy a gift for the new baby. The press spotted us and ran stories about me spoiling the twins – little did they know we were actually spoiling our other new grandchild!

Eva-Deia arrived at 4.39 p.m. on 19 February. She had a squashed button nose and the cutest little face. It was funny how little she looked like her parents to begin with, but we were all instantly in love.

'You're a granddad three times over,' Joan said, turning to me.

'No, no,' I corrected her, 'I'm a grand-*dude* three times over!'

Eva-Deia was named after my mum and a beautiful village up in the mountains of Majorca, where Sam and Holly had spent happy holidays at the stunning La

Residencia hotel. For our grandchildren's first family holiday together we decided to go back to Deia, and enjoyed a magical few days up in the hills. Before the twins were born, Holly also had the name Deia in mind. After Eva-Deia arrived I said to her and Sam: 'Well, I think the right babies got the right names and they all couldn't be more perfect.'

After wanting grandchildren for years, within a matter of weeks we had three. Then, in early 2017, I became a grand-dude for a fourth time. When Sam and Bellie's second child was being born, I was out on the water kitesurfing around Necker. I knew Bellie was in labour, but thought I had enough time for a quick kite. Rather than pace the floor fretting, I knew the waves would calm me down. However, halfway around the island a boat rushed up to me with the news that I should head for home immediately. I scrambled onto the beach and called Sam. We all love surprises in my family, and have quickly established a tradition of keeping the sex of our grandchildren unknown until they are born. I held my breath as Sam made me wait momentarily before sharing the wonderful news that he had a son. I was crying with joy as he told me the baby was named Bluey Rafe Richard Branson.

I wondered if the grandkids would change my view on the world, or make me want to protect it more. But, really, I already had that perspective, which came from being a lad of the sixties, a decade when change was happening. From protesting against the Vietnam War to introducing the pill, from the civil rights movement to the environmental move-ment, freedom felt possible. It was a hippy time, but the hippies talked a lot of sense without necessarily having the wherewithal to back it up. Now, we need to follow through. When I had my own children, it strengthened that view, and having grandchildren did the same again. Having said that, I don't want to be stuck in the same ways of thinking, and I know my grandchildren will be able to teach me so much, like my children before them and my parents before them.

While I always got on well with my parents when I was growing up, it wasn't until I was a little older that we were able to spend long stretches of time together. Dad worked all hours as a struggling barrister so we would usually only see him on weekends, while Mum was always starting and struggling with a new entrepreneurial scheme, and looking after my sisters Lindy and Vanessa, too. When I went away to boarding school we saw each other even less, but we made up for it later on.

When Joan and I had children I was determined to be there with them as much as possible, which is why I always worked from home, first on our houseboat and then in Holland Park. But I was still away a fair amount with work. Now, with our grandchildren, Joan and I are eager to spend every second we can with them. During their frequent visits to Moskito or Necker Island, I will clear my schedule, and I always factor in time solely for playing (sorry, babysitting).

Once when Holly, Freddie and the kids arrived at Red Dock on Necker, I grabbed Etta from the boat, and Joan picked up Artie.

'What about me? Where's my hug?' asked Holly.

I was changing nappies later the same day and noticed Joan staring at me in a strange way.

'What?' I asked.

'Do you know what? I think you've finally grown up – if that's possible!'

After sixty-six years, I was finally behaving like a responsible adult – well, sort of. I was also blowing raspberries at Etta. Joan sees a lot of Holly in Etta, both in her looks and her calm, bright nature. I'm sure that Eva-Deia and Bluey, Etta and Artie will be close to their parents and I can already see what wonderful mums and dads Sam, Bellie, Holly and Freddie are becoming. I'm confident their children will grow up happy to tell them anything, which is the philosophy we always had with Holly and Sam. We have always wanted what's best for them, which means being honest both ways, telling them everything and letting them make their own decisions and mistakes. The strength of our family is unreserved love and openness. We are lucky that Joan and I have been together for so long, which has given tremendous stability to the kids, nephews, nieces and friends they have had for many years. I hope it continues for generations to come.

On the evening after Bluey was born, I felt in a reflective mood and wrote to Holly and Sam: 'The beauty of having children is that the relationship gets better, stronger and more magical with every day that goes by. Love you both so, so much.' I thought back to a farewell letter I wrote to them twenty years earlier, as I prepared to embark on a ballooning challenge I wasn't sure I would return from. More than ever, I felt so lucky to have survived to share so many more memories and adventures with the people I care about. To build more organisations, hear more laughter, take on more challenges, share more love and go on finding my virginity in business, in life and in love.

43 Travelling into the Future

You are waiting on the platform for your transportation to arrive. Rather than a carriage or a car, a pod arrives; you step inside and are shot through a vacuum from one side of the country to the other in a matter of minutes. It sounds like science fiction, doesn't it? It sounds like a good idea to me.

While I was at school, I would find anything to distract me from the homework I really needed to do. One diversion tactic was reading books, ideally swashbuckling adventures or fantastical tales to take me far away from the classroom grind. One of these was *The Man in the High Castle*, Philip K. Dick's disturbing and enthralling alternative history that recently got turned into a TV series. Reading the book as a teenager, I was intrigued by the tubes used to rocket people across continents at lightning speed. Years before, in the 1930s, Will Whitehorn's grandfather Harold Kenneth Whitehorn had a similar idea when he filed a patent for the first ever vacuum-tube electromagnetic train. (It's no surprise Will ended up running Virgin Galactic!) His granddad even had a basic working model on display in the Science Museum in London. He also knew Joseph Foa, professor at New York's Rensselaer Polytechnic Institute, who took his ideas forward in the 1950s and '60s with a transport system he called Tubeflight, which proposed using magnets to send capsules floating on cushions of air through long tubes. But back then, the technology didn't match the ambition. In

2013 Elon Musk made a splash bringing these ideas to life again by publishing a paper on them. But still, nobody was close to turning these concepts into reality. Until now ...

Patrick McCall heard about a new company called Hyperloop One. He rang me to explain the concept and I asked for five minutes to think about it. I called him straight back and said, 'Let's do it.' I had met Josh Giegel a few times when he worked for us as an engineer at Virgin Galactic, and I found that the vision of his new firm, Hyperloop One, fitted with my own reasons for starting businesses: find what you are frustrated about – and solve it.

'Travel sucks,' said Josh, which was quite the statement to make to a man who has founded three airlines, two train businesses and three space companies. 'Let's make travel not suck.' He had my attention. The concept was, as Will's grandfather had dreamed of in the 1930s, to move people and things faster than at any other time in history. Passengers and cargo would be loaded into pods and accelerated gradually via electric propulsion through a low-pressure tube. The pod would quickly lift above the track using magnetic levitation and glide at airline speeds for long distances due to ultra-low aerodynamic drag. Essentially, it would be a revolution in the way we all travel. Others had talked about it. But these guys had a full-scale test facility sitting in the middle of the Nevada desert. I asked if I could come and see it for myself.

On 17 May 2017, I got in a car in Las Vegas and we drove out to the desert. After half an hour or so, a long, white tube appeared on the horizon, framed by cloudless blue skies.

It was hot and sticky, but I was happy to put on my hard hat, hi-vis and protective goggles to take a closer look. As we walked over, I quizzed Josh about leaving Virgin Galactic.

'So you left the most exciting company in the world?'

'I guess so – until this one.'

'Well, if you were going to leave, this is probably as good a reason as any.'

We walked into the DevLoop, a 500-metre-long tube with a diameter of 3.3 metres. Seeing the inside of the test system up close, eyeing the track and the curved walls was exhilarating.

'It's pretty much a maglev train in a vacuum tube,' some-body said. Inside here, days earlier, the first full-system Hyperloop One test in a vacuum environment had taken place. Propelled by electrical charges and using magnetic levitation, the test sled zipped through the DevLoop tube for 5.3 seconds. Within this short time period it reached 70 miles per hour, with nearly 2 Gs of acceleration.

I felt an excitement similar to the moment when I had walked into the spaceship hangar in Mojave for the first time. During the walkabout, I asked lots of questions and took even more notes. I had brought along expert engineers from Virgin Trains in the UK and Virgin Orbit in the US, to dig down into the technical details. One of my first questions was about the sustainability potential of Hyperloop One.

'It will be all-electric and we're working on making it as sustainable as possible,' Josh told us.

I also wanted to know how passengers would respond emotionally and physically to the Hyperloop. 'How will it make them feel?' I asked. 'How will it be different to any future competitors? What will it say about the people who ride it?' Virgin is an experience brand, and that thread flows through our airlines, our spaceline, our health clubs and even our banks. I wanted to know if Hyperloop would give people a unique experience, not just a faster transportation method. I liked what I heard.

Josh said he had sat through interminable meetings with all sorts of potential investors, who told him that the business plan didn't add up, the challenge was too big and they were wasting their time. There was an element to him of wanting to prove experts wrong, while pursuing what he was passion-ate about, that I liked. That's often a recipe for success. We were in, agreeing to invest and form a global strategic part-nership. While our teams began negotiations, testing continued. During phase two, the longest test lasted 10.6 seconds, with the top speed of 192 miles per hour (310 kilometres per hour) – or 86 metres per second. The maximum distance travelled was 436 metres, with a peak acceleration of 1.48 Gs – equal to 0-to-60mph in

1.85 seconds. But this is nothing on the end goals. Every journey, from every origin to every destination, will be non-stop, with proposed speeds of 671mph – or 300 metres per second. It typically takes four to five hours to travel 300 kilometres by road; by train it would be more than two hours; with Hyperloop One it will take eighteen minutes. We envisage combining the convenience of a metro with the capacity of a train at the speed of a plane, all on a national scale.

On 12 October I was in London, celebrating the hardback launch of this very book. It was a busy day, with back-to-back interviews, meetings, and dancing on the table live on BBC One all to fit in before a huge talk and party at Troxy in east London. But my life has a habit of throwing up happy complications. Arriving into London, I was told the news that we were investing in Hyperloop One was about to come out. Now, if we were announcing this, we wanted to do it on our terms, not with a leak. We hastily arranged for some TV interviews and shared our newest company with the world: Virgin Hyperloop. I was able to expand on some of the projects we have in the works, including routes in the Middle East, Europe, India, China, Russia, Canada and the US. People were, unsurprisingly, most intrigued by our projected journey times, including Edinburgh to London in just fifty minutes.

I was so excited by the potential of the company that I was happy to get even more involved. In December 2017 I became chairman of Virgin Hyperloop, the first time I had taken such a position in many years. I began rolling up my sleeves, joining long board meetings and actually enjoying them – a very rare occurrence! My confidence was backed up by the company raising an additional $50 million from its key shareholders Caspian Venture Capital and DP World, bringing the total it had raised since its foundation in 2014 to almost $300 million. Meanwhile, over at the DevLoop, the team of engineers, machinists, welders and fabricators, led by Josh and CEO Rob Lloyd, were hard at work. In the third phase of intense testing, we set a new test speed record of 387 kilometres per hour (240 miles per hour, or 107 metres per second). That's fast.

However, there is a long way to go to proving that the system can work at full scale and speed. Upcoming tests will include sending a prototype passenger pod zooming through the Hyperloop, with initial speeds of up to 250mph and greater distances travelled. I am incredibly excited about how the technology and the team behind Virgin Hyperloop could transform passengers' lives. We got the first taste of how people will react to the concept when I travelled to India in February 2018. The Indian State of Maharashtra announced their intent to build a Virgin Hyperloop between Pune and Mumbai (one of the busiest routes in the world), beginning with an operational demonstration track. The Virgin Hyperloop route would link central Pune, Navi Mumbai International Airport, and Mumbai in twenty-five minutes and connect 26 million people. Supporting 150 million passenger trips per year, it would help create a thriving, competitive mega-region. Indian prime minister, Narendra Modi, and the chief minister of Maharashtra, Devendra Fadnavis, joined us as we signed a Framework Agreement for the project, and I could feel the anticipation in the room as I spoke.

'I'm incredibly excited about the potential to truly transform not just transportation, but wider society. Virgin Hyperloop can help India become a global transportation pioneer and forge a new world-changing industry.'

This was an important point – the business has potential to have a much greater impact than simply improving travel. The Pune–Mumbai route will have massive time savings, create tens of thousands of jobs and help attract new business and investment – which could add up to $55 billion in socio-economic benefits. The system, which is 100 per cent electric, will also ease severe congestion, reduce smog and cut up to 86,000 tonnes of greenhouse gas emissions over thirty years. I found it particularly exciting how Hyperloop could allow India to leapfrog entire stages of technological development. In telecoms, most people in India never had fixed-line telephones, so mobile penetration was dramatic. Similar rapid progress with Hyperloop could allow India to skip the infrastructure and cost issues of high-speed rail and jump ahead of other nations.

The announcement led to more interest from exciting directions, notably Dubai Airports, where former Virgin Trains and Virgin Atlantic director Paul Griffiths is now CEO. His vision is using Virgin Hyperloop to connect airports that are many miles apart (effectively into one airport) and to transport passengers directly to airline gates, completing check-in and security on-board. I love the idea, which will dramatically speed up travelling times while saving costs, hassle and space. Once you're in the Virgin family you never leave, so I'm confident we can make it work with Paul and Dubai.

Some people asked why I was so keen to invest in a company that could dramatically disrupt existing successful business models in industries like rail and aviation. I simply pointed up to the skies. It was the same reason cavemen invented wheels, when feet had been perfectly good for getting around beforehand. It was the same reason Henry Ford built the Model T, when horses and carts were just fine, thank you very much. It was the same reason the Wright Brothers created the plane, and the pioneers of space travel keep pushing the envelope. If we can create a business that can move people and things at airline speeds for the price of a bus or train ticket, then why shouldn't we? If we can do it in a safe, efficient, sustainable way, helping broader society at the same time, then count me in.

I believe Virgin Hyperloop could have the same impact in the twenty-first century as trains did in the nineteenth. I'm sure there will be rivals nipping at our heels, but we are the only company in the world that has built a fully operational Hyperloop test system. And we're determined to be the first to make Hyperloop a commercial reality. While making timing predictions is no exact science, we are hoping to be ready to go in 2021. It's a wonderful example of what can happen when a fascinating idea meets a huge customer need served by our brilliant brand. Projects like this are what keep me getting up in the morning, trying to push boundaries, having fun and moving – fast!

*

There are lots of frustrations, big and small, which we take for granted will not change. But most of these problems are actually opportunities waiting to be grasped. Sometimes solutions can be sitting in front of you – right on your plate. I gave up eating beef in 2014, wanting to make a small personal effort to get healthier and support a more sustainable world. Conventional meat production can have truly devastating environmental impacts. Livestock produces 18 per cent of all man-made greenhouse gas emissions – making it a bigger contributor to global warming and environmental degradation than all forms of transport. As more people come out of poverty in emerging markets, demand for cattle will continue to soar, and if nothing is done about it we will soon have little rainforest left and little biodiversity, and climate change will accelerate. I was surprised how little I missed beef, and once I looked into it further, I was amazed at the alternatives, especially with meat substitutes. They also looked like very interesting business opportunities. With global consumers currently spending nearly $1 trillion per year on meat, and demand for meat forecast to double in the coming decades, we need a solution.

We started by investing in Beyond Meat, a company developing plant-based foods that taste just like meat but eliminate the need for cattle and other animals to be eaten. This could result in using thirty-five times less land alone and fifteen times less water, and the end product could be as much as twenty times less costly. Obviously, this is no use if the food doesn't taste great. We did a blind testing on Necker; I played chef and served up plant-based burgers to our guests without telling them they weren't meat. They said they were the best hamburgers they had ever tasted, and laughed with delight when I revealed what they had just eaten.

While these plant-based solutions are interesting, I was also fascinated by the 'clean meat' space. One company, Memphis Meats, is developing a way to produce real meat from animal cells, without the need to feed, breed and slaughter actual animals. We invested alongside the likes of Bill Gates and huge meat producers Tyson Foods and Cargill. At scale, Memphis Meats will use millions of litres less water and millions of acres less land; produce up to 90 per cent fewer greenhouse gas emissions, and be less expensive than conventional meat production. And it's a huge step forward for animal welfare. I believe that in thirty years or so we will no longer need to kill any animals and that all meat will either be 'clean' or plant-based, will taste the same as traditional meat and also be much healthier for everyone. One day we will look back and think how archaic our grandparents were in killing animals for food. And hopefully we can get there quickly enough to save the remaining rainforests.

Moving these concepts into widespread commercial success is going to take time. But when it comes to turning ideas into reality, it is entrepreneurs who have the potential to change the world. I met a lot of people with this potential when I joined the TV show *Shark Tank* as a guest shark in 2017. While I'm very used to being pitched to, I felt quite nervous as I joined the sharks, who were already sharpening their teeth to get stuck into the hopeful entrepreneurs. Before the show, Mark Cuban told me to be myself. So he shouldn't have been surprised when we had a little misunderstanding during the pitch for, of all things, a meditation app called Simple Habit. Mark called the entrepreneur a gold-digger, which I thought was rather offensive. As a knight, I defended her honour by playfully throwing my glass of water over him. He wasn't at all impressed with the impromptu shower, and threw his water right back at me. Anyway, it made for good television!

I went on to invest in two purpose-driven businesses. Outdoor-gear firm Sierra Madre Research, run by husband-and-wife team Richard and Julie Rhett, appealed to my adventurous side. I saw a lot of my younger self in a twelve-year-old entrepreneur called Carson. He couldn't fit his skateboard in his school locker and realised many others had the same problem, so created Locker Board, which redesigns upcycled skateboards that fit into backpacks and lockers. His idea is a lot better than my youthful business attempts – growing Christmas trees and breeding budgerigars.

If either company does half as well as another of my investments, Ring, then it will be an incredible success. I first met Jamie Siminoff by chance in a lift in Brussels many years ago. Fast-forward to 2013 and Jamie went on *Shark Tank* to pitch his idea for a smart doorbell and home-security company. He was rejected by all but one shark, who offered less than what Jamie believed it was worth so he declined and walked away with nothing. Mark Cuban specifically said it wouldn't be successful. But the sharks didn't know Jamie's story. I found myself talking to him at the bar on Necker Island and was fascinated to learn how he had tried to come up with a great business idea for years, making prototypes in his garage in California. While he worked, he was frustrated that he kept missing calls at his front door. So he rigged up a link from the doorbell to his smartphone so he could answer the door remotely via video. Jamie told his wife, who loved the idea because it meant she could always see who was at the front door and felt much safer. Before he knew it, friends who visited were all interested in the doorbell. It dawned upon Jamie that this accidental invention was the best business idea he'd ever had, and he created Ring. When I heard Jamie's tale, I knew we were investing in an entrepreneur, not just a business.

Over one million homes now have Ring's protective gear; they employ more than 2,000 people and are fulfilling their purpose of reducing crime in neighbourhoods. In March 2018, I was very proud for Jamie when they were acquired by Amazon for over $1 billion. Like most good ideas, it is an artful solution to a complex problem. As I tell every young entrepreneur I meet asking for tips: keep it simple, stupid.

*

In September 2017 I travelled to Saudi Arabia. It had been many years since I had visited and I wanted to see first-hand the changes taking place in the country. On my first visit I gave a speech to a large group of businesspeople. Just before going onstage I was told that I would only see men in the audience. All of the women had been put into a segregated area, caged off behind a wall at the back of the hall. When I picked up the microphone I said: 'I know the saying is that when you're in Rome you're meant to do as the Romans do, but it does seem wrong that all of you men have got the best seats and all the women are caged off at the back.' There was a deathly silence. Then there were loud whoops and stamping of feet from behind the wall; the women had climbed onto their seats, cheering and throwing their handbags into the air. Once the noise died down I carried on with the speech, adding that I hoped I'd maybe sparked a little revolution.

From what I had heard, by 2017 things were changing for the better, and it seemed like an exciting time to visit. On the day I arrived, women were given the right to drive for the first time. The fact that this was a major milestone shows just how far Saudi Arabia still has to go to reach equality. However, it was a much-welcomed sign of progress. I asked every woman I met what she thought of the news and was met with overwhelming positivity. I had heard that Saudi Arabia's thirty-two-year-old Crown Prince Mohammad bin Salman, who had just come to power, was committed to moving his country into the modern world, and bringing its citizens with him. It would be good to see this in action.

Arriving in Riyadh, I met with the Crown Prince. He was friendly, charismatic and quick to get to the point. His team wanted to show us a side of Saudi Arabia that most people do not get a chance to experience. We were taken to the Red Sea to explore an enormous new project to turn a huge lagoon into a world-class tourism destination. It spreads over more than fifty islands between the cities of Umluj and Al Wajh and we were told the project would create as many as 35,000 jobs in an area remote from major cities. My first thought was about the ocean. I had never been in the Red Sea and was eager to take a dip. The water was bright turquoise and extraordinarily clear, the reefs pristine. Standing on the islands, we could see majestic eagle rays and dugongs swimming by, while turtles pulled themselves in and out of the water to lay their eggs. I really was surprised how utterly untouched the landscape was, and how completely unspoilt the ocean.

'This must be one of the last marine wonders of the world,' I said to Patrick McCall, who had joined us on the trip. I could see how, given the right protections, it could remain that way for decades to come.

Next, we visited the UNESCO World Heritage Site, Mada'in Saleh. I've been fortunate to visit Petra in Jordan, a ruin from the same ancient civilisation, but this was even more breathtaking. The surrounding mountains are a natural masterpiece, with 131 tombs cut from the rock in eye-catching colours.

'It would be so spectacular to see it from a hot-air balloon,' I said, offering to arrange for some Virgin Balloons to go to Mada'in Saleh. Nearby, a railway had me reminiscing about my childhood when I idolised Lawrence of Arabia. The railway had been a target for him in the revolt against Ottoman domination and a train he blew up in the conflict had been restored to the track. I felt a childlike excitement as I did my best Richard of Arabia impression, wearing a keffiyeh in the midday sun while standing next to the train. Exploring the country, I could see the vision for a more open Saudi Arabia starting to come to light. Very few visitors choose to holiday in Saudi Arabia, because of the environment there for the past thirty years. Likewise, many Saudis travel abroad to enjoy their holidays. Projects such as the Red Sea development could help modernise and liberalise the country, bringing in new ideas, while also helping to showcase and protect the unique natural beauty of this land.

Back in Riyadh, I had a long dinner with the Crown Prince. He asked me if I would become an adviser on the Red Sea and Al-Ula development projects and I was happy to accept. He told me the history of his country and tried to explain the situation he faced. More than half of the population are under twenty-five and eager for reform; he believes they want to see a new, modernised society. However, since the Islamic Revolution in 1979, the country has been held in the grip of an ageing religious establishment whose hard-line approach controls much of private and public life. He explained how he wants to stand up to these extremists and show how they have misinterpreted the Quran for their own gain. He said that in the process he has had death threats and even assassination attempts. He is trying to move the country forward step by step into the modern era and plans to reintroduce cinemas and live music in Saudi Arabia after an absence of twenty-five years. Listening, I realised what an enormously difficult job he has to promote change while reconciling the various forces that seek to pull this vast country in very different directions. But he was very determined and I believe he will succeed.

We also talked business. The Crown Prince was very interested in our space ventures, and we discussed the possibility of a new partnership between Virgin Galactic, Virgin Orbit, the Spaceship Company and Saudi Arabia. A year earlier our team had received a call from Jonathan Gray of First Idea stating that the Kingdom of Saudi Arabia's Public Investment Fund (PIF) had identified the Virgin Group as the people they most wanted to work with in the space sector. We had been in discussions with another party but saw Saudi Arabia as a more exciting partner. I had some serious concerns given Saudi's record on equal rights and continued use of the death penalty. So before agreeing I wanted to be sure the country was moving in a positive direction.

I spent time walking around Riyadh, talking to members of the public on the street, who were excited about the changes taking place. I also brought up our concerns with the Crown Prince and his team. I believe the Crown Prince is a reformer. He has set out a vision for his country that will fundamentally change Saudi's society and economy, and has started by loosening restrictions and encouraging a more progressive stance on areas such as women's rights. But he needs to carry the public with him so it has to be a gradual approach. He's also making some brave economic moves as he guides the Kingdom away from its dependence on oil, including plans for a $500-billion new city in the north of the country. This bold Vision 2030 will see the country put its oil wealth into growing other sectors such as education, entertainment, tourism, and the technology of the future (such as Virgin Hyperloop). Their wish to invest in our space technology is part of the larger societal trans-formation the Crown Prince seeks to bring to his country. We shook hands on a deal and announced the partnership at Riyadh's Investment Forum FII on 26 October.

We expected to finalise the deal by the end of February 2018. But, as often happens when you get into the nitty-gritty with lawyers and negotiators, the deal changed into something very different. As term-sheet discussions dragged on, we were getting further away from a deal that worked for both parties. The new conditions made it impossible for Virgin to agree and I assumed they no longer wanted to go ahead with the investment. Then, in March 2018, I received a WhatsApp message from the Crown Prince confirming his commitment to the partnership. He was visiting the Queen and the Prime Minister in London, and wanted to meet up with me. On my flight to England, I decided to sit down with all the details in front of me and write a letter to the Crown Prince's key adviser, PIF CEO Yasir bin Othman Al-Rumayyan. I set out the history and explained our con-cerns about how the negotiations were going. I thought through the deal from both points of view and tried to come up with a really fair compromise that worked for both parties. Then I gave a list of seven key points which we needed to agree to close the deal.

'I really hope that the above works for you and we can shake hands on it today,' I wrote. 'Anyway very much look forward to seeing you for breakfast. Best, Richard.'

Yasir came to Holly and Freddie's house for breakfast. During my last visit to Saudi I'd been invited to his home, so it seemed right to do the same. Etta and Artie were running around our feet, asking for Holly, and the place was warm and welcoming. The fact that we are a family busi-ness is important, and with family being so important in Saudi Arabian society, I suspect they relate better to us than they would to faceless corporations. We had lots of coffee and a healthy breakfast of muesli and fruit salad. We then moved to the sofa and Yasir read my letter. There was a pause before he asked me some quick questions. Then he said: 'We have a deal.'

As we went out into the street he gave me a big hug. That night I joined a small, private dinner with the Crown Prince. He was very relaxed, didn't have a tie on and knew how to make everyone else feel at ease too. I sat opposite him and asked a lot of questions. He has a lovely glint in his eye, a great sense of humour. Yet there is an incredibly tough side to him, which you rarely see but know is there.

When we announced the deal, I highlighted the new opportunities for women in Saudi Arabia. I spoke of all these seeds languishing on the ground for years and how, now they were finally being watered, they were springing up to play full parts in a fairer, better society that empowers its citizens. Hopefully our involvement in Saudi through space and other projects can play a positive role in that.

Speaking of which, 2018 is shaping up to be the most exciting year yet for Virgin Galactic. It's been wonderful seeing the progress from a series of successful tests on the ground and in the air, to the continuing development of our team culture and leadership. On 5 April, SpaceShipTwo VSS Unity safely and successfully completed her first supersonic, rocket-powered flight, with our program's longest rocket burn duration of 30 seconds, fastest speed of Mach 1.87 and highest altitude of 84,271 feet. At the time of going to print, I'm looking forward to seeing an increasing number of powered test flights in the next few months, including the momentous day that will be our first spaceflight. If that wasn't thrilling enough, Spaceport America and New Mexico are currently getting ready for our team and vehicles to transition from Mojave into their new permanent home. You probably know by now that I am prone to making predictions, but I wouldn't do so if I wasn't confident. I'm not offering any dates, but I will be following our test program very closely indeed, and hope that my own flight into space will take place later in 2018. Now that will make for the best new chapter of all …

44 Surviving the Hurricane

Necker Island is one of those rare places on this planet where you feel not only connected to nature but also consumed by it. You can feel the sun beaming down onto your face, its rays seeping into your skin. You can smell the ocean in the air and feel the wind whipping through your hair. You can see flamingos and scarlet ibis above you, iguanas and giant tortoises beneath you, and countless other varieties of animal in between. Nature surrounds you in all its glory – and, every now and then, in all its brutality. 6 September 2017 was one of those days when nature reminded us how fragile life on earth really is.

I spent the night before sleeplessly huddled up in my room, looking out at the howling gale and biting rain. I felt apprehension, a little bit of fear, mixed with tremendous excitement at seeing nature at its most ferocious. I know some people will think I'm irresponsible, but I love to experience things others haven't and be there first-hand. Minute by minute, Hurricane Irma was edging closer and closer. The weather reports told us that the power of the hurricane was unheard of – it had strengthened to more than Category 5, the highest possible on the scale, which itself had never hit the BVI full on before. Surely the winds couldn't really sustain 185mph, with gusts of over 200mph. Could they? As morning broke, the atmosphere was eerie. I spent the day with our team, everyone busy battening down the hatches across the island and putting our robust safety plans into place. We had some delightful guests staying who cut their trip short, while another group postponed. We put out messages urging our local employees on other islands to stay inside, ideally in organised shelters or other solid concrete structures with water and supplies. For our teams who lived on Necker and Moskito, the best option was to remain there, where we had constructed very strong buildings with hurricane blinds. We had food, provisions and medical supplies and were as well prepared as possible.

We all gathered together in two rooms inside the Great House. I hadn't had a sleepover quite like it since I was a kid. We played the dice game Perudo and my favourite card game wild bridge, and exchanged stories of previous hurricanes we had experienced. In the next room, we placed as many lemurs and parrots as possible in boxes for safety; a blind flamingo named Lucky was in one of the showers, while the tortoises settled nearby, as if they sensed what was coming. It was a bizarre situation; I was willing the eye of the storm to veer away from the BVI in these last few hours but in all honesty, if it was to come, I would have hated to miss it. I told the team what a privilege it was to spend this surreal time with such a great group of young people.

This was not my first rodeo. We have a hurricane in the British Virgin Islands around once a decade and I had experienced three over the last thirty years. Two powerful hurricanes, Earl and Otto, hit the BVI in 2010 and caused extensive damage. I rode them out inside a guest tub on top of the house and beheld nature at its most fierce. Because it was so high up, I always thought I was safe from any flying debris, which is the biggest danger. It was exhilarating feeling the power of the sea breaking over the clifftops, the roar of the winds, the lightning and the rain. But those were less powerful hurricanes. On this occasion, knowing how strong Irma was expected to be, Holly made me promise not to go to the tub. Being an older dad who now likes to rebel against his daughter, I couldn't help popping in as the hurricane started to arrive. It was spectacularly beautiful looking out at the tempestuous seas and the unnerving sky 360 degrees around us, at the start of what was now forecast to be the hurricane of the century. But I didn't last long. Holly's warning rang in my ears and I got out before it truly hit.

About sixty of us and our dogs, Sumo, Miso and Milo, bunkered down in the three-room cellar underneath the Great House, the safest place on the island. Most people hadn't experienced a hurricane before, and didn't have to wait long until it arrived with its full fury – if the Saffir-Simpson scale measured above Category 5, this would have been a Category 7. The pressure built up and up and up until it felt as though our ears were going to burst. Our engineers drilled holes into the shutters to alleviate the pressure without letting in the hurricane. However, water was pouring in through the roof. We took it in turns to line up with buckets and towels emptying water into the toilet to stop the room flooding (and using the same water to flush the toilet). In between, we used the conga line to massage the shoulders of the person in front of us. This went on hour after hour. There were tears. There were hugs. Then one window blew in, hit by a flying tree, and we all had to retreat rapidly to two rooms. As the storm reached a crescendo, really roaring like an express train screeching past hour after hour, Keny, our island manager, decided to open some fine wine to keep our minds off it (while his children, Zara and Theo, sat in the corner and played UNO). Soon Ben had put on battery-powered disco lights and since the room was shaking anyway, everyone started dancing to the Beach Boys' 'Good Vibrations'.

I could only imagine what was going on outside. I feared for the people elsewhere in the BVI in flimsy houses, and hoped they were safe. I feared for the wildlife, worrying that the flamingos and lemurs and hummingbirds couldn't survive such a storm. I feared for the beautiful island itself. I thought about Joan, Holly, Sam and the grandchildren, thankful they were all away from here. The hurricane got stronger and stronger. Whole trees were blown against the side of the building, coconuts hit the shutters and we could hear the crash of glass. Miraculously, the cellar held firm through the full ferocity of the storm. And then, suddenly, within a split second there was a strange, tranquil moment of absolute silence. We knew that it was either the end of the storm, or that we were now right in its eye.

We waited fifteen minutes. Then Adam Simmonds, our engineer, very, very slowly undid the big screws holding the door in place and we ventured outside. We had to climb over tonnes of broken glass and smashed doors to get to the edge of the patio, which overlooked the island. When we saw the wasteland that Necker, our home for many, many years, had become, my heart sank and tears formed in my eyes. It was absolutely devastated, like pictures I had seen after nuclear blasts. What had been a beautifully green, lush island was now black. I could see huge trees flattened, every leaf gone, doors, windows and whole buildings completely shattered. I'm not one to worry about losing material things – in the end, all that matters is that nobody was hurt – but you're never emotionally prepared for something like that. I felt broken. But I didn't have long to grieve. The other side of the hurricane hit and we threw ourselves back into the cellar, resealed the door and bunkered down to ride out the last four hours of Irma, which turned out to be even more damaging than the first half.

When we emerged afterwards, there was desolation in every direction. I was stunned to see that entire buildings had simply disappeared. A whole beach of palm trees had been uprooted without trace. Outside the bunker, bathroom and bedroom doors and windows had flown 40 metres away. As for the hot tub I had been sitting in? A 1-tonne bath had flown about 30 metres through the air, and buried itself exactly where I'd been. There is no chance I would have survived if I had stayed put. I had to laugh, turning to the team: 'Well, that would have been an interesting way to go!' Bizarrely, as I looked out at the wreckage, my first thought was anger. I was furious at every climate change denier who refuses to see the plain truth that human-made climate change is a key factor in the increasing intensity of these hurricanes. We are not doing enough to tackle this enormous challenge. If Irma is any indication, we must brace ourselves for more of these catastrophic weather events.

By now it was early evening. We attempted to walk around Necker, wading through debris and destruction. The tennis court was gone. A giant wave had taken everything from the pavilion – the bar, televisions, tables, chairs – and dumped it all on what had been the tennis court along with several feet of sand. Most of the island was 4 feet underwater. The staff village had been flattened. We made a priority list of what needed doing, including setting up an animal hospital to rescue as much wildlife as possible. Of course, I knew that if Necker was this bad it would be a drop in the ocean compared to what was happening elsewhere in the BVI and that our priority must be to check on the local community. All communications were down, but we soon managed to get one satellite phone working for outgoing calls, so I could get some messages for help out.

Keny and I decided we needed to get to Virgin Gorda as soon as it was light. We had pulled one boat inland before the hurricane and found it next morning with two palm trees draped over it, but still seaworthy. The ocean was remarkably calm and we made it over to Virgin Gorda, where boats were piled up like matchsticks in the harbour. Huge cargo ships had been thrown out of the water onto rocks. We had to climb over upturned cars, torn trees and telegraph poles. Resorts were obliterated. Houses and churches where people sheltered had their roofs blown off. We got up to a clinic where people had spent the night and met a number of our team, including Brian and Trevor, who had helped build the original Necker house thirty-five years earlier and had been with us ever since. We heard stories of what they had all been through. One family I met had their entire house blown away. They raced to take shelter in another house, which promptly got blown away as well. They gathered their children to crouch down next to a wall for shelter, but then the wall crumbled. Finally, they found refuge in the bottom of a cistern and saw out the storm. It was just incredible there was no loss of life. We heard some-body say: 'It's Irmageddon around here!' Humour amongst the chaos made us smile.

In the BVI, every single island was battered; more than 90 per cent of all residential buildings became uninhabit-able, all local infrastructure – power, telecommunications, water and sanitation – was either destroyed or seriously damaged. In Tortola prison walls had collapsed and some of the escaped prisoners created panic. Thankfully the British military stepped up and did an incredible job in restoring order, putting 300 Royal Marines on the ground pretty quickly. The Prince of Wales, Prince William and Prince Harry took the closest interest and did what they could to nudge things along behind the scenes.

As we were too far from Tortola to make a big difference there, we decided the priority was to help the people of Virgin Gorda to get back on their feet. Kim Takeuchi and Lauren Keil, who run our local foundation, Unite BVI, got to work making a list of what was needed most. Adam and Chris Yates began sorting the water supply. I talked to the Governor of Puerto Rico, who agreed to start sending in emergency supplies. As one day turned into the next, the whole community rallied round. Sam got back to the BVI as soon as he could on a Virgin Atlantic flight filled with aid supplies. We embraced and fought back the tears.

Sam told his sister, organising aid back in the UK: 'It's like a bomb has gone off. The BVI has gone from an idyllic gem of the world to a humanitarian disaster zone. Everything is destroyed. One of the Marines, who had been deployed in war zones, told me he has still never seen anything like this. There's a 180-tonne ship on the side of the hill, and the land has not one leaf left – most of the trees have been ripped out of the ground. The people of Virgin Gorda are struggling to survive.'

Sam helped to set up a North Sound Aid Centre on Virgin Gorda, opening a kitchen to provide basic meals, and dealing with evacuation schedules, housing needs, primary-needs lists and supplies inventories. The team spent full-on days distributing canned foods, water, medical supplies, sanitary supplies and other essentials to the surrounding islands. I joined in, going around meeting and talking with people. Moments of sweetness and kindness grew amongst the rubble. A thirteen-year-old girl set up her own school in the wreckage, teaching her fellow kids now their school was closed.

Little rituals were beginning to fall into place. After working flat out around the clock clearing debris and working on recovery efforts, we would gather in the sea off Necker to cool off, washing each other's hair before sharing a meal and planning the next day's most urgent tasks. After the 'bath', I took Sam for a walk around the island so we could check on the animals. Considering this was the strongest storm ever to hit the Atlantic, it is incredible how many survived. The scarlet ibis, roseate spoonbill, stout iguanas, giant tortoises and our trusty dogs were all fine. The vast majority of lemurs survived, and most of the flamingos returned to Necker and Moskito. Sadly, though, there were some heart-breaking losses. There wasn't one hummingbird left on the island – I just hoped they had managed to travel in the eye of the storm to safety, which some birds do. But there were some positive stories. I was touched to meet a wonderful vet from Grenada, Dr Carter, who with Tayia and Ella managed to bring some flamingos right back from the brink and onto the road to recovery.

I felt understandably emotional walking across the wreckage of the hurricane with Sam. This was where he had played as a boy, where he had grown into a wonderful young man, where he brought his own children to see their grand-dude and grandma. I noticed a bashed-up container strewn across some ragged ground. After the Necker fire I had put treasured things we'd salvaged from the flames into what I thought were fire-safe boxes. This one had contained my dad's medals and other precious artefacts, which I had planned to give to Sam and Holly, and hoped they would one day pass on to their own children. Like so many other possessions, they were gone. But looking at Sam, I realised it really didn't matter. As with the Great House fire, love and memories are what's important – not stuff. We got back to work.

Once we'd helped get people the basics of food, water and tarpaulins, we set about looking at the bigger picture. Tourism was decimated, the hotels were all gone, cruise ships would be avoiding the BVI and the financial services industry had largely left. The BVI had been turned into one of the poorest nations in the world overnight. The lack of communications made organising support extremely difficult, so on 10 September I decided to fly to nearby Puerto Rico to mobilise wider aid efforts. We hastily arranged meetings with various governments and aid agencies. I spoke with community leaders, as well as BVI Governor Gus Jaspert, Premier Orlando Smith and Deputy Premier Minister Kedrick Pickering. Behind the scenes, I was lobbying the UK government and Foreign Office for support. Some people questioned why the UK should help the BVI when its standard of living was high. The answer was simple – the BVI no longer had a standard of living. This disaster was different because an entire country was paralysed, with everything from supplies to security to communications to transport unable to function. Other disasters happen regionally, with different parts of the same country able to continue operating and providing support – the whole of the BVI had been wiped out. At the time, the BVI was not eligible for aid from the UK and a lot of complex red tape was holding things up. I spoke to International Development Secretary Priti Patel, Defence Secretary Sir Michael Fallon and Foreign Secretary Boris Johnson. They rallied well, agreeing to give the BVI a substantial loan on the condition that a professional crisis-management team was set up. We did our bit in pulling this together with the islanders to get the region back on its feet.

The flagship HMS *Ocean* was diverted to the region, filled with more than 60 tonnes of aid, building materials, landing craft, nine helicopters and personnel. It was a real lift for everyone, and when I got back to the BVI from Puerto Rico, I went aboard to speak to as many of the team as possible and simply say thank you. Nick Wood, HMS *Ocean*'s commanding officer, showed me around. I walked the bridge, saw the storerooms full of supplies, and even enjoyed the captain's chair for a moment! Lauren from Unite BVI joined us and gave the Commander a list of all the most urgent things we felt they could help with, especially getting food, water and power to remote regions in most desperate need that only helicopters could reach. The Puerto Rican government were incredible, offering to fly in supplies and help in any way they could. I conveyed their offer of support to the BVI Governor and we were able to get permissions quickly.

More aid boats started arriving with essential supplies, and the armed forces organised their distribution. We saw the priorities as resolving sanitation issues, putting tarpaulin on roofs, providing medical assistance, reopening supply chains to get supermarkets and banks open, restoring power and water, and clearing debris. These were short-term fixes, though. While they were essential, we needed a long-term solution. I called for a Disaster Recovery Marshall Plan for the BVI to aid in recovery, sustainable reconstruction and long-term revitalisation of the local economy. This would need to include building resilience against what is likely to be a higher intensity and frequency of extreme weather events, as the effects of climate change continue to grow. I was due to travel to Climate Week in New York. I debated long and hard whether I would be more useful on the ground in the BVI, but determined I could have most impact banging the drum for urgent climate action at the talks in the US and securing more funds for the Caribbean.

Jean Oelwang and the team gathered together groups of potential donors and I met with the heads of the Inter-American Development Bank, the IMF and the World Bank to discuss plans. I called for a Marshall Plan for a cleaner, greener Caribbean, and a commitment to empower the region's people to shape their own future and rebuild their nations. To get this off the ground, we teamed up with a group of inspirational Caribbean leaders who had a vision for the Caribbean to become the world's first 'climate-smart zone'. Later, at the Caribbean Renewable Energy Forum in Miami, I met with more than fifty representatives of Caribbean governments and utility companies to discuss plans to expand the use of renewable energy in the region. We highlighted the importance of solar, wind, geothermal and other forms of renewable energy to cut costs, reduce the harm being done to the environment and increase the resilience of their electric systems to withstand future hurricanes. Coincidentally, one of the few structures on Necker Island to emerge from Irma virtually unscathed was our array of solar panels. As an investor and entrepreneur, I've never seen a more compelling business case. After all, you don't have to ship sunshine or wind. The Caribbean – and the world at large – must finally take the leap from twentieth-century technology to twenty-first-century innovation. And we must resist the all-too-familiar impulse to return to business as usual and do the same things as before, simply because they are easy and cheaper in the short term. I am optimistic, with the political will emerging now, that these island states have the opportunity to become models of what climate-smart recovery around the world can and should look like.

*

While we worked to repair the damage done by the hurricane, some devious people saw an opportunity to profit from it. This story sounds as though it has come straight out of a John le Carré novel, but I assure you it is true. Six months earlier, my assistant received a written note on what appeared to be official government paper from UK Defence Secretary Sir Michael Fallon, requesting an urgent call. When I rang, he told me it was an incredibly sensitive matter and that he wanted to be sure there was nobody else in the room while we talked. He asked that we speak in strict confidence. A British diplomat had been kidnapped and was being held by terrorists, and British laws prevented the government from paying ransoms. Normally, he completely concurred with this but on this occasion there was a particular, very sensitive, reason why they had to get the diplomat back. So they were extremely confidentially asking a syndicate of British businesspeople to step in. I was asked to contribute $5 million of the ransom money, which he assured me the British government would find a way of repaying.

I said that I was sympathetic to his request, but that in the last week I had come across a couple of incidents where people had been scammed. I needed to be absolutely certain that this wasn't such an event, and that he was who he said he was. He said he fully understood and that I should send one of my senior team over to his department at Whitehall to have a quiet word with his secretary. She was the only other person who knew about it and if we said the code word 'Davenport', she would confirm it was for real. Although the Sir Michael I spoke to sounded exactly like Sir Michael, I was understandably cautious. After I had asked one of my lawyers to go to Whitehall, I rang Downing Street and asked to be put through to his office. His secretary assured me that he hadn't spoken to me and that nobody had been kidnapped. It was clearly a scam and we passed the matter over to the police. Businessman David Reuben told me he had been targeted by a con man using identical tactics, but he too was suspicious and the attempt failed.

Six months on, I received an email from a friend in the US, a very successful businessman, asking when I would be returning the three-week loan I had asked for to help the BVI communities. I had no idea what he was talking about. He told me he had received an email from my assistant, to arrange a call with me. When the call happened the con man did an extremely accurate impression of me and spun a big lie about urgently needing a loan while I was trying to mobilise aid in the BVI. They claimed I couldn't get hold of my bank in the UK because I didn't have any communications going to Europe and I'd only just managed to make a satellite call to the businessman in America. The businessman, incredibly graciously, gave $2 million, which promptly disappeared.

I spoke to the businessman and had to tell him specific details of our last get-together (at a football game) before he was convinced it was really me and not the con man. We quickly realised he had been duped out of his money by a criminal pretending to be me. He has spent his life cautiously building his businesses and told me he couldn't believe how stupid he had been. He is an incredibly generous person who gives to all sorts of causes, and it is just too sad for words that of all people it was he who had fallen for it. If only his money had gone to the people of the BVI, not the con man. People used to raid banks and trains for smaller amounts – it's frightening to think how easy it is becoming to pull off these crimes, but normally it's poor, vulnerable people online who suffer the most from sophisticated cons.

*

Back in the BVI, the recovery efforts continued. By 12 December 2017, we were ready to unveil a project I was particularly passionate about. We travelled to France with Bill Gates, Michael Bloomberg and others to meet the new president, Emmanuel Macron, to discuss progress two years on from the historic Paris Agreement and agree what we could all do together to help. We also joined forces with Grenada's prime minister, Keith Mitchell, St Lucia's prime minister, Allen Chastanet, Dominica's prime minister, Roosevelt Skerrit, and other Caribbean leaders to announce the creation of a Caribbean Climate-Smart Accelerator. This $8-billion climate-investment plan will hopefully create the world's first 'climate-smart zone' as envisioned by the Caribbean leaders, saving the public millions in energy bills and moving the whole Caribbean towards 100 per cent clean energy. The Accelerator can reinvigorate the islands and help make them more resilient for hurricanes in the future.

A couple of months later, I chaired a meeting with the head of the Inter-American Development Bank and another group of Caribbean leaders. At the back of this book I've listed my numerous close shaves. But I suspect my most-embarrassing-moments list could be even bigger! I had been travelling a lot and was a little tired when I arrived in

Jamaica, so had drunk an awful lot of coffee. As the talks continued, I was desperate to go to the loo. After about an hour, I decided enough was enough. Although I was easily noticeable as co-chair of the meeting, I sneaked out, hoping not to be spotted. I made it to the loo, put my arm against the wall and as I was relieving myself of the coffee gave a good sigh. I seemed to pee for an awful long time. Then the automatic flusher went on. Finally, I zipped myself up. I grabbed a cup of coffee on my return so people would think I'd left for a drink. But when I came back into the room, everyone turned and looked at me. I caught Jean's eye and saw she was trying to suppress a laugh. I realised with horror I had left my microphone on and everyone in the room had heard my pee. I had to smile.

Our vision for the Caribbean will not be defined by disaster; it is filled with hope. I think it will become a beacon for island nations all over the world, creating thriving economies fuelled by clean energy and resilient design. The way of life here, as everywhere, should work with, rather than against, nature. We have the opportunity of a lifetime to help make this vision a reality. At Virgin Unite and Unite BVI, we continue to support long-term recovery, focusing on three key pillars: community (specifically education), entrepreneurship and environment. I've been living in the Caribbean for a long time and know its amazing people well. I've seen the deep pain experienced by those in the BVI and other Caribbean countries, losing their homes and their livelihoods, though certainly not their spirit. Their resilience and heart are an enormous inspiration. The tasks ahead of us are daunting, but it's the people who give me hope that the Caribbean islands will bounce back stronger than ever.

*

Since the hurricane, if anything my life has speeded up. Just before going to print on this updated autobiography, I enjoyed ten days that really shook my world. We raced around the globe celebrating the launch of Holly's first book, *WEconomy*. We signed off on an exciting new Virgin Voyages deal. Virgin Hotels announced a deal for the Hard Rock Hotel and Casino in Las Vegas (Joan suggested renaming it Virgin Rocks!) and I gave a speech while in Vegas that raised hundreds of thousands of dollars for Virgin Unite. I visited our new Virgin Hotel sites in San Francisco and New York. While on the West Coast, I cycled and played tennis for the first time in three months (having recovered from a shoulder injury). I also went to Virgin Hyperloop to meet all of the brilliant engineers and progress our plans for the company in India and Dubai. Then I visited Virgin Orbit, where I had a blast hosting a game show with the team.

Elsewhere, Virgin Atlantic doubled our flights to Johannesburg to twice daily and Virgin Active opened a stunning new concept club in Sydney. LanzaTech's clean fuel got permission for use on commercial flights, at up to 50 per cent mix. On 1 April 2018, Virgin Australia launched our first spin class in the sky! I met with some fascinating new potential partners about our plans for aviation in America. I caught up on the Elders' latest progress as they returned from a visit to the Middle East, and the B Team as we agreed five global areas on which to concentrate our efforts. I urged Brazil in a tweet to create a huge new ocean reserve, which Ocean Unite's efforts behind the scenes helped to make happen. At TED, the Audacious Project was unveiled to the world. Virgin Money appointed Irene Dorner as chairwoman, creating the only female duo leading one of the UK's FTSE 350-listed companies.

In the British Virgin Islands, we signed off on plans to fund a crisis-management team to support recovery, as well as a pan-Caribbean accelerator team to bring clean energy to the region. I had a dreadful cold throughout the trip, so despite doing so many deals I was unable to shake hands with anybody! Back in the US, I enjoyed a very successful visit to Virgin Galactic with Saudi Arabia's Crown Prince and his four key advisers. As well as viewing the spaceship and discussing their investments in Virgin Galactic and

Virgin Orbit, they said that they want to connect cities in Saudi with Virgin Hyperloop and invest in the business. We also spent time talking about the Red Sea development project. A few days later, VSS *Unity* completed her first supersonic, rocket-powered flight. Finally, I was brought down to earth with a bump when Joan said a cabin-crew member had told her how sad the team were to hear that I had Alzheimer's! I assure you I haven't. I headed to meet Holly and the family, who were skiing in Verbier, and spend time with my grandchildren. Soon I was unknotting Eva-Deia's hair, loving playing my role as doting grand-dude.

Despite being so busy, I have been reflecting even more on the things that are most important to me. They are simple: I want to be active and healthy; I want to make a difference in whatever I do; I want to be inspired by the people and world around me; and of course, I want my grandchildren to come and spend as much time with me as possible. I've been on the road a lot since the hurricane, and started surprising them whenever I can. When Sam and Bellie took the kids to Bali for a few months, I decided spontaneously to fly there. I had a large box delivered to their house. When Sam cut the top open with a big knife, much to his, Eva-Deia and Bellie's delight, I jumped out like a jack-in-the-box. I love surprises and so do they. Everything boils down to family. With my own family, I want to be a better husband, son, brother, father and grand-dude. With my Virgin family, I want to keep changing business for good. With the BVI family, I want to help get this magical part of the planet back on its feet. With the global family, I want to help build a world that our grandchildren can be proud to inherit. There's lots to do – screw it, let's do it.

Epilogue

As I was going through the final edits of this book, Joan took me, Holly and Sam to one side on Moskito Island. 'Richard, I've got an envelope here that you gave me before your last balloon trip.' I looked at the aged envelope in her hand and my mind flew back to the Sheraton Marrakech hotel in 1998, where I had written it. 'To be opened only if ...' it said on the front – it was in case I didn't make it home again. Now, two decades on, Joan let me rip open the letter. There was one for her, and one for Holly and Sam:

Darling Joan –

Well, that was a stupid thing to do – and at Christmas too!! What can I say ...

I have written you a more personal letter that is in my will. I'd like to cover here one or two other thoughts.

I have left in place an excellent team at Virgin. I hope I've also left them with enough to continue to stay and grow Virgin into the best Group of companies in Britain. As long as you can keep them motivated they will be wonderfully loyal. I'd suggest you meet up with them all once every three months for an update.

Rather than having so much of our investments tied up in the airline it might be worth selling a stake in it when the timing is right. Rail is a more difficult decision – I think we owe it to the rail users and the Virgin name to get it right. But I would suggest that you try to keep control of all of them in case Holly or Sam one day take a real interest in the business.

I should be grateful if you could involve my mum and dad in the hotels. Send them out scouting – South Africa, etc. And please humour my mum as I've been so bad at doing.

Finally I am glad I got back to see Necker Island for a few hours.

If it doesn't in any way spoil the Island for you all I wouldn't mind resting amongst the gulls at the far end of it. Invite the rest of the family and our friends and have a true Scottish wake. Tell Sam this is the one night he's allowed to get drunk. And one day in the very distant future – I'd like to feel you'll join me there.

Letters like these are completely unreal but have to be faced someday. The chances are that we'll both die in our beds of old age – but even then these things need to be addressed. In any event I feel much better having left everything in some kind of order.

Still trying to say it – sorry!

Love you very much

Richard

We smiled as we read the letter together and I thought back to all I could have missed out on. Holding Joan's hand, we began reading my letter to my children.

Dear Holly and Sam,

Most dads in these modern times don't put their children through what I regularly do to you.

It should only be at the time of war that children say their farewells to their dads with that unspoken concern that they may never see each other again.

So why do I do it to you? In the past I suspect I was seeking adventure, young, seeing what I was capable of, testing myself and my team to the limit, testing the equipment, having a lot of fun and perhaps being thoroughly irresponsible.

Now I sincerely believe that all the flights we've had in the past – all the difficulties we've been through – all the experience we've gained have come together to create a balloon and capsule that can and will make it around the world, and hopefully home for Boxing Day.

I wouldn't change a word of the letter I wrote for you (which you will read in a book I've written for you both called *Losing My Virginity*) in case everything went wrong on my first ballooning trip. The only thing I will add is that at Virgin we have a company that you should be proud of. We have wonderful people who make up those companies who you should be even more proud of, who together have built up one of the best companies in Britain. If one or both of you are interested, in time this team will take you under their wing and help train you into all the workings of Virgin.

For a number of years you should be great listeners for there is a lot to learn. You should roll up your sleeves – have fun – and try out everything and in time hopefully become capable of being leaders of people too. The way to become a great leader is to look for the best in people – seldom criticise – always praise.

You will also have to earn your leadership – but must accept you may never earn it. It won't be easy. People will be cynical. Suspicious. You mustn't earn it because you are my children – but despite of the fact that you are my children. You have to prove how good you are with people and what good listeners you are.

You may on the other hand have no interest in getting involved with Virgin and that's fine too. Holly, you may wish to continue to pursue your career as a doctor – and prove to yourself what you are capable of. One day in the future, however, you could find that your medical experience could overlap with Virgin.

As to you, Sam, it's too early to tell – prove to yourself what you're capable of. It's an awful lot. And let Steve Ridgway, mum and others help and guide you. There's wonderful friends and people around you to give you advice. Keep this letter and read it again on your eight-eenth birthday.

Anyway – whatever happens – I'm off on a wonderful voyage.

Love Dad

P.S. Love you both very much.

Turning to my family, a little misty-eyed, I couldn't help but laugh. 'Well, it's funny how things turn out. I'm glad you never had to read these letters, until now, when we can look at them and smile.' I couldn't get the letters out of my mind, and the next morning I woke up early and wrote just one more letter, to my new grandson, Bluey.

My dear Bluey,

A few weeks ago you came into this world, my fourth grandchild and newest miracle to arrive in our lives. I wanted to set down in ink how much you have to look forward to. As I write this, you are sitting on your grandma's lap, sleeping peacefully. Your big sister Eva-Deia is playing nearby with your cousins Artie and Etta. They are drawing squiggles all over my notes, creating treasure out of paper. They have the biggest smiles on their faces, even larger now their newest playmate has joined them in the world. Your mummy and daddy are over-joyed you have arrived, and your granny and I are beside ourselves with excitement. As you will discover more every day, you are the most precious new member of a family who will do anything for each other.

2017 is a scary time to enter the world. The challenges facing us all, from threats to democracy to climate change, cannot be underestimated. The key is to see these as opportunities and embrace the challenge rather than shy away. I take great heart from new generations, who are far more understanding, compassionate and pur-poseful than any that have gone before. I love surrounding myself with young people, and I'm sure they keep me youthful, educate me and open my eyes to new ideas. As we get older it is a danger to get set in our ways and believe what we believe. I love having my mind changed. That is one of the challenges I entrust to you, your sister and cousins too.

We are sitting at the Temple on Necker Island early in the morning, looking out over to the flamingo pond as two of our beautiful pink birds soar gently overhead. It was in this exact spot that my heart sank when I learned of VSS *Enterprise*'s accident. It was a stomach-wrenching moment. Since then, the team have worked day and night to build and test our new spaceship. A few days ago I saw VSS *Unity* fly by herself for the third time. I cried as the glistening silver craft glided through the cold Mojave air, carrying the hopes and dreams of many with her. Just watching the awestruck faces of the people working on the project, and the delight in the eyes of their children, was simply magical. I believe you will go to space when you are old enough. It may take longer than we expected, but space is hard and the end result will be that much safer and better. Ultimately any project needs a bit of good fortune, and I believe we will get there.

You have entered a world where you have limitless opportunities. You are part of a bigger family than your relations alone – you are part of the Virgin family. For many, many years at Virgin we were literally struggling to survive. It was a long learning process, with no outside financial backing, and we were fumbling in the dark. We hadn't been taught what to do, we were learning on the job with no experience whatsoever. Everything was fresh and new, and there was a first time for everything. All of that is ahead of you. There will be so many failures, so many mistakes, but so many triumphs, so much joy and so much laughter.

Now I have learned a thing or two about the world, I hope to pass my experience on to my grandchildren and, through business and philanthropy, try to make the world a better place for you to grow up in. I know more now. I am less innocent. But it is important to realise I still have a hell of a lot to learn. There is so much more left for me to experience and explore, so many people better than myself to learn from. I will continue questioning, questioning, questioning. I will never completely get to the truth, but I want my life to be one long strive to get there.

I have learned so much from Etta, Artie and Eva-Deia already. Watching them as toddlers reminded me that you don't learn to walk by following the rules. You learn by doing and by falling over. It will be the same for you, as it still is for me. All we can do is keep moving forwards, falling over, supporting each other and getting back up again. As we get older it is hard to maintain the sense of adventure you have been born with, and I want you to help me keep hold of my childlike spirit of wonder. I can't wait to read you *Where The Wild Things Are* and *The Owl and the Pussycat*. I'm looking forward to taking you out in the fresh air, surrounded by nature, and teaching you to swim in the ocean. I want to show you how to play tennis and chess and go on adventures together. I'm sure you will have far more to teach me too.

By the time you read this, the world will have transformed again. When I think to what 2050 will look like, my mind whirrs to you visiting for my 100th birthday on a supersonic flight, staying at space hotels and being connected to every person on the planet. Back on Earth, if I start predicting the future I worry I sound like a *Miss World* contestant. Yes, I do want to see a world without conflict. I want to see the ocean protected and species preserved. I want equal rights for all, an end to the death penalty and the war on drugs. I want education transformed to become useful and practical, cities reimagined as environmentally friendly open spaces, diseases controlled, poverty eradicated and entrepreneurship stimulated globally. But the exciting thing is these big aspirations are all achievable. I hope setbacks like Brexit and the US election do not hinder the positive progress of the past few decades. It is up to us all to press on.

Your great-grandmother and great-grandfather always told me how seeing your daddy and Auntie Holly grow up was amongst their greatest joys, and I understand that now. Your granny and I would love to see you grow up in the same way and we'll be doing everything we can to keep fit and healthy and stay around. It is frightening, when I think of the close-calls on my adventures, that I may never have met you. When I fell off my bike last year, my life flashed before my eyes for a second – this book has been a chance to dwell on life for a little longer. When I saw your little face for the first time, and held your tiny hand, I thought about everything that had brought us to this most joyful moment. I don't think I would change any parts of it, and I can't wait for the next chapter. As I prepare to put my pen down, you are opening your eyes. The sun is rising. A new day is dawning.

Love,
Grand-Dude

Appendix Seventy-~~five~~ six! Close Shaves

'You must have had a near miss for every year you've been alive,' said Helen after my cycling accident. 'I think it's probably more than that – there's been four this year alone. I'll try to remember them all.' I went back to my bedroom at about 11 p.m. and began noting down all the close shaves I could think of. By morning, I had come up with this list (I'm sure I've missed some!):

1. 1953 – Aged three, tobogganing on a tray down an icy hill. I ended up falling off and going on my face instead. Mum says it's why I look like I do!
2. 1954 – There was petrol rationing after the war. Naughtily, my parents were storing petrol in the kitchen of the house, which one day caught fire. My sister Lindy and I had to be hurried out of the house while the fire brigade put out the blaze.
3. 1955 – Jumped into a fast-flowing river in New Milton, Devon, to win a bet that I could learn to swim by the end of the holiday. I survived and earned the ten shillings prize from my Auntie Joyce.
4. 1956 – Playing dare with my best friend Nik Powell, we were seeing who could ride his bike closest to a river. I got the closest and ended up in the river! I managed to get myself out, but lost his bike – Mum and Dad had to save to buy him a new one.

5. 1957 – Climbing up a steep cliff in Devon on holiday, I was showing off to my friends and got stuck halfway up it. I couldn't go up or down and had to be rescued.

6. 1958 – My first time horse jumping, I fell onto a jump mid-air and broke some ribs. I've still got the broken rib on my left side sticking out to show from it.

7. 1960 – Playing football at school, I ripped my knee cartilage – that was the end of any professional sporting aspirations.

8. 1968 – Came off a motorbike in Bali while holidaying as a teenager. I was left badly cut up.

9. 1972 – Survived a fishing boat sinking on honeymoon with my first wife Kristen off Mexico. We decided to jump off the boat and swim for shore, while the rest of the passengers stayed put – we were the only survivors.

10. 1973 – My houseboat in London, *Duende*, sank. I pumped out water and when the pump was turned off it siphoned all the water back in.

11. 1974 – Went for a walk with Kristen and my dog Friday in London. We were just going past St Mary's Hospital, Paddington, when a body came flying through the air and exploded on the railings right in front of us. It was somebody committing suicide, who had jumped out of a hospital window.

12. 1975 – Hit by lightning in a plane. This has now happened three times over the years.

13. 1976 – Flew a microlight aircraft by mistake. It was the first time I'd sat in it, I had no idea how to fly it, and accidentally took off. I was pulling wires out desperately. I cut the engine and managed to crash-land into a field. My instructor died in an accident the next day.

14. 1977 – We used to have weekends away with Virgin staff, which once got a little out of control. We were out on the water and two of us ran our jet-skis into each other. Thankfully there were no broken bones, but the jet-skis were write-offs.

15. 1979 – At 2 a.m., decided to sail around Necker Island with my friend Steve Barron. We got lost in the pitch

black, huge waves rolled in and we crashed onto the coral. Thankfully the moon came out and we made it back to the island in just about one piece.

16. 1980 – I stubbed my toe while walking around Necker Island and suddenly fell down a gaping gorge. I managed to get my hand to the other side, and Steve Barron managed to rescue me, pulling me up before I fell to what would have been certain death on the jagged rocks below.

17. 1981 – My party trick at staff parties was to walk across the top of marquees, and pretend to slip and grab the top of the tent. Once I missed grabbing it and went shooting all the way to the ground. Luckily I only suffered cuts and bruises.

18. 1983 – Beaten up by three burglars in my home in Albion Street. Managing to escape, I ran naked to Virgin's offices.

19. 1984 – The engine exploded on the first Virgin Atlantic test flight, with a jet of flame 100 feet long going past my face as I sat in a window seat on board. The Civil Aviation Inspector was on the flight, too, on the day before our inaugural. Some birds had flown into the engine. I wasn't sure whether to be terrified of losing my life or terrified of losing my licence.

20. 1985 – Got caught in a strong storm off the Isle of Wight while on the *Virgin Atlantic Challenger 1*. The engineer on board broke his leg.

21. 1985 – Sank in the *Virgin Atlantic Challenger 1* as we were crossing the Atlantic, had to be pulled out of the ocean.

22. 1986 – Crashed a hire car while driving through the Alps to Zermatt with my family. I hit some ice and went down a small cliff and turned the car over. I also crashed another car in Switzerland while driving alone on another occasion.

23. 1986 – On my first solo hot-air balloon flight I crashed badly, smashing into the ground. It was a sign of things to come!

24. 1986 – On another early balloon flight, I went flying over Oxford with Mike Oldfield, and soon found there was no safe place to land. After almost crashing onto some railings in a park, I managed to land the balloon on the roof of a bakery.

25. 1986 – On my first time skydiving, there was one cord that opened the parachute, and one that got rid of it. I pulled the wrong cord by mistake. I was falling through the air before an instructor managed to yank my spare ripcord.

26. 1987 – On our attempt to cross the Atlantic in a hot-air balloon, the balloon's solar heating was too good and we headed up, up and up with seemingly no way to stop it. My co-pilot Per managed to bring the balloon down just before the capsule imploded and we tumbled to our deaths.

27. 1987 – On the same flight, we crash-landed in Northern Ireland in the hot-air balloon – officially breaking a Guinness World Record in the process.

28. 1987 – On the same challenge, I lost my co-pilot when Per jumped into the Atlantic, leaving me alone in the hot-air balloon as it disappeared back above the clouds. I was convinced I was going to die.

29. 1987 – On that memorable flight's fourth brush with disaster, I managed to crash the balloon into the North Sea, and was rescued by helicopter.

30. 1988 – We were sitting on boulders in the Caribbean on a cliff top. The boulder Holly was sitting on suddenly fell down the cliff with her following it. The boulder hit a tree, which fell gently on top of Holly and stopped her going all the way down the cliff.

31. 1989 – I decided to make an entrance to my wedding with Joan, dangling from a helicopter in an all-white suit. I dropped into the shallow end of the pool by mistake, smashed my legs, and spent the whole wedding hobbling.

32. 1990 – Flew to Iraq in a successful attempt to get Saddam Hussein to release hostages he was holding. It was

incredibly tense and could have turned nasty – we celebrated with rescued family and loved ones as we left Iraq's airspace.

33. 1990 – We were about to get into a hot-air balloon to attempt to cross the Pacific, when it literally fell apart in front of our eyes. If it had happened after take-off . . .

34. 1991 – Our next attempt to cross the Pacific in a hot-air balloon saw it catch fire at 30,000 feet. We managed to extinguish the fire before the balloon was destroyed.

35. 1991 – On the same balloon flight, we lost half our fuel when full tanks dropped as we jettisoned empty fuel. We thought we would run out of fuel halfway across the Pacific, before the strong winds in the jet stream saved us.

36. 1991 – At the climax of the Pacific flight, we crashed in the Arctic – successfully completing the challenge, but crashing in -50 degree temperatures 3,000 miles from our planned destination in Los Angeles.

37. 1992 – I was on holiday with the family in Sri Lanka, and the Prime Minister offered to take us up to Trincomalee to see how safe it was, after years of fighting with the Tamil Tigers. We arrived by helicopter to see a big, deserted hotel, a huge empty swimming pool and nobody else there. As we drove around the city, there were roadblocks everywhere. We went back to the hotel. I just felt very uncomfortable and told our guide we wanted to leave, saying: 'I don't think this is a safe place for children.' They were good enough to fly us out before dark. That night the Tamils invaded and everyone in the town was slaughtered.

38. 1993 – Heard a thief in my children's bedroom in Holland Park, while I was sitting downstairs watching the Hitchcock film *Psycho*. I heard Joan let out a blood-curdling scream and raced upstairs. I threw a plastic bottle of water at the intruder as he ran away.

39. 1994 – Driving down the M40 with the family in a Range Rover. At about 11.30 p.m., I flipped the car upside down on a corner. Another car came along and clipped us,

smashing its wing mirror on the side of us. We were very fortunate that the police were in the vicinity. They ran up, got a light set up and broke us out with a truncheon. The family wisely banned me from driving after that!

40. 1994 – Plans for a kidnapping attempt on the family were overheard in the local pub in Kidlington. Our gardener found out about it and told the police. Thankfully, nothing ever came of it.

41. 1995 – I was water-skiing behind a blimp in Florida as part of a scene for the *Baywatch* TV show. I got into difficulties and was rescued by the *Baywatch* team.

42. 1996 – We were about to take off on our first trans-global hot-air balloon flight attempt in Morocco when a British Airways plane turned its engine in the direction of the balloon and blew it away.

43. 1997 – On our second trans-global ballooning attempt, the balloon plummeted into the Atlas Mountains. We just managed to stop it hitting the ground at full speed.

44. 1997 – The second trans-global balloon attempt ended when we crashed in Algeria. We survived the crash but were then held hostage by a local warlord, who lavished food on us, but made it clear he wasn't in any hurry to let us go. We kept on gently explaining that we really needed to get back to England, while they refused to let us make any telephone calls. Somehow we managed to get a message to the British ambassador. He talked to the Algerian president, who sent his personal executive jet to pick us up.

45. 1998 – On our third trans-global hot-air balloon flight, the Chinese authorities threatened to shoot us down. Having escaped unscathed, we found we were going to fly over North Korea, who we were extremely worried might shoot us down, too. In the end, we received a welcoming email from them: 'We're happy to let you through – good luck on your challenge.'

46. 1998 – On the same ballooning attempt we were caught up in strong winds in the Himalayan chain and ended up crossing directly above Mount Everest and K2.

47. 1998 – The round-the-world hot-air balloon attempt ended when we plummeted into the Pacific and were rescued by the Hawaiian coast guard on Christmas Day. I had now been rescued by helicopter in the North Sea, twice in the Atlantic, in the Pacific, the Arctic, and off a banana boat. We sponsored London's Air Ambulance for many years to say thank you.
48. 1999 – Shortly after buying the Kasbah Tamadot in Morocco, I went out horse riding and was knocked off my horse.
49. 2000 – There was a major electrical fire at our London house in Holland Park. Thankfully, nobody was hurt, but a huge quantity of paperwork, diaries and personal possessions were lost.
50. 2000 – Flew through the air, 100 feet below a helicopter in Sydney Harbour to launch Virgin Mobile Australia. Suddenly I saw the imposing structure of Sydney Harbour Bridge approaching fast, and thought I was going to hit it. At the last possible second the helicopter veered upwards and I narrowly avoided becoming a permanent addition to the side of the bridge.
51. 2001 – Narrowly missed stepping on a live track with 25,000 volts charged above, while inspecting our new tilting trains in England.
52. 2002 – Another fire, this time at the then family home in Kidlington, where a blaze ripped through a cricket pavilion we used to store all manner of items from Virgin's history, including my diaries.
53. 2003 – Swimming with humpback whales and their young off Dominican Republic, one decided to slam its heavy tail, narrowly missing me.
54. 2004 – Agreed to do a bungee jump off Victoria Falls as part of my TV show *The Rebel Billionaire*. As I fell through the air I clipped my head on something and came back up with blood streaming down my face.
55. 2004 – On the same show, I climbed a rope ladder to get to the top of a hot-air balloon at 10,000 feet. The lady I was with, contestant and Spanx owner Sara Blakely,

nearly fell through the gap at the top. I was close to following her down.

56. 2005 – Went out onto the water in a Hobie Cat, sailing between Anegada and Necker Island. The boat capsized and a young lad fell onto my back. I came back to Necker on a stretcher.

57. 2006 – Came off a quad bike in the mountains of France on a very rough road and had to have a major operation on my shoulder.

58. 2007 – Jumped off Palms Casino in Las Vegas as we announced Virgin America's new route to the city. After initially refusing to do the jump, I reconsidered and plunged down the building at high speed in strong winds. I smashed painfully hard into the building. Fortunately I hadn't spun around, so my backside hit the wall rather than my head. It completely ripped the back of my trousers off, cut my legs and arm open and badly bruised my hand.

59. 2008 – Tried to break the transatlantic sailing record with my children and become the fastest mono-hull sailing yacht to cross the Atlantic. We were severely seasick but making good time before the boat broke and we had to abandon the attempt.

60. 2009 – Went wing-walking on a Virgin Atlantic plane, while holding Kate Moss upside down. I slipped and we narrowly avoided plunging off the plane onto the tarmac.

61. 2009 – Tried to beat a world record in an English Electric Lightning jet for the fastest 0–30,000 feet straight-up flight. It was extremely exhilarating and we narrowly missed out on the record. Sadly the pilot died a few days later on another attempt, as the plane lost control.

62. 2009 – At the unveiling of SpaceShipTwo, a hurricane hit the Mojave Desert and we just managed to race onto buses as the winds sent scaffolding crashing down, blowing our marquee and everything inside it away into the desert night.

63. 2010 – Larry Page and I went kitesurfing from Anegada and it suddenly got very dark. After a very nervy few hours lost in the night, we were very relieved to find the safety of Necker.

64. 2011 – Got hit by a young lad while skiing in Verbier. I had to have a major operation on my knee.

65. 2011 – Fell into a cactus stark naked while rushing to help as fire engulfed the Great House on Necker. The house and our possessions were destroyed, but nobody was hurt.

66. 2012 – Went swimming with sharks and sailfish, when one sailfish got extremely close. Its razor-sharp, sword-like bill was a centimetre away from blinding me.

67. 2012 – Climbed Mont Blanc, the highest mountain in France, with my children and friends. We had a near-miss with boulders falling around us but just managed to avoid them.

68. 2012 – Kitesurfed across the English Channel after a failed attempt the day before. I lost my board 110 times, avoided huge ships, and ended up practically frozen when we got to France, to be met by armed and angry police.

69. 2013 – Joined Holly to kite around Necker for the first time. I foolishly lost my kite in seriously choppy seas. Holly had to kite back to Necker to get a boat to rescue me.

70. 2014 – Another near-miss with boulders as we hiked through Switzerland on the Virgin Strive Challenge.

71. 2014 – Was on board a speedboat racing in the Poker Run in the British Virgin Islands. Two boats went out of control in front of us, smashing into each other. We just managed to avert them.

72. 2016 – Smashed my teeth twice within a month while playing tennis on Necker Island.

73. 2016 – Ran into a bullet-proof door while trying to enter a jewellery shop in the Cayman Islands to buy Joan a present for our anniversary.

74. 2016 – Was 'kissed' by a shark as I swam with rays in the Cayman Islands.

75. 2016 – My life flashed before my eyes as I went over the handlebars while cycling on Virgin Gorda. My bike disappeared off the cliff. I escaped with a cracked cheek, severe cuts and bruises and a torn shoulder.

76. 2017 – We huddled in a concrete bunker on Necker as the strongest storm to ever hit the Atlantic destroyed the island around us. A 1-tonne bath had flown about 30 metres through the air, and buried itself exactly where I'd been sitting not long before.

Bonus close shave: (OK, this one wasn't exactly life and death, but when I was caught by my wife kitesurfing with naked model Denni Parkinson on my back, it certainly felt like it!)

If I keep getting this lucky, and live long enough, I hope to write the final entry in my trilogy of autobiographies when I am well into my nineties, possibly with my great-grandchildren, potentially from up in space. The working title for my last book? *Virginity Found.*

Acknowledgements

I would need another book to properly thank the tens of thousands of wonderful people who make Virgin what it is today. But a special mention to Nick Fox and the Virgin management team, Ed Faulkner, Lucy Oates, Joel Rickett and the Virgin Books team for their guidance on this project. Thanks to Helen Clarke for her assistance, and of course Joan and my family for their love and support. An extra special thank you to every person who has ever been and will always be a part of the Virgin family.

Picture Credits

SECTION ONE

Page 1   **all** Branson family

Page 2   **top** Branson family, **middle** Virgin Mobile, **bottom** Branson family

Page 3   **top** © National Portrait Gallery, London, **middle** Virgin Mobile, **bottom** Virgin Trains

Page 4   **top** Virgin Trains, **middle** Virgin Money, **bottom** Virgin Galactic

Page 5   **all** Branson family

Page 6   **main image (and main image page 7)** Virgin Limited Edition, **inset** Branson family

Page 7   **both insets** Branson family

Page 8   **top left and top right** The Elders, **bottom** © David Turnley

Page 9   **top** Virgin Mobile, **middle** The Branson Centre of Entrepreneurship, **bottom** Branson family

Page 10   **top** © Herb Lingl/aerialarchives.com, **middle** Claire Brown, **bottom** © Nick Stern

Page 11   **top** Virgin Atlantic, **middle** © markgreenberg-photography, **bottom** Virgin America

Page 12   **top** Virgin America, **middle** © Nic Serpell-Rand, **bottom** Virgin Galactic

Page 13   **top** Branson family, **middle** Virgin America, **bottom** © Jim Marks

Page 14   **top** Virgin Galactic/Mark Greenberg, **bottom** © Benjamin Eye

Page 15   **top** Virgin Active, **middle** © Shawn Heinrichs, **bottom** © James McCauley

Page 16   **all** Branson family

SECTION TWO

Page 1	**top** © Jack Brockway, **middle** Branson family, **bottom** © Jack Brockway
Page 2	**top** Virgin Australia, **middle** Virgin Galactic, **bottom** © Jack Brockway
Page 3	**top** © Paul Nicklen, **middle** © Getty Images/ Larry Busacca, **bottom** © Martin Hartley
Page 4	**top** Virgin Trains, **middle** © markgreenbergphotography, **bottom** Virgin.com
Page 5	**top** © Shawn Heinrichs, **middle** © Spray Films, **bottom** Virgin Money
Page 6	**top** © Owen Billcliffe Photography, **middle** Virgin Active, **bottom** Air Asia
Page 7	**top** © Jack Brockway, **bottom** © Rebecca Bowring
Page 8	**all** © takeaimphotography.com/amy trahant
Page 9	**all** Virgin Limited Edition
Page 10	**top** © takeaimphotography.com/amy trahant, **middle** Virgin Active, **bottom** © Owen Buggy
Page 11	**top** © Tom Oldham, **middle** © Steve Boxall and Zero Gravity, **bottom** © Vito Amati Photography
Page 12	**top** Virgin America, **middle and bottom** Virgin Management
Page 13	**top** © Jack Brockway, **middle** Scaled Composites, **bottom** Virgin Galactic/Mark Greenberg
Page 14	**top** Twentieth Century Fox, **middle** Virgin Atlantic, **bottom left and right** © Jon Griffith
Page 15	**main image** Virgin Galactic/Mark Greenberg, **inset bottom** © Reuters
Page 16	**top** Virgin Galactic, **middle** © Damon Dahlen, **bottom** Branson family

SECTION THREE

Page 1	**top** © Jack Brockway, **middle and bottom** Virgin Hotels
Page 2	**top** © Owen Buggy, **middle and bottom left** © Rebecca Family Photography, **bottom right** © Owen Buggy

Page 3   **top left** Mark Kelly, **top right** © Owen Buggy,
             middle © John Armstrong, **bottom** Virgin Australia
Page 4   **top** UNODC, **bottom left** courtesy McGee Media
             from Finding Your Roots with Henry Louis Gates,
             Jr., **bottom right** Justin Trudeau
Page 5   **top** Branson family, **middle** Virgin Galactic/
             Mark Greenberg, **bottom** © Jack Brockway
Page 6   **main image** Branson family, **inset top** © Owen
             Billcliffe Photography
Page 7   **top** © Shivraj Gohil/Spacesuit Media, **middle**
             Branson family, **bottom** © Mitch Phillips
Page 8   **top** Getty Images, **middle** © White House/Pete
             Souza, **bottom** Branson family
Page 9   **top left** Branson family, **top right, middle and**
             bottom © Adam Slama
Page 10   **top** © Adam Slama, **middle** © Bill and Melinda
             Gates Foundation/Mike Kemp, **bottom** © Owen
             Buggy
Page 11   **top and middle** Virgin Galactic, **bottom** Branson
             family
Page 12   **top and middle** © Jack Brockway, **bottom**
             © Joann McPike
Page 13   **top left** © Owen Buggy, **top right and middle**
             © Joann McPike, **bottom** © Matt Young
Page 14   **top** Branson family, **middle** Virgin Sport,
             bottom left and bottom right © Owen Buggy
Page 15   **top left** Virgin Orbit, **top right** Virgin Voyages,
             middle Virgin Orbit, **bottom** Branson family
Page 16   **top left** Greg Rose, **top right, middle and**
             bottom Branson family

The publisher has made every effort to credit the copyright
owners of any material that appears within, and will correct
any omissions in subsequent editions if notified.

INDEX

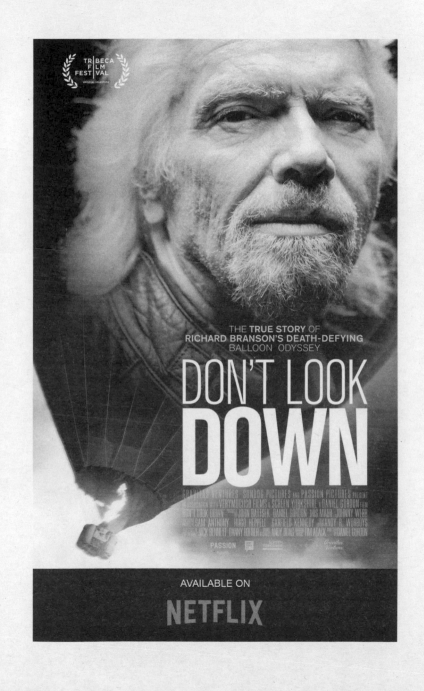